The Winchester Psalter

The Winchester Psalter
an Iconographic Study

Kristine Edmondson Haney

LEICESTER UNIVERSITY PRESS 1986

First published in 1986 by Leicester University Press
Distributed in the United States of America
by Humanities Press, Inc.,
Atlantic Highlands NJ 07716

Designed by Douglas Martin
Phototypeset in Linotron 202 Baskerville
by Wyvern Typesetting Ltd, Bristol
Printed in Great Britain by
Redwood Burn Ltd, Trowbridge

British Library Cataloguing in Publication Data

Haney, Kristine Edmondson
The Winchester Psalter: an iconographic study.
I. Title
091 ND3357.W5

ISBN 0-7185-1260-x

In Memory of Francis Wormald

Contents

List of Illustrations

Photograph Acknowledgments

Aachen, Ann Münchow: 103
Barcelona, Archivo Maas: 84, 87, 98, 104, 117, 122 (Fotografia cedida y autorizada por el Patrimonio Nacional)
Cambridge, Pembroke College: 153, 154, 155 (by kind permission of the Master and Fellows of Pembroke College)
Cambridge, Trinity College: 163 (by kind permission of the Master and Fellows of Trinity College)
Cologne, Rheinisches Bildarchiv: 76, 92, 114, 120, 127, 133, 137
Florence, Alinari/Art Resource, NY: 52
London, British Library: 1–38, 79, 101, 111, 147, 148, 162 (by permission of the British Library)
London, Conway Library, Courtauld Institute of Art: 40, 49, 50, 53, 58, 60, 73, 75, 80, 81, 82, 85, 86, 88, 91, 94, 99, 112, 115, 121, 124, 125, 128, 132, 139, 140, 141, 143, 144, 149, 150, 152, 160 (photographs 85, 88, 91 and 139 copyright Reginald Dodwell)
London, National Monuments Record: 131 (by permission of the Royal Commission on the Historical Monuments of England)
London, Warburg Institute: 43, 86, 89, 93, 95, 102, 118, 126, 130
Marburg, Bildarchiv Foto Marburg: 41, 74, 83, 90, 96, 97, 116, 123, 129, 136, 138
Munich, Hirmer-Verlag: 72, 151
New York, The Metropolitan Museum of Art: 145 (gift of J. Pierpont Morgan 1917)
New York, The Pierpont Morgan Library: 70 (by permission of the Trustees)
Oxford, Bodleian Library: 39, 48, 51
Paris, Bibliothèque Nationale: 47, 100, 105, 106, 109, 110, 113, 134, 135, 146, 158, 161 (phot. Bibl. nat. Paris)
Paris, Photographies Giraudon: 66, 67, 69
Rome, Biblioteca Apostolica Vaticana: 46, 56, 71 (Foto Biblioteca Vaticana)
From the cited literature: 42, 44, 45, 54, 57, 59, 61, 62, 63, 64, 65, 68, 70, 77, 78, 107, 108, 119, 142, 156, 157, 159

List of Abbreviations

AB	*Art Bulletin*
B.A.V.	Biblioteca Apostolica Vaticana, Rome
Beckwith, *Ivory*	John Beckwith, *Ivory Carvings in Early Medieval England* (1972)
Bergman, *Salerno*	Robert Bergman, *The Salerno Ivories* (Cambridge, MA, 1980)
B.L.	British Library, London
B.M.	Bibliothèque Municipale
B.N.	Bibliothèque Nationale, Paris
Bodl.	Bodleian Library, Oxford
Boeckler, *Das Goldene*	*A. Boeckler, Das Goldene Evangelienbuch Henrichs III* (Berlin, 1933)
B.R.	Bibliothèque Royale, Brussels
BSFRMP	*Bulletin de la Société française de reproductions de manuscrits à peintures*
Buchthal, *Paris Psalter*	Hugo Buchthal, *The Paris Psalter* (1938)
C.C.C.	Corpus Christi College, Cambridge
Codex Epternacensis	Nuremberg, Germanisches-Nationalmuseum, MS 151642
Codex Escorialensis	Escorial, Codex Vitrinas 17
Dodwell and Clemoes, *Hexateuch*	C. R. Dodwell and Peter Clemoes, *The Old English Illustrated Hexateuch British Museum Cotton Claudius B.IV* (Baltimore, 1974)
Goldschmidt, *Die byzantinischen*	A. Goldschmidt and K. Weitzmann, *Die byzantinischen Elfenbeinskulpturen des X.-XIII. Jahrhunderts* (2 vols., Berlin, 1930–4)
Goldschmidt, *Die Elfenbeinskulpturen*	A. Goldschmidt, *Die Elfenbeinskulpturen aus der Zeit der karolingischen und sächsischen Kaiser, VIII.-XI. Jahrhundert* (4 vols., Berlin, 1914–26)
Hesseling, *Miniatures*	D. Hesseling, *Miniatures de l'octateuque grec de Smyrne* (Leiden, 1909)
JBAS	*Journal of the British Archaeological Association*
JWCI	*The Journal of the Warburg and Courtauld Institutes*
Kaufmann, *Romanesque*	C.M. Kauffmann, *English Romanesque Manuscripts 1066–1200* (1975)
Koehler, *Die karolingischen*	W. Koehler, *Die karolingischen Miniaturen* (7 vols., Berlin, 1930–71)

Kracher, *Millstätter*	*Die Millstätter Genesis und Physiologus Handschrift*, ed. A. Kracher (2 vols., Graz, 1967)
Kraus, *Die Miniaturen*	F. Kraus, *Die Miniaturen des Codex Egberti* (Freiburg, 1884)
Metz, *Golden Gospels*	P. Metz, *The Golden Gospels of Echternach, Codex Aureus Epternacensis* (New York, 1957)
Millet, *Recherches*	G. Millet, *Recherches sur l'iconographie de l'évangile* (Paris, 1916)
Ouspensky, *Octateuque*	T. Ouspensky, *L'Octateuque de la bibliothèque du Serail à Constantinople* (Sofia, 1907)
Pächt, *St Albans*	O. Pächt *et al.*, *The St Albans Psalter (The Albani Psalter)* (1960)
PL	*Patrologia cursus completus*, Series Latina, ed. J.P. Migne (221 vols., Paris, 1844–91)
Ronig, *Codex*	F. Ronig, *Codex Egberti* (Trier, 1977)
Schiller, *Ikonographie*	G. Schiller, *Ikonographie der christlichen Kunst* (4 vols., Gütersloh, 1966–80)
Swarzenski, *Monuments*	Hanns Swarzenski, *Monuments of Romanesque Art*, 2nd edn (Chicago, 1967)
Temple, *Anglo-Saxon Manuscripts*	Elzbieta Temple, *Anglo-Saxon Manuscripts 900–1066* (1976)
Tolhurst, *Breviary*	*The Monastic Breviary of Hyde Abbey, Winchester*, ed. John B.L. Tolhurst (6 vols., 1933–42)
Volbach, *Spätantike*	W.F. Volbach, *Die Elfenbeinskulpturen der Spätantike und des frühen Mittelalters*, 3rd edn (Mainz, 1976)
Wilpert, *I sarcofagi*	Giuseppe Wilpert, *I sarcofagi cristiana antichi* (5 vols., Rome, 1918–32)
Wormald, *Winchester*	Francis Wormald, *The Winchester Psalter* (1973)

Preface

THIS STUDY began in January of 1971 as the topic for a report in a seminar dealing with illuminated manuscripts. The assignment was a logical one since the Winchester Psalter was a little studied masterpiece of English Romanesque painting. It was with considerable sadness that plans for a dissertation on the Psalter were set aside later that year upon learning of Francis Wormald's forthcoming monograph. For British Library MS Cotton Nero C.IV had already become, to borrow a phrase from R. W. Southern, an object of great scholarly affection. The appearance of Wormald's book invited a reconsideration of this decision. He viewed his study as one that would break new ground in the hope that this would stimulate further research. It did, in fact, accomplish far more, offering any number of important contributions on the calendar, litany, provenance and style of the manuscript. On questions concerning the iconography, his book provided a significant introduction to an extremely complex subject. However, further investigation of the iconography seemed warranted in view of the numerous additional questions prompted by the literature that appeared after Wormald's death. The decision to return to this topic was made in the hope that it would be viewed as the continuation Wormald himself encouraged. This study was certainly undertaken in that spirit, as one which builds on the work of a scholar who in this area, as in so many others, offered new insights which increased our understanding and appreciation of English medieval painting.

In addition to continuing and expanding upon the traditional iconographic enquiry initiated by Wormald, the concluding section of this study attempts to break new ground in another area. An initial effort was made in this direction a decade ago but abandoned when notes collected over a period of two years were inadvertently burned by the custodial staff of a major European library. Perhaps this was a sign that this line of enquiry was best set aside, and it was. However, discoveries made in the same library several years later suggested that the topic should be reopened.

In pursuing this subject anew, I have attempted to expand upon a strict consideration of the iconography to explore the factors that governed the inclusion of a pictorial frontispiece in Nero C.IV. Since the questions raised with regard to this issue draw on disciplines beyond the normal domain of an art historian, they are raised in the hope of engaging the interest and attention of specialists in other fields who could develop them further.

A study of this nature would have been impossible without aid and guidance from many sources, for which I am extremely grateful. My research for a doctoral dissertation on this topic was supported by a Penfield Fellowship from New York University (1973–4) and a Robert Goldwater Fellowship from the Institute of Fine Arts (1975–6). Additional support was provided by the University of Massachusetts, Amherst, in 1979 and the National Endowment for the Humanities in 1983–4. In addition, a number of institutions made their materials readily available to me; among them are: the Bibliothèque Royale in Brussels, the Bibliothèque Nationale in Paris, the Biblioteca Apostolica Vaticana in Rome, the Bodleian Library, the British Library, Corpus Christi College Library at Cambridge University, the Courtauld Institute, Durham Cathedral Library, the Harvard University libraries, the Kupferstichkabinett in Berlin, Lincoln Cathedral Library, Pembroke College Library at Cambridge University, St John's College Library at Cambridge University, Universitätsbibliothek in Bremen, the University Library at Cambridge University, the Warburg Institute and Winchester Cathedral Library. Among the librarians and curators of these institutions, I would like to express my gratitude to F. Avril, J. Backhouse, R. I. Page, J. Ker, G. Knoll, G. Dogar, F. Mielke and R. Simpson.

Among the individuals who contributed valuable suggestions to this study, I would like to thank Janet Backhouse, Harry Bober, Julian Brown, Hugo Buchthal, Vincent Cleary, Adelheid Heimann, Christopher Hohler, Michael Kauffmann, Tom Mathews, Nigel Morgan, Anthony Parker and Ian Short.

Finally, I would like to thank Heather, the family word processor, and my husband, Walt, who managed with constant good humour to keep both females in his household productively engaged in this project.

Chapter One: Description of the Manuscript, Reconstruction of the Miniature Cycle

FOR A GENERATION, the Winchester Psalter has been a familiar sight in the Grenville Hall of the British Museum Library. There, in a handsome case, it rests comfortably in the company of many of the other treasures of medieval illumination. Surrounded as it is by some of the finest examples of English medieval painting, it pales in comparison to its companions. However ingeniously conceived and deftly executed, its pen drawings are somewhat overshadowed by the dazzling brilliance of the Benedictional of St Aethelwold or the contrast of rich, deep colours against the pristine vellum of the Shaftesbury Psalter. For, unlike most medieval manuscripts, Nero C.IV has suffered from numerous additions and emendations which have altered and marred its original appearance. It is, therefore, essential to begin this study of its iconography with an examination of the physical condition of the book. Such an evaluation yields a number of clues which can be brought to bear on the problem of the original structure and appearance of this manuscript.

1. DESCRIPTION OF THE MANUSCRIPT

The manuscript is composed of 142 vellum leaves. Each leaf measures 32 cm × 22.5 cm.

Collation

The original structure of the quires has not survived. The bifolia have been cut apart and mounted as a series of separate leaves.

The Miniatures

The illustrations occupy the first 38 leaves, folios 2–39. They depict scenes from the Old Testament, life of Christ, the Virgin and the Last Judgment.

The miniatures have been trimmed, inlaid in vellum frames and mounted as a series of single-leaf rectos. The vellum employed for the miniatures is fairly thin and brownish in colour. The edges of each sheet have been bevelled to facilitate the inlaying process. There is virtually no variation in the texture of the exposed side of the vellum. Each sheet has a fairly rough, suede-like surface. Microscopic examination reveals that the miniatures appear on the hair sides of the leaves. Examination of the versos is impossible because the miniatures are glued to the frames.

Some folia are occupied by a single subject, while other leaves are divided into two or three registers to accommodate a larger number of scenes. The dimensions of these registers vary considerably.[1] The picture space is bordered in black ink. In cases where the margins of the original sheets are intact no marks from the ruling or pricking remain. The scenes were drawn in black ink and some were tinted with limited applications of brown, buff, green, red and blue wash.

The attribution of the miniatures presents a problem other than the common one of associating the work of various masters with clearly differentiated stylistic traditions. Although there is considerable variety, it can best be described as a variation in quality which is sometimes quite considerable. One exceptional group of miniatures stands apart from the rest. The Betrayal of Christ and Flagellation (Fig. 20) are among them and serve to illustrate the salient characteristics of this group. The body proportions of the figures in these scenes are fairly normal, with firm, rounded limbs and well-defined mid-sections. The relation of head to body is slightly abnormal, as large heads well up to dominate slender bodies. The head type used for Christ was repeated throughout the cycle. It has a broad forehead, high cheekbones, tiny drooping earlobe and narrow jaw. Dramatic eyebrows arch above large, rounded eyes which droop at the corners. The eyes continue down into a sharp nose, moustache and small mouth. The full head of hair swells above the head, projects onto the forehead and clings to the neck in a rolled braid. The drapery patterning, which places the figure in the high Romanesque phase of English illumination, receives careful attention here. The body is dissected into a series of interlocking segments by the continuous motion of a fluid, curving line. The line forms an askew oval over the shoulder joint, slices down and inward across the arm, then hooks sharply in the opposite direction. The abdomen stands out clearly, defined by a larger version of the ovoid shoulder division. Below, the double curved line slithers across the thigh and ripples into the hem. The undergarment further divides the body at the knee and ankle while the complicated hems swing gracefully. The artist was not content to articulate the figure with linear divisions but accentuated corners and edges by an intricate, varied web of pattern. Rivulets of V-shapes were his choice for this figure, but a wide range of patterns appears in other miniatures, one of which is the U-shaped wedge used on Pilate in the Flagellation. The artist also paid close attention to the smallest finishing details. The hems of garments were edged with ornamented borders of varied description. The fillet binding Christ's hair in the Flagellation and the inside surface of the sleeves of Pilate are other examples. The subtlety and variety displayed in the drapery patterning are equalled by this artist's shading technique. The brilliant definition of Christ's arms and torso in the Flagellation is an outstanding example. The arms are divided by pairs of half-ovals while the chest is divided into three sections by a tree-like pattern. Shading is applied elsewhere to indicate the texture of hair, beards, chain mail and fur. Apart from this, the only colour is found around the contour lines of each of the segmented areas which form the stylized bodies and borders. Colour follows the outlines of the drawing, giving the effect of a shadow, softening the otherwise harsh impression created by the pen line. There is no trace of colour in the centre of these segmented areas. It is, then, a tinted drawing technique where a limited application of thin, even coloured wash is relieved against the vellum ground. The overall impression is one of a superb draughtsman capable of work of the highest quality which displays meticulous attention even to the slightest detail. The master's superior level of technical skill becomes a secondary issue compared to the dramatic force which infuses scenes like the Betrayal where the lyrically poised figures of Christ and Judas hover in the midst of a crowd gripped by a mood of violent frenzy. Among the other miniatures in this group are those on fols. 2, 4, 7, 9, the lower half of 15, 16, 18, 19, 20, the top half of 24, the lower half of 35, 37, 38, and 39.

The other miniatures in the manuscript can be separated from this group for a variety of reasons. Generally, the rest of the miniatures lack the consistently high quality of the first group. An examination of the Presentation in the Temple (Fig. 14) illustrates these points. The shape of Simeon's face suggests that the artist consulted the model used for the doctor seated to the left of Christ in the scene directly below. The use of the same model makes the deviations from group one more obvious. The curve of the face hints at the high cheekbones of the elder with a line that swells outward then slides in to meet the extremely long beard. The facial contour suggested by this line is somewhat misunderstood in relation to the other facial features. It is impossible to determine the relation of the schematically drawn eyes to the rest of the face. They hover in the cheekbone area. In the face of the elder, the bone curves out below the eyes, clearly indicating their place in the facial structure. This lack of sureness extends to the hesitantly arched eyebrows, askew nose, and lack of skill in coordinating parts of the body. The shoulder joint is absent, making it appear that the thin arm grows out of the chest. The other arm, which encircles Christ, is abnormally long. The treatment of the drapery is weak, crisscrossed by a pattern of sagging lines. The miniatures in this group include all those not cited above, with the exception of those on fols. 29 and 30. There are slight variations in scale of certain figures on fols. 3 and 5, which may be due to the influence of the Old Testament iconographic source.

In spite of the differences in quality, the miniatures in these two groups are closely linked to one another. They follow a single stylistic norm typical of mid-twelfth-century English painting. Because there is only one style represented here, it is difficult to ascribe the groups to different artists. Certain factors do suggest that one artist could have executed the entire series. The variation in quality sometimes occurs on the same page, as, for example, fol. 15. There is also considerable variation within individual scenes. In the Marriage at Cana (Fig. 16), elements like the tablecloth and tree are skilfully drawn while the figures are quite weak. The combination of varying levels of quality within individual miniatures announces a fusion of the seemingly disparate groups. Whether to interpret this as uncommonly drastic fluctuations within the work of one artist or an indication that the master worked so closely with an assistant that they collaborated on certain scenes is difficult to determine. Both situations are quite unusual. What is clear and most important for a consideration of the iconography is that the drawings form a closely knit group, conceived and executed contemporaneously.

More difficult is the question of the two 'Byzantine' miniatures on fols. 29 and 30. Wormald suggested that they are by an artist other than the one responsible for the other miniatures.[2] Since they differ stylistically from the rest, an assessment of their relationship is placed on a different footing. However, there are certain features which indicate they may well have been the work of the main artist. The head of Christ in the scene of the Death of the Virgin (Fig. 28) is the easiest to connect with the work of the master. It is extremely close in a number of respects to that of Christ on fol. 21 (Fig. 20).

The miniatures bear three sets of inscriptions. One, in Latin, appears on the scrolls carried by some of the figures. It may well be the work of the scribe responsible for the text on fols. 40–142. The same black ink was used in both cases.[3] Moreover, characteristic features of his hand described in this chapter, most notably the 'us' sign, are present here. A second set, in Anglo-Norman French, appears on the margins of some of the scenes. A different ink was used for these inscriptions and has faded to a brownish colour. Although added in the twelfth century, the French inscriptions are the work of another hand.[4] A third, thirteenth-century group of inscriptions in French appear in the margins of certain scenes in red ink.

Four systems of foliation are found on the miniatures. There are two sets of Roman and two sets of Arabic numerals. Wormald tentatively identified the larger set of Roman numerals which first appear on fol. 8 as the work of a sixteenth-century hand. This set of numerals was drawn in a dark brown ink. A second, smaller set of Roman numerals first appears on fol. 12. These numerals are drawn in a different, faded brown ink. A set of Arabic numerals begins in black ink on what is now fol. 2 with '1'. Wormald noted that these numbers were added after the Roman numerals. It may also be observed that the same hand foliated other manuscripts in the Cotton collection, including Cleopatra B.XIII, Nero A.II, Vitellius A.XIX, and Galba A.XVIII. The identification of the same hand in the Galba manuscript is particularly significant since it can contribute to a closer dating of the Arabic foliation in Nero C.IV. A set of small numbers now only partially visible appears at the browned edges of the Galba leaves, suggesting they were added before the folia were singed in the Cotton fire of 1731. The larger set of numbers, corresponding to those in Nero C.IV, were placed lower down on the pages, suggesting that they were added after the fire. This gives a date after the first quarter of the eighteenth century for this set of foliation numbers in the Psalter.

A second set of Arabic numbers in lead point appears in a modern hand on the frames of the miniatures. Other traces of writing appear on various miniatures. '5r' is inscribed above the gate of Paradise (Fig. 1) in a seventeenth- or eighteenth-century hand. Two marks in black ink 'II' appear in the lower register of fol. 2 and upper register of fol. 3. On fol. 7 (Fig. 6), the lower register, what appears to be a 'xiii' is visible when the page is held upside down. The black ink used for these marks does not correspond to that used elsewhere in the manuscript.

There are also traces of writing on the outer margins of fols. 5, 9, 13 and the inner margins of fols. 6, 10, 14, 18. The script can be identified as a late sixteenth- or early seventeenth-century Elizabethan secretary hand which slants to the left, that is, backwards. Traces of paste appear together with the script on fol. 5. This suggests that these impressions of groups of letters were caused by pasting strips of an Elizabethan document onto the leaves of the Psalter. When the strips were later removed, a mirror image of some of the letters was left on the vellum. This practice was not uncommon among bookbinders of the seventeenth century and later. Similar strips still remain pasted to the inner edges of certain folios of the Benedictional of St Aethelwold, B.L., MS Add. 49598.[5]

Offsets caused by verdigris pigment are visible on many of the miniatures.[6]

The Text

The text occupies fols. 40 to 142. The vellum is uniform throughout. It is white to greyish white in colour, smooth and fairly thin. It is difficult to discern any significant differences between the hair and flesh sides with the naked eye. Both sides are fairly smooth and no pores are visible. However, under a microscope it is possible to determine that the folia were arranged in the normal manner, with hair facing hair and flesh facing flesh. The text begins with a calendar which occupies fols. 40 to 45. The writing space measures 22 × 11 cm. There are 35 lines per page. The lines are not filled out. The longest has approximately 32 characters per line.

The text continues with the Gallican version of the psalms together with an Old French version.[7] The pages are ruled with lead point into two columns, each of which measures 26.2 × 7 cm. There are 1.4 cm between the columns. There are 40 lines of text per column. The text was written in the same black ink used for the Latin inscriptions and miniatures. The lines are filled out with approximately 36 characters per column. From fol. 46r to 50r the Latin text occupies the right column and the French text the left. From 50v to 123r the Latin version occupies the left column and the French the right.

Major divisions of the text occur at psalms 1, 26, 38, 51, 68, 80, 97, 101 and 109. This can be explained by a combination of the eight-part Benedictine division with the three-part Insular system.[8] The largest initials mark psalms 1, 26 and 101. These initials, drawn in pen and containing both floral motifs and human figures, can be attributed to the artisan responsible for the miniatures. Psalms 51 and 109 are marked by large letters (4–5 cm) in red and blue. The remaining divisions at psalms 38, 68, 80 and 97 are marked by letters approximately 2.5 cm in height. The bodies of the first three letters are in blue. Foliate tendrils within the body of the letter in red complete these initials. The fourth for psalm 97 is in green and filled with blue tendrils. There is also a 2 cm initial marking a monastic division of psalm 108:8. The first letter of each remaining psalm was drawn in a single colour in a typical twelfth-century display script. The colours alternate between red, blue and green. These letters occupy the height of the ruled space for one column of text, approximately .8 cm, making them twice the size of the remaining text.

The remaining textual material includes canticles, 123v–130r; Gloria in excelsis, 130r; Pater Noster, 130v; Apostles Creed, 130v; Quicunque vult, 130v–132r; the litany, 132r–132v, collects 133v–134r; and 36 prayers, 134r–142v.[9]

The text is the work of a single scribe. The many features of his handwriting which occur consistently throughout include the following. In the ampersand, the lower counter between the first and second strokes is a narrow oval slanting downwards from left to right at an angle of about 45 degrees; the upper counter formed by the third stroke is small or non-existent; the first stroke ends in a long, steeply rising hairline to which a conspicuous squat serif is attached on the left; and the second stroke, ending in a short rising hairline, descends below the bottom of the first. The abbreviation line is short and ends in a rising hairline which usually carries a modest serif on the left. The symbol for *-us* is made in two strokes, with a small counter between them, the second of which is notably angular and ends in a hairline which usually touches the corner of the letter to which it refers. The zigzag tag under the tagged *e* is usually quite long and consists of two delicate hairlines formed by a short thick line running more or less parallel to the baseline of the letters above.

The scribe who wrote the text may well have had a larger role in the production of this manuscript. The Latin inscriptions within the miniatures were written with the same ink employed for the text and may well have been written by the main scribe. The miniatures which incorporate these inscriptions were also fashioned with this ink. They are quite probably the work of one artisan, possibly with some assistance. The master responsible for the miniature cycle also drew the large pen initials for psalms 1, 26, and 101 with this ink. This indicates that the scribe was at work on the miniatures and the artisan on the text. This, at the very least, suggests that there was extremely close collaboration between the scribe and artisan. This is also supported by an examination of the pen initials for the psalms. The text overlaps the initials for psalms 26 and 101, indicating that the initials were in place before the text was written.[10] This is very unusual. More often the opposite was the case and with good reason. It is simpler to position the initials correctly in relation to a completed page of text than on a blank sheet of vellum. The latter situation which was the case here would have required especially careful planning and close coordination of the activities of scribe and artisan. It is certainly possible that this occurred but another explanation suggests itself. All of these circumstances make it possible to consider the possibility that the scribe and artisan may have been one and the same individual.

Binding

The binding is modern. Traces of an earlier binding are visible at the extreme left-hand edge of the leaves. There are five wedge-shaped marks indicating that the spine had five bands flush with it in the sunken cord style. A series of prick marks in the same margin leaves traces of an earlier stitching in the overcast method.

Provenance

As early as 1873, a serious attempt was made to determine the date and provenance of the Psalter. Through an examination of the calendar and prayers, Thompson and Bond found connections with both twelfth-century Winchester and Shaftesbury.[11] They suggested that the prayer addressed to St Swithun probably indicated that the manuscript was written at the Benedictine Priory of St Swithun's, Winchester and the addition to the calendar for the dedication of the church at Shaftesbury that it later became the property of this house. A more precise *terminus ante quem* for the date was later based on the fact that the feast of Edward the Confessor was not entered in the calendar, suggesting that the manuscript was completed before Edward's canonization in 1161.[12] Wormald secured this attribution by identifying several Winchester saints in the calendar and dated the Shaftesbury additions to the thirteenth century.[13] In addition, Wormald was the first to point to Hyde Abbey, Winchester, elements in the calendar but maintained the traditional attribution to St Swithun's. The connection to St Swithun's has been supported in more recent studies, especially in view of the prayer to St Swithun which specifically states that the petitioner offers the prayer to Swithun in his *aula*. Two scholars have suggested that Hyde elements are understandable in a St Swithun's manuscript of this period since Hyde had no abbot and was under the jurisdiction of St Swithun's Priory and the bishop of Winchester, Henry of Blois.[14]

Elements in the Latin prayers also offer clues concerning the identity of the patron. The masculine singular form is used in these private prayers for the petitioner. Some prayers make collective pleas, on behalf of the petitioner's *benefactores*. These elements point towards a monastic patron. However, the last three Latin prayers as well as the Gloria, Pater Noster, Apostles Creed, Quicunque vult and the psalms also have an Anglo-Norman French version. The presence of the French forms complicate the question of patronage because they appear with some frequency in twelfth-century manuscripts with Benedictine connections as well as in those intended for secular patrons.[15] This suggests that the manuscript was made before 1161, probably for a Benedictine[16] associated with St Swithun's Priory and possibly also intended to be used by that individual for the spiritual direction of others.

The Psalter was not to remain long in Winchester. Later entries in the calendar indicate that some time in the thirteenth century the manuscript passed into the hands of the Benedictine nunnery dedicated to the Virgin and St Edward at Shaftesbury. As Wormald observed, these additions cannot be earlier than 1257 when Stephen Bauceyn, a soldier of Henry III, was killed by the Welsh. His obit is written in the same hand as the rest of the Shaftesbury additions.

The ownership of the manuscript from the thirteenth century until it entered the Cotton collection cannot be determined. The exact date when it became a part of the Cotton library is also unclear. The founder of the collection, Sir Robert Cotton, is believed to have begun collecting manuscripts around 1588 and continued his activities until 1629.[17] Additions were made to the collection by his son Thomas and grandson John before it was presented to the nation in 1700.[18] There are several methods used to ascertain whether a manuscript was acquired by Robert Cotton. One is his signature on the opening leaf of the manuscript.[19] The condition of the Psalter makes verification on this basis impossible. A second means of determining whether a manuscript entered the collection through his efforts is an unpublished 1621 catalogue of the collection, B.L., MS Harley 6018. The entries are numbered from 1 to 413 and bear no reference to the shelf marks used in the Cotton library and subsequently. Identification must rest upon isolating details of an entry which can be related to the manuscript in question. None of the cryptic entries for psalters points unequivocally to Nero C.IV, which does not rule out the possibility that it is listed here. It is more certain that the manuscript entered the collection before 1638. The evidence appears in the second catalogue of the Cotton collection drawn up after the death of Robert Cotton in 1631, but before 1638. On fol. 121v of the unpublished catalogue, London, B.L., MS Add. 36789, there is an entry which reads: 'plurime picturae david psalmi latino et gallico'.

2. A RECONSTRUCTION OF THE MINIATURE CYCLE

Wormald was the first to notice that the present arrangement of the miniatures, mounted as a series of 38 rectos, is not the original one.[20] He observed that the three earliest sets of foliation appear only on alternate leaves. This is best explained by the common practice of numbering only the recto of each leaf. Accordingly, Wormald rearranged the miniatures, mirrored in the arrangement of plates in his monograph, so that the miniatures face each other in pairs. This suggestion was later confirmed by Mara Witzling.[21] She pointed out that the original right-hand margins of even-numbered miniatures from fol. 8 on are apparent. From fol. 19 on left-hand margins are visible. This would correspond with the normal practice of giving pages originally painted on rectos a larger right-hand margin, and the versos a wider left-hand margin.

In order to achieve the arrangement he proposed, Wormald commented that 'at some time before the middle of the nineteenth century the leaves with the full-page miniatures were split and the verso pictures mounted as rectos'.[22] The date when such a procedure was carried out was established by Witzling. She drew attention to the fact that the text pages, also separated into leaves, are foliated in Arabic numerals in the upper right-hand corner of each recto, ending on fol. 122. This corresponds with the description given in the 1802 catalogue of the Cotton collection. According to the current foliation, the manuscript concludes on fol. 142. This discrepancy of 20 matches the gain of 19 pages achieved by the separate mounting of the versos in the miniature cycle, since Wormald's foliation begins with fol. 2. Since the manuscript went to the bindery only once between 1802 and 1873, when the leaves were first described mounted as rectos, the change was quite probably made in 1842.[23] The other remark in Wormald's statement regarding splitting the leaves has not been satisfactorily explored in depth. Exactly what Wormald intended by this remark is unclear. There are two possible ways of interpreting it. Each bifolium, each measuring 32 × 45 cm could have been painted on both sides and peeled apart to produce two thinner bifolia still measuring 32 × 45 cm. Or the bifolia could have been painted on one side and cut along the fold, resulting in two leaves each measuring 32 × 22.5 cm. Painting bifolia on both sides was the common practice in twelfth-century England. It occurs in earlier twelfth-century manuscripts with prefatory cycles including the St Albans and Shaftesbury Psalters.[24] However, while this practice might reasonably be anticipated for the Winchester manuscript,[25] practical considerations suggest that this was not the case.[26] The alternative explanation suggests that the bifolia were painted only on one side. Although this procedure was not commonplace, there are precedents for this practice. Miniatures appear on only one side of the leaves in the Book of Durrow, in Amiens, B.M., MS Escalopier 2, an eleventh-century psalter from Angers, in Valenciennes, B.M., MS 500, a twelfth-century saint's life from St Amand, and in the York and Ingebourg Psalters as well as a number of thirteenth-century psalters.[27] In most of these cases, the miniatures are arranged so that two miniatures face each other. After each pair of miniatures intervene two unpainted back sides, so that the cycle alternates between a painted and unpainted pair. If the Winchester miniatures had been arranged in this manner, the job of separating them would have been relatively simple. Each bifolium could have been cut down the middle along the fold line, resulting in two smaller leaves. Perhaps this is what Wormald intended to suggest for it is possible to construe his remarks in this manner.

Wormald made one last observation about the makeup of the cycle. He pointed out that there is a difference between the Arabic and Roman numerals in the manuscript. The Roman numerals first appear on what is presently fol. 8 as VI, while the Arabic foliation gives this page as 4.[28] From this he concluded that two leaves were lost from the beginning of the manuscript. He suggested that they contained scenes of the Creation and Adam and Eve. The range of possibilities here is really somewhat broader than Wormald indicated. It is conceivable that as many as two miniatures could have been lost. On the other hand, it is possible that the cycle is complete. The missing leaves could have been addenda to the manuscript. Leaves tipped in at a later date were usually numbered together with the original material. It is also possible that the missing leaves, even if a part of the original twelfth-century manuscript, did not contain miniatures. While some psalters with prefatory cycles begin with miniatures, others do not. In these cases, the illustrations are preceded by textual material. An eleventh-century psalter from Winchester, B.L., MS Cotton Tiberius C.VI, a twelfth-century psalter in Madrid with a Winchester calendar and the York Psalter are examples.[29]

Wormald's remarks prompted a reconsideration of the original arrangement of the miniatures by several other scholars. In his review of Wormald's monograph, Carl Nordenfalk proposed making fols. 6 and 7 with the story of David face one another, placing 7 before 6 to achieve the correct chronological order. Similarly, he arranged fol. 3 (Noah, Abraham) with 5 (Jacob, Joseph) and 4 (Joachim) with 8 (the infancy of the Virgin).[30] More recent studies have proposed other arrangements; most notable among them is that of Mara Witzling.[31] In the main, her suggestions offer substantive proof for Wormald's arrangement of the miniatures. Her reconstruction was based on the discovery of offsets on some of the miniatures. Fibre-optic light examination does confirm that these offsets are present on all of the miniatures. It is particularly noticeable on fol. 4 where the doorway from the Joseph scenes left a clear impression on the Moses page (Fig. 3). In this case, and all the others, the offsets were caused by a verdigris pigment. Verdigris is a green or greenish blue pigment resulting from the action of acetic acid on copper.[32] It is an unstable substance that begins to react with vellum immediately upon contact and continues to react with it as long as the contact is maintained. This pigment can bleed forward into a facing leaf and/or through the back of a leaf and even into an adjoining leaf. In the Winchester Psalter, it is clear that the latter was most often the case. The majority of the green imprints do not appear on the surface of the leaves. They look hazy and indistinct until a strong light is held behind the page. It is only then that the offsets become sharp and their outlines can be matched against green shapes in other miniatures. The marks that verdigris leaves are, then, like footprints in wet cement. Every step has been recorded and is a clear indicator of the proximity of the leaves at every moment when contact existed. This is of particular value in the case of the Winchester Psalter because the original structure of the quires has been destroyed. The information which the verdigris offsets provide is two-fold in nature. They suggest the original arrangement of the miniatures. The Adam and Eve scenes on fol. 2 bear only traces of fol. 3. This would most logically correspond with the placement of fol. 2 as a recto with 3 immediately following as a verso, as Wormald first noted. Fol. 4 depicting scenes from the life of Moses bears the clear impression of the Jacob and Joseph scenes on fol. 5. In this case, the Moses scenes should logically follow the Joseph scenes, as Witzling suggested. However, if this was the original arrangement, the shift in position would have occurred before the addition of the seventeenth-century binding strips and Arabic foliation, both of which support Wormald's arrangement of 4 before 5. In similar fashion, fol. 6 with scenes of David and Goliath bears traces of fol. 7 with scenes of David as a shepherd. Again, the chronology of these events in I Kings suggests that 7 originally preceded 6, as Nordenfalk proposed, although back to back rather than as a facing pair. Fol. 8 with the life of the Virgin bears traces of fol. 9, the Jesse Tree. Here the order appears to be undisturbed and to follow the arrangement of Wormald. The remaining miniatures continue in a chronological sequence which corresponds with the verdigris traces and in the order proposed by Wormald.[33] The presence of the offsets also offers a second important source of information concerning the miniature cycle. Since the distinct impressions left by the verdigris can be accounted for by examining the extant miniatures it is unlikely that single miniatures were ever removed. However, since the range of subject matter and arrangement of miniatures has no exact parallels elsewhere, venturing further would exceed what the fragmentary evidence is capable of revealing.

Not all the miniatures originally envisaged as tinted drawings were completed. Many areas were drawn in pen outline and never accented with colour. The most striking example is the frequently reproduced scene of the Angel Locking the Damned in Hell (Fig. 38). The upper half of the Hell-mouth was drawn in pen and covered with an even green wash. The lower half received the identical treatment in pen outline but only a few strokes of colour were applied to the nose. Since by far the largest concentrations of untinted drawings appear near the end of the cycle,[34] it is reasonable to assume that the initial plan was interrupted before it was carried to completion.[35]

The confusion that has arisen over the original condition of the manuscript appears to be the result of the misinterpretation of the application of opaque paint, black ink and gilding to the partially unfinished drawings. These features can be explained as a series of alterations and additions which can be approximately dated and are particularly valuable for explaining the present condition of the drawings. In addition to over 250 figures, architectural settings and borders executed in the tinted drawing style, approximately 30 figures and some architectural details and elements of the borders are or were fully painted.[36] Although a small number of these figures appear throughout the manuscript, the largest concentration appears in the drawings left incomplete near the end of the cycle. Even here they are scattered randomly throughout the unfinished scenes. The scant proportion of these figures and their curious, sporadic appearance differs from the consistent character of the tinted-drawing cycle. This suggests that they represent a deviation from the original plan. Other features also point in this direction. On fol. 25 (Fig. 24), for example, only the face of Christ was painted while the body was tinted. Although there are rare instances where tinted and painted figures appear in the same work in the twelfth century,[37] it is unique to find them combined in the same figure. It is difficult to believe that this unorthodox juxtaposition of painted and tinted areas was planned from the beginning. However, in the cases where the paint surfaces are intact, it is evident that these figures were executed in a style contemporary with that of the tinted drawings. The mid-century date and placement of these painted features suggest that some of the miniatures were altered shortly after the pen sketches were completed.

Additional observations lead to similar conclusions. A series of Anglo-Norman French inscriptions accompany some of the miniatures. They are not uniform in their placement or in the size of the script. Some appear on the gold framing bands, as on fol. 7 (Fig. 6), but where these borders are too narrow, they appear above the border of fol. 10 (Fig. 9) on arches, fol. 14 (Fig. 13), squeezed between and over architecture and figures, fols. 27 and 28 (Figs. 26, 27), or in the middle of a miniature, fol. 20 (Fig. 19). The French inscriptions are not by the scribe who wrote the text and possibly also the Latin inscriptions on the scrolls. There is an extreme regularity of forms which lacks the variety found in the text. The display script shows a mixture of capital and uncial forms in a fairly rigid formula. The alphabet as a whole depends largely on capital forms with the exception of *e*, *m*, and *h* which are always uncial.[38] *M* is only exceptionally a capital, on fols. 13 and 15. By contrast the text shows far greater variety. On fol. 44v, for example, three forms for the *A* were employed. Furthermore, letter forms in the text are, in general, rounder and more flexible. The serifs were usually formed with curved strokes, while those in the inscriptions are rigid and straight. There are also two letter forms in the inscriptions which do not occur in the text. They can be described as a closed *e*, found on fol. 7, and a closed *m*, likewise found on fol. 7 and elsewhere. These closed forms for these letters are not regularly encountered in manuscripts dated before 1150, but become increasingly common in the third quarter of the twelfth century, especially in the 1170s and beyond.[39] They occur mixed with other forms in B.L., MS Royal

2.A.XXII, dated 1173–1220, but in other instances were used fairly consistently by the third quarter of the twelfth century, e.g. in B.L., MS Royal 3.A.XII, from Cirencester.[40]

An examination of the language of the French inscriptions by Ian Short, who contributed the following commentary, established similar boundaries for their dating.[41]

> Archaic spellings in Nero C.IV include the preserved dentals in *enfantet*, *meinet*, *offret*, which become less common as the twelfth century advances. As for *espirs* for *espirz* (=*espiriz*), *innocens* for *innocenz*, and the two examples of nom. pl. *li apostles* for *li apostle*, these might seem to point to later in the century rather than earlier, but Philippe de Thaon in his *Bestiaire* of 1121–35 uses mixed rhymes in *-s* and *-z*, and the *Alexis* of the Albani Psalter of pre-1123 shows similar developments in the declension system. The orthography could just as well be that of the 1130s as the 1160s, and Norman perhaps (we have no points of comparison) just as well as Anglo-Norman. The variations in spelling could possibly indicate a somewhat later scribe copying earlier tituli. There is no definite evidence to preclude a dating up to the 1160s or even the 1170s; to put it any later would involve postulating a model being copied which had archaic traits in its spelling. I would be quite happy to accept a *ca.* 1150 dating on what little linguistic evidence there is, and just as happy to admit a possible margin of 20 or so years on either side.

The assessment of the inscriptions as alterations may be extended to a series of heavy, crude outlines which are drawn in another type of black ink. They were used to strengthen the fine pen outlines of figures and edge the gilded borders. The less accomplished character of these black lines also applies to the gilding of the hems of garments, crowns, and many borders. Here the gold obliterates details such as the delicate beading on the border of the Virgin's robe (Fig. 15). Moreover, where black ink articulates the gilding, as on fol. 10 (Fig. 9), it is simpler and cruder than the fine detailing visible beneath the gilding. The application of opaque blue paint to the backgrounds is of a similar nature. It obliterates numerous details which are now visible due to the flaking of the blue paint. These over-painted areas appear throughout the cycle. While the manuscript does not offer internal evidence for a dating of the blue grounds, their frequent appearance in mid-twelfth century manuscripts suggests that they, like the painted figures, gilding and inscriptions, date before 1170.

Chapter Two: The Iconography of the Old and New Testament Scenes

THE DESIGN OF the Winchester cycle called for the inclusion of an introductory series of scenes drawn from the Old Testament. Although this cycle is spare and seemingly abbreviated it yields a wealth of information about Old Testament cycles in England both before and after the Conquest. The artist drew the largest group of scenes from Genesis. He employed a source that has much in common with a group of medieval monuments related to the sixth-century Cotton Genesis.[1] The influence of this group is evident in the first scene on fol. 2 (Fig. 1). The cycle opens with God Reprimanding Adam and Eve conflated together with their Expulsion from Paradise. While no single monument of the Cotton group contains all the features depicted in Nero C.IV, it is striking that all of the details of the Winchester scene are paralleled in a monument of this group. There are certain similarities to Carolingian monuments related to the Cotton Genesis. As in the Bamberg Bible, the angel actually touches Adam on the shoulder.[2] Unlike the Bamberg scene but in agreement with the San Paolo Bible, the couple are naked as they leave Paradise.[3] However, more numerous and distinct parallels lie elsewhere, pointing away from any direct connection with a Carolingian source. A number can be found on an eleventh-century ivory box in the Staatliche Museen in Berlin (Fig. 41).[4] On the ivory, the angel turns to look back over his shoulder as he guides the couple from Paradise. Not only is the glance significant in itself, it also establishes a link to the preceding scene of the Calling. Here God raises his hand in judgment toward a cringing, naked Adam and Eve. The Winchester scene abbreviates this sequence by representing God at the actual Expulsion. This suggests that in forming his illustration of the Admonition and Expulsion, the Winchester artist may have been influenced by a Cotton Calling–Expulsion sequence like the elaborate one on the Berlin ivory. Further evidence for this contention is found in the twelfth-century Millstatt Genesis, Klagenfurt, Mus. Cod. VI, 19, fol. 12r (Fig. 42).[5] Here even the gestures and stances of Adam and Eve in the Calling are nearly identical to their counterparts in the Psalter.

A scene in the lower register further contributes to defining the Cotton model. The Offerings of Cain and Abel is one of the most unusual scenes in the Winchester Genesis cycle. Certain details correspond closely with monuments associated with the Cotton group. The figure of Abel, stepping forward with one knee raised, resembles its counterpart in the Millstatt Genesis (Fig. 44). The bust-length figure of God is paralleled in the wall painting formerly in S. Paolo fuori le mura, Rome,[6] and the Rovigo Bible, Biblioteca dell' Accademia dei Concordi, MS 212[7] (Fig. 45), which also omits the altar between Cain and Abel.[8] However, the Winchester scene differs significantly from all of these examples because it shows Cain turning away. This rare detail can only be found in three other monuments, all of which have been associated with the Cotton group.[9] Its meaning can best be explained by two scenes in the Rovigo Bible (Fig. 45). In the scene just referred to, Cain and Abel raise their offerings to God. This is followed by a second scene where Cain turns away. The inscription identifies the latter as an illustration of Genesis 4:5–7 which describes the wrath of Cain after Abel's preferment. The Rovigo illustration suggests that the unusual Winchester scene was ultimately based on two successive events described in Genesis 4:3–7. It also hints at the derivation of the scene from an ancient source because it follows the characteristically late antique practice of copiously illustrating scriptural passages.

These impressions are reinforced by an examination of the Noah scenes on fol. 3 (Fig. 2). The scene in the middle register illustrates Noah Receiving the Dove into the Ark. The closest comparisons are to a mosaic in San Marco (Fig. 52). Here the Flood is elaborately depicted in four separate scenes: the Drowned Floating in the Waters during the Storm, Noah Sending out the Dove, Noah Receiving the Dove and the Debarcation. Details from each have been combined in the Winchester scene, again hinting at the comprehensive nature of the source. The dead floating in the flood waters closely resemble figures in the mosaic. The open-mouthed, profile view head on the far right in each case, the horse craning its neck to stay above water and the head in the centre shown in three-quarter view with long, wet strands of hair streaming behind suggest a relationship to a Cotton model. The detail of the crow alighting on a corpse in the second frame at San Marco appears on the left in the Psalter. Noah receiving the olive branch from the dove appears in the middle register on the left at San Marco. Additional similarities can be found in the San Marco Debarcation scene. Although the shapes of the arks differ, each is divided into two storeys. The crowds of gesticulating figures also bear some resemblance to one another, if somewhat less specifically.

Jacob's Dream shows points of contact in several respects, with another Cotton monument, an ivory from a group in Salerno (Fig. 62).[10] In both cases, the ladder is positioned from left to upper right. Two angels ascend toward the Creator. This is in direct contradiction of the text which specifically mentions angels both ascending and descending. Other similarities include the arc of heaven at the top of the ladder which the angel on the Salerno ivory touches. The figure of Jacob in both works is shown lying with his upturned face pointing in the direction of the ladder,[11] unlike the majority of representations of this scene where he turns away.[12] Although not as close in other respects, the Millstatt dream scene[13] may help to explain the cube-like structure under Jacob's head. In both the Millstatt and San Paolo fuori le mura scenes[14] the dream scene is followed by Jacob anointing an altar which resembles the shape of the pillow in the Psalter. In the Millstatt scene, the prismatic shape has also been repeated to the left of the anointing scene. This raises the possibility that this feature was incorporated by the Winchester artist from such a scene.

This scene also offers clues about the antiquity of certain elements of the iconography. A painting in the catacomb on the Via Latina, Rome[15] (Fig. 61) agrees with the iconography of the Cotton and Winchester scenes but is especially close to the Nero C.IV depiction. Unlike the Salerno Jacob but in agreement with the Psalter, Jacob is bearded and is only semi-recumbent. Even the movement of an arm across the body and arrangement of the legs agree with the position of the Winchester figure. Another monument which has been discussed in conjunction with the Via Latina catacomb is also of importance here. In the catacomb of SS. Marco e Marcelliano, the ladder is positioned from left to right. Jacob faces it, as he does in the Psalter.[16]

The scene of the Sacrifice of Isaac (Fig. 2) is another which follows the pattern of adhering with considerable fidelity to remote sources. The movement of Abraham's arm, bent at the elbow with the blade pointing behind him, is most closely paralleled in Early Christian monuments. Both the Leucadius sarcophagus in Tarragona[17] and an ivory pyxis in Bologna[18] (Fig. 54) duplicate this pose for Abraham. Equally noteworthy are the parallels for the relatively rare position of Isaac kneeling frontally on the altar.[19] The only other extant examples of this type date from the Early Christian period.[20] A last detail, the blindfold worn by Isaac also displays an awareness of an ancient tradition.[21] In addition to the Salerno ivory, it is found on the Leucadius sarcophagus and an Early Christian gold glass in the Vatican Museum.[22]

These scenes form a pattern that points toward a tradition that can be associated with monuments from Rome in the Early Christian period. There are other scenes in the Psalter which lend added weight to such a theory. On fol. 5 (Fig. 4), there are four scenes from the life of Joseph. The first scene depicts the attempted seduction of Joseph by Potiphar's wife. This relatively rare seated position for Potiphar's wife can be contrasted to the standing type found at San Marco,[23] Millstatt,[24] the Rovigo Bible,[25] as well as in the Octateuchs.[26] It is highly significant that the Winchester type is also found at San Paolo fuori le mura (Fig. 64). Like the Psalter, the Roman frescoes shared much of their iconography with the Cotton group but deviate from it in their Joseph scenes. Instead, as has long been recognized in the case of the frescoes,[27] they draw closer to another ancient Joseph cycle preserved in the Vienna Genesis.[28] In certain respects, the Vienna illustration (Fig. 63) is quite similar to the Winchester scene. Although the twelfth-century scene is reversed, it duplicates many details in the Vienna seduction scene, including the elaborate boudoir setting. The second and third scenes are somewhat less conventional but the fourth scene again finds parallels in the San Paolo wall painting and the Vienna manuscript (Fig. 68) and a related ivory casket in Sens Cathedral (Fig. 69).[29] While all four monuments include the scene of Joseph before Potiphar, the greatest similarities are with the Vienna manuscript and Sens casket. These scenes include an architectural framework and Joseph standing near an open doorway, feet apart with one arm held close to his body and the same relative positions of Joseph and pharaoh.

These comparisons suggest that the artist was familiar with a tradition which had much in common with one known in Early Christian Rome.[30] While this accounts for the distant heritage of the model, there is little reason to suspect that the artist had a venerable Italian codex before him. Throughout the cycle, there are numerous indications that this ancient source had already passed through the hands of Anglo-Saxon artisans. Distinctive Insular motifs such as the jawbone used to murder Abel (Fig. 1) and the shape of the ship in the Noah scenes (Fig. 2) are among them. In addition, there are any number of similarities to scenes in the two extensively illustrated examples of Anglo-Saxon Old Testament illustration, the Caedmon manuscript, Oxford, B.L., MS Junius 11,[31] and Aelfric's Paraphrase of the Pentateuch and Joshua, London, B.L., MS Cotton Claudius B.IV.[32] The latter, as noted in earlier studies, shares iconography with the San Paolo fuori le mura fresco cycle, providing continuity between the Early Christian world and the twelfth century. The Dream of Jacob in Aelfric, for example (Fig. 60), shows numerous points of similarity with the Winchester scene, as well as with San Paolo.[33] The positioning of the ladder and Jacob draws it into a close relationship with the Cotton example from Salerno (Fig. 62) as well as with the Winchester scene. Also similar are the scenes from the life of Noah. In the Psalter, the scene of God Commanding Noah to Build the Ark appears in the upper register of fol. 3 (Fig. 2). The Winchester scene combines two events, God Commanding Noah to Build the Ark and Noah Constructing the Ark. These scenes do appear in Cotton monuments, however in these cases[34] God's presence is indicated by a hand or bust-length figure. The Anglo-

Saxon examples translate this abbreviated image into a full-length figure. God stands before Noah in Aelfric (Fig. 50) and also in the Caedmon manuscript (Fig. 51). The inclusion of a full-length standing figure of God sets them apart from most other Cotton depictions, a distinction which they share only with the Salerno ivories.[35] The second scene involving the actual construction of the ark again draws close to the Anglo-Saxon variants. Unlike San Marco,[36] San Paolo fuori le mura frescoes[37] and the Salerno ivories,[38] where Noah supervises a large work crew, in the Psalter he is alone. This is a feature the Winchester scenes share only with the Millstatt Genesis,[39] Caedmon and Aelfric. Additional similarities to the Anglo-Saxon examples are the shape of the axe with its long, straight blade turning up at the ends and the delicately curving bow of the ark.

The relationship of the Winchester and Caedmon manuscripts can be extended through a comparison of their Murder of Abel scenes. The abbreviated treatment of the Rovigo scene found in the Psalter where Cain's wrath appears as part of the offering scene, can be found in only one monument which predates the Psalter. It appears in the eleventh-century Spanish Ripoll Bible, Rome B.A.V., MS Vat. lat. 5729, fol. 6r in the upper right (Fig. 46).[40] The importance of the relationship to the Ripoll Bible is magnified when it becomes evident that the iconography and, in some instances, even the style of the Spanish manuscript and its sister, the Roda Bible, Paris, B.N., MS lat. 6 (Fig. 47) correspond to the Caedmon manuscript (Fig. 48).[41] A comparison of the scenes from the lives of Cain and Abel in the three manuscripts reveals a number of striking similarities. In the Caedmon manuscript, Abel approaches the hand of God from the left, followed by Cain. It is significant that this is the only scene in the Junius manuscript where the *manus Dei* appears, a feature it shares with both Spanish works. The arrangement of both Cain and Abel to the left is also an unusual aspect of the Caedmon scene. This feature is found in the Roda Bible in the lower left scene (Fig. 48). The succeeding depiction of the Murder also demonstrates the relationship of the three works. In the Caedmon manuscript and Roda Bible, Cain leans forward with the leg closest to Abel bent slightly as he raises a club high above his head. The kneeling Junius Abel raising his hands in front of his body is quite similar to his counterpart in the Ripoll Bible. The close relation of these three manuscripts to one another and the Cotton tradition suggests that the Winchester scene was present in an Anglo-Saxon source.[42]

The scenes from the life of David in the Psalter were modelled upon other sources. The David and Goliath sequence (Fig. 5) was drawn from what was originally a very full cycle. These scenes, and the Anointment of David (Fig. 6), have much in common with a tradition known in both the East and West from an early date and generally referred to as the 'aristocratic recension'.[43] This is evident in the first scene illustrating David before Saul. The only precedent for this extremely rare depiction is found in the Byzantine Book of Kings, Rome, B.A.V., MS Vat. grec 333 (Fig. 71).[44] Another scene which displays parallels to monuments in this group is the combat of David and Goliath. It is quite similar to one in the Byzantine Marciana Psalter (Fig. 72).[45] The last scene on fol. 6, David Returning with the Head of Goliath appears in the Carolingian St Paul's Bible (Fig. 77).[46] While these sources point toward the wide distribution of this cycle, the focus can be narrowed considerably in determining the immediate source of the Winchester scenes. Any number of details indicate that the model was Western, and more than likely, Anglo-Saxon. Parallels for giving David and Goliath different heights is almost never encountered in the East; the Marciana Psalter forms a rare exception. This convention had already been accepted into the Insular repertoire long before the Conquest when it appeared in London, B.L., MS Harley 603, fol. 73v (Fig. 73).[47] Even more clear-cut evidence is provided by the combination of events found in the Winchester manuscript. The second scene simultaneously depicts David preparing to hurl the stone together with Goliath struck by the missile. This particular combination points toward a Western tradition. It is already found in the c.800 Corbie Psalter, Amiens, B.M., MS 18, fol. 123v (Fig. 74), a manuscript which has often been discussed in connection with the Insular tradition.[48] Also highly characteristic of a Western and, more specifically, Anglo-Saxon tradition is the Beheading scene. There are especially close ties to the eleventh-century Arundel Psalter from Winchester (Fig. 75).[49] Here David stands atop Goliath and grips the sword with two hands, a posture never assumed in Byzantine images. Equally significant are the extremely close parallels to the Werden Psalter, fol. 74r (Fig. 76) where David again stands on Goliath.[50] The recent identification of an English source for this eleventh-century manuscript further strengthens a basis for identifying the model as Anglo-Saxon. The Werden scene has added significance because it also provides a parallel for David Returning with the Head of Goliath, drawing the last scene on fol. 6 into a close relationship with a manuscript derived from Anglo-Saxon sources. The Return with the Head can also be found in the Utrecht Psalter (Fig. 78) which was known in England from the early eleventh century.[51]

The second group of David scenes (Fig. 6) can again be traced to another group of sources available in Anglo-Saxon England. David as a Shepherd bears a striking resemblance to one in the Utrecht Psalter (Fig. 78). David's Struggle with the Lion is most closely paralleled in an Anglo-Saxon source. A similar representation appears in the Vespasian Psalter (Fig. 79), strongly pointing toward an Insular model.[52]

In addition to the scenes drawn from Genesis and Kings, there are two other Old Testament scenes from the life of Moses (Fig. 3). They stand in sharp contrast to the fairly traditional character of the Old Testament cycle as a whole. Since they have been altered to the point that they do not point directly toward any specific source, they will be discussed in a separate chapter.

The design of the Winchester cycle also included a request for a New Testament sequence beginning with the Infancy of Christ, continuing with the Passion of Christ and concluding with a lengthy Last Judgment cycle. In fashioning his New Testament miniatures, the Winchester master drew upon four traditions. Three of them point toward the influences that had shaped English illuminations earlier in the twelfth century as well as before the Conquest. A fourth group points toward other sources, indicating that the artist moved away from the mainstream by giving his cycle features not shared by other English manuscripts of the period.

One major source for the Winchester artist was the rich tradition of his own country in the century before the Conquest. Miniatures throughout the cycle preserve many features that are highly characteristic of Anglo-Saxon art. In some cases, especially in the Infancy cycle, the artist adopted these formulae with little change. This is evident in a scene like the Nativity which conforms as a whole to an iconographical formula used in England since Anglo-Saxon times.[53] It is preserved in two pre-Conquest manuscripts, the Sacramentary of Robert of Jumièges, Rouen, B.M., MS Y.6, fol. 32v (Fig. 85) and the Benedictional of St Aethelwold, London, B.L., MS Add. 49598, fol. 15v (Fig. 86).[54] As in the Sacramentary, the artist placed the Virgin parallel to the picture plane. The midwife attending her was fashioned after a counterpart like the one in the Benedictional. In both cases, the midwife stands behind Mary's head and looks toward Joseph, seated at the opposite end of the bed. The position of Joseph at the foot of the bed and his contemplative pose can also be compared to the Benedictional figure. In both cases, Joseph is seated resting his face on his hand. The positioning of Christ's crib below the bed offers a last point of similarity.

Elsewhere the artist reacted in a more original way to the Anglo-Saxon heritage. This is apparent in the highly unusual Cana scene (Fig. 16). The curious scene in the lower panel sets it apart from every other earlier Western Cana scene. While it is fairly common to include servants pouring from water vessels or carrying jugs to the table, the activities in the Psalter are almost unprecedented as a bevy of servants work below stairs. The figure carrying a jug up the ladder can be compared to one in a calendar illustration in London, B.L., MS Cotton Julius A.VI, fol. 5v (Fig. 111). A similar type, now found used as a servant in a banqueting scene, appears in

Harley 603, fol. 66v (Fig. 112).[55] The banqueting scene itself also finds parallels in Anglo-Saxon art. The third figure from the left is comparable to one on the Bayeux Tapestry.[56] This shows an especially wide acquaintance with past traditions and willingness to borrow eclectically as the need arose and draw upon individual motifs, directly or indirectly, to fashion new scenes.

Finally, the Last Judgment cycle (Figs. 30–8) displays a profound awareness of the Anglo-Saxon heritage. Although the length and complexity of this group of scenes is unparalleled in manuscript illumination of this period, details display numerous affinities with a visual tradition established before the Conquest.[57] Wormald has already noted the similarity to the angel locking the door of Hell in the eleventh-century *Liber Vitae* of Hyde Abbey.[58] To this may be added other examples in manuscripts and monumental painting (Figs. 150–1), as well as in ivory carving.[59] However, the cycle as a whole displays a more far-reaching awareness of Anglo-Saxon attitudes than the few extant visual precedents might suggest. The lengthy, detailed Last Judgment cycle echoes the preoccupation with the Doom that gripped the English imagination for generations before the Conquest. It is reflected in the prayers, sermons and poetry of the Anglo-Saxon period. There images of the pains of Hell, the ferocity and violence of its inhabitants, the terrible suffering of the damned and the finality of their imprisonment issue forth with the same vivid clarity.[60]

Another major source of influence on the artist was Ottonian art. This is quite clear in the Annunciation scene (Fig. 10). Here the artist favoured the standing position for the Virgin Annunciate encountered in a number of Ottonian manuscripts. The late tenth-century *Codex Egberti*[61] already displays many of the elements found in the Winchester scene. Here the angel stands on the left in a three-quarter pose raising his hand toward the Virgin. Mary faces him on the right and raises her hand with palm upturned, as in the Psalter. A major difference between the two scenes is the treatment of the architecture in *Egberti*. An architectural frame was designed later for Annunciation scenes in the Echternach scriptorium,[62] drawing them into a closer relationship with the Winchester Annunciation. One is found in the *Codex Aureus Epternacensis*, Nuremberg, Germanisches-Nationalmuseum, MS 156142, fol. 18v (Fig. 83). A more specific parallel for the Winchester frame is found in a slightly later Echternach manuscript, now in the Escorial, Codex Vitrinas 17, fol. 94v (Fig. 87). The exterior architecture is closely comparable. In both cases, rounded towers are connected by sloped walls which meet at a centre block surmounted by a triangular pediment. This suggests that the Winchester artist was influenced by a scene produced at or under the influence of the Echternach scriptorium about a century earlier.

A number of other Infancy scenes in the cycle reflect a fairly broad acquaintance with this Ottonian product. Some, like the Annunciation, merely serve to reinforce the impression that the models resembled the extant examples from that school. In other cases, however, the Winchester iconography reveals that the Ottonian tradition known in twelfth-century England was far richer than these Echternach monuments would suggest. Such a scene is the Massacre of the Innocents (Fig. 13). The general layout of the Winchester composition was already reflected in the *Codex Egberti*, fol. 15v,[63] and was taken over into the Echternach Perikope now in Bremen, Universitätsbibliothek, MS b.21, fol. 13r. More specific and detailed comparisons are possible with *Epternacensis*, fol. 19v (Fig. 97). The stance, gestures and positioning of Herod and the soldier behind him were followed closely by the Winchester illustrator. The artist also looked at Echternach models for other soldiers. The soldier closest to Herod suspending a child from one hand while plunging a sword through the chest was taken over by the Winchester master. Even rare details like the sword carried by Herod are found in the Echternach scene. In other respects, however, the scene created by the Winchester artist departs from the Echternach types. The woman standing on the right in the Psalter cannot be explained on the basis of the extant Echternach models alone. The mothers in the Psalter display shock or stunned surprise as they recoil from the massacre. The Echternach group shows the mothers either huddled on the ground cradling their dead children, fighting with the soldiers or reacting with wildly theatrical gestures and movements. The stunned women in the Psalter display gestures and emotions muted by grief. This attitude is more closely reflected in the Middle Byzantine cycle which has been discussed as the source of the Echternach iconography rather than in the Ottonian group itself. In grec 74, fol. 5r,[64] one of the mothers stands quietly, raising her hands to the sides of her face. An even closer comparison occurs in another manuscript which has also been discussed in relation to this Ottonian group.[65] In Paris, B.N., MS copte 13, fol. 6v[66] (Fig. 100) two mothers stand at the left of the massacre scene. One raises her hand to her mouth while another behind her grasps the side of her face. The women in the Psalter respond with similar gestures, suggesting that the Ottonian source was richer or different in this respect.

Another example involves the sequence of Christ with the Doctors (Fig. 14) followed by the extremely rare scene of Christ with his Parents (Fig. 15). The narrative is described in Luke 2:42f. Jesus accompanied his parents to Jerusalem, stayed behind when they returned home, disputed with the doctors and finally was discovered in the temple by his parents. The first Winchester scene of Christ with the Doctors is extremely similar to the one in the *Escorialensis* (Fig. 104). While Christ's parents are excluded from the *Escorialensis* scene, they are found in the *Codex Egberti* and the Bremen Perikope. This suggests that an Echternach model could have shown the two scenes independent of one another.[67] There are, in fact, several extant Byzantine monuments which demonstrate that the events surrounding Christ's appearance in the temple were at one time illustrated separately.[68] The first two events are illustrated separately in the twelfth-century Gospel book in Florence, Laurentiana, MS VI 23, fol. 106v.[69] The second two scenes in Laurentiana are confined to a single image, like the examples discussed above. Much more significant in this context is the precedent for illustrating Christ among the Doctors separately. In Paris, B.N., MS grec 510, fol. 165r (Fig. 105) Christ's reunion with his parents is shown to the right of the doctors in the temple. Here the Virgin also stands to the left of Christ but instead of the formal detachment of Nero C.IV, she warmly embraces her son. Joseph is also included in the Byzantine manuscript, although further to the left instead of standing on the opposite side, as in the Psalter. Possibly the Winchester artist had before him a model similar to grec 510 which he modified to make the scene strictly symmetrical. In this manner he brought it into harmony with the previous scene of Christ in the temple.

Another reminiscence of these Byzantine cycles is found in the lower panel of the Cana scene (Fig. 16). The artist apparently built up this scene piecemeal, drawing in some cases on Anglo-Saxon traditions. In another instance, there is a significant analogy in grec 74, fol. 170v (Fig. 109). Here a servant stands to the left drawing water from a well. It is the only example of servants at the well which predates the Psalter.[70]

A third source of influence for the Winchester master was the living tradition forged in England a generation earlier.[71] In particular, the artist responsible for the Winchester miniatures has been discussed as someone associated with Bury St Edmunds. The stylistic affiliation between his figure style and that from Bury has long been recognized. A generation ago, Thomas Boase made an extremely perceptive comparison to a drawing of the Crucifixion in a Bury manuscript.[72] Francis Wormald continued, doing more than anyone to define this relationship to Bury in a series of striking comparisons between the Winchester Psalter and Bury Bible, attributed to Master Hugo.[73] He also suggested a further Bury connection for the New Testament Passion cycle in the Pembroke leaves. Michael Kauffmann later confirmed that the Bury New Testament cycle was extremely influential as a source for the Winchester scenes.[74] More recently, Walter Oakeshott proposed that the Nero C.IV master was called from Bury St Edmunds to Winchester.[75]

These impressions must certainly form the basis for any study of this topic. However, they can be modified in certain respects. In addition to the comparisons to the developments at Bury St Edmunds in the 1130s, there are features in the Winchester cycle that show the artist was familiar with the work of the Bury scriptorium after the creative phase associated with the c.1137 execution of the Bury Bible by Master Hugo.[76] Comparisons may also be made to a c.1140 manuscript from Bury, Cambridge, Pembroke College, MS 16, which provides parallels not only for the design elements found in the Winchester border but for the colour and technique as well.[77] The border of fol. 12 of the Psalter (Fig. 11) may be compared to Pembroke 16, fol. 7v (Fig. 154) and fol. 18 of the Psalter (Fig. 17) to fol. 17r of Pembroke 16 (Fig. 155). Although it is impossible to discern in black and white photographs, the colours used in the two manuscripts are identical. These are shades of green, red and a yellowish tan. The same may be said of the application of colour. Soft, pale washes of colour were applied to the body of the decoration. Decoration in this manuscript in design as well as execution is closer to Nero C.IV than any other twelfth-century manuscript. In fact, nothing comparable can be found elsewhere. Similar comparisons can be offered for the floral ornament in the Psalter. Perhaps the most prominent aspect of the ornamental decoration of the Psalter are the large, luxurious flowers that appear in several of the figural scenes as well as in several initials in the text. The earliest fully developed examples of the flower appear in the Bury Bible.[78] While the ultimate debt to the illustrator of the Bible is unmistakable, the configuration of the Winchester Psalter ornament finds closer parallels elsewhere. Among the manuscripts which can be grouped most closely with the Psalter are the Bury manuscripts produced in the wake of Master Hugo's tenure at Bury St Edmunds. Pembroke 16 (Fig. 154) has pen-drawn floral forms which are close to those in Nero C.IV. Another manuscript from the same group, Pembroke College, MS 64, fol. 148r (Fig. 155), can also be included here. The proximity of the Winchester floral decoration to these later Bury manuscripts provides additional confirmation for the theory that one major source of inspiration for the Winchester artist was the Bury scriptorium, in the period after Master Hugo worked there. Moreover, although the hand of the Winchester scribe does not appear in any Bury manuscript, there are indications that he may have been influenced by a scribe active there in the second quarter of the twelfth century. Similarities to the work of the Bury scribe include the formation of the 'tagged *e*', '*us*' sign, '*bus*' mark, open *g* and a trailing tail on the letter *q* as well as the use of a superscript *s* at the end of a line.[79]

An examination of the Passion scenes in the Psalter further supports the association with Bury. It is among this group of Winchester scenes that the closest comparisons to scenes associated with Bury may be found. An example is the rendering of the Christ on the road to Emmaus (Fig. 24).

The basic compositional structure of the encounter on the road to Emmaus used by the Winchester artist was inherited from the Ottonian art circle.[80] There is little reason to believe, however, that the Winchester artist based his composition directly upon such a model. The Ottonian prototype underwent several alterations at the hands of English artists in the first half of the century. It is to these Insular monuments that the Winchester illustration is most closely aligned. Pembroke 120, fol. 4v (Fig. 132) explains the appearance of the Winchester Emmaus scene. Not only the general arrangement of the Bury St Edmunds composition but minor details not found in the Ottonian examples relate it to the Winchester scene. Christ wears a pilgrim's hat and carries a staff. The pilgrim closest to them gestures to Christ, wears a fur cloak, a hat and is bearded. His companion, similarly garbed and bearded, points away from the group to the sun above Emmaus. In all these respects, the Winchester artist was clearly indebted to the innovations introduced into the Emmaus scene in twelfth-century England.[81]

However, other scenes show that the Winchester artist had access not only to Pembroke 120 but to a wider circle of twelfth-century English models. The Flagellation (Fig. 20) is among the scenes which indicates the artist had access to sources beyond the Bury group. In Pembroke 120, fol. 3v (Fig. 125) Christ, wearing a loincloth, stands behind a column with his arms crossed in front of him and tied to the support. Two scourgers flank the central column. They lurch back, about to deliver blows with their whips. Pilate sits at the left, raising one hand, as if to direct the assault. However, the Winchester artist was not content merely to copy the model before him but altered it until a strikingly individual creation evolved. In certain subtle respects, the changes made by the Winchester artist reflect a dependence on the Albani Psalter (Fig. 126). In the St Albans Flagellation, Pilate sits frontally as he watches Christ's suffering. Another point of comparison is the rope binding Christ's arms. In both the Albani and Winchester scenes, the flagellant on the left holds the end of the rope in his left hand as he prepares to deliver a blow with the right. The blindfold worn by Christ in the Winchester Flagellation might also be explained by an innovation found elsewhere in the Albani Passion cycle.[82]

In another case, the disparity between the Winchester scene and the Pembroke scene is even greater. The scene of the Women at the Tomb on the Bury leaf is modelled after a Carolingian type found in the Drogo Sacramentary, fol. 58r, and later in the Benedictional of St Aethelwold, fol. 51v.[83] The scene in the Psalter follows a different formula. It is found, for example, in the eleventh-century Boulogne Psalter, fol. 109r (Fig. 129). In each scene, the angel sits on an empty tomb[84] and gestures to the approaching women. The sleeping soldiers in both scenes are placed below the angel. This pre-Conquest model for the angel–soldier arrangement was taken up again in the early twelfth century. In the Albani Psalter, page 50 (Fig. 130) the basic arrangement of the angel and soldiers was retained with modifications. The coffin cover found in the Boulogne Psalter was removed by the Albani artist, a device that heightens the dramatic impact of the empty tomb. While following the Anglo-Saxon precedent of placing them on the ground directly below the coffin, the Albani artist also rearranged the sleeping soldiers. In this respect he clarified the confusing array of figures in the lower register of the Boulogne illustration. It is to this type of twelfth-century model rather than the Bury formula that the Winchester artist referred. The Albani type was also incorporated, in almost identical fashion, in the Shaftesbury Psalter, fol. 13.[85] To this may be added other close parallels between certain Winchester and Shaftesbury scenes which have been recognized for some time.[86] Since the Lansdowne manuscript offers the only clear parallels for some highly unusual aspects of the Winchester cycle, including the Sending of the Angel for the Annunciation (Figs. 9, 82) and the Jesse Tree (Figs. 8, 81), its possible impact on the Winchester cycle cannot be underestimated.

A consideration of the relationship to the Bury, St Albans and Shaftesbury manuscripts inevitably prompts the question of whether the Winchester artist simply followed a slightly earlier twelfth-century manuscript that had already assimilated earlier Anglo-Saxon and Ottonian elements. This would have been the simplest course and is suggested by scenes like the Road to Emmaus and Women at the Tomb. If this was the case, it would establish that there was at least one English miniature cycle, now lost, which differed substantially from any of the extant works and served as the sole model for the Winchester Psalter. However, a close inspection of each New Testament scene does not tend to support such a conclusion. The overall impression given by the New Testament cycle is of a distinct lack of uniformity. The fluctuations in the divisions for the picture space, scale of the figures and variety of architectural elements all point away from the use of a single source. The iconography also gives any number of indications that the Winchester artist employed a wide variety of sources including those of the eleventh century together with more recent interpretations of them. This is most readily evident in the Pentecost scene (Fig. 27). The Albani Psalter, page 55,[87] Pembroke 120, fol. 6r[88] and Shaftesbury scenes[89] make the Virgin the central focus, following a tradition that can be traced to a Carolingian formula.[90] The Winchester artist alone chose to follow the Anglo-Saxon tradition. Certain elements of the scene can be traced back to one of the earliest pre-Conquest Pentecost scenes in the Benedictional of Robert of Jumièges, Rouen, B.M., MS Y.7, fol. 29v (Fig. 141). The general arrangement of the apostles, Peter and the dove is similar. The architectural framework of this manuscript and another closely related to it suggests an additional link to Anglo-Saxon sources. In the Benedictional of St Aethelwold, fol. 67v,[91] the tower elements take on abstract geometric forms. The prismatic structures, drawn from a wide range of viewpoints, suggests the somewhat confused architectural superstructure in the Psalter.

While the arrangement of the apostles in the Benedictionals resemble the general disposition of the apostles in the Psalter, there is a basic difference in the placement of the figures in space. In the Benedictionals, the apostles are seated around a semicircular curve so that all are visible. In the Psalter, they sit in a straight line, in two rows. The alteration is found in several other Anglo-Saxon works. The Tiberius Psalter, London, B.L., MS Cotton Tiberius C.VI, fol. 15v,[92] the Hereford Troper, fol. 31r (Fig. 142) and the Sacramentary of Robert of Jumièges, fol. 84r (Fig. 141) offer precedents for the lower half of the illustration.[93] In the Troper, the apostles are disposed in two rows behind Peter and Paul who are closest to the centre. The equal emphasis on the apostle princes is shifted in the Psalter to a somewhat greater concentration upon Peter. This feature is reflected in the Sacramentary of Robert. Taken together, the Anglo-Saxon sources establish a sufficient degree of similarity to suggest the artist chose to refer back to the pre-Conquest tradition in forming this scene.

The willingness of the artist to reject the modern solutions and instead to sift back through the older sources, is evident elsewhere, including the scene of Christ Washing the Feet of the Disciples (Fig. 19). The Albani artist followed Byzantine models while the Pembroke illustrator followed an Anglo-Saxon type where Christ kneels on both knees before Peter who points to his head.[94] The Winchester master took another direction, and modelled his scene after one like that in *Escorialensis* (Fig. 122). The Ottonian composition also includes all twelve apostles on a long bench to the left of Christ. They are arranged in two rows, only the heads of those in the rear appear between the shoulders of the apostles in the first row.

Other scenes also show that the Winchester artist combined Anglo-Saxon and Ottonian scenes in a way the Albani, Bury and Lansdowne artists did not. The illustrator of the St Albans Psalter, page 22 (Fig. 89) drew on Anglo-Saxon models[95] like that in the Sacramentary of Robert of Jumièges, fol. 33r (Fig. 88) in constructing his Annunciation to the Shepherds. He followed the Anglo-Saxon model closely, incorporating the angelic choir surrounded by an aureole, and the messenger angel confronting the shepherds reclining on a hillside with their flocks. The Winchester artist did not pattern his illustration (Fig. 10) upon the St Albans composition but rather upon the older model common to both. He selected other elements like the startled shepherd closest to the messenger angel on the ground who draws back in surprise. He used the gesture of this figure for the shepherd furthest to the left. He was also influenced by the other shepherd in the Sacramentary in fashioning the third shepherd from the left in the Psalter. Although the two figures are reversed in direction, points of comparison become clear on closer inspection. Both figures crane their heads to the side and extend the arm on that side of the body outward. The other arm is held close to the body, bent at the elbow so that the forearm crosses in front of the figure. This bent arm holds a crook which extends down to rest at or under the foot. These detailed resemblances to the Anglo-Saxon miniature leave little doubt about one of the sources used for this scene.

In addition to making an independent selection of Anglo-Saxon motifs, the artist varied his image even further by incorporating details from a second source. In the Sacramentary, the news of Christ's birth is delivered to the shepherds by the angelic messenger standing on the ground while the heavenly choir simply watches and reacts to the scene below. Precedents do exist for the heavenly choir delivering the message directly to the shepherds. In the *Codex Egberti*, fol. 13v (Fig. 90) and the Bremen Perikope,[96] a large envoy of bust-length angels address the startled shepherds. Several detailed comparisons to the *Egberti* shepherds are also possible. The middle shepherd in *Egberti* holds his crook with one arm and rests the elbow of the opposite arm on it. The arm resting on the staff is bent at the elbow to enable the figure to support his head with his hand. This pose is strikingly similar to that of the shepherd on the right in the Nero Psalter. The shepherd standing closest to the angels in *Egberti* displays similarities in gesture and pose to the second shepherd from the left in the Psalter. In both cases, the shepherd grasps his crook with the deft motion of his sharply turned wrist. In addition, both shepherds raise the opposite arm, palm upright toward the heavenly choir. The wide-legged stance of the *Egberti* shepherd is less similar to his counterpart in Nero C.IV. A shepherd in the *Escorialensis* (Fig. 87) provides a closer parallel for this detail. Here the shepherd to the left holds his crook with one hand and raises the opposite hand to the angel. His stance is closer to the erect, straight-legged posture of the shepherd in the Psalter. The shepherd third from the left in the Psalter is paralleled in the Brussels Perikope, fol. 8. Here a shepherd turns his head sharply to the right and also swings his arms in this direction. One last, extremely minor but amusing, detail can be explained by a comparison to the same Echternach manuscript. The curious calf who bends his head back, tongue extended, to observe his master finds a parallel in the Brussels Perikope where two similarly preoccupied creatures watch their astonished masters.

The spirit of independence and ingenuity displayed by the Winchester master helps to explain his willingness to experiment with other sources. They point away from the traditions established in his own country toward developments across the Channel. The way in which he incorporated these elements sets the Winchester cycle apart from earlier English manuscripts in the selection of sources and the innovative way they were used to fashion new scenes. The Baptism scene illustrates this point. In this case, the artist largely rejected the Anglo-Saxon formula which was revived in the twelfth century by the Albani artist[97] as well as the Ottonian types. The parallels which can be established for the Winchester Baptism lie in another sphere. Christ stepping to the side as he is baptized is a relatively rare iconographical type. The largest concentration of examples date from the Early Christian period.[98] One of these monuments, the sarcophagus of Anastasius in Arles,[99] is especially noteworthy since the position of Christ's body and the movement of his legs and arms almost exactly parallel those in the Psalter. A variation on this side-stepping type survived in the Latin West in the Carolingian period,[100] but closer comparisons are possible with later medieval examples. These include, among others,[101] an early twelfth-century manuscript from Bremen (Fig. 106) Chantilly, B.M., MS 7, fol. 9v,[102] and an enamelled plaque from the 1181 altar in Klosterneuberg, Austria[103] (Fig. 107), by Nicholas of Verdun. The similarities between the late twelfth-century enamel and Nero C.IV are the most pronounced. In both cases, a bearded Christ steps towards the Baptist. The positioning of the head, torso and arms in the two works is nearly identical. In fact, when reproduced on the same scale, a tracing of one corresponds line for line with the other. The arrangement of the legs is also based on a common source, the only difference being a slight exaggeration of the side movement in the Psalter. The comparison with the Mosan enamel exceeds a similarity in iconographic type. It appears that the two scenes were copied in detail from the same artistic blueprint.[104]

The dove of the Holy Spirit figures prominently in the Gospel text and is invariably present in Baptism scenes from the Early Christian period onward. Many of the earliest Baptism compositions show the dove approaching Christ from the side in a fashion similar to the Psalter.[105] This type was greatly overshadowed by another which appeared during the same period. In this second type the dove hovers directly above Christ's head in a dorsal view, with its wings extended to either side. The extreme popularity of this type almost completely eclipsed the Winchester type from the fifth century onward.[106] The appearance of the side-view dove is so rare in the succeeding centuries that the few existing examples are of particular interest. One appears on an early eleventh-century ivory from Liège, formerly in the Kaiser Friedrich Museum, Berlin (fig. 108). Others are found in the *Codex Egberti*, fol. 19v,[107] several twelfth-century German examples[108] and at Klosterneuberg.

In view of the numerous close comparisons to Mosan monuments for Christ and the dove, the proximity of Mosan examples for St John is noteworthy. The iconographical type of John the Baptist found in the Psalter can be traced to Early Christian sources[109] and is also found in Ottonian examples.[110] However, the Mosan ivory formerly in Berlin bears such a striking resemblance to the Winchester image that it appears to be a more direct source than the others. The posture of the two figures, with John's bare leg emerging from his robe in a definite forward stride, is extremely similar. The robe also links the Mosan example and the Psalter. The Bible is fairly precise in its description of the Baptist's garments. Mark relates that John was clothed with camel's hair and a girdle of skins. Early Christian artists, including the author of the Arles sarcophagus, interpreted the animal skin covering as a short garment, fastened over one shoulder and ending above the knees.[111] Carolingian artists continued to use this type and also deviated from the biblical description by garbing John in classical robes.[112] A type more closely associated with the garment on the ivory and in Nero C.IV began to appear in the Ottonian period. In the Brussels manuscript fol. 18v and *Epternacensis* fol. 19v (fig. 97), one finds a long, all-encompassing cloak which falls from the shoulders to below the knees. Important as the Ottonian examples are in determining the inception of the hair robe, they are not as close to the Psalter as the Mosan example. The long hair robe worn by John on the ivory and in the Psalter falls from the arms and ends in a continuous curving border. The relationship of the Psalter to Mosan sources is further strengthened by the fact that two other Mosan examples of the type can be cited. The robe is worn by John on the twelfth-century baptismal font of Reiner of Huy in the church of St Barthélemy in Liège and the twelfth-century manuscript fragment in Berlin, MS 78.A.6, fol. 10r.[113]

There are other details and schema in several rare or unusual christological scenes in the Winchester cycle which again point toward Mosan sources.[114] However, since the dates of these sources are very close to that of the Psalter, they must be treated with greater circumspection. One such scene is the unusual Marriage at Cana (fig. 16). The scene in the upper register, depicting the wedding banquet, bears certain general similarities to Anglo-Saxon patterns, including those on the Bayeux tapestry. However, it seems likely that the formula underwent further refinement in the twelfth century. The closest comparisons for a number of intricate details are found in twelfth-century Mosan and Franco–Flemish sources. Nothing identical is found in England. In view of the clear Mosan parallels for the Baptism scene, the same pool of sources may have included motifs for Cana. However, the relationship should be treated as a complex one which in the absence of precisely dated works can only demonstrate the proximity of English and Mosan traditions at this moment and the involvement of the Winchester artist in this movement. The Mosan parallels for the Cana scene are found in the Floreffe Bible, London, B.L., MS Add. 17737–8,[115] and a Job manuscript, Paris, B.N., MS lat. 15675 (fig. 110).[116] The second guest from the right in the Psalter rests his right hand on the table. The thumb is extended as are the index and middle fingers, which are crossed over one another. The other fingers are curled back into the palm. The lady fourth from the right in the Paris manuscript places one hand on the table in exactly the same fashion. The profile of this same Winchester guest, second from the right, closely resembles those second from the left and furthest to the right in Job. The bump on the nose, curl of the nostril, drooping angle of the mouth and sharp, narrow chin link the three figures to one another. These close comparisons can be extended to include all the figures in the Winchester Cana scene.[117]

In addition to these christological scenes, there are several of particular interest in the unusual Last Judgment cycle. Certain details in this complex series of scenes have no exact precedents.[118] Among these is a scene depicting the choirs of the damned, fol. 37 (fig. 36). The treatment is novel, showing rows of heads in the upper register and the full-length figures of clergy below. As in the case of the christological scenes, it is in this unusual scene, without exact parallels, that the closest comparisons to Mosan art occur. The odd, almost comical heads are grouped into seven rows. The uppermost row depicts a single young-man type. Each figure has an unusually large, prominent nose and open mouth. The same profile is repeated for each head in the row with slight variations. This curious practice again suggests the use of a standardized pattern. Striking parallels for this type appear in several contemporary Mosan works. A number are found in a Bible from the abbey of Sainte Marie du Parc, London, B.L., MS Add. 14788–90. The head is found in volume 1, fol. 6v and volume 3, fol. 120 (fig. 147).[119] The extended eyebrow, slanted eye, long crooked nose and mouth are drawn from the same model as those in the Psalter. An additional parallel for this figure appears in the Mosan medical treatise in the British Library, MS Harley 1585.[120] The long-nosed patient of the doctor on fol. 9v falls into this group. More remarkable, however, are the striking similarities between another figure in this manuscript and the beautifully sculpted head of the figure often referred to as a physican on fol. 13r (fig. 148). The physican can be compared to the fifth head from the right in the second row. Both display the same proportioning and configuration of the facial features including prominent cheekbones, a broad forehead, arched eyebrows, oval eyes extended at the corners, rounded nose and a small mouth. The three-quarter view oval female face in row four is like one found in both the Parc and Harley manuscripts.[121] For the fifth row, another initial from the Parc Bible, fol. 118v, is similar. It has the same strong straight nose and drooping mouth. These Mosan features recur elsewhere in the Last Judgment cycle, along with others.[122] Especially interesting is the imaginative scene of the tortures of the damned, fol. 38. Although the devils appear remarkable in their variety, here again, they are like Mosan examples. A grotesque head ornamenting the tail of the initial S on fol. 83r, volume 2 of the Parc Bible, is nearly identical to the devil on the far right in the upper register. The three-quarter view, crooked nose, open mouth, beard, wild hair and large ear of each are copied from the same model. Still others in the Winchester manuscript approach those in the Job manuscript.[123]

There are other scenes in the Winchester cycle which also show that the artist set aside traditional English formulae in favour of more recent cross-Channel developments. Such a scene is the Betrayal of Christ (Fig. 20). He is led forward by an evil-looking individual who grasps his outstretched, manacled hands. The central group differs significantly from those in the Albani Psalter, Pembroke 120 and the sources upon which they are based.[124] In these earlier examples, Christ stands frontally, as opposed to the side view found in the Psalter. The arrangement of the other characters varies somewhat but the early Betrayal iconography is clearly differentiated from the later type by the frontal placement of Christ. On the basis of the monuments now extant, it appears that the Betrayal iconography of Nero C.IV can be related to a type which evolved in the late eleventh century. One example is found on a fragmentary ivory plaque in Berlin.[125] Another Western ivory from the late eleventh century also preserves the type, in a more complete version, showing the Betrayal and Arrest together. The ivory, which was tentatively identified by Goldschmidt[126] as Belgian, is now in the treasury of the cathedral of Zagreb, Yugoslavia. Aside from the Zagreb ivory, the majority of the monuments are from central and southern France and northern Spain. One of the earliest is found among the pen drawings in a late eleventh-century manuscript in Auxerre, believed to be from Tours.[127] Another is found on the Puerta de los Platerías, Cathedral of Santiago de Compostela, dated into the early part of the twelfth century.[128] Two further examples are found on capitals of the first and second series carved for La Daurade, Toulouse, in the early twelfth century.[129] The capital (Fig. 123) from the second series, dated 1115–20, is particularly noteworthy, since not only the central group but the surrounding crowd is similar to that in Nero C.IV.[130] The figures in the La Daurade crowd also carry an array of formidable weapons. The figure immediately to the left of Judas holds a torch aloft. The same function is performed in Nero C.IV by the short beak-nosed man behind Judas who holds a large lantern above his head. By the middle of the century, the Arrest–Betrayal type was fairly widespread in both France and Spain.[131] For example, the type was employed twice at Chartres Cathedral, both on the west façade (Fig. 124) and in the Passion lancet.[132] The lengthy tradition for this scene on the continent, in this instance, again suggests the artist was influenced by a cross-Channel development.

Another scene which again shows the Winchester artist was in possession of some recently developed type known on the continent is his Entombment of Christ (Fig. 22). This scene combines two events that followed the Crucifixion, the Entombment and the Anointment of Christ. The Entombment scene had been represented in a similar fashion in the *Codex Epternacensis* (Fig. 127). However, in this case, the Winchester scene cannot simply be explained on the basis of a pre-existing Ottonian or English tradition. In the Psalter, the Entombment was elaborated upon by the addition of a second subject, the Anointment of Christ. This scene is never encountered in Ottonian or Anglo-Saxon art and only hinted at in early twelfth-century English scenes.[133] Exactly when in the twelfth century the scene first appeared is unclear since there is considerable controversy concerning the date and provenance of several examples.[134] However, it can be said that the scene enjoyed considerable popularity in France. The scene appears on a capital in the cloister of Aix-en-Provence[135] and on another in Dreux.[136] It is also found at Chartres in the Passion lancet and also on a capital on the west façade (Fig. 124). This is the only monument of the period which combines the two extremely rare iconographic types for the Betrayal and Anointment found in the Winchester cycle. The relationship of the Winchester depiction scene to others of this type is again an extremely complex one. However, the Anointment scene does point toward the modern nature and continental distribution of a source employed by the Winchester artist but not by English illuminators working earlier in the century.

While the variety exhibited by the iconography is striking, it is the ingenuity shown in fashioning new scenes that is particularly noteworthy and identifies the artist as an individual of singular ability. What characterizes his illustrations is their high degree of originality and inventiveness. While drawing on a number of traditional sources, he exercised independent judgment about what elements to use and how to relate them to one another. The result was a series of highly original scenes. In this case, an individual artist guided the production of a luxury book that bears his imprint more than that of the sources he consulted.

However, while the Winchester artist was receptive to a number of traditional and recent developments he can scarcely be characterized as a mere draughtsman, laboriously piecing together patterns inherited from other artists. In his hands, what might have been a mundane narrative was transformed into a series of unique and sometimes unforgettable creations. The sure yet delicate strokes of his pen made scene after scene an arena where the forces of good and evil were pitted against one another. The gentle Abel sinks before his snarling brother (Fig. 1). The touching devotion of the grief-stricken mothers in the Massacre (Fig. 13) is played off against the gruesome brutality of the soldiers. The depiction evokes contemporary descriptions of the ubiquitous climate of violence during King Stephen's reign but the scene as a whole has the nightmarish quality of a spectre recalled from an uneasy sleep.[137] The contrasts become even more pronounced as Christ reaches adulthood. He lunges athletically across the page to face the devil in the desert. His opponent waits quietly, garbed provocatively as a temptress. Only the fangs and hairy green body emerging from the close-fitting gown mar the illusion of the *femme fatale*. In the Passion cycle, the struggle reaches a feverish pitch. The lyrical grace of Christ in the Arrest (Fig. 20) is contrasted with the surrounding crowd whose distorted features and savage, animal-like jaws convey their hostility. These pent-up emotions are unleased in the Flagellation scene where the graceful curve of Christ's torso bends beneath the whip as the spectators view him, their expressions convulsed with hatred. All of this is merely a prelude to the concluding statement on fol. 39 (Fig. 30). The menacing jaws of Hell and snarling devils within are no match for Michael. He pirouettes with the elegance of a ballerina, sealing them away with a deft flick of the wrist. The poles of good and evil are still clearly present but now the final balance has been achieved. In this last scene, as in the cycle as a whole, the Winchester master allows the drama to unfold in a way which bears the stamp of his unique genius. All this identifies him as an artist of rare ability. So he appears to the contemporary eye and may also have done at the time. It is therefore not difficult to imagine that for all these reasons he could have been called upon to fashion the Winchester cycle.

Chapter Three: The Marian Cycle

IN FASHIONING the miniature cycle, the artist patterned three groups of scenes upon a variety of established iconographic types. Both the Old Testament and christological cycles were fairly traditional. Although unusual in its length and complexity, most Last Judgment scenes conformed to this pattern since they stemmed from earlier depictions of the Last Judgment. One group of miniatures, illustrating the life of the Virgin, stands apart from the others. As Wormald and others have already pointed out, many of the scenes from the life of the Virgin do not conform to any known depictions of Mary's life.[1] Instead, they appear to be *ad hoc* compilations of elements drawn from standard christological scenes, many of which appear in the Winchester Psalter itself. The Annunciation to Anna is a reduced version of the Annunciation to Mary, the Meeting at the Golden Gate is similar to Christ with his Parents, the Nativity of the Virgin follows the iconography for the Nativity of Christ and the Presentation of the Virgin, a Presentation of Christ.[2] The unusual iconography of this group of scenes suggests that the artist was requested to include a series illustrating particular events from the life of the Virgin. Owing to a lack of appropriate sources, he was obliged to adapt other scenes, forming the cycle piecemeal based on what was available to him. It scarcely seems likely that he would have undertaken such a task unless the subject had a special significance for the patron. Some of the reasons why such a request was made may be discerned from the particular choice of subjects included here. There are two groups of scenes devoted to the Virgin, one illustrating the beginning of her life (Figs. 3, 7) and a second the end (Figs. 28–29). The first series begins a scene which illustrates the conception of the Virgin. The Annunciation to Joachim appears at the bottom of fol. 4 (Fig. 3).[3] It is clearly identified by an inscription on the scroll held by the angel: 'noli timere ioachim ego . . . angelus domini' ('do not be afraid, Joachim, I am the angel of the Lord'). This scene finds textual basis in the sources dealing with the infancy of the Virgin, the *Latin Infancy Gospels*, *Protoevangelium* of the monk James and the Gospel of the Pseudo-Matthew.[4] There is also a clear visual precedent for the scene.[5] It occurs in the eleventh-century troper from Hereford, London, B.L., MS Cotton Caligula A.XIV, fol. 26v (Fig. 57). The conception sequence continues with two additional scenes, the Annunciation to Anna and the Meeting of Joachim and Anna at the Golden Gate (Fig. 7). This concentration upon the conception is significant in itself, since at this time, even a single illustration of this event was a relatively rare occurrence.[6] Also noteworthy is the placement of the Annunciation to Joachim together with the Moses scenes which also serve as the conclusion to the illustrations of the Pentateuch. In the upper register, Moses before the Burning Bush and Moses Receiving the Law are depicted (Fig. 3). More enigmatic is the unparalleled scene in the middle register which unites all the images on the page into a single statement. Here a nimbed figure hands a book to a king on his right and a sceptre to a king on his left. There are no exact visual comparisons for this scene and the inscription which may originally have identified these figures has crumbled away, leaving only traces on the border separating the upper two scenes. It remains to be determined who the three figures are and why they draw together the Moses and Joachim scenes. The motivation for this arrangement can be explained by the major liturgical and theological importance of the conception of the Virgin in twelfth-century England.

The conception of the Virgin had been celebrated in the English liturgy since the Anglo-Saxon period. Although the Greek feast of the Conception came to the Latin West by way of southern Italy, the oldest reliable traces of the feast are found in liturgical documents which were in use in the south of England during the last decades before the Conquest.[7] More important in this context is the specific mention of the annunciation of the angel made in several texts for the liturgical celebration of the feast. Three texts incorporate the annunciation of the angel into the service for the eighth of December in the formulas of benediction of prayers for the feast. One of them is found in the Missal of Leofric, Oxford, Bodl., MS Bodley 579, given by the bishop to the cathedral of Exeter:[8]

Deus, qui beatae Mariae virginis conceptionem angelico vaticinio parentibus praedixisti, praesta huic praesenti familiae tuae eius praesidiis muniri, cuius conceptionis sacra solemnia congrua frequentatione veneratur.	O God, you who foretold the conception of the Blessed Virgin Mary to her parents through the prophecy of an angel, grant the safety of her protection to this present family of yours who honour with due observance the sacred rites of her conception.

The appearance of this prayer and others like it in other service books[9] marked a decided change in the attitude of the English church to the events which had been regarded as merely apocryphal accounts of the conception. Their incorporation into the prayers of the church gave them official ecclesiastical endorsement.

The feast was only celebrated in England during the generation before the Conquest. This Anglo-Saxon feast, honoured at a few centres in southern England, including Winchester,[10] can best be understood as an expression of mere piety to the Virgin without any doctrinal afterthought or inkling of theological justification.[11] As one author has pointed out, it is probable that in the minds of the Anglo-Saxons, the conception was worthy of veneration not so much because it was accomplished without original sin but because of the supernatural events described in the Infancy Gospels which surrounded her conception.[12] The celebration of the feast was to end abruptly with the Norman Conquest. The feast was one of the specially English observances that Archbishop Lanfranc disliked and purged from the calendar of his cathedral church at Canterbury. He also caused it to be suppressed throughout England.[13]

For the next half century, no trace of the feast is found in either liturgical books or other historical documents.[14] Suddenly, in the 1120s, the feast of the Conception again became the object of attention in monastic circles.[15] Although opinions vary concerning reasons for the reinstitution of the feast, there was no apparent change in its meaning.[16] In the eyes of its defenders, it was still a commemoration of the historical fact that the Virgin was conceived after an angel visited her parents.

The movement towards the re-establishment of the feast in the 1120s was to encounter opposition near the end of the decade. It has been suggested that among monasteries with strong Old English traditions the feast represented an admiration for Anglo-Saxon piety.[17] This revival, which was viewed as a national movement of Anglo-Saxon devotion, soon encountered Norman opposition.[18] At the instigation of unidentified opponents of the feast,[19] two powerful bishops, Roger of Salisbury and Bernard of St David's, raised objections to the celebration of the feast on the grounds that it had been prohibited in a council and its origin lacked the authority of the Roman church. More significant are the theological objections they raised.[20] They argued that the feast had no reason for existing because all conception submitted to the law of sin.[21] Proponents of the feast quickly rose to its defence. Among the most significant were Eadmer, a monk of St Augustine's, Canterbury, who wrote 'De Conceptione Sanctae Mariae', and Osbert of Clare, prior of Westminster, who composed 'Sermo de Conceptione Sanctae Mariae'.[22] Their writings mark a clear break with the spirit of the preceding period. Under the stress of the argument that the act by which Mary inherited the stain of original sin was not a fitting object for veneration, they began to discuss more exactly the place of Mary in the scheme of the Incarnation and her relation to the *massa peccatrix* which was tainted by original sin.[23] Thus, for the first time, the celebration of Mary's conception was closely tied with the dogma of her sinlessness.[24]

The controversy over the feast was to be settled by a council held in London at Michaelmas 1129, where it was discussed in the presence of the papal legate, John of Cremona, and Henry I. The feast was officially approved 'by papal authority', thereby ending the controversy over the adoption of the feast in England.[25] By 1130, the feast was firmly established in the English liturgy.

The decision of the council of London brought only a temporary cessation to the theological debate over the Immaculate Conception. In 1138, the canons of Lyons instituted the feast of the Immaculate Conception in their church. Their action quickly drew sharp criticism from St Bernard who stated his objections in a lengthy epistle to the canons in 1140.[26]

The controversy which began with Bernard's reply to the canons initiated a debate over the question of the Immaculate Conception that was to last for 30 years. It was not merely the preoccupation of several isolated theologians but a question widely discussed on the continent and in the British Isles.[27] One of the defenders of the doctrine of the Immaculate Conception in this period deserves particular attention in this context. Nicholas of St Albans was an Englishman whose treatise 'De Celebranda Concepcione Beatae Marie Contra Beatum Bernardum' appeared about 1146.[28] Little is known about Nicholas except that he was a *magister* connected with schools and was prior of St Albans. It was his treatise which first brought him prominence.[29] Nicholas differed significantly from Eadmer and Osbert in his manner of attacking the problem by arguing that the Virgin was sanctified before animation and never came under sin.[30] Both Eadmer and Osbert saw only the exterior aspect of the problem. Nicholas, on the other hand, had finally arrived at an analysis of the Immaculate Conception considered in relationship to the inward order of the soul of the Virgin.[31]

At a time when the Immaculate Conception again became a widespread matter of serious dispute, Nicholas answered detractors of the feast with more erudite arguments than his predecessors. Shortly before the middle of the twelfth century, he argued that the Virgin was lifted above human sin by the hand of God. This renewed preoccupation with the question of the Immaculate Conception occurred during the period when the Winchester Psalter was produced. The impact of this widespread climate of belief in England and on the continent can be seen in the Winchester illustration.

The image of the burning bush, which continued to burn without being consumed, had long been used as a symbol of the Virgin in literature and art to illustrate the doctrine that the Virgin was purified at the moment of the Annunciation.[32] The burning bush in relation to the Incarnation was also drawn into the discussion of the Immaculate Conception since the Immaculist position maintained that the Virgin was sanctified from the moment of her conception, not the Incarnation. It appears in the writings of Adam of St Victor,[33] in a sermon of Peter Comestor on the Conception of the Virgin[34] as well as in one by Osbert of Clare on the same subject:

Cuius mysterii figuram Moyses aspexisse legitur, quando eum Domino vocante rubus ardebat et non consumebatur.[35]	Moses is said to have looked upon the figure of this mystery when the Lord called him as the bush burned but was not consumed.

Surrounding the idea of Moses with the law are metaphors by each of the three authors. Eadmer calls the Virgin 'the temple of the incarnate word'.[36] Mary was predestined to be the Mother of God, therefore the dwelling place and temple of the Most High. The foundation of the building is the beginning of her existence, her conception. In order that her conception should be a fitting foundation for such a palace, it should be without the slightest corruption from sin.[37] Similar ideas are echoed in Nicholas's treatise.[38] The works of Eadmer and Nicholas argue that because the Virgin was preserved from sin by Divine Wisdom she was a fitting tabernacle for divinity. Egbert of Schoenau and Peter Abelard in sermons on the Conception[39] and Osbert, on the other hand, refer to the Virgin not as the tabernacle but as the ark of the commandments:

David autem pater tuus in cythara laudes tuas psallit, et coram archa testamenti Domini manibus plaudens spiritualiter saltat et ludit. Ea videlicit est filia tua, Dei genitrix virgo MARIA, . . .[40]	Moreover your father David sings your praises on the cithara and in the presence of the ark of the commandments of the Lord he claps his hands singing and dancing spiritually. It, as you can see, is your daughter the mother of God, the virgin MARY, . . .

In view of the close relation of the Moses scenes to Immaculist writings, the unidentified scene in the middle register may be considered in the same context. The problem here is more difficult because there are no iconographical parallels or inscriptions which help to identify the scene. However, the Immaculist arguments suggest an interpretation. The identification of the nimbed figure in the centre of the page rests on the twelfth-century texts. Eadmer, Osbert and Nicholas state that the builder of the temple, the Virgin, is the Divine Wisdom of God the Father.[41] He preordained her purity and preserved her from Original Sin. Significantly enough, this relationship, identified by inscriptions and prayers, had been illustrated in an earlier Winchester drawing, London, B.L., MS Cotton Titus C.XXVII, fol. 75v[42] (Fig. 157). The idea of divine intervention is also crucial to the Immaculist position in the twelfth century and explains the central placement of the figure in the Psalter. He is the author of her timeless divinity and as such forms the nucleus which holds the various elements on the page together.

God does not occupy the middle register alone but stands in the company of two crowned men. Although the crowned figures could be interpreted as allegorical personifications, feudal lords or biblical kings, the writings of Eadmer, Osbert and Nicholas shed light on the question. In the context of the present argument, the most plausible explanation is that the figures personify Old Testament ancestors of the Virgin. To the twelfth-century authors, they are the building materials from which God fashioned his temple, the Virgin. At the end of a lengthy description of the building of the temple, Osbert concludes by saying:

Ceterum pro marmore quod aream pavimenti condecorat in aedificatione huius regalis palacii, omnium pene regum Iudae in sacra genealogia series est conputata. Quorum quidam quamvis essent in perversis operationibus coram domino reprobi: extiterunt tamen insignes praecelsa maiestate sanguinis generosi.[43]	Further, on the marble which decorates the pavement area in the building of this royal palace, a sacred genealogical series of almost all of the kings of Judaea has been rendered. Although certain of these kings were rejected in God's sight because of corrupt works, they nevertheless stood out for the exalted majesty of their noble blood.

Eadmer also hints at this when he refers to Mary as the *flos de radice Iesse* (the flower of the root of Jesse).[44] Moreover, he stresses that Mary received sanctifying grace at her conception because the Holy Ghost descended upon her. Mary would not have triumphed over the law of death had it not been for the tree of Jesse, her genealogical tree, in which she was sanctified and which was the rebirth of the world.[45] The reference to the Virgin as the stem of the root of Jesse also occurs in the c.1300 breviary from Hyde Abbey, Winchester, for the feast of the Conception.[46]

The question remains, which biblical ancestors are represented here? Without inscriptions, any identification can only be tentative, but a number of factors support Wormald's suggestion that they may be David and Solomon.[47] Osbert refers to them several times, including references to them as ancestors of Christ.[48] There are also visual precedents for this relationship. Jesse Trees which terminate in the Virgin instead of Christ have been viewed as an Immaculist symbol.[49] There are twelfth-century examples of this type of tree which emphasize the direct descent of the Virgin from her most exalted royal ancestors, David and Solomon. One is found in an antiphonary from Salzburg, St Peters Abbey, MS a.XII.7, p.383 (Fig. 156), and another in the Lambeth Bible.[50] It is also possible to point to numerous later Immaculist images where David and Solomon figure prominently.[51]

This tentative identification of the two figures can also be supported by an additional visual comparison. While the hair colour of the kings does not suggest a difference in age, another device is employed. As in the Salzburg manuscript, the beard of one king is longer than that of the other. There is also an English precedent for this manner of distinguishing David from Solomon. An Anglo-Saxon Gospel book in Boulogne, B.M., MS 11, has two prefatory illustrations to the Gospel of St Matthew. Under a series of arches, the ancestors of Christ are arranged in chronological order. David and Solomon are represented in the second row from the top at the right, fol. 11r (Fig. 158). David wears a longer, more pointed beard than his son. The attributes held by the kings in the Psalter, book and sceptre, also agree with the Boulogne image.

In the Winchester illustration, the two kings do not merely hold the book and sceptre, but receive them from God. The bonding of the figures illustrates the transmission of God's will through the Virgin's royal ancestors, the concept which is emphasized by the twelfth-century authors. This interpretation agrees with the iconography of the scene. The transmission of divine authority was traditionally depicted as God bestowing objects upon lesser beings. Moreover, there was a formula for a double presentation scene firmly established in the iconographical repertory from the Early Christian period. Among the scenes which depict the Godhead or Christ standing frontally and bestowing special powers or priviledges upon lesser beings flanking in three-quarter view is the *traditio legis*.[52] One such example, found on the Hiberno-Saxon cross at Monasterboice (Fig. 159), shows striking formal similarities with the scene in the Psalter, suggesting that the Winchester artist fashioned his presentation upon such an iconographic formula. This type offered a clear precedent for a scene showing the dispensation of the divine will through God's elect. In spite of its unique appearance, the scene can be related thematically and formally to an established type.

The message of this page bears a clear thematic relationship to the scenes that follow. The next group (Figs. 5–6) illustrates the life of David. Since the scenes are encompassed within the Marian cycle, their placement emphasizes the royal ancestry of the Virgin at the moment the viewer contemplates the message of her impending birth. This echoes the themes outlined on fol. 4. Yet another layer of meaning is added to this construct immediately following the infancy scenes. On fol. 9 (Fig. 8), the theme is repeated a third time in the illustration of the Jesse Tree. The tree is limited to three figures, David, the Virgin and Christ, again stressing her royal lineage and direct descent from the house of David.

Placing the elaborate demonstration of Mary's immaculate origin together with other infancy scenes suggests that a specific factor motivated the request for their inclusion here. The scenes of the Annunciation to

Joachim, to Anna and their meeting at the Golden Gate illustrate the Immaculate Conception, the event that was honoured by a feast on the eighth of December in Winchester. The Nativity of the Virgin was similarly celebrated on the eighth of September.[53] These events from the infancy cycle were, then, not only important stages in the Virgin's early life but were honoured as such at Winchester in the twelfth century. The liturgical importance which these scenes share also encompasses two other often-discussed scenes in the Winchester cycle, the Death of the Virgin (Fig. 28) and the Virgin Enthroned as the Queen of Heaven (Fig. 29).[54] They can be viewed as the logical continuation of the infancy scenes. They bring the cycle to completion, thereby celebrating the other major Marian feast of the liturgical year.

The inclusion of the last group, however, can also be viewed from several additional vantage points. Like the Immaculate Conception, the Assumption of the Virgin was the object of considerable attention at this time. Although the feast had been accepted as early as the seventh century, the theological position of the church concerning the Assumption did undergo considerable modification in the twelfth century. A number of scholars in Britain and on the continent argued in favour of the corporal assumption of the Virgin.[55] As a result, this position finally received clear definition and widespread acceptance by the end of the twelfth century. Moreover, as the *Munificentissimus Deus* explained just a generation ago, the belief in the bodily assumption was a privilege interconnected with that of the Immaculate Conception:

Quae quidem, singulari prorsus privilegio, immaculata conceptione sua peccatum devicit, atque *adeo* lege illi permanendi in sepulcri corruptione obnoxia non fuit, neque corporis sui redemptionem usque in finem temporum expectare debuit.[56]

She indeed, by virtue of her singular privilege, overcame sin through her immaculate conception, and for this reason she was not subject to the corruption which is the rule for bodies remaining in the tomb, and she did not need to wait until the end of time for the restoration of her body.

Such a relationship is already hinted at in the Hereford Troper (Fig. 57) where the Annunciation to Joachim illustrates the feast of the Assumption. There were also certain connections between the two questions in the twelfth century when arguments for the Immaculate Conception and Assumption did run along the same lines, even employing the same terminology at times. However, any specific doctrinal association between them in the Winchester Psalter is unlikely since until the end of the twelfth century they were to develop parallel to one another, as two largely separate issues.[57]

In addition to these theological and liturgical considerations, there were certainly additional factors which may well have motivated the choice of the Assumption as well as its placement opposite the Virgin Enthroned and before the Last Judgment cycle. As Wormald so perceptively observed, the Death of the Virgin and the Virgin Enthroned would originally have faced each other, forming a diptych.[58] He also carried this idea further, suggesting parallels with Byzantine or quasi-Byzantine icons. These are intriguing ideas that deserve close attention. They hint at the function of these scenes as votive images, Byzantine icons once removed.

The image of the Virgin on fol. 30 (Fig. 29) can certainly be understood in these terms. She sits frontally, raises her hands before her and stares out of the picture space. In these respects, the image conforms to an iconographic type that was often employed in a votive context. Some of these images are especially noteworthy since they also share their Byzantine or quasi-Byzantine style with the Winchester Virgin. One is found in the Homilies of the Monk James, fol. 66v (Fig. 146). Here Adam and Eve kneel before the Virgin, who assumes exactly the same pose as the Winchester figure. Another appears in the Egberti Psalter.[59] The image was probably added to an Ottonian manuscript by a Russian artist working in a provincial Byzantine style. This image accompanies prayers of intercession addressed to the Virgin, including one also found in the Winchester Psalter.[60] Another parallel is offered by a crusader kingdom manuscript, the Melisende Psalter.[61] Here, in a twelfth-century manuscript with Winchester elements in the calendar,[62] the image of the Virgin enthroned is placed just before a prayer of intercession addressed to her. The similarity the Winchester Virgin shares with these examples by virtue of the quasi-Byzantine style and iconography suggests that it, too, was considered a votive image. These factors also make it tempting to contemplate the possibility that these characteristics may have been viewed as imparting a special efficacy to the icon-like image. There are also significant precedents of a somewhat different sort in English manuscripts. There is one in the Lansdowne Psalter (Fig. 161). Although typically English in style, the frontal position of the Virgin and supplicant below establish it as a votive image. Moreover, the miniature faces the beginning of a lengthy series of intercessory prayers addressed to the Virgin, one of which is also found in the Winchester Psalter.[63] Another example is found in Oxford, Bodl., MS Auct. D.2.6 which contains the prayers and meditations of St Anselm.[64] Here a female supplicant again kneels before the Virgin and Child. The prayers to the Virgin begin on the folio opening just opposite this image.

The suggestion that the miniature of the Virgin on fol. 30 may have been understood in a votive context is further enhanced by the presence of the Assumption scene. In her Assumption, the Virgin was freed from death and at this moment stepped forth as an eminently powerful intercessor.[65] The importance of the Assumption in this context can be traced through a long history in Christian pleas for intercession. Such pleas formed a part of the liturgy in the East at an early date and in the West from the seventh century. The reflections are found in the Gelasian Sacramentary.[66] Forms of intercession are also found in other service books, such as the ninth-century Antiphonary of Compiègne[67] or the tenth-century antiphonary from Prüm, Patis, B.N., MS lat. 9448. Here the text for the feast of the Assumption is accompanied by two miniatures. The first depicts the Death of the Virgin[68] and the second her enthronement (Fig. 162). The accompanying text praises and honours the Virgin at her Assumption, continues by speaking of her place in the scheme of redemption and concludes with a plea for intercession. The idea of intercession in conjunction with the Assumption is also found in the works of eleventh- and twelfth-century authors including Fulbert of Chartres,[69] Bernard of Clairvaux,[70] Peter of Blois[71] and Herbert of Losinga. In his sermon on the Assumption the latter states:

Si enim in resurrectione dominica multa corpora sanctorum qui dormierant resurrexerunt, et in sanctam civitatem multi(s) apparuerunt, quomodo caro resurgere non poterant (sic) quae ipsum resurrectionis generavit auctorem? Plena, fratres, et secura fide tenete quod beatissima virgo Maria, et anima et corpore immortalis facta, cum filio suo Domino nostro Ihesu Christo ad (sic) dextris residet Dei; mater penitentium, et interventrix efficacissima pro peccatis nostris apud clementissimum filium suum.[72]

For if at the Lord's Resurrection many bodies of saints who had been asleep, arose and appeared to many in the holy city, how could that person not rise up in flesh who begat the very author of the Resurrection? Brothers, in full and secure faith remember that the most Blessed Virgin Mary, immortal in both body and soul, with her son our Lord Jesus Christ, sits at the right hand of God, as the mother of penitents and the most efficacious intercessor for our sins before her most merciful son.

A last consideration remains which on the one hand concludes an examination of the Virgin cycle and on the other raises new questions involving them together with other miniatures in the manuscript. The placement of the two illustrations of the Virgin as an intercessor must also be viewed in relation to the extensive judgment cycle that follows. While this complex pictorial sequence is unique, it emerges as the product of a lengthy tradition. It is expressed visually in the Homilies of the Monk James (Fig. 146).[73] There is also an eleventh-century prayer of Fulbert of Chartres, addressed to the Virgin as an intercessor at the Last Judgment,[74] and lengthy prayers from the twelfth century.[75] In Britain the theme is already found in the late tenth-century Vercelli Homilies[76] and, significantly, in a miniature from the eleventh-century Grimbald Gospels from

Winchester (Figs. 149, 162).[77] The miniatures accompany the double-page opening to the Gospel of St John. On the left, sits Christ in Majesty. Below him appear the apostles, and St Michael holding a group of 'souls'. The judgment theme implied here is linked to an image of the Virgin on the opposite page. She is enthroned, wears a crown and is flanked by angels. This depiction is a variation on the theme *Regina Angelorum* at the Last Judgment which reappears in another form in the Winchester Psalter. All of this suggests that the inclusion of the unusual groups of scenes illustrating the life of the Virgin and Last Judgment in this manuscript, had a purpose. In spite of their heterogeneous stylistic and iconographic character, they were meant to honour the Virgin and in so doing, enhance her prestige and effectiveness as an intercessor, especially at the Last Judgment. In these respects, they can be viewed not as entirely new but rather as a revival and elaboration of earlier traditions, particularly those from Winchester in the century before the Conquest.

Chapter Four: The Pictorial Cycle

THE CLOSE ASSOCIATION of the 'Byzantine diptych' and Last Judgment scenes in what may be a votive context raises a final and more complex issue. The thematic unity they display prompts a consideration of the cycle as a whole in order to determine what may have motivated the patron to request the entire group of scenes as the visual frontispiece for a psalter. If the patron had commissioned a series illustrating the life of David, the normal selection in Byzantine and Western psalters, the answer would have been fairly straightforward since the scenes would focus upon the author of the text. In Nero C.IV, however, the illustrations of the life of David are merely a small part of a cycle that is primarily christological in its orientation. While such a selection may initially seem puzzling, it is possible to view it as the product of a lengthy tradition which developed slowly over several centuries. In a general sense, the psalms had been associated with Christ or specific events in the life of Christ since the Early Christian period. Ireneas felt they announced the coming and Passion of Christ. Tertullian also viewed them in relation to the Passion. Ambrose stated that the psalms proclaimed openly the coming of Christ, his Incarnation, redemptive work, Passion, Resurrection and glorification. Jerome again related them to His work of redemption while Augustine found references to Christ in the first psalm.[1] In the same period, other formulae drawing more specific parallels between individual psalms and the life of Christ were composed. They were series of *tituli* which gave the psalms a Christian orientation by associating some or all of them with the person of Christ.[2] For the most part, these notices were fairly general, merely mentioning that the psalms pertain to Christ. However, the fifth series went further, drawing allusions to Christ from the sense of each psalm. In some cases, these christological references were collated into the text so that each one stood just before the corresponding psalm. However, *tituli* could also be grouped together and placed before the text of the psalms as a whole. This is the arrangement followed in the Vespasian Psalter where the *tituli* of the fifth series were included in a series of texts which preface the psalms.[3] This marks the beginning of a movement toward the incorporation of references to Christ in the frontispiece of an Insular psalter. It is carried further in the Vespasian Psalter itself which includes another text of even greater interest. The *tituli* are preceded by a letter ascribed to Pseudo-Jerome which not only makes general references to Christ but also singles out specific events from his life:

Licet enim universi psalmi, qui requisitum fuerit, legis divinae propemodum omnia habeant; tamen donante Deo, et Domino Iesu Christo, et Spiritu sancto in confessione Trinitatis, qui psalmi proprie ad singulos dies feriatos Domini Salvatoris nostri Filii Dei pertineant, sequestratim exposuimus. Qui ad Natalem; qui ad sanctam Epiphaniam, id est, ad baptismum Dominicum, sive apparitionis stellae diem; et qui in quinta feria ante passionem Domini; et qui in ipsa passione Dominica; qui in pascha Resurrectionis ipsius Domini nostri Redemptoris; et qui in Ascensione eius in coelos; qui etiam in Adventu eius; et qui de iudicio futuro; et qui de civitate aeterna, in qua Christus Dominus noster sanctos suos a principio mundi usque ad finem huius saeculi, sibi congregat secum conregnaturos in aeterno regno coelesti, sanctus Dominus, trinus et unus, Deus aeternus; qui etiam ad Dominum Deum deprecandum in litania; vel qui a poenitentibus psalli debeant; qui etiam in natali sanctorum diei debent. Caeteros vero psalmos invenies qui quotidie legendi sunt.[4]

For although the psalms as a whole, as is only proper, contain almost all of divine law, nevertheless with God permitting, together with the Lord Jesus Christ and the Holy Spirit in the confession of the Trinity, we have separately set forth the psalms which relate to particular feast days of the Lord, our Saviour, the Son of God, as follows: psalms which pertain to his Birth, or to the holy Epiphany, i.e., to the Baptism of the Lord, or to the day of the star's appearance; and psalms which relate to the fifth ferial before the Passion of the Lord; and those which refer to Passion Sunday itself, and those which concern the feast of the Resurrection of the Lord our Redeemer; and those which pertain to his Ascension into Heaven; and psalms concerning his future judgment; and those relating to the eternal city in which Christ our Lord gathers to himself from the beginning of the world even to the end of time those saints who will reign in the eternal heavenly kingdom, with Him, the holy Lord, three yet one, God eternal; and psalms for prayer to the Lord God in a litany; or those which are to be chanted by repentant sinners; and those too which should be sung on the birthdays of the saints. Other psalms you will discover which are to be read each day.

It is particularly significant that this early text, which prefaces an Insular manuscript, goes beyond general mention of Christ to discuss particular uses of the psalms in the liturgical celebration of specific events in the life of Christ essential for man's redemption. It is also noteworthy that it stresses the importance of the psalms in penitential exercises.

The role of the psalms in a devotional scheme, outlined in the letter of Pseudo-Jerome, invites a closer examination of the psalter itself in this context. The psalms were the basis for the public prayer of the Divine Office as well as a source for private prayer during the Middle Ages.[5] The movement toward a greatly expanded use of the psalms for private devotions can be associated with the Carolingian period. Benedict of Aniane in the later part of the eighth century is said to have introduced the recitation of 15 additional psalms and other prayers before the singing of Matins as well as the Office of the Dead as a further devotional supplement. In the same period, the use of the psalter for the private devotions of the laity was described in detail by Alcuin in his *De psalmorum usu liber*. Alcuin prepared a regular daily course of prayer based upon the psalms for Charlemagne. Here he presented the psalms as the basis for confession of sins and perfect basis for requesting divine mercy.[6] The use of the psalms in a daily round of prayer soon assumed a more elaborate form. Later in the tenth century, Vespers and Lauds of all saints began to be added as a supplement to the regular Vespers and Lauds of the day in some monasteries. By the end of the century, the foundation for the Little Office had been prepared. This development included a cursus in honour of the Virgin and additional psalms for the Divine Office. Various patterns were also drawn up to incorporate the psalms into a daily round of private devotions for the laity. One result was the development of a collection of devotions for laymen, the primer.[7] The adoption of the primer by the laity has been interpreted as a desire of the lay world by the end of the tenth century to imitate the devotions of the clergy. The psalms and the book that contained them were then from the Carolingian period the basis of private devotions of both the monastic and lay worlds.

The directives of the Vespasian Psalter frontispiece together with a broader consideration of the psalter as a prayer book prompts an investigation of other psalters and prayer books of this period. One of these is a ninth-century psalter commonly referred to as the Book of Cerne, Cambridge, University Library, MS Ll.I.10.[8] The manuscript is perhaps best known not as a psalter but as the prayer book of Bishop Aedeluald of Lichfield. That the Book of Cerne served the latter function is demonstrated by the lengthy series of private prayers that follow the psalms. More important in this context is the preface. It is composed of excerpts from the Gospels describing the events of the Passion and is placed directly before the text of the psalms. The inclusion of a frontispiece describing the Passion in a book intended for private devotions may suggest that these Gospel passages formed a part of the devotional scheme. This leads to a consideration of other prayer books from the same period which also include prefaces of importance. London, B.L., MS Royal 2.A.XX, contains prefatory material of a similar nature. Here excerpts from the Gospels on the Passion come before a series of private prayers.[9] It may also be noted that in each case, the selections from the Gospels correspond to major christological feasts, suggesting a certain continuity with the emphasis on events of liturgical significance cited in the Vespasian Psalter.

Another manuscript of great importance in this connection is the book of Nunnaminster, London, B.L., MS Harley 2965, a prayer book of the eighth or ninth century.[10] Here the series begins with accounts of the Passion according to Mark, Luke and John. Next come several prayers by Gregory and Augustine followed by a series of 43 collects, referring to events from the life of Christ. They begin with prayers concerning the birth of Christ and continue with the Circumcision, Epiphany, Baptism, Temptation, Cana, an extensive Passion series, Ascension, Pentecost and conclude with the Last Judgment.

Similar practices continue into the eleventh century in the *Liber Vitae* of Hyde Abbey, Winchester. Here the accounts of the Passion, drawn from Matthew, Luke and John, precede a series of prayers. There are also eleventh-century psalters from Winchester which can be drawn into this framework.[11] The frontispiece to the psalms in Arundel 155 includes prayers to be recited before and after the psalms themselves. Here the devotional use of the psalms to commemorate the events of the life of Christ crucial in the redemptive scheme is made clear on fol. 11v:

Oratio ante psalterium	*A prayer before the psalter*
Praesta, quaeso, omnipotens et misericors Deus, ut intelligenter et libenter atque perspicue merear audiri. Tuis enim adiutoriis omnimodis indigeo, ut valeam cum concessa gratia aliquatenus verba tuae maiestatis cantare. Per Iesus Christum Dominum nostrum.	Grant, I beg you, almighty and merciful God, that I may deserve to be heard intelligibly, gladly and clearly. For I need your help in every way, so that by your grace I may to some extent be fit to sing the words of your majesty. Through Jesus Christ our Lord.
Alia oratio	*Another prayer*
Suscipe, sancta Trinitas, hos psalmos consecratos quos ego indignus et peccator decantare cupio in honore sancti nominis tui et beatissimae semperque virginis MARIAE et sanctorum angelorum et archangelorum, patriarcharum, prophetarum, apostolorum, martyrum, confessorum, atque virginum et omnium sanctorum tuorum, pro me miserrimo famulo tuo seu pro cunctis fidelibus viventibus sive defunctis. Concede, domine IESU Christe, ut isti psalmi omnibus proficiant ad salutem et ad veram paenitentiam faciendam et emendationem ad vitam aeternam. Amen.	Receive, Holy Trinity, these consecrated psalms which I, unworthy and a sinner, wish to sing in honour of your holy name, and of the most blessed and ever Virgin Mary, holy angels and archangels, patriarchs, prophets, apostles, martyrs, confessors and virgins and of all your saints, for myself, your most miserable servant, and for all the faithful, living or dead. Grant, Lord Jesus Christ, that these psalms may help all men to salvation and to make true penitence and improvement, for eternal life. Amen.
Alia oratio	*Another prayer*
Suscipere digneris, Domine Deus Pater	Deign to receive, Lord God Father

omnipotens, creator generis humani et redemptor, hanc orationem psalmorum quos ego peccator et indignus decantare praesumo pro commemoratione nativitatis, passionis, resurrectionis, ascensionis et adventus Domini nostri Iesu Christi, et pro commemoratione omnium sanctorum qui tibi placuerunt ab initio mundi.

almighty, creator and redeemer of the human race, this prayer for the psalms which I, a sinner and unworthy, presume to sing in commemoration of the Nativity, Passion, Resurrection, Ascension and Second Coming of our Lord Jesus Christ, and in commemoration of all the saints who have pleased you since the beginning of the world.

Another reference to the importance of the psalms in devotions comes in Tiberius C.VI. Following the illustrations is a textual preface that includes prayers and a long formula for confession. The private prayers, directed toward obtaining remission from sins, begin on fol. 21v. They continue on 22v with the following prayer:

Et licet usque ad obitum vitae huius psalmi virtutem contemplaveris atque scrutaveris, nunquam perfecte illum, ut puto, intellegere potes. In quo nullus versus est in quo non sit via Dei vel lex vel mandatum seu praeceptum Dei vel verba aut iustifationes vel iudicia aut sermones Dei descripti. Et ideo non tibi opus ut per diversos libros animo diffundaris. In psalterio solo usque ad obitum vitae habes materiam legendi, scrutandi, docendi, in quo invenias prophetas, Evangelium atque apostolos, et omnes divinos libros spiritaliter, atque intelligenter ex parte tractatos atque descriptos. Et priorem atque secundum adventum Domini ibi reperies prophetatos, incarnationem quoque ac passionem resurrectionemque atque ascensionem dominicam. Et omnem virtutem divinorum dictorum in psalmis invenies, si intima mente perscruteris; et ad medelam intimi intellectus per Dei gratiam perveneris.

And though you will meditate on and examine the virtue of this psalm until the end of your life, you will never – I think – be able to understand it perfectly. In it there is no verse which does not contain the way of God and his law and his command, or the precept of God and his words or justifications, and the judgments or sayings of God written down. And so you need not be spread in spirit over a variety of books. In the psalter alone, until the end of your life, you have matter to read, to examine and to teach, in which you may find the prophets, the Gospel and the apostles, and all the divine books spiritually and intellectually, in part, handled and set forth. And you will find there the first and second coming of the Lord prophesied, also the Lord's Incarnation, Passion, Resurrection and Ascension. And you will find in the psalms the whole virtue of the divine sayings, if you examine them intimately; and by the grace of God you will come to the healing of intimate understanding.

These Anglo-Saxon texts continue the themes found in earlier textual prefaces by emphasizing that the psalms are the basis for prayer and studying them leads to an understanding of the events in the life of Christ which prepared for man's salvation.

This Insular practice of introducing a devotional book with an account of the life of Christ is also reflected in visual examples from the Anglo-Saxon period. Illustrations at this early date did not achieve the clarity of focus found in the textual sources, but the subject matter does parallel them in certain respects. Among the tenth-century miniatures added to the Aethelstan Psalter, London, B.L., MS Galba A.XVIII, is a frontispiece of Christ at the Last Judgment (Fig. 150).[12] Elsewhere in the cycle are or were miniatures of the Nativity and Crucifixion. In most other cases, the focus is more clearly upon the Passion, as it had been in the textual prefaces of the preceding period. Both the late tenth-century Harley MS 2904 and an eleventh-century psalter from Winchester, London, B.L., MS Arundel 60, display the Crucifixion as a pictorial frontispiece, a feature they share with a number of continental manuscripts.[13] This theme is expanded upon in the prefatory miniature cycle of Tiberius C.VI, the only pre-Conquest psalter possessing an extended visual frontispiece.[14] Here the picture cycle enlarges upon the Passion theme with liturgically-oriented scenes for the Easter season. It opens with the Temptations of Christ and continues with the Entry into Jerusalem, Washing of the Feet, Betrayal, Christ before Pilate, Crucifixion, Resurrection, Harrowing of Hell, Incredulity of Thomas, Ascension and Pentecost. These illustrations are of special importance, not only in their increasing complexity but also because they are joined together with the textual preface quoted above. The common placement of the textual and visual elements suggests that they should be viewed as a single frontispiece to the psalms. As such they embrace a common focus for meditation, the saving grace of Christ, achieved through the Passion and Resurrection. The frontispiece achieves a new clarity here, surpassing that in earlier textual or visual frontispieces.

After the Conquest, psalter prefaces no longer included the sort of elaborate textual introductions they did in the Anglo-Saxon period, but the visual tradition was revived by the artist of the Albani Psalter. Like Tiberius C.IV, the manuscript possesses an elaborate Passion cycle, now enriched with scenes of the Fall, Expulsion and Infancy of Christ. The fragmentary nature of the Lansdowne Psalter cycle is much to be regretted and precludes suggestions regarding the principle of selection involved. It can be observed, however, that the few remaining scenes fall into two groups, those illustrating events surrounding the Nativity and the Passion. By the middle of the twelfth century, then, there was an established tradition of prefacing psalters with illustrations which vary in their selection of individual scenes but share a common liturgical orientation. The Winchester cycle can be viewed within this group. This is readily apparent in the case of certain scenes from the Infancy and Passion cycles, although not as clear with others. However, it is possible to draw all the scenes within this framework in a way that gives a fairly precise accounting for the selection of each scene. The cycle as a whole closely parallels the selection of readings for Matins in the Benedictine Breviary of Hyde Abbey[15] for the season from Advent through Epiphany and from Septuagesima through Pentecost.[16]

The group of scenes in Nero C.IV centring around the events of Advent begins with the extremely rare scene of the Angel Gabriel sent out by God for the Annunciation. Its appearance is explained by the Hyde Breviary where it is the first christological response in the first nocturn for Matins on the first Sunday in Advent: 'Missus est Gabriel angelus ad Mariam virginem desponsatam Ioseph.' ('The angel Gabriel was sent to the Virgin Mary espoused of Joseph.') This response is followed immediately by a reference to the Annunciation itself: 'Ne timeas Maria invenisti gratiam apud Dominum. Ecce concipies et paries et vocabitur altissimi filius.'[17] ('Do not fear, Mary, you have found favour with the Lord. Behold you will conceive and bear a son who will be called the son of the most high.') Multiple references to the Annunciation echo throughout the second nocturn, followed in the third by the versicle drawn from Isaiah which corresponds to the illustration of the Jesse Tree on fol. 9: 'Egredietur virga de radice Iesse. Et flos de radice eius ascendet.'[18] ('A stem will come forth from the root of Jesse and a flower will grow up from his root.') The following scenes of the Nativity and Shepherds are paralleled in the Matins readings from the vigil for the birth of Christ through those for Christmas day.[19] The Matins office for the feast of the Innocents encompasses the scenes from the encounter of Herod with the Magi through the Flight into Egypt.[20] The remaining scenes from the early life of Christ unfold in a sequence related to the feast of the Epiphany. They are paralleled in the breviary in the observance of the Epiphany with this antiphon: 'Magi viderunt stellam et dixerunt ad invicem. Hoc signum magni regis est eamus et inquiramus eum et offeramus ei munera aurum thus et mirram.'[21] ('The magi saw the star and said to one another: This is the sign of the great king. Let us go and seek him and offer to him gifts of gold, frankincense and myrrh.') The Matins office for the feast of the Epiphany continues with readings describing the Journey of the Magi, their meeting with Herod and their Adoration of Christ.[22] Both the Presentation and Baptism are represented in the Winchester calendar and take their place in a liturgical cycle. The Presentation in the Temple, as the feast of the purification of the Virgin, was celebrated at Winchester and appears as a part of the festival cycle in the Hyde Missal.[23] The Baptism also forms the subject for the octave of the Epiphany and the Sunday within the octave of the Epiphany.[24] The same series of Matins readings introduces Christ among the Doctors.[25] The subject is encountered again in the Matins readings for the first Sunday after the octave of the Epiphany. Here the lesson is expanded to describe not only the meeting of Christ with the doctors but also his subsequent encounter with his parents.[26] This scene in the Psalter has few, if any, close parallels but is, like the sending of the Angel, encountered in the breviary. The last Winchester subject to fall into this group is the Marriage at Cana. It forms the subject of two Matins readings for the second Sunday after the octave of Epiphany.

The preparation for Easter begins 70 days before on Septuagesima Sunday. Although not included in the Easter cycle at an early date, it and the general subjects of the readings assigned to it were fixed from the eighth century.[27] Subjects from Genesis formed the basis for the day which by the twelfth century signalled the beginning of the Easter season. This is the orientation of the readings in the Hyde Breviary. Lessons for Septuagesima are devoted to the history of Adam, Eve, Cain and Abel. The ninth, tenth and eleventh lessons for Matins are devoted to the Calling and Expulsion of Adam and Eve.[28] Significantly, a detail of the Winchester Calling–Expulsion sequence finds a striking parallel here. The inscription on the scroll held by God in the Winchester miniature reads: 'Videte ne forte sumat de ligno vitae' ('Watch lest perhaps he take of the tree of life.'). This is not a direct quotation of the corresponding verse in Genesis 3:22: 'Et ait Dominus Deus "Ecce homo factus est quasi unus ex nobis, ut sciat bonum et malum; nunc ergo, ne mittat manum suam et sumat etiam de ligno vitae et comedat et vivat in aeternum." ' ('And the Lord God said: "Behold, man was made as if one of us, so that he might know good and evil; now therefore, let him not put out his hand and take also of the tree of life, and eat, and live forever." ') Instead it bears greater similarity to the response to the eleventh lesson: 'Ecce Adam quasi unus ex nobis factus est sciens bonum et malum. Videte ne forte sumat de ligno vite et vivat in eternum.'[29] ('Behold Adam was made as if one of us, knowing good and evil. Watch lest perhaps he take of the tree of life and live forever.') The twelfth lesson which follows describes the Labours of Adam and Eve, the subject depicted after the Expulsion in the Psalter. This lesson concludes with a versicle and response devoted to Cain and Abel. Here the illustrations echo the sense of the breviary passages which centre around the murder of Abel.

The lessons for Sexagesima are again drawn from Genesis and deal with the history of Noah. The readings begin with Genesis 5:31–6:2 while the versicle and response begin with a later moment described in Genesis 6:13–15:

R Dixit Dominus ad Noe finis universae carnis venit coram me. Repleta est terra iniquitatae eorum. Et ego disperdam eos cum terra.
V Fac tibi archam de lignis levigatis; mansiunculas in ea facies. Repleta.[30]

And the Lord God said to Noah: The end of all flesh is come before me. The earth is filled with their wickedness; and I will destroy them with the earth. Make for yourself an ark from smooth wood; make rooms in it. Let it be filled.

The versicles and responses for the third lesson describe the ark afloat, those of the fourth the destruction of all but Noah's family, the fifth and sixth again refer to the ark afloat and the seventh to Noah sending forth the dove. The eighth and final Old Testament lesson of the day concludes with Genesis 6:14–15, describing God commanding Noah to build the ark. The readings and especially the versicles and responses for Sexagesima centre around the subject depicted in the Winchester miniatures.

The lessons for the Matins office on Quinquagesima Sunday are devoted to Abraham. The lessons for the second nocturn centres in the main around the story of Abraham and Isaac. Here response and versicles for the sixth lesson begin:

R Temptavit Deus Abraham et dixit ad eum. Tolle filium tuum quem diligis Isaac et offeres illum mihi in holocaustum super unum montium quem dixero tibi.
V Vocatus quoque a Domino respondit: adsum. Ait ille Dominus. Tolle filium.[31]

God tempted Abraham and said to him: Take your son Isaac whom you love and offer him to me as a burnt offering on one of the mountains which I shall tell you of. Called also by the Lord he replied: I am here. The Lord said: Take your son.

The responses and versicles for the seventh lesson describe the journey of Abraham and Isaac and building of the altar. Those for the eighth lesson focus upon the sacrifice:

R Angelus Domini vocavit Abraham dicens. Ne extendas manum tuam super puerum eo quod timeas Dominum.
V Cumque extendisset manum ut ymolaret filium, ecce angelus Domini clamavit dicens. Ne extendas.

The angel of the Lord called Abraham saying: Do not extend your hand over the boy, for you fear the Lord. And when he had extended his hand in order to sacrifice his son, behold the angel of the Lord called out saying: Do not extend it.

The response again parallels the inscription on the scroll which reads: 'Ne extendas manum tuam super puerum.' ('Do not extend your hand over the boy.') Somewhat further removed is the biblical passage: 'Non extendas manum tuam super puerum, neque facias illi quidquam.' ('Do not extend your hand over the boy, nor do anything to him.')

Quadragesima Sunday has no Old Testament lessons. Old Testament subjects are reintroduced on the second Sunday in Quadragesima. This group of Matins lessons has responses and versicles describing events from the life of Jacob. Those for the fifth, sixth and seventh lessons focus upon the dream of Jacob.[32] The eleventh lesson concludes with Jacob's encounter with the angel.

The Old Testament Matins lessons for the third Sunday in Quadragesima are devoted to Joseph. The confrontation of Joseph with the wife of Potiphar is not included in the Hyde Breviary, although it does appear in another medieval English breviary from Hereford.[33] However, the unique sequence of two scenes which follow it in the Psalter are described in the fifth lesson of the Hyde Breviary:

R Memento mei dum bene tibi fuerit. Ut suggeras pharaoni ut educat me de isto carcere, quia furtim sublatus sum et hic innocens in lacum missus sum. V Tres enim adhuc dies sunt post recordabitur pharao ministerii tui et revocabit te in gradum pristinum. Tunc memento mei. Ut suggeras.[34]

Remember me for as long as it shall be well with you. Suggest to pharaoh that he should lead me out of this prison, since I was carried off secretly and, innocent as I am, was thrown into a pit. For after three more days the pharaoh will recollect your ministry and will call you back to your original state. Then remember me. Suggest . . .

The Matins lessons for the fourth Sunday in Quadragesima describe events from the life of Moses. The response and versicle for the first lesson focuses upon the dialogue of God and Moses as he spoke from the burning bush.[35] Those for the sixth and seventh lessons describe Moses receiving the tablets of the law on Sinai.[36] The story of Moses concludes the Old Testament Lenten readings in the Hyde breviary on the last Sunday in Quadragesima.

A comparison of the Old Testament scenes in the Winchester cycle with those in the Hyde Breviary reveals a striking number of parallels. Both commence with the history of Adam, Eve, Cain and Abel. They continue with Noah, Abraham, Jacob, Joseph and Moses. The choice of the general subject matter is identical, there are no significant omissions or inclusions in one not paralleled in the other. In many instances, the comparisons go beyond the common choice of the same series of individuals to centre upon the same points in time. This is true of the Calling, Expulsion and Labours of Adam and Eve, Murder of Abel, God's instruction to Noah, the Ark Afloat, God's Instruction to Abraham, the Sacrifice of Isaac, the Dream of Jacob, his struggle with the angel, Joseph released from prison, Moses before the Burning Bush and Receiving the Law. In certain instances the parallels extend further because of the close correspondence between the Latin inscriptions found in the Winchester miniatures and the breviary text. Only two scenes, the sacrifice of Cain and Abel and Joseph with

Potiphar's wife are not included in the Hyde offices. One of these can, however, be found in another medieval English breviary. Regardless, both of these subjects are understandable in this context. The Offerings and Wrath of Cain resulted in the Murder of Abel and, more to the point, the Offerings had long had a place in the sacrificial scheme of the Mass.[37] The life of Joseph was also viewed by the Fathers as parallel to that of Christ in many respects, including his temptation and temporary entombment.[38]

Explaining the relationship of the remaining subjects in the Psalter to the Easter season presents fewer problems. The first christological subject following those encompassed within the Epiphany observance is the Temptation of Christ. This subject was traditionally associated with Lent and is predictably included in the eighth, ninth, tenth, eleventh, and twelfth lessons for Quadragesima Sunday in the Hyde Breviary. The Winchester cycle continues with the Raising of Lazarus. The readings accompany the Vespers office during the fourth week in Lent.[39] The events of Palm Sunday, Christ's entry into Jerusalem and acclamation are illustrated on fol. 9 and marked by these readings in the Hyde Breviary. The pictorial series continues with a sequence of events beginning with the Washing of the Feet and concluding with the Crucifixion and Deposition. They are the focus of attention in the services for Holy Week.[40] The Easter services include extensive readings describing the Magdalene's encounter with Christ, a subject repeated throughout Easter week, which may explain why the subject received such an elaborate treatment in the picture cycle. The reading for the Incredulity of Thomas comes on the octave of Easter[41] followed by those for the feast of the Ascension and Pentecost. The Easter cycle is, then, a particularly rich one. Illustrating not only the major feasts associated with the most important season in the liturgical year but with a series of subjects beginning with the Temptation which were traditionally associated with this period of the year and included in its liturgical observance. This rich, lengthy Easter cycle may be viewed as a continuation and elaboration of a tradition extending back to earlier psalters with textual prefaces describing the Passion. More complex, perhaps, in terms of their relationship to the liturgical direction of the cycle is the placement of the *Maiestas Domini* and the extensive series of images dealing with the Last Judgment. Its placement in the Psalter, directly after the Pentecost scene, cannot be explained on the basis of scripture alone but instead finds a clear liturgical precedent. In the Hyde Missal, the readings for the first Sunday after Pentecost are drawn from Revelation 4:1–10 which includes the description of the *Maiestas Domini*. In a more general manner, readings in the Hyde Breviary for the octave of Pentecost touch on the theme of Christ as judge,[42] a theme expanded upon in the Office for the octave of Easter. The Last Judgment miniatures which follow may also be viewed in relationship to and completion of the readings for the Easter season. There is ample precedent for this practice continuously from the Anglo-Saxon period. In the view of the anonymous author of the Anglo-Saxon Blickling Homilies, the Doom would come on Easter day.[43] He opens his homily for Easter day with the image of the creator upon the judgment seat. While the apocryphal inclusions in this collection made them suspect to homilists of the eleventh century,[44] the connection of Christ as the judge with the Easter season is carried over in a manuscript containing homilies by Aelfric of Eynsham. In Trinity College, Cambridge, MS B.15.34, fol. 1r[45] (Fig. 163), he is clearly identified by an inscription on his breast as: *IUSTUS IUDEX* and a second on his knees as *REX REGUM*. A third inscription appears on his open book: 'ego sum qui de morte surrexi; ego vivo in eternum lux mundi; Ego venio in die iudicii.' ('I am he who rose from the dead; I live forever, as the light of the world; I come on judgment day.') On fol. 2r the text begins with the homily for Easter Sunday. The connection of the Judgment with the Easter season continues after the Conquest when it is evident in the Hyde Breviary. Here the readings for the first and second Sundays after the octave of Easter are devoted to readings from Revelation.[46] An antiphon which precedes them begins:

Magna et mirabilia opera tua Domine Deus omnipotens, iustae et verae viae tuae, rex seculorum. Quis non timebit te Domine et magnificabit nomen tuum quia solus pius es, quoniam omnes gentes venient et adorabunt in conspectu tuo, quoniam iudicia tua iusta sunt.	Great and miraculous are your works, Lord God almighty; just and true are your ways, king of the ages. Who will not fear you, Lord, and glorify your name, because you alone are holy; because all peoples will come and worship within your sight; because your judgments are just.

The entire christological cycle in the Psalter can be viewed, then, as an elaboration of the two most important feast cycles in the liturgical year, Christmas and Easter. As in earlier works, the coming of Christ is clearly overshadowed by the preponderant emphasis surrounding his Crucifixion and Resurrection. This is hardly surprising. As the central focus of the cult, Easter was the supreme celebration of the liturgical year, one which long before the twelfth century had come to encompass the period from Septuagesima through Pentecost. It was a season of the greatest importance, a time to reflect upon the dilemma of the human race, who as descendants of Adam and Eve, shared in the sin which was only removed through Christ's Crucifixion and Resurrection. As the period marked by Christ's sacrifice to erase man's sin, it was also a time to think beyond atonement in the current year to the last day, towards which all efforts at atonement were directed. These thoughts were channelled and directed during the Easter season in the form of additional petitions for forgiveness. They mark the pages of the Hyde Breviary, as they had coloured and shaped the devotions of the season for centuries, as in the twelfth lesson for the fourth Sunday after the octave of Easter:[47]

Fit etiam aliquando ut salutaria prorsus et precibus solicitis et devotis quaeramus actionibus. Ne tamen statim quae petimus obtineamus. Set in futurum petitionis nostrae differatur effectus. Set genibus flexis cotidie rogamus patrem dicentes adveniat regnum tuum. Idem tamen regnum non mox oratione finita set tempore congruo sumus accepturi.

It also happens sometimes that we might seek our salvation certainly both through devout prayers and pious acts. However, let us not obtain immediately what we seek. But let the completion of our petition be delayed into the future. Yet daily on bent knees we ask the Father saying your kingdom come. Still, we are going to receive the same kingdom not soon after the completion of the prayer but at a suitable time.

While the Winchester cycle echoes the most important feasts of the liturgical year in a fairly straightforward fashion, the reason why they were included in this particular book is more complex. The simplest explanation, namely that they were intended to accompany the public celebration of the Office, is not satisfactory since this manuscript was not a choir book. Instead, the Psalter was intended for the private use of an individual associated with a Benedictine priory. With the additional clarification that follows, it will be possible to demonstrate that a liturgical cycle was an appropriate choice for a private prayer book because by the twelfth century, events of liturgical significance were included in regular rounds of private devotions as well as in the public celebration of the Divine Office.

There were schemata by this date which encouraged the faithful, including those in Benedictine circles, to meditate on certain events in the life of Christ daily by associating them with the hours of prayer.[48] Even from an early date, the little hours, Prime, Sext and Terce had involved a commemoration of the events from the Passion. There is a work attributed to Pseudo-Bede which associates the events of the Passion with the hours of prayer.[49] According to John Cassian, the sixth hour, as an hour of prayer, commemorated Christ ascending the cross:

Hora autem sexta immaculata hostia Dominus noster atque Salvator oblatus est Patri, crucemque pro totius mundi salute conscendens, humani generis peccata delevit . . .

Also in the sixth hour the spotless sacrifice our Lord and Saviour was offered to his Father, and mounting the cross for the salvation of the whole world, he washed away the sins of the human race.

The same idea is expressed in the Bangor Antiphonary: '*Ad sextam.* In cruce positus.'[50] ('*At sext.* He was placed on the cross.') This makes it a very early, if not the earliest, service book authority for assignation of various night and day hours to commemorate and correspond to the incidents of Christ's Passion and Crucifixion. By the twelfth century, there was a movement toward the association of each hour with an event from the life of Christ, a movement which obtained a more developed form in the breviaries of the mid-thirteenth century.[51] Still, the outlines of this development were clear in the early twelfth century. In the *Speculum de Mysteriis Ecclesiae*, chapter 3,[52] formerly ascribed to Hugh of St Victor, there are christological associations for each of the hours. For Matins: 'Tempore noctis natus est de Virgine.' ('He was born of a virgin during the night.') This admits an age-old idea that the birth of Christ occurred during the hours of darkness. Lauds is associated with the Resurrection. For Prime comes the recollection of 'ab angelis mulieribus annuntiata resurrectio'. ('The Resurrection announced by the angels to the women'.) The little hours retain the traditional association with the events of the Passion, marked especially at Terce when 'crucifixus est Dominus scilicet mundi Redemptor.' ('The Lord, that is, the Redeemer of the world, was crucified.') None marks the death of Christ on the cross 'In eadem . . . hora mori voluit pro homine, in qua homo expulsus est de paradiso.' ('In the same hour in which man was expelled from Paradise, He wished to die for mankind.') Vespers and Compline make reference to the second coming: 'In vesperis commemoramus adventum Domini in mundi vespere. In completorio completum erit gaudium sanctorum in die generalis retributionis.' ('In Vespers we celebrate the coming of the Lord in the evening of the world. In Compline, the joy of the saints on the day of general retribution will be completed.') Around the same time, Rupert of Deutz suggested a somewhat different set of associations for the canonical hours in *De divinis officiis*.[53] For Matins he made the association with the birth of Christ but he also saw further connections. This was the hour when Christ rose from the dead and as well as the time for his return. Lauds is associated with the Resurrection: 'Sanctis mulieribus resurrectione Domini ab angelis annuntiata, tristitia fidelium iam incipit converti in gaudium.' ('With the Resurrection of the Lord announced to the holy women by angels, the sadness of the faithful now begins to be converted into joy.') Prime is associated with an event of the Passion, the Mocking of Christ before Pilate, but unlike others, the hour is also connected with events after the resurrection of the dead. In Terce the reference is to Christ crowned with thorns and Sext speaks of Christ raised on the cross, None the hour of his death, Vespers to the Last Supper and Washing of the Feet. Compline completes the theme with a more general reference to the Easter season since Christ greets his apostles with 'pax vobis' ('peace be with you'). In addition to the schemata which associated the hours with a cycle which embraced events from the Infancy and Passion cycles, the *De divinis officiis* draws closer to the Winchester cycle by adding references to the Last Judgment.

The suggestion that the illustrations may be related to a regular round of devotions can also be gleaned from the structure and content of certain prayers that follow the psalms in the Winchester manuscript. These devotional forms were intended for private use and were among those repeated in a regular round of prayer for centuries by Benedictines and laymen. They include the Office of the Cross, litany of the saints and a series of prayers addressed to Christ and the Virgin. The Office of the Cross appeared as early as the tenth century as an addition to the Divine Office. In strict imitation of the Divine Office, it became a daily exercise throughout the year and combines the themes of the Passion with the future judgment:[54]

Adoro te Domine Iesu ascendentem in cruce. Deprecor te ut ipsa crux liberet me de angelo percutiente	I adore you Lord Jesus, mounting the cross. I beseech you that the cross itself may liberate me from the chastising angel.
Adoro te vulneratum in cruce. Deprecor te ut ipsa vulnera sint remedium animae meae.	I adore you wounded on the cross. I beseech you that the wounds themselves be the remedy for my soul.
Adoro te mortuum et sepultum. Deprecor te ut ipsa mors sit vita mea.	I adore you dead and buried. I beseech you that your death itself be my life.
Adoro te descendentem ad inferos liberantem captivos. Deprecor te ut non permittas me ibi introire.	I adore you descending into hell, liberating the captives. I beseech you that you not permit me to enter there.
Adoro te resurgentem a mortuis et ascendentem ad dextram Dei Patris. Deprecor te miserere mei.	I adore you rising from the dead and ascending to the right of God the Father. I beseech you to have mercy on me.
Adoro te salvatorem, venturum et iudicaturum. Deprecor te ut in tuo sancto adventu non intres in iudico cum me misero peccatore, qui cum Deo Patre et Spiritu Sancto vivis et regnas in secula seculorum. Amen.	I adore you, Saviour, who are going to come and judge. I beseech you that in your holy coming you not enter into judgment over me a miserable sinner, you who live and reign with God the Father and the Holy Spirit for ever and ever. Amen.

The other formulae which include the litany and prayers to Christ and Virgin elaborate on the petition for mercy outlined in the conclusion of this prayer. As more complex intercessory pleas, they request aid and forgiveness at the hour of death and Last Judgment. In so doing, they bring to mind the second function of the psalms outlined centuries before in the

Vespasian Psalter and Tiberius Psalters, for they are penitential exercises. In their identification as pleas for forgiveness, they can be viewed in relation to the 'Byzantine diptych' where the Virgin as intercessor sits between the viewer and the Last Judgment cycle. The same theme is found in these prayers. The litany which invokes the aid of God, the Virgin and the saints in obtaining forgiveness, had been an established part of public and private devotions for centuries. From an early date, this plea incorporated an awareness that deliverance would come through the Saviour. Early Insular forms of the litany, like the one in the Stowe Missal, are extremely brief but incorporate this awareness by mentioning the Crucifixion after the invocation of the intercessors.[55] Litanies in some later manuscripts tend to become more elaborate, describing at greater length the events in the life of Christ which prepared the way for man's salvation. This is already clearly evident in the Arundel Psalter where, in addition to the Crucifixion, Christ is invoked in his Advent, Nativity, Circumcision, Baptism, Entombment, Resurrection and Ascension.[56] In the early twelfth century, the litany in the Lansdowne Psalter follows a similar pattern but with significant variations. The petitioner asks to be freed from the devil, death, the pain of Hell, and the wrath to come through the mystery of the Incarnation, Nativity, cross and Passion, Crucifixion, Resurrection, Ascension, and Pentecost. This is followed directly by:

In hora mortis succurre nobis, Domine.	In the hour of death aid us, Lord.
In die magni iudicii libera nos, Domine.[57]	On the day of the great judgment, free us, Lord.

Here the events representing the moments in the life of Christ necessary for salvation are tied to the coming judgment when, the petitioner hopes to be spared eternal damnation, in part through his prayers. This litany is extremely similar in many respects to the one in the Winchester Psalter. It begins with the same request for freedom from the devil and the rest, then continues:

Per misterium sanctae incarnationis tuae libera nos, Domine	Through the mystery of your holy Incarnation, free us Lord.
Per annuntiationem tuam libera nos, Domine	Through your Annunciation, free us Lord.
Per adventum tuum libera nos, Domine.	Through your coming, free us Lord.
Per nativitatem tuam libera nos, Domine.	Through your Nativity, free us Lord.
Per circumcisionem tuam libera nos, Domine.	Through your Circumcision, free us Lord.
Per baptismum tuum libera nos, Domine.	Through your Baptism, free us Lord.

Per ieiunium tuum libera nos, Domine.	Through your fasting, free us Lord.
Per passionem et crucem tuam libera nos, Domine.	Through your Passion and cross, free us Lord.
Per sanctam resurrectionem tuam libera nos, Domine.	Through your holy Resurrection, free us Lord.
Per ammirabilem ascensionem tuam libera nos, Domine.	Through your wonderful Ascension, free us Lord.
Per gratiam sancti spiriti paracliti libera nos, Domine.	Through the grace of the consoling Holy Spirit, free us Lord.
In hora mortis succurre nobis, Domine.	In the hour of death, aid us Lord.
In die iudicii libera nos, Domine.[58]	On the day of judgment, free us Lord.

This establishes the litany in the Psalter as a form elaborate enough to embrace the cycles from Advent through Epiphany, Lent, Passion week, the Passion, Resurrection and Ascension. All were invoked with a view to deliverance at the hour of death and ultimately on Judgment Day. It is a form of daily prayer which epitomizes the subject matter and intent of the pictorial cycle. There are also certain formal, structural similarities. In the miniatures, the scenes from the Old Testament and life of Christ are separated from the judgment cycle by the two 'Byzantine' miniatures. The two scenes devoted to the Virgin interrupt the sequence, breaking any purely chronological progression. There is also a pause and alteration in the form of the litany between the events from the life of Christ and the final plea for deliverance at life's end and again on the Last Day.

In addition to the litany, the Psalter contains a collection of private prayers. The majority of them are prayers of intercession addressed to Christ, the Virgin, the archangel Michael and the saints which enrich and expand upon the more abbreviated form of the litany. This is a collection which enables the Psalter to take its place among a small group of manuscripts intended, in part at least, for the private devotions of Benedictines and laymen. It is a practice well documented among surviving manuscripts from the eighth century. In addition to the expanded use of the psalms as the basis for private devotions, other increases in devotional material can be associated with this period. There are psalters from this period employed for this purpose which commonly have suitable collects interspersed with the text of the psalms. They are followed by brief prayers which may have been written by Alcuin.[59] Contemporary with the psalters of the Carolingian period were the first extant collections of private prayers. These *Precum Libelli* contained prayers composed by the early Church Fathers, along with the usual Pater Noster, Ave and some popular psalms.[60] Other patterns for devotions from the Carolingian period are found in the prayer manual of the Tuscan saint, Jean Gualbert, who died in 1073. The prayers, however, are older and were probably composed in the ninth century.[61] They consist of three series, the first a long group addressed successively to the Trinity, the cross, the Virgin, the angels, apostles and confessors. A second series of prayers, of monastic inspiration, express the intentions or personal needs of the person offering the prayers. The last series appears principally under the names of the early Fathers. These formulae are directed toward obtaining forgiveness for the petitioner and mention events in the life of Christ, as in the following, addressed to God the Father: '. . . de cuius sancta incarnatione, passione et resurrectione et in caelis ascensione tibi cotidie gratiarum actiones refero . . .'[62] ('. . . I set forth for you daily acts of thanksgiving regarding His holy Incarnation, Passion, Resurrection and Ascension into heaven . . .). It is followed by another, addressed to Christ which mentions the Passion and Last Judgment: '. . . -ut in die magni adventus tui, cum veneris iudicare vivos et mortuos . . .'[63] ('. . . so that on the great day of your coming, when you will come to judge the living and the dead, . . .')

From the same period come several Insular collections of private prayers. By far the most important among them is the Book of Cerne. The collection includes 74 prayers and hymns following the text of the psalms. The content of individual prayers also is related to those in later manuscripts, including one of those in the Winchester Psalter.[64] This collection is also of importance because of the way it weaves the events from the life of Christ into the intercessory structure of the prayers. In some prayers, brief mention is made of the Passion, Resurrection and Ascension in connection with a plea for protection against the torment of the devil and of Hell.[65] Another, more complex prayer elaborates upon this framework. It opens with a declaration of the adoration of Christ and requests freedom for the petitioner for his sins. The prayer continues:

Domine Iesu Christe adoro te in utero virginis descendentem et ex virgine natum et in praesepe positum et circumcisum. Depraecor te qui humilis venisti ad creandos nos, firma in me humilitatem veram. Domine Iesu Christe adoro te baptizatum quando aquas in vinum mutasti.	Jesus Christ I adore you descending in the womb of a virgin and born of a virgin and placed in a manger and circumcised. I beseech you who came as a humble being to us mortals to strengthen in me true humility. I adore you Lord Jesus Christ, having been baptized, when you changed water into wine.

After a series of references to the miracles of Christ the prayer continues:

Domine Iesu Christe adoro te Lazarum suscitantem et lacrimantem. Depraecor te ut me resuscites ad vitam aeternam, et fiat in me fons aquae vivae salientis in vitam aeternam. Domine Iesu Christe adoro te in crucem ascendentem et spiniam coronam	Lord Jesus Christ I adore you raising Lazarus and crying. I beseech you to restore me to eternal life. And may the source of living water which springs forth to life eternal be made in me. Lord Jesus Christ I adore you ascending the cross and wearing the

portantem in capite. Depraecor ut ipsa crux liberet me de angelo percutiente. Domine Iesu Christe adoro (te) in cruce vulneratum, felle et aceto potatum. Deprecor te ut tua vulnera remedium sint animae meae. Domine Iesu Christe adoro te in sepulchro positum. Depraecor te ut tua mors fiat mihi vita. Domine Iesu Christe adoro te descendentem ad inferos, liberantem captivos. Depraecor te ut me non demittas introire ubi Adam tibi dixit, ecce manus quae me plasmaverunt, et dixerunt alii quis est iste rex gloriae. Dominus virtutum, scio quia ultra hic non descenderis. Domine Iesu Christe adoro te ascendentem in caelos sedentem ad dexteram patris. Depraecor miserere mei. Domine Iesu Christe adoro te venturum iudicaturum. Te depraecor ut in tuo adventu non intres in iudicium cum me peccante.[66]

crown of thorns on your head. I pray that the cross itself free me from the chastising angel. Lord Jesus Christ I adore you wounded on the cross when you had been given gall and vinegar to drink. I beseech you that your wounds might be the salvation of my soul. Lord Jesus Christ I adore you placed in the sepulchre. I beseech you that your death may become life for me. Lord Jesus Christ I adore you descending into hell, liberating the captives. I beseech you that you not send me down to enter where Adam said to you: Behold the hands that fashioned me, and others said who is that king of glory. Lord possessed of moral perfection, I know that you might not have descended below this. Lord Jesus Christ I adore you ascending into heaven and sitting at the right of the Father. I beseech you to have pity on me. Lord Jesus Christ I adore you when you will come and judge. I beseech you that when you come you enter not into judgment over me, a sinner.

The emphasis upon the life of Christ in relationship to salvation on Judgment Day parallels the structure found later in the Psalter. The preoccupation with the judgment reverberates through this collection of prayers, repeatedly drawing attention to the frail, sinning nature of the petitioner and the majestic power of the judge to grant or withhold eternal life.[67] These private petitions addressed to Christ which honour his life and death also occur in other manuscripts of the period. They are found in a less elaborate form in Harley 7653, and Royal 2.A.XX.[68] The theme is also presented in the series of collects in the Book of Nunnaminster which traces the life of Christ. The second theme, an anticipation by the unworthy but repentant sinner with the coming day of judgment as an element independent of the life of Christ, also occurs in Royal A.2.XX.[69]

These forms of expression are continued in psalters of the eleventh century. In a series of psalters which have private prayers following the text of the psalms, both the prayers detailing the events in the life of Christ and those which focus on Judgment Day form an integral part of these manuscripts. There are lengthy prayers of this nature in the pre-Conquest manuscripts Arundel 60 and Arundel 155.[70] Another prayer, mentioning both the life of Christ and the Last Judgment in one prayer, follows the cycle of the Passion illustrations in Tiberius C.VI.[71]

Prayers which mention the events of the life of Christ in relationship to judgment continue to be included among the private devotions in twelfth-century psalters like Lansdowne 383.[72] In the Winchester Psalter, the prayers as a group again focus upon obtaining pardon and some of them are addressed to God the Father or Christ. However, there are some significant differences here. The Winchester prayers do not display the impassioned anguish of those in the early collections. The emphasis shifts from an unworthy petitioner shrinking before a remote, stern judge to a lavish and more intimate outpouring of adoration and praise for Christ, particularly in a prayer of St Anselm.[73] Moreover, in addition to the prayers in Nero C.IV addressed to God the Father and Christ, there is another sizeable group. In these prayers, which continue a tradition established at Winchester in the Anglo-Saxon period,[74] the events of Christ's life are enumerated in petitions addressed to the Virgin rather than to God the Father or Christ. One prayer in particular is extremely important since it closely parallels the form of the Winchester illustrations:

Ave Maria gratia plena dominus tecum. Benedicta tu in mulieribus et benedictus fructus ventris tui. Ave beata Maria gratia plena gaude et laetare Dei genitrix virgo integerrima super solem et lunam pulcherrimam. Ave, gaude et laetare speciosa et glorissima cuius speciem rex caeli et terrae concupivit. Ave, laetare et gaude humillima, piissima, misericordissima cuius humilitatem, pietatem et misericordiam respexit omnipotens Deus. Ave, gaude et laetare salutata ab angelo. Ave, gaude et laetare obumbrata a spiritu sancto. Ave, gaude et laetare quae vere filium Dei vivi ex tua virginea carne incarnatum, ex tuis visceribus genuisti virgo integerrima permanens. Ave, gaude et laetare quae filium Dei pannis involuisti. Ave, gaude et laetare quae filium Dei incunabulis strinxisti. Ave, gaude et laetare quae filium Dei lactasti. Ave, gaude et laetare quae filium Dei reclinasti in praesepio. Ave, gaude et laetare quae filium Dei praesentasti in templo. Ave, gaude et laetare quae filium Dei gestasti in tuo beatissimo gremio. Ave,

Hail Mary full of grace the Lord is with you. Blessed are you among women and blessed is the fruit of your womb. Hail blessed Mary full of grace, rejoice and be glad virgin mother of God you are the most spotless, even above the sun and moon the most beautiful. Hail rejoice and be glad, beautiful and most glorious one whose form the king of heaven and earth strove after. Hail, be glad and rejoice most humble, pious and merciful one, whose humility, piety and mercy omnipotent God looked to. Hail, be glad and rejoice you greeted by the angel. Hail, rejoice and be glad you filled with the Holy Spirit. Hail, be glad and rejoice you who from your womb bore the incarnate son of the living God from your virginal flesh while remaining the most pure virgin. Hail, be glad and rejoice you who enveloped the son of God in garments. Hail rejoice and be glad you who bound the son of God with swaddling clothes. Hail, be glad and rejoice you who suckled the son of God. Hail, rejoice and be glad you who laid the

gaude et laetare quae filium Dei nutristi et eidem humanitatis officia impendisti. Ave, gaude et laetare quae filium Dei audisti praedicantem salutem nostram. Ave, gaude et laetare quae filium Dei de te incarnatum vidisti crucifixum, mortuum, et sepultum in carne pro salute nostra. Ave, gaude et laetare cuius beatissimam animam gladius passionis Christi filii tui Domini nostri pertransivit, affectu piissime dilectionis. Ave, gaude et laetare quae filium Dei vivi vidisti resurrexisse a mortuis per gloriam patris. Ave, gaude et laetare quae verum filium Dei vivi vidisti post resurrectionem mortuis ad celos ascendentem ad patrem cum eadem sanctissima carne quam de te immaculata virgine assumere dignatus est. Ave, gaude et laetare virgo in partu, et virgo post partum. Ave, gaude et laetare mater angelorum atque archangelorum. Ave, gaude et laetare regina caelorum. Ave, gaude et laetare laus omnium sanctorum. Ave, gaude et laetare recuperatio perditorum. Ave, gaude et laetare exultatio justorum. Ave, gaude et laetare spes miserorum. Ave, gaude et laetare spes nostra. Ave, gaude et laetare salus nostra. Ave, gaude et laetare omnium bonorum nostrorum virtus. Ave, gaude et laetare per misericordiam Domini nostri Iesu Christi nostra in omnibus piissima auxiliatrix, et salvatrix, et gubernatrix. Ave, gaude et laetare gloriosa et valde gloriosissima in omnibus virgo Maria, angelorum et hominum laude dignissima et nimis veneranda per omnia saecula seculorum.[75]

son of God in a manger. Hail, rejoice and be glad you who presented the son of God in the temple. Hail, rejoice and be glad you who carried the son of God on your blessed bosom. Hail rejoice and be glad you who nourished the son of God and you who fulfilled the obligations of humanity for him. Hail, rejoice and be glad you who heard the son of God predicting our salvation. Hail, rejoice and be glad you who saw the son of God from you incarnate, crucified dead and buried in the flesh for our salvation. Hail, rejoice and be glad you whose blessed soul the sword of the Passion of Christ, your son and our Lord, has pierced most piously with the affection of love. Hail, rejoice and be glad you who saw the son of the living God to have risen from the dead through the glory of the Father. Hail, rejoice and be glad you who saw the true son of the living God after his Resurrection from the dead ascending to heaven to his Father with the same most holy flesh that he was worthy to receive from you, immaculate virgin. Hail, rejoice and be glad you who were a virgin during birth and after birth. Hail, rejoice and be glad mother of the angels and archangels. Hail, rejoice and be glad queen of heaven. Hail, rejoice and be glad, you the esteemed one of all saints. Hail, rejoice and be glad, you the restorer of those in perdition. Hail, rejoice and be glad, you the exaltation of the just. Hail, rejoice and be glad, you the hope of the wretched. Hail, rejoice and be glad, you our hope. Hail, rejoice and be glad, you our salvation. Hail, rejoice and be glad, you the source of strength of all our good people. Hail, rejoice and be glad, you, through the grace of our Lord Jesus Christ, in all things our most holy helper and preserver and director. Hail, rejoice and be glad, you glorious and truly most glorious in all things Virgin Mary, you most worthy of the praise of angels and men and who will be greatly venerated for ever and ever.

The last prayer from the Psalter itself, now combines a recounting of events in the life of Christ related to the work of salvation with a form of address that encompasses the Virgin and directs the prayer to her as Queen of the Angels and intercessor, the role she assumes in the Winchester illustrations.[76] She is addressed in these prayers as she appears in the miniature on fol. 30, as *Regina Angelorum*. Elsewhere she is asked for aid and comfort as an intercessor at the hour of death and before the Judge.[77] The necessity for aid at this moment may originally have seemed even more compelling. A rubric at the bottom of the last folio alludes to a lost series of prayers which apparently described the pains of Hell.[78] Even without them, the similarity in form between the miniature cycle and this prayer underlines the striking commonality of pictorial and verbal forms.

The parallels between the miniature cycle, liturgy and other devotional forms suggests that the Winchester cycle stands in the middle of a long development. It is first noticeable in early books like Cerne, Royal A.2.XX and Harley 2965 which were intended for private devotions. Here the Gospel accounts of the Passion appear before the text of the psalms and private prayers outline events in the life of Christ, suggesting a meditational and devotional concentration upon what is central to the redemptive scheme. The prefatory texts in the Vespasian Psalter also point in this direction as well as emphasizing the use of the psalms in penitential exercises. These ideas are carried on visually from at least the eleventh century when a Passion series appears in Tiberius C.VI, joined together with a prefatory text that again underlines the devotional and penitential uses of the psalms. This pattern continues with increasing complexity in the twelfth-century psalters, including Nero C.IV. Here both the Incarnation and the Passion are placed in relationship to the judgment theme, stressing the importance of salvation through Christ in anticipation of Judgment Day. As with the earlier devotional books, the exact role these illustrations played in the pattern of private devotions is unclear. However, the icon-like image of the Virgin, her placement before the Last Judgment cycle and the similarities between the illustrations and intercessory pleas suggest a relationship may have been intended. Although no devotional manual exists from this period, the *Ancrene Riwle* of the early thirteenth century points in this direction. The instruction for the pattern of devotions includes a section which mentions turning to the image of the Virgin, kneeling and saying five Aves. This was to be followed by bowing and kneeling before other images and relics immediately before Matins.[79] However, in the absence of rubrics in Nero C.IV, such a use for the pictures must remain in the realm of speculation. Another century passed before the ambiguity of the picture–text relationship in twelfth-century psalters assumed real clarity. The increasing emphasis upon the Incarnation and Passion took a more securely fixed place in relation to daily devotions in the c.1240 Oxford Book of Hours, London, B.L., MS Add. 49999. The form here shows some clear parallels with the pre-existing psalter tradition. The scenes centre around the Infancy and Passion cycles but the relationship to the devotional scheme is now clearly expressed. The Infancy scenes appear in connection with the Matins office and the Passion scenes in relationship to the Office of the Cross, Terce, Sext and None.[80] It is a pattern which continues to be expanded upon in later books of hours where the illustrations are not only connected with the little hours but expanded to embrace the entire daily cursus of private devotions.[81] Thus, this interpretation of the Winchester miniature cycle as a logical preface for a prayer book suggests that such books formed a bridge, pictorially as well as verbally, to devotional manuscripts of the later Middle Ages.

Chapter Five: Conclusion

WHILE THE Winchester Psalter has long been an object of scholarly study, its physical condition has raised numerous doubts as to the structure of its picture cycle as a whole. The analysis of the manuscript in the present study reveals that although in a damaged condition, the Psalter is actually better preserved than previously believed. The presence of verdigris offsets make it possible to match up existing miniatures. On the one hand, this confirms Wormald's arrangement of the miniatures in facing pairs and on the other, strongly suggests that with the possible exception of two miniatures at the beginning, no single leaves were removed from the cycle. In similar fashion, a detailed study of the drawings leads to a reassessment of their condition. They were planned and executed by one artist, possibly with assistance, as a series of tinted, line drawings. At a slightly later date, some of them were overpainted by a less skilful artisan. In spite of this regrettable tampering, the additions do not obliterate details significantly enough to interfere with a study of the iconography.

Elements in the calendar point to a date before 1161. Other features of the calendar and prayers of the manuscript associate it with the Benedictine priory of St Swithun's, Winchester. Although there is a certain degree of ambiguity present because of the inclusion of certain saints not typically associated with Winchester, the prayer to St Swithun on fol. 137v which specifically mentions the petitioner offering the prayer in St Swithun's *aula* points unequivocally to Winchester. The prayers yield further information about the intended owner of the manuscript. They are extra-liturgical formulae, suggesting that the manuscript was not a choir book but was intended for private use. The forms of the prayers provide further clues. They refer to the petitioner using the masculine singular form and enter pleas on behalf of his *benefactores*. This strongly suggests that the manuscript was intended for the private use of a Benedictine and possibly also used by this person for the spiritual direction of others. The French text and prayers could have been used by either patron, since they are found in manuscripts belonging to Benedictine houses as well as those in secular hands.

Whoever the patron was, he was clearly a wealthy individual capable of affording an illustrated luxury book for his private use. He ordered a prayer book with a picture cycle that may well have been related to the devotional scheme. There was nothing particularly new or radical herein. Benedictine houses in the twelfth century were often centres where Anglo-Saxon patterns of piety and devotion were revived. This is certainly evident in the Psalter itself, where many of the prayers were taken over without change from Anglo-Saxon petitions. Nor did the choice of the subjects for the picture cycle represent a significant departure from the norm. There had been a lengthy tradition in England of prefacing prayer books with textual and visual material centring around the Passion of Christ, or in expanded versions, upon the Infancy and Passion, with particular emphasis upon events of liturgical significance which underlined the Christian message of redemption. The Winchester cycle can, in many respects, be viewed as an elaboration upon this theme. Both the Old Testament scenes and those illustrating the Last Judgment can be viewed as an elaboration and enrichment of the Easter cycle. However, the miniatures not only mirror events of annual liturgical significance but also those frequently in the thoughts and prayers of pious individuals. The Passion of Christ had long been the focus of daily private meditation, a pattern which continues in the prayers of this manuscript.

While tradition governed the general scope and focus of the picture cycle, there are any number of unique variations upon the basic theme. Since no two picture cycles in English psalters of this type are alike, it seems reasonable to assume that the patron did not order a book of set format, but could have contributed suggestions about the subject matter of the picture cycle. This is especially noticeable in a second group of illustrations, centring upon the Virgin. The scenes of her Immaculate Conception can be viewed as more than a mere revival of earlier attitudes. The unusually full cycle of three scenes of her conception as well as their juxtaposition together with scenes from the life of Moses and possibly also David and Solomon point toward contemporary debate over the Immaculate Conception. This attempt to honour the Virgin and elevate her status also encompasses the scenes of the 'Byzantine' diptych where her prestige is further enhanced. Twelfth-century attitudes again come to the fore, since this was a period when the question of the bodily Assumption of the Virgin was widely discussed and her power as an intercessor increased substantially. That she was intended to fill this role in the Winchester cycle is indicated both by the iconographic type and by its placement just before the Last Judgment cycle. She confronts the beholder and stands between the viewer and the coming judgment. It is a formula strikingly similar to prayers in Nero C.IV, especially one addressed to the Virgin, as *Regina Angelorum*. Regardless of the exact stylistic source for these quasi-Byzantine scenes, their placement here suggests that they may well have been included because they functioned as icons, or at least votive images. It is intriguing to consider the possibility that their Byzantine origin gave them greater power in this respect. In any case, they are understandable in a book which concludes with a long series of petitions for forgiveness directed to the Virgin requesting aid on Judgment Day. Whether the owner actually prayed with these images before him is, of course uncertain, but it is clear that the scope of the picture cycle coincides closely with the intent of these intercessory petitions. In these respects, it again represents an enrichment of ideas set forth in psalter prefaces before the Conquest.

To carry out the design for this manuscript, the patron obtained the services of an artisan who may well have copied the text and fashioned the miniatures. He was an individual who had been associated with the scriptorium of Bury St Edmunds. The most significant stylistic comparisons for the Psalter can be made to manuscripts from Bury. The most important earlier source for the Nero C.IV style was the Bury Bible and Bodley 297. Other comparisons for border designs, floral motifs and shading technique suggest more than a passing acquaintance with Bury, possibly even establishing this as the centre where the artisan obtained his early training. However, the range of sources known to him suggests an understanding which surpasses what the Bury scriptorium produced. He was also familiar with the work of St Albans and Shaftesbury. Exactly how he acquired his knowledge of English sources of the period is unclear. Either Bury had a far richer tradition than previously suggested or the artist travelled widely. However, since his hand does not appear in any other work of the period, his exact movements before coming to Winchester cannot be precisely determined. The use of recently developed patterns might also help to explain the parallels with contemporary continental works. In some of these cases, the parallels were so close that miniatures appeared to have been traced from the same patterns as Mosan works. Exactly where he would have seen them is unclear. However, even Winchester is a possibility. The enamels made for Henry of Blois, now in the British Museum, have recently been proven to be the work of Mosan goldsmiths who may have been working in England. Such works could themselves have been patterns for the artist. Since there is no evidence to suggest that twelfth-century Winchester manuscripts predating the Psalter had elaborate picture cycles, it is possible that when the artisan came to Winchester, he introduced these contemporary English and some continental motifs. In addition to this, there are factors that suggest that he so drew on Anglo-Saxon iconography after coming to Winchester. Both the David scenes and some of the New Testament scenes are extremely close to those in pre-Conquest Winchester manuscripts. Either at the request of the patron or independently, he apparently varied his contemporary store of patterns by borrowing from traditions established in Winchester before the Conquest.

Regardless of exactly where the artisan obtained the models employed in the creation of the Winchester cycle, these schemata yield a substantial amount of information about the pictorial tradition in England before and after the Conquest. Although the evidence is too fragmentary to pinpoint the scriptorium that provided the model for the Old Testament scenes, they do, in other respects, enrich an understanding of picture cycle construction in England. The manner in which the Psalter reflects an Anglo-Saxon model suggests that the pre-Conquest heritage was richer both in the choice of subjects and complex detail than the extant monuments would indicate. The scenes selected for illustration included a number rarely encountered, among them, the Giving of the Labours and Cain's Wrath. Others like the Flood, Sacrifice of Abraham and Jacob's Dream incorporated a wealth of detail that reflects an ancient tradition. Other comparisons characterize this ancient archetype as one which had much in common with the Cotton Genesis and the related group of monuments. In a few cases, there are similarities to members of the Carolingian branch of this family. However, these parallels are so general and infrequent that they suggest a common heritage rather than any direct connection. The parallels to the Rovigo Bible, San Marco, the Salerno ivories, the Millstatt Genesis and San Paolo fuori le mura frescoes point toward a method of illustration and specific details more easily explained by an ancient model than a Carolingian one. The Genesis scenes in the Psalter help to define more clearly the provenance of this ancient archetype. Among the Early Christian parallels for its scenes are a number that point toward Roman monuments, namely, the wall paintings formerly in San Paolo fuori le mura as well as those in the Via Latina and SS. Marco and Marcellino catacombs. The San Paolo frescoes are particularly significant because they contained the same combination of Cotton Genesis and Vienna Genesis iconography found in the Psalter. This lends added weight to the theory of a Roman archetype.

However, the immediate source of the Winchester miniatures was an Anglo-Saxon, not an ancient, model. Because it is based on an Anglo-Saxon source, the Psalter cycle also has a bearing on the intricate problems involving the Junius and Caedmon manuscripts. The Psalter shares scenes and specific iconographic motifs with both manuscripts. Details in the Nero C.IV Giving of the Labours and Labours of Adam and Eve are also found in both Anglo-Saxon manuscripts. The Abraham and Jacob scenes correspond, in certain respects, to scenes in Aelfric. The Cain and Abel scenes may be related indirectly to those in Caedmon. This confirms the research of those scholars who viewed the two Anglo-Saxon works as the products of a common tradition. However, while these shared features do indicate some sort of relationship between the three works and the Cotton recension, the numerous differences described in earlier studies and others noted here must also be taken into consideration. These differences are sufficiently numerous and significant that they cannot be explained by a single late antique archetype which served as the direct source for Junius 11, Claudius B.IV and the Anglo-Saxon model used for Nero C.IV. One explanation would be to suggest, as others have, that two ancient manuscripts with Cottonian features were available in England. The characterization of the model for the Psalter presents another alternative. There was, in addition to Junius 11 and Claudius B.IV, at least one other Anglo-Saxon manuscript exhibiting Cottonian features. Such a manuscript, or manuscripts, could have served as the main model for one of the two extant Anglo-Saxon works while the other was based more directly upon the ancient source. The intervention of such an intermediary or intermediaries would help to explain why they share certain features while differing entirely in other places. For they would, under these circumstances, stand at varying distances from the ultimate ancient source. Which of two such manuscripts lies closer to the ancient archetype and what additional sources may have helped to shape an Anglo-Saxon intermediary are important questions but they go well beyond the bounds of this study.

Although obtained from other sources, the David scenes reflect a pattern similar to the one established for the Genesis scenes. The closest comparisons were to pre-Conquest Insular sources which, in turn, reflected Western, Early Christian models. The Old Testament miniatures were, then, quite traditional, adhering to pictorial formulae which had formed the basis for illustration in England for well over a century.

The New Testament scenes also offer important information about earlier and contemporary traditions available in England before and after the Conquest. Here again, the design for the iconography in many respects followed a predictable pattern. Three fairly traditional types of sources lie behind the Winchester cycle: Anglo-Saxon, Ottonian, and those developed in twelfth-century English centres. The twelfth-century sources found parallels in works from several leading scriptoria including Bury St Edmunds and St Albans. Here, as in the case of the Old Testament scenes, certain details bear witness to the wealth and richness of sources now lost. This was especially true of the Ottonian cycle which betrays a wider range of parallels with Byzantine monuments than previously recognized. While the main outline of the relationships to these three groups has been clear for a generation, what has not been fully appreciated is the way this artist reacted to these sources. He found them extremely useful and drew upon them freely. In the end, however, the models lost their separateness because of the unique way he combined them. He did not copy from one source but chose instead to sample a variety of alternatives, fashioning scenes from traditional elements so that his miniatures are not exactly like those in other twelfth-century manuscripts. His willingness to experiment extended further and is particularly noticeable in his incorporation of fairly recent iconographic formulae and motifs which find their closest parallels in contemporary works from the continent. This last group establishes even more distance between this cycle and other English cycles of the period.

However, in the final analysis, what is most significant is the way all of these elements were woven into the unique new fabric of the Winchester cycle. As such, they bear witness to an artisan who was a singularly gifted individual. In shaping this cycle, the extraordinary force of his innovative genius emerges. He managed to unite seemingly endless details together within a single framework. His task was to present a series of scenes telling the story of the consequences of sin and Christ's intervention to obtain man's redemption. He was able to do so not only by juxtaposing a series of ready-made scenes but by fusing them together in a new, utterly coherent way. The cycle as a whole is shaped by the lively, dramatic characterization of the history of salvation as a struggle between the forces of good and evil. Perhaps for this reason, more than any other, these miniatures continue to exercise a fascination undimmed by the passage of 800 years upon those who visit the Grenville Hall of the British Museum Library.

Catalogue of Miniatures

God Reprimanding Adam and Eve; the Expulsion (Fig. 1), *Genesis 3:22–3*

God stands at the left holding a scroll inscribed: 'Videte ne forte sumat de ligno vite'. The tree of life stands in the centre of the frame with the scroll entwined in its branches. The Lord raises his left hand in the direction of an angel with a flaming sword who guides Adam and Eve through the gate of Paradise.

The scene appears to be a conflation of two events: God admonishing Adam and Eve together with their expulsion by an angel. The scene bears numerous points of similarity with monuments associated with the Cotton Genesis tradition, as discussed in Chapter Two above. There are additional indications that the model was modified in Anglo-Saxon England. There are two related scenes in the Caedmon manuscript. Here one scene is devoted to God Reproaching Adam and Eve[1] and a second to the Angel Driving Adam and Eve from Paradise (Fig. 39). In the Anglo-Saxon scene, it is the angel and not the Lord who directs the couple from Paradise. All three again correspond by showing Adam turning back toward the angel as he departs.[2] While the iconography of the Winchester Expulsion differs from that in Aelfric's Paraphrase, it shares certain details and principles of organization with the Anglo-Saxon scene. The tree of Paradise figures with unusual prominence in a number of the Aelfric illustrations, as on fol. 7v (Fig. 40),[3] where it displays the tightly woven pattern of small branches, decorative lozenge-shaped leaves and slender trunk of the tree in the Psalter. More interesting is the way the tree is used in the corresponding Aelfric scenes. In the scene of God Calling to Adam and Eve, related in Genesis 22:8–18, the tree acts as a divider behind which the sinners huddle. In the succeeding illustration depicting the Expulsion, God forcefully ejects the couple as they pass behind the tree. The presence of the tree of Paradise in the Calling and Expulsion scenes in such a prominent place has no exact parallels elsewhere but does play a similar role in the Aelfric and Winchester scenes.

By contrast, there are few points of comparison with the Expulsion scenes in the Octateuchs.[4] Here the presence of God is suggested by a hand, the angel does not look back or carry a sword and pushes against a clothed Adam and Eve with two hands.

The Angel Giving Adam and Eve their Labours (Fig. 1)

An angel stands between Adam and Eve, handing Adam a shovel and Eve a spindle.

The scene of the Angel Dispensing the Instruments of Labour to Adam and Eve has no basis in the biblical narrative. A source which more closely approaches the subject represented here is the apocryphal *Vita Adae et Evae*.[5] In chapter 22:1–2, the *Vita* describes the events surrounding the scene depicted in the Psalter.[6] The Winchester depiction differs from the majority of examples based upon this text. Most of the monuments that depict this subject isolate the angel instructing Adam and

Eve. It is this scene which is illustrated in the Aelfric commentary (Fig. 40), on a twelfth-century baptismal font from Tournai in East Meon, Hampshire,[7] and among the late twelfth-century wall paintings done by an English artist in Sigena, Spain.[8] A precedent does exist, however, for the Distribution of the Labours in the ninth-century Byzantine manuscript, the Homilies of Gregory Nazianzus, Paris, B.N., MS grec 510, fol. 52v.[9] Here the angel presents a mattock to Adam, Eve is absent. However, it seems unlikely that the Winchester illustration was derived from a Byzantine source. There are striking differences in the arrangement of the two scenes, most notably, in the omission of Eve in grec 510.

While there are no extant Cotton Genesis or Anglo-Saxon examples of this scene, certain details suggest a relationship to this tradition. In the Expulsion scene in San Marco[10] and Caedmon (Fig. 39) Adam and Eve leave Paradise carrying the implements of their labour. While the tools are not specifically mentioned in the biblical text, their inclusion implies that they were presented to the couple before they left Paradise. The implements themselves can be linked to the same tradition. In the Winchester scene, Eve is presented with a spindle. She holds a spindle in the San Marco Expulsion scene and later appears in the same mosaic spinning, as she also does in the *Hortus Deliciarum*.[11] She also carries the whorl of a spindle from Paradise in the Caedmon manuscript.[12] Adam accepts a spade from the angel. The spade was apparently an Anglo-Saxon innovation which supplanted the traditional tool, a hoe.[13] The shovel first appears in the Caedmon manuscript (Fig. 39) and in the Aelfric scene depicting the Angel Instructing Adam and Eve (Fig. 40). Indirect support for the existence of this scene as a whole in an Anglo-Saxon model comes from the twelfth-century porch of Malmesbury Abbey in Wiltshire (Fig. 43). One of the medallions offers the only identical comparison for the scene in the Psalter.[14] Here an angel stands between the sinners, handing Adam a spade and Eve a distaff. Significantly enough, the Genesis scenes at Malmesbury have been traced directly to the Cotton Genesis recension as it is preserved in the Aelfric Paraphrase.[15] The Aelfric manuscript does not include this scene, but does illustrate the closely related Instruction scene (Fig. 40). This has led more than one scholar to suggest that the source behind the Malmesbury and Winchester scenes was English and probably of Anglo-Saxon date.[16]

Adam and Eve at Labour (Fig. 1), *Genesis 4:23*

Adam stands, turning the earth with a shovel while Eve stands at his left spinning.

The Genesis passage which touches upon the labours describes Eve's sorrow as childbearing. In accordance with the biblical narrative, the Touronian Bibles show Eve seated suckling her child.[17] The Octateuchs differ by showing Adam and Eve seated near a plough.[18]

Several members of the Cotton family deviate from this pattern by showing Eve spinning. Representations containing this detail can be found at San Marco[19] and in the *Hortus Deliciarum*.[20] While these examples differ by showing the couple seated, the standing positions in the Psalter are paralleled in the Rovigo Bible.[21] Adam and Eve are also found standing in a monument which has been traced to Anglo-Saxon sources. In a wall painting in Tavant, a remarkably similar representation occurs.[22] Here Eve, occupied with her distaff, turns to watch Adam. He bends forward at the waist, placing one foot on the upper edge of his digging implement. Several details also point toward an Anglo-Saxon source. In the Psalter, Adam again digs with a spade. Not only the tool in the Aelfric Instruction scene (Fig. 40) but the garment Adam wears, the attitude of his body and bare feet all find a comparison in the Psalter.

The Offerings of Cain and Abel (Fig. 1), *Genesis 4:3–7*

A bust-length figure of God leans out of the arc of heaven. He clutches a book and points toward Abel. Abel kneels as he offers a lamb to the Creator. On the right, Cain stares open-mouthed at the Lord while turning away holding a sheaf of wheat.[23]

The more conventional and prevalent type for the Offerings of Cain and Abel shows both figures approaching the Creator. While the scene allows for considerable variation, the common denominator in each case is the motif of both figures in the act of making their offerings.[24] The scene in the Psalter differs significantly from the vast majority of representations since it appears to refer to the moment after the one habitually chosen for representation. Genesis 4:5 describes the moment after Abel's preferment which describes Cain's wrath and his downcast countenance. This appears to agree more closely with the Winchester scene where Cain, open-mouthed with astonishment at the unfavourable decision, turns sharply to leave. This rare moment is depicted only in monuments associated with the Cotton Genesis and its English derivatives discussed in Chapter Two.

The Murder of Abel (Fig. 1), *Genesis 4:8*

Cain stands on the left and brings a large jawbone down on the head of Abel who kneels with his arms crossed on his chest.

There is no connection to the scene in the Octateuchs where Cain stones Abel to death.[25] While the depiction of the Murder of Abel showing Cain actually striking him on the head[26] is not as rare as the preceding scene, there is no other monument that exactly duplicates it in every detail. However, a large concentration of features occur in monuments associated with the Cotton Genesis group and associated Insular monuments discussed in Chapter Two.

For the figure of Abel, it is necessary to seek comparisons elsewhere since the kneeling, submissive Abel in Nero C.IV conveys a distinctly different attitude than most of his counterparts in the Cotton group.[27] While Abel kneels in the Caedmon manuscript (Fig. 48), the hands are raised before the body in a gesture that is difficult to interpret. The hand movements are represented more distinctly in the Ripoll Bible (Fig. 46). Here Abel kneels with head bowed and eyes closed. He lifts his hand, palm outstretched in a gesture that bears no trace of belligerence. Instead, we sense the gentle Abel is submitting to his brother. It is in the artist's interpretation of Abel's reaction rather than the formal iconographical device used to express it that the Psalter resembles these scenes.

It is possible to suggest that the Winchester artist used the crossed arms to suggest this same sense of resignation. On the tympanum of Rochester Cathedral (Fig. 49) Abraham prepares to slay his son. Isaac stands before him, unmoving, with his arms crossed in front of him. Isaac had long been presented in church doctrine as the ideal son, submitting with perfect obedience and complete resignation to his father's will.[28] From an early date, crossed arms in this context, then, convey Isaac's lack of willingness to hinder his approaching death in complete acceptance of the divine will. This is also the spirit which can be attached to Abel in the Winchester drawing.

Noah Commanded to Build the Ark (Fig. 2), *Genesis 6:13–22*

God stands on the left holding a scroll and pointing to Noah who stands in the centre of the composition. Noah holds an axe and points toward the unfinished ark.

It appears that the Winchester scene is a conflation of God Instructing Noah to Build the Ark together with details of the building scene borrowed from a reduced rendering of the Cotton Genesis type. This model was probably an Anglo-Saxon work related to the Cotton Genesis group, as discussed in Chapter Two.

Noah Receives the Dove into the Ark (Fig. 2), *Genesis 8:6–11*

The ark carrying Noah, his family and the animals rests on the waters. Noah stretches his arm toward a dove carrying an olive branch. The corpses of the drowned fill the turgid water below.

The scene is represented in the Octateuchs but in a much reduced fashion. Here Noah leans from a box-like ark to receive the branch. The other passengers and drowned are not included.[29] The scene is not represented in Caedmon, Roda, S.-Savin, Salerno, Millstatt or Malmesbury which deal with other aspects of the narrative. In Caedmon, the Flood is copiously illustrated with the Embarkation, Ship Afloat During the Flood and Debarcation. The Aelfric manuscript also devotes several scenes to the Flood.[30] Although there are no exact correspondences to the Nero C.IV subject, it is important to note that the source of these Anglo-Saxon Noah scenes has been related to the Cotton Genesis recension.[31] The source for the Winchester illustration does lie in the Cotton group. The monument most closely resembling the Psalter is a mosaic at San Marco (Fig. 52) discussed in Chapter Two. The appearance of a number of details in the Psalter which find exact comparisons in the mosaics at San Marco leads to the conclusion that the Winchester artist drew freely upon an extensive model of the Cotton Genesis recension in creating this image. Although the scene is not found in the extant Anglo-Saxon manuscripts, it is possible that there was such an intermediary because of the Viking design of the ship and Cotton sources behind the other Noah scenes in the Anglo-Saxon manuscripts.

God Instructing Abraham to Sacrifice his Son (Fig. 2), *Genesis 22:2*

The Lord stands at the left holding a scroll inscribed: 'Tolle filium tuum quem diligis Ysaac'. With his other hand, he points toward Abraham who listens attentively as he begins to draw his sword.

The scene appears in the Octateuchs[32] where the Lord is represented by a hand instead of the full-length figure in the Psalter. A closer comparison is possible to Aelfric, fol. 37v (Fig. 53), where the Lord is represented anthropomorphically, as in Nero C.IV. He gesticulates toward Abraham and carries an unfurled scroll which also relates this representation to the Winchester scene. Neither the Octateuchs nor the Aelfric manuscript depict the obedient response of Abraham who draws his sword in compliance with God's command.

The Sacrifice of Isaac (Fig. 2), *Genesis 22:10–12*

An angel emerges from a cloud and holds a scroll inscribed: 'ne extendas manum tuam super puerum'. With the other hand, the angel grasps the sword of Abraham. Abraham turns his head in the direction of the angel while grasping Isaac by the hair. Isaac kneels upon an altar, blindfolded, with his hands bound behind his back.

The immediate source of this scene is difficult to identify since, unlike the previous illustrations from Genesis, no single source corresponds with the scene in Nero C.IV even in a majority of details. Numerous scattered comparisons are possible, however, and many of them are found in works which have already been related to the Psalter. This is especially true for Abraham turning his head back to confront the angel. The type can be found on Early Christian[33] and Byzantine[34] monuments. It also appears in Cotton Genesis works. While the Sacrifice is not represented in the Cotton Genesis or at San Marco,[35] it is found on a Salerno ivory[36] and in the Aelfric manuscript, fol. 38r.[37]

Unfortunately, none of these examples agrees completely with the Psalter. They do not show Abraham's arm bent at the elbow with the sword blade pointing behind him. The range of possible comparisons here is limited. The type can be found as early as the fifth century on the so-called Leucadius sarcophagus in Tarragona[38] and an ivory pyxis in Bologna (Fig. 54).[39] The type was used during the early Middle Ages for a drawing in the Prudentius manuscript in Leyden, Bibliothek der Universität, MS Burm.Q.3, fol. 120r.[40] The same representation can be found considerably later, in a manuscript which suggests a closer relation to the Psalter both temporally and geographically. The Abraham figure is found in a twelfth-century manuscript from the monastery of St Bertin in northern France, St Omer, B.M., MS 34, fol. 1v.[41]

To find comparisons for the angel speaking to Abraham, it is again necessary to turn to Western sources. While the biblical narrative specifically mentions the angel speaking to Abraham from a cloud, the figure is replaced by a hand emerging from a cloud in the Early Christian and Byzantine examples cited earlier. The angel can be found in English medieval monuments including Aelfric and Malmesbury.[42] The closest correspondence is, however, to the St Bertin scene where the angel simultaneously seizes the blade of Abraham's sword and unfurls a scroll.

None of the representations discussed above which provide exact comparisons for the figure of Abraham and the angel offers a parallel for Isaac. The position of Isaac kneeling frontally on the altar is relatively rare. Both the Octateuchs and Cotton group show the scene differently. In the Octateuchs, Isaac kneels in profile with his back to Abraham. In the Cotton recension, he is also shown in profile but here Isaac is pulled across the altar toward Abraham who grasps him by the hair. Both the Octateuch and Cotton types can be traced back to Early Christian prototypes.[43] The type found in the Psalter can also be found in several Early Christian monuments,[44] discussed in Chapter Two.

The Abraham miniatures have proven to be more problematic than the preceding illustrations. Certain details can only be found in sources whose relation to the Psalter is not readily explicable. However, in the main, the scene can be explained by an English tradition because of the connections to the Aelfric manuscript and a twelfth-century manuscript from St Bertin, a monastery which had extremely close ties with England.[45]

Moses Before the Burning Bush (Fig. 3), *Exodus 3:2f.*

Moses stands barefooted, holding a rod and pointing toward a flame-encircled medallion. Inside a half-length figure raises a hand in blessing.

The depiction of Moses as a mature, bearded man relates this representation to the Western tradition. In the East, Moses is shown as a beardless youth, as for example in the Octateuchs.[46] The bearded Moses standing before the bush rather than kneeling to remove his sandals occurs frequently in the West from an early date. It is preserved in the St Paul's Bible, fol. 20v[47] (Fig. 55), in Aelfric,[48] in a late eleventh-century Bohemian Gospel book in Cracow, Mus. Czartoriski, MS 1207,[49] and on the mid-twelfth-century leaf in the Morgan Library, M. 724r.[50] More unusual is the inclusion of the rod in Moses' hand. Although it is not represented frequently, its inclusion here is explained by repeated references to it in Exodus 4:1f. It is also included in a number of Moses scenes in Aelfric.[51] However, the Winchester composition has no exact parallels in any of these scenes and may have been adapted to suit the particular circumstances which governed the subject matter of the page as a whole.

The stylized bush before Moses is a relatively rare iconographic motif. The common way of representing the divine presence is by a hand or bust above the bush (Fig. 55). The only representation of the heavenly apparition in a medallion which certainly predates the Psalter is found in the early twelfth-century Byzantine Homilies of the Monk James.[52] The fact that the motif occurs earlier in a Byzantine manuscript has recently led one scholar to suggest that its appearance in the Psalter demonstrates the influence of Byzantine iconography on the Nero C.IV artist.[53] While the possibility of a Byzantine derivation must be kept open, certain other factors must be taken into consideration here. It should be pointed out that showing the visitor in the bush and not above it follows the biblical text, Exodus 3:2–4, which refers directly to God appearing in the bush.

There are other possible interpretations of the bush, however. The Psalter is not the only twelfth-century Western example which includes the bush. The Creator speaking to Moses from the midst of the bush appears in one of the earliest stained glass windows at S.-Denis, which has been dated before 1149.[54] It can also be found in the mid-twelfth century English Walsingham Bible, Dublin, Chester Beatty Collection, MS 22,[55] at Malmesbury,[56] and elsewhere later in the century.[57] Since the window at S.-Denis and the Walsingham Bible are close contemporaries of the Psalter, it would be impossible to demonstrate with certainty that the motif was derived directly from a Byzantine source rather than transmitted through a Western intermediary. That is, of course, unless the Western tradition evolved independently, under the influence of the Vulgate text.

Moses Receiving the Tablets of the Law (Fig. 3), *Exodus 19:20f.*

A horned Moses moves up a hilly slope to receive the tablets of the Law from a hand emerging from a cloud.

Moses Receiving the Law had already found visual expression in the synagogue at Dura Europas. Here Moses stands flat-footed and reaches up to receive the tablets.[58] The Winchester iconography showing Moses ascending the mountain is commonly found in

Byzantine art, as for example, in Rome, B.A.V., MS Vat. gr. 342, fol. 133r[59] (Fig. 56). A wider variety of iconographic types was employed in the West.[60] Moses ascending the mountain appears along with a number of types from an early date.[61] It also appears later in the St Paul's Bible,[62] fol. 30v, which also provided a comparison for the scene of Moses before the Burning Bush. However, the Winchester depiction can be distinguished from others of this type because Moses tucks his head down so that it is hidden from view. Considering that none of the others have this feature, it is impossible to identify an immediate precedent for the scene.

The horns of Moses are a Western phenomenon which first appear in Aelfric.[63] After Aelfric, the feature is not found again until the first quarter of the twelfth century when it appears in the Shaftesbury Psalter and Bury Bible.

The Lord Presenting a Sceptre and Book to Two Kings (Fig. 3)

The Lord stands between two crowned men. He hands the figure on the left a sceptre. To the king on the right, he hands a book. There are no visual precedents for this scene.

The Annunciation to Joachim (Fig. 3)

An angel stands on the left holding a scroll bearing the inscription: 'noli timere ioachim ego . . . angelus domini'. In the centre of the composition stands a youthful Joachim flanked on the right by his flock.

The text on the angel's scroll immediately identifies the scene as the announcement of the Virgin's impending birth to her father, Joachim. The verse is a quotation from the Gospel of Pseudo-Matthew, one of the Latin Infancy Gospels dealing with the Virgin's youth.[64] The scene was rarely represented in either Byzantium or the Latin West. When it did occur, it was generally part of an expanded cycle dealing with the Virgin's early life. In the majority of these cases, Joachim is represented seated instead of standing as in the Psalter.[65]

There are only two representations which predate the Psalter where the unusual iconography of Joachim standing at the Annunciation can be found. The earlier of the two appears in an eleventh-century English manuscript which has been tentatively assigned to Hereford.[66] The scene illustrates the Feast of the Dormition of the Virgin in London, B.L., MS Cotton Caligula A.XIV, fol. 26v (Fig. 57). The close relation between the scene in the Hereford Troper and the Psalter leaves little doubt that the immediate source of the illustration in Nero C.IV was an English manuscript. The second example is found in the Byzantine Homilies of the Monk James[67] and bears little direct relationship to the Winchester scene.

Jacob Wrestling with the Angel (Fig. 4), *Genesis 32:22–32*

A youthful angel stands on the left gripping Jacob about the waist and holding a scroll inscribed: 'Dimitte me quia jam aurora est'. Jacob stands on the left locked in the angel's arms. He unfurls a scroll with the inscription: 'Non dimittam te nisi benedixeris mihi'.

The scene does not follow the biblical chronology since it is placed just before Jacob's Dream which is described in Genesis 28:11. The same arrangement of the two scenes can be found in grec 510, fol. 174v.[68] However, the specific comparisons that can be made to the scene in the Byzantine manuscript are few. While the angel is represented as an athletic young man with vari-coloured wings in both cases, the other details do not correspond. Jacob is shown as a mature, bearded figure in the Psalter, while in the Gregory he appears as a contemporary of the angel. The attitudes of the combatants also differ. In the Psalter, they are shown in profile turned towards one another with their arms wrapped around the opponent's waist. In grec 510, the angel is shown full front while a much shorter Jacob is shown from the rear, clinging to the angel's elbow and shoulder. A survey of other Byzantine monuments does not provide any further points of comparison. In the Octateuchs,[69] the struggle with the angel is shown in two scenes. In the first, Jacob and the angel, who is winged and has a halo, approach each other. In the second scene, which represents the actual combat, the angel has been replaced by a man of Jacob's height, providing little basis for comparison.

Closer comparisons can be made to Western monuments. In Aelfric, fol. 50r (Fig. 58), a winged, barefoot angel whose youthful face is encircled by a halo stands in profile as he grips Jacob about the waist. The angel in the Aelfric manuscript closely resembles his counterpart in the Psalter in all these respects. The correspondence between the Jacob figures is equally noteworthy. Jacob is represented bearded, striding forward in profile while gripping the angel about the waist. The proximity of the Winchester iconography to the Aelfric manuscript in this instance, as in so many others, adds additional support to a theory linking the Psalter to an Anglo-Saxon tradition.

The relationship of this Insular tradition to the Cotton Genesis group can be expanded by considering the Millstatt representation. Here, fol. 45r (Fig. 59), a youthful, haloed angel and bearded Jacob grip each other firmly in a motion which closely parallels that in the Psalter. The correspondence of the Aelfric, Millstatt and Winchester scenes again demonstrates the relationship of the English monuments to the Cotton tradition.

Jacob's Dream (Fig. 4), *Genesis 28:11*

Jacob lies on the ground with his head resting upon a large, square stone. Above him a ladder bearing two angels extends upward to the arc of heaven containing a bust-length figure of the Creator.

The corresponding scene in grec 510, which agrees with the Psalter in the ordering of the Jacob scenes, provides parallels for the iconography in only a few minor details. Both manuscripts show two angels ascending the heavenly ladder. In this respect, they deviate from the biblical text which specifically describes angels ascending and descending the ladder. In general, however, the correspondences between the scenes are outweighed by the differences. In grec 510 and also the Octateuchs[70] Jacob is shown as a youth whose head is inclined downward and supported by his hand. The Octateuchs deviate even further from the Psalter. Here the descending angel mentioned in the text is included.

The closest parallels are to Anglo-Saxon monuments which reflect an ancient Cotton tradition, as discussed in Chapter Two.

One additional detail which cannot be explained on the basis of the Cotton group is found in the Lambeth Bible, fol. 6r.[71] The angel on the top rung of the ladder approaches the Creator holding a scroll. The angel occupying a similar position at the top of the ladder in the Psalter also holds a scroll.

Joseph and Potiphar's Wife (Fig. 4), *Genesis 39:11–13*

The wife of Potiphar lies on a bed and grasps the cloak of Joseph who is seen fleeing through an open doorway.

Unlike the summary treatment of the other patriarchs, the story of Joseph is illustrated here by four scenes. Such a concentration of Joseph scenes can be explained in part by a long-standing tradition. As a biblical figure beloved since Early Christian times,[72] Joseph received considerable attention in early medieval cycles illustrating Genesis.[73] These monuments reveal that from an early date there were several iconographical traditions for representing Joseph's life. It has been widely recognized, however, that though these traditions may differ from one another in a number of respects, they also seem to be interrelated.[74] The enormous complexity caused by the overlapping of these traditions has a bearing on the Winchester Joseph cycle.

The encounter of Joseph and Potiphar's wife was frequently represented in medieval art. The more common type showed the wife standing as she snatches the cloak, as for example in the Octateuchs[75] and San Marco.[76] It is to another ancient type that the scene in Nero C.IV is related. As already discussed in Chapter Two, the more unusual treatment of the scene, with the wife lying in bed, can be found in the Vienna Genesis (Fig. 63). The type is also found in grec 510,[77] fol. 69v where Potiphar's wife sits on a stool. The basic formula still corresponds with the Psalter but the details of the boudoir architecture and doorway are absent. The scene also appeared in the fresco cycle formerly in S. Paolo fuori le mura, Rome (Fig. 64).

Potiphar's Wife Displays Joseph's Cloak to her Husband (Fig. 4), *Genesis 40:16*

Potiphar's wife stands on the left holding Joseph's cloak and pointing to her husband who is seated, wearing a crown and holding a sceptre.

Potiphar's wife relating Joseph's supposed advances was given an elaborate treatment in the Vienna Genesis.[78] In the upper register, Potiphar's wife relates her story to the servants of her household while Potiphar can be seen approaching the open doorway. Potiphar's wife sits on a low, cross-legged stool, as does Potiphar in the Psalter. In the lower register is the scene which corresponds to the one in the Psalter. Potiphar's wife extends the cloak to Potiphar who stands on the left. There are representations, however, which more closely parallel the Psalter by showing Potiphar seated. In the Octateuchs,[79] Potiphar's wife stands to the left holding the cloak while Potiphar sits at the right, gesturing toward his wife as in the Psalter. A somewhat closer comparison can be found on a Byzantine ivory casket now in the treasury of Sens Cathedral,[80] which is related iconographically to the Vienna Genesis.[81] On the late eleventh- or early twelfth-century casket (Fig. 66) the scene is more unified than in the Octateuchs and is framed by architectural additions, as in the Psalter.

Joseph Released from Prison (Fig. 4), *Genesis 41:14*

Joseph climbs up a ladder out of a box-like structure. The gaoler simultaneously grasps his outstretched hands and points toward the doorway.

There are few surviving examples of Joseph's release from prison. It is not represented in the Cotton group, Vienna Genesis, Octateuchs or grec 510. The Sens casket is unusual in this respect, since it not only depicts the event but devotes two scenes to it. In the first,[82] Joseph is seated while the gaoler unbinds his fetters. In the second scene, the gaoler grasps Joseph by the hand and leads him through the doorway (Fig. 67). This moment is preserved in identical fashion in a twelfth-century Byzantine psalter in the Vatican[83] and the thirteenth-century Hamilton Psalter in Berlin. The Aelfric manuscript also devotes a scene to Joseph's release.[84]

While the idea of Joseph's release is related to the Sens ivory and that of pharaoh's palace to the Aelfric illustration, it is the individuality of this scene that characterizes it. The curious prison from which Joseph emerges has no clear parallel elsewhere. Most representations show the prison as a tall stone structure or as a rounded enclosure.[85] In the Psalter, on the other hand, Joseph climbs out of a box supported on a foundation decorated by a wave pattern. No parallels exist for the box but the foundation is closely comparable to the rock upon which Jacob pours oil in the Lambeth Bible. Whether this should be interpreted as stone or foliation in both cases is unclear. The idea of incarcerating Joseph below ground is also unique. The Vulgate mentions only 'carcere' and the Septuagint 'ὀχύρωμα' or fortress.

Joseph before Pharaoh (Fig. 4), *Genesis 41:37f.*

The pharaoh, seated and crowned, hands a sceptre to Joseph who stands on his left.

The scene is not represented at San Marco or in the other monuments linked to the Cotton Genesis. The scene does appear, however, in the Vienna Genesis, page 36.[86] Although this scene had originally been identified as Joseph interpreting the dream of pharaoh, it has been pointed out[87] that since the preceding scene on page 35 clearly represents the dream sequence, the following scene must illustrate the text passage referring to pharaoh honouring Joseph. As in the Psalter, the Vienna Genesis pharaoh is crowned and seated on a low bench. He raises one hand in salute. Joseph stands near an open doorway, feet apart, clutching at his clothing with one hand. Another monument already linked with this group also includes the scene. Like the Vienna Genesis, the Sens casket (Fig. 69) shows pharaoh flanked by two attendants. The proximity of the casket to the Psalter, however, is more striking. In both cases, pharaoh sits frontally gesturing with upraised hands toward Joseph who stands immediately to his left.

The Aelfric manuscript shows a later point in the story when Joseph drives away in his chariot.[88] In both cases, pharaoh is bearded, wears a crown terminating in three fleur-de-lis and sits on a cross-legged stool. The stool, with its ball finials and claw feet, bears a relation to that of pharaoh and Potiphar in the Psalter.

David before Saul (Fig. 5), *I Kings 17:31–40*

Saul sits under an arch surrounded by his entourage. He holds a suit of chain mail and points to David who faces him holding his shepherd's crook and sling.

The events directly preceding David's battle with Goliath were rarely illustrated in the Middle Ages.[89] When this moment was selected, two passages from the Bible were usually illustrated. Verse 38 describing Saul arming David can be found on the Heraclean silver plate from Cyprus,[90] and on the Early Christian door of St Ambrose in Milan.[91] More numerous are the representations of the next verse describing David standing before Saul wearing his armour. The earliest example can be found among a series of frescoes in Chapel 111 at the Coptic monastery of Bawît in Egypt. Here David is dressed for battle in a suit of armour and helmet.[92] This type appears later in a ninth-century Byzantine manuscript, the *Sacra Parallela*, Paris, B.N., MS grec 923.[93] It also appears in the Latin West. It can be found on the mid-twelfth-century English leaf in the Morgan Library (Fig. 70) and a late twelfth-century French Bible.[94]

Quite clearly, the moment depicted in the Psalter does not duplicate either of these types. The Winchester David stands before Saul without armour. This suggests that the scene may either be the moment when Saul first offers David the armour[95] or the one after David rejects Saul's gift. The second possibility seems the most likely since verse 40, which follows David's return of the armour, specifically mentions that David took his staff, filled his shepherd's bag with stones and had his sling in hand. Both the sling and the crook are clearly visible in the Psalter. The forceful manner in which David holds them up before Saul also coincides with his decision to carry them into battle, described in verse 40.

There is only one other representation which has been identified as David Rejecting Saul's Armour. It is found in the Byzantine Book of Kings, Rome, B.A.V., MS Vat. gr. 333, fol. 23r (Fig. 71), mentioned in Chapter Two. In this scene, which has certain formal analogies with the Winchester depiction, David stands before Saul holding the staff, sling and shepherd's bag. Saul is seated under a canopy carried by slim columns. He simultaneously points in the direction of the discarded armour held by the figure to David's left and to the sling in David's hand. The arrangement has been modified somewhat in Nero C.IV, possibly due to a lack of space which affects not only this illustration but the other three on the page. The crowd of figures standing behind David belongs to the combat scene which follows. This is evident from the rapt attention which they give to David and Goliath while completely ignoring David before Saul. The crowd behind David in Vat. gr. 333 has been shifted under the canopy with Saul in Nero C.IV. This rearrangement accounts for the uncomfortably crowded appearance of Saul's tent in the Psalter. Perhaps because of this shift which caused the elimination of the figure holding the chain mail shirt, the artist placed it in the hands of Saul. In spite of the differences of arrangement in the Byzantine manuscript and the Psalter, a link between the two exists in the subject and the disposition of the protagonists. This establishes a relationship between the Psalter and the only extant Book of Kings which has an extremely dense cycle of illustrations for the life of David.

David and Goliath (Fig. 5), *I Kings 17:41–9*

David steps forward with his sling which contains a rock. Opposite him stands Goliath who has already been struck by a stone. A crowd holding spears stands behind David.

The combat between David and Goliath is represented in the Vatican Book of Kings,[96] the silver plates from Cyprus,[97] and a number of related 'aristocratic' psalters.[98] Most Byzantine monuments of the aristocratic group differ from the representation in the Psalter. They endeavour to suggest

David and Goliath are equally matched by making them the same height. There is one Byzantine monument, however, which draws closer to the Winchester depiction. The scene in the Marciana Psalter, Venice, Biblioteca Marciana, MS gr. 17, fol. 1v (Fig. 72), like that in the Winchester manuscript, is a literal representation of the text. Both scenes follow the biblical description of Goliath as a man of enormous size and David as a youth. The Marciana scene also corresponds by showing the giant standing motionless before the battle. This scene, as observed recently, must have been abstracted from a much longer sequence of David's encounter with Goliath.[99] The crowd of spectators offers another point of comparison. A figure in profile turns to a figure behind him represented in three-quarter view. These parallels are especially noteworthy because they establish a connection between the Psalter and a manuscript that shares its David cycle with the aristocratic group while deviating from it in certain crucial respects. The ways in which it differs have been shown to affiliate it with David scenes of the Early Christian period.[100] This places Nero C.IV in reasonable proximity to a member of the aristocratic family which shows close affinities with an early, not Middle, Byzantine tradition. The Middle Byzantine examples of this scene not only deviate by showing David and Goliath of equal height,[101] they also differ by illustrating a moment of the story other than the one in the Psalter. Middle Byzantine examples show David and Goliath before the battle and, more frequently, the moment when both are actively engaged in combat.[102] The second group show David about to hurl his missile at an aggressive Goliath who strides toward him, sword in hand. The Middle Byzantine representations never depict David about to throw the stone together with Goliath who has already been struck by the missile.

More exact comparisons for the disparate size of the two figures together with the moment illustrated in the Psalter find closer parallels in Western representations. While Early Christian scenes show David and Goliath equally matched,[103] by the eighth century, Goliath appears as a giant. As discussed in Chapter Two, he towers over David in the Corbie Psalter, Amiens, B.M., MS 18 (Fig. 74) and Harley 603 (Fig. 73). The Corbie illustration combines the same two moments in the narrative as the Winchester scene. A question then arises as to how this conflated illustration was arrived upon. The illustration in both manuscripts does not isolate one moment in the story but combines details that refer to events that transpired at different points in time: David hurls the rock and it strikes Goliath. The scene therefore cannot be understood as a literal interpretation of the Bible but one that conflates two successive moments into one image. In trying to identify the model, it is logical to assume that the two events were once illustrated separately. Western monuments do exist which depict either the first scene[104] or the second[105] in both France and England in the eleventh and twelfth centuries, lending credence to this theory.

It is important to recognize that this scene also occurs in other twelfth-century English manuscripts. It can be found in the Dover Bible, Cambridge, C.C.C., MS 3, fol. 117r[106] and the Morgan leaf (Fig. 70).

David Beheading Goliath (Fig. 5), *I Kings 17:51*

Goliath lies upon his shield. His helmet has been removed and blood streams from the wound in his forehead. David stands on his chest, bending forward as he attempts to sever the head. The Beheading scene exists in the Byzantine Book of Kings and the related monuments.[107] None of these monuments agrees with the Winchester iconography. The Byzantine monuments display two types. In one, Goliath kneels facing David who grasps him by the hair with one hand while decapitating him with the other. The other version shows Goliath lying on his back while David stands behind his head.

David standing on Goliath's body while dispatching him does appear with some frequency in the West.[108] The closest parallel for the position of David is found in the Bible of Stephen Harding which may be based on an English source.[109] Closely related variations indicate that the type was established in England before the Conquest, as evidenced by the Tiberius Psalter[110] and London, B.L., MS Arundel 155 (Fig. 75).[111] The Arundel Psalter is closer to Nero C.IV since it shows David actually severing the head instead of stabbing Goliath in the chest. The manner in which the Arundel David grabs Goliath's hair with one hand while severing the head with the other is reflected later in the Dover Bible[112] and M. 724.

While the variation given in Nero C.IV where David stands on Goliath and grips the sword with both hands does not exist in earlier or contemporary English monuments, it can be found in the eleventh-century Werden Psalter (Fig. 76). As discussed in Chapter Two, this connection is especially noteworthy in view of the recent demonstration that the iconography of the Werden Psalter is based on that of an English manuscript. Furthermore, it appears to stem from a Western, Early Christian source since it does not display features characteristic of Eastern cycles.[113]

A last detail of this miniature requires further clarification. The crowd standing behind David and Goliath looks incongruous and out of place in this scene. Often a fleeing crowd forms a part of the battle scene, as in Tiberius C.VI. Such a group could have been shifted to the beheading scene. The crowd might also have been taken from a beheading scene that was arranged differently. In the frescoes at Bawît,[114] and in the Paris Psalter,[115] a crowd of onlookers stands to the left of the beheading scene, fixing their attention on the action before them.[116] This may also have been the arrangement in the model used for the Winchester scene.

David Presenting the Head of Goliath to Saul (Fig. 5), *I Kings 17:54*

Saul is seated under a portico surrounded by his entourage. David approaches from the right holding the severed head of Goliath.

David returning with the head of Goliath is not represented in the Vatican Book of Kings or the related monuments. It does appear in two Byzantine monuments, a psalter, Rome, B.A.V., MS Vat. gr. 752,[117] and the ivory casket in the Palazzo di Venezia in Rome.[118]

There is considerably more evidence for this scene in the West. It can be found on an Early Christian sarcophagus in Marseille.[119] It appears in the ninth century in the St Paul's Bible, fol. 81r (Fig. 77) and Utrecht Psalter (Fig. 78), in the tenth on the Muirdach cross at Monasterboice,[120] and in the eleventh, in the Odbert Psalter, Boulogne, B.M., MS 20,[121] and the Werden Psalter (Fig. 76). The presence of the scene in the St Paul's Bible establishes a connection with the Vatican Book of Kings tradition since the two manuscripts share the same

David cycle. The Werden Psalter further establishes that this cycle was known in England before the Conquest.

By the twelfth century, the scene had received wide distribution in the West.[122] One example deserves special attention in this context since it appears on the Morgan leaf (Fig. 70). In both M. 724 and the Psalter, David Presenting the Head to Saul appears to the left of the beheading scene. This arrangement differentiates the English examples from others like the Boulogne Psalter, Souvigny Bible and Paris, B.N., MS lat. 8846, where David presents the head to the right of the Beheading scene.[123] These monuments conform more closely to the established rule of reading a text and its illustrations from right to left. The Psalter and M. 724 instead follow the sequence found in the St Paul's Bible.

The Morgan leaf is also important in another respect. It helps to strengthen the contention that an expanded Western David cycle paralleling gr. 333 was available in twelfth-century England. In addition to the scenes it shares with the Psalter and St Paul's Bible, the leaf adds another. The first scene on the leaf shows David Armed before Saul. This scene exists at Bawît[124] and in the *Sacra Parallela*,[125] both of which share the gr. 333 David cycle. This also indicates that the two twelfth-century English manuscripts were drawing independently on the same extensively illustrated David cycle. The fact that the Arming, Refusal and Return were all included in the model indicates that it was an extensive one. It combines together scenes found in isolated Eastern monuments, no one of which possesses a cycle of comparable density, which is not to say that such a cycle did not exist in the East. The David cycles in Nero C.IV and M. 724, seen in relation to the St Paul's Bible, are important evidence for the existence in the West, from at least the ninth century, of an extensive David cycle. The artist of the two twelfth-century manuscripts drew independently upon this model in fashioning their David scenes. The last is important in itself since it offers another insight about the relation of Nero C.IV to a nearly contemporary English monument. The Psalter is not modelled upon a contemporary work but draws on an older source common to both.

David as a Shepherd (Fig. 6), *I Kings 17:34*

David stands on the left holding a shepherd's crook. Next to him two goats spring from the ground and strike their horns together.

The scene found represented here is a relatively rare one. David as a shepherd is not found in the Vatican Book of Kings. It does appear in several of the related aristocratic psalters. In these manuscripts, David is shown seated and playing a harp, surrounded by his flock.[126] In a second group of Byzantine psalters which have marginal illustrations, David stands in the midst of his flock, making the type closer to the Winchester David. While David holds a musical instrument in these marginal psalters, a detail absent from Nero C.IV, the positioning of his legs and manner in which he holds his shepherd's crook is similar to the Winchester version.[127]

The marginal psalter type where David stands with a harp is reflected in a Western example, the Stuttgart Psalter, Stuttgart, Würtembergisches Landesbibliothek, Biblia folio 23, fol. 158v.[128] Another parallel exists in an isolated Western example which predates the Psalter. On an ivory in a private collection in Basel is a representation of David as a shepherd.[129] In the lower register,

David stands in a relaxed pose with crossed legs as he leans against his staff. His lambs frolic around him. The trees included here blossom forth with an exotic variety of flowers which provide a tapestry-like backdrop for the scene. This detail, which finds a comparison in the flowering tree of the Psalter, makes the relationship between the two monuments all the more striking. Another extremely close parallel is also found in the Utrecht Psalter (Fig. 78). Here David stands with his legs uncrossed, in a position nearly akin to that assumed by the Winchester David.

The figure of David on the ivory and in the two psalters appears to have had a long history in pastoral scenes. A number of Early Christian representations of shepherds tending their flocks offer parallels.[130]

David Rescues the Ram from the Lion (Fig. 6), *I Kings 17:34–5*

David stands behind the lion to free the ram. Inscription: ICI ESCVST DAVID AL LIVN VN VEILLE. (The Anglo-Norman inscriptions follow Wormald's transcription.)

The struggle with the lion was not depicted in Vat. gr. 333 but does appear in the aristocratic psalters.[131] These monuments differ from Nero C.IV by illustrating a different textual passage. They depict the first phrase of I Kings 17:35 which states that David went after the lion and struck him. The Psalter illustrates the next passage in verse 35 where David delivers the lamb from the lion's mouth. This second passage was illustrated in the Byzantine marginal psalters mentioned in connection with the previous scene. It appears in the ninth-century Chuldov Psalter in Moscow, Historical Museum, MS gr. 129, fol. 147v and in the eleventh-century Theodore Psalter, London, B.L., MS Add. 19352, fol. 188v.[132] There are striking similarities between the Chuldov–Theodore representation and that in the Psalter. In both cases, David stands behind the animal while reaching around to free the lamb from the lion's jaws.

The comparison to the marginal psalters is all the more striking when it becomes apparent that the Chuldov–Theodore type was established in the Insular repertory[133] as early as the eighth century. It can be found in the Vespasian Psalter, London, B.L., MS Cotton Vespasian A.I, fol. 53r (Fig. 79).[134] The Vespasian representation differs slightly from the Chuldov–Theodore and Winchester type because David bends the lion's head back in profile to free the lamb. The point of commonality is the position of David who stands behind the lion. In view of the relation between the Basel ivory and Nero C.IV in the preceding scene, it is especially important to note that the ivory supplies a detail missing from the Vespasian Psalter. On the ivory, as well as Nero C.IV and Chuldov, David reaches around the lion's head, shown frontally, to snatch the lamb.

It appears, then, that the Winchester scenes of David as a shepherd find their closest parallels in several Byzantine marginal psalters which are reflected in two Western monuments which predate Nero C.IV. While no single monument in the group supplies all the details found in the Winchester Psalter, the marginal psalter iconography is undoubtedly the common source. The fact that the marginal psalter model was available in England from the eighth century strongly suggests an Insular intermediary for the Winchester scene.

The Anointment of David (Fig. 6), *I Kings 16:12–13*

Samuel stands at the right anointing the head of David. Inscription: ICI ENVNIST SAMVEL LI PRHETE DAVID EN REI PAR LV CVMADT DEV.

The Anointment of David does appear in the Vatican Book of Kings and aristocratic psalters.[135] The general arrangement of the scene, as well as certain details, is quite close to those in Nero C.IV. In the Byzantine scenes, Samuel stands on the left anointing the head of David who stands on the right. As in Nero C.IV, the aristocratic versions show the brothers standing in two rows so that only the heads of the figures in the second row are visible. The exact number of brothers depicted does not correspond, however. The verse in I Kings mentions seven brothers while the Psalter shows only six. One of the manuscripts related to Vat. gr. 333, the Leo Bible, Rome, B.A.V., MS Reg. gr. 1, does show only six brothers as in the Psalter.[136] There are also a number of substantial differences between Nero C.IV and this group of Byzantine monuments. The architectural background and allegorical personification of clemency in the Byzantine manuscripts are missing from the Psalter. In these respects, Nero C.IV more closely resembles an older member of the aristocratic group.[137] In grec 510, fol. 174v,[138] the anointment does not include clemency. Another difference between the Psalter and all of these Byzantine examples is the figure of Samuel. In the Psalter, Samuel raises his hand above his waist.[139]

The appearance of the aristocratic recension Anointment scene in Britain at an early date has long been documented. The type can be found as early as the eighth century on a leaf now in Leningrad, Public Library, MS Lat.Q.V.XIV.[140] The scene on this Insular leaf is reduced to the three principal figures, David, Jesse and Samuel. Still, it offers an early precedent for the arrangement of the figures in the Psalter. The Tiberius Psalter (Fig. 80) possesses an Anointment scene with a number of similarities to the Nero Psalter. In both representations, Samuel stands at the right emptying a horn of oil upon the head of David who stands before him. He raises both arms in a manner quite similar to the Winchester figure. David responds by raising the arm closest to the picture plane as he gestures to Samuel. In both cases, David stands with the leg closest to Samuel bent slightly to carry the weight of his body. In addition, the gesture and attitude of the figure directly behind David in the Tiberius Psalter bear a striking resemblance to the brother behind Jesse in Nero C.IV. The gesture of the raised hand and positioning of the legs and feet are especially noteworthy. Another detail, his striped stockings, resembles David's in the Tiberius Anointment. The two scenes also agree by eliminating the architectural background and personification found in the Vatican Book of Kings and aristocratic psalters. The English scenes correspond further by showing the oil horn with the wide end pointed down, while the reverse is the case in the aristocratic group.[141]

There are also a number of differences between the Tiberius and Winchester Anointments. In the Tiberius Psalter, only David's right arm, which is raised toward Samuel, is shown. In the Nero Psalter, David's left arm is also included, gripping his shepherd's crook. The crook extends downward with its curved end resting upon the ground. David's foot rests on it. Since David also holds a staff in his left hand in the Leo Bible, it is likely that the Winchester artist derived this misunderstood motif from his model, rather than inventing it himself. In the Psalter, Samuel and Jesse are large, majestic figures who dwarf David standing between them. In Tiberius C.VI, David and Jesse are the same size, so that the striking juxtaposition of the three figures is lost. In Nero C.IV, the brothers are placed in two rows so that the figures in the first row are completely visible while only the heads of those behind them are shown. In Tiberius C.VI, the crowd is squeezed behind Jesse and piled up in several rows so that only the heads are visible. These observations strongly suggest that the Anointment scene in the Nero Psalter was not copied from the Tiberius Psalter but from a type common to both.

The Annunciation to Anna (Fig. 7)

The angel stands at the left holding a scroll and gesturing to Anna who stands facing him. This scene introduces a series of scenes from the life of the Virgin which have been grouped together to form a full-page illustration. As such, it is the earliest full-page cycle in a Western manuscript.[142] While there was an established tradition of illustrating the life of the Virgin in the East before this date, there is no indication that it influenced the composition of this scene. The Eastern examples follow the text of the *Proto-Evangelium.* In the Byzantine scenes, Anna stands in a garden near a fountain as an angel flies overhead.[143] This type is also found in earlier Italian examples.[144] In the Psalter, all references to the garden are absent, pointing away from any connection with the Byzantine tradition. Instead, the scene is closely modelled upon the iconography of a Western formula for the Annunciation.[145] More specifically, it can be viewed as a reworking of motifs that occur in the Annunciation on fol. 10 (Fig. 9) and elsewhere in the Nero manuscript. The figure of Anna is virtually identical to the Virgin in the Annunciation. The angel can be compared to Gabriel on fol. 10, as well as to God instructing Noah on fol. 3 (Fig. 2).

The Meeting of Joachim and Anna at the Golden Gate (Fig. 7)

Joachim and Anna stand facing each other before a schematized representation of the gate of Jerusalem.

This subject had long been recognized as the illustration for the Feast of the Conception in the East. The Byzantine feast picture is characterized by the embrace of Joachim and Anna,[146] a type which carries over in Western representations under Byzantine influence.[147] The Winchester scene departs from the norm by placing Anna and Joachim on opposite sides of the gate. There are certain precedents, however, for elements of this compositional scheme. The gate and Joachim's gesture are similar to motifs on the Bayeux Tapestry.[148] Anna is similar to the Virgin on fol. 16 (Fig. 15), again suggesting that motifs in the Winchester Infancy cycle were re-employed here.

The Birth of the Virgin (Fig. 7)

Anna lies in a bed above which curtains and lamps are suspended. A servant sits to the right holding the Virgin.

In the East, scenes of the Nativity of the Virgin possessed no unique characteristics and were, from the beginning, modelled on scenes of the birth of Christ.[149] The Winchester scene, which is one of the earliest

Western examples, also seems to have been based on models designed for the Nativity. There are certain similarities to the Winchester Nativity (Fig. 9), as for example, the canopied bed. However, the scene as a whole is more closely paralleled in an Echternach manuscript (Fig. 83) upon which the Winchester Infancy cycle depends. The woman at the right has been identified by Wormald as the midwife who responds to Anna's enquiry about her child.[150] While the text does explain this detail, there is no visual precedent for the inclusion of the midwife. The midwife holding the Vigin bears striking similarities to a Virgin and Child group in a twelfth-century copy of the Prayers and Meditations of St Anselm, Oxford, Bodl., MS Auct. D.2.6,[151] and may have been patterned after such a model.

The Presentation of the Virgin in the Temple (Fig. 7)

Anna holds the Virgin before an altar. Joachim and a woman, holding doves, stand to the left. Inscription: ICI OFFRE AL TEMPLE . . . SECVN LA LEI.

The presentation had been celebrated as a feast in the East since the sixth century and is encountered there as an isolated feast picture as well as in more complete cycles. In the Eastern examples, the Virgin is depicted as a child old enough to walk to the priest, rather than as an infant. Her parents stand apart and behind her in the Byzantine examples.[152] The Byzantine arrangement is retained in some Western examples.[153] The Winchester scene differs from these examples and as Wormald has suggested is probably based upon a scene of the Presentation of Christ.[154] Like the previous scene, it seems to be based on the prototypes used by the Winchester artist for his Presentation of Christ, rather than directly upon this scene (Fig. 14). In addition to the parallel cited by Wormald to the Benedictional of St Aethelwold, there are others in the *Codex Epternacensis* (Fig. 96) and the Albani Psalter (Fig. 101). The arrangement of the figures and placement of the altar are found in the Ottonian manuscript. The manner in which Anna holds Mary and in which the woman offers the doves is similar to some in the Albani scene. The temple, altar, lamp and hanging curtains are paralleled in the Utrecht Psalter and its English copies.[155]

The Jesse Tree (Fig. 8), *Isaiah 11:1*

Jesse lies asleep at the bottom of the page. From his body rises a tree which represents David, the Virgin and Christ as the supporting members of the trunk. Above the head of Christ appears the dove of the Holy Spirit. From the trunk curl fleshy stems which terminate in large flowers. Standing on these stems are two bearded men holding scrolls and gesturing towards the central figures.

The Jesse Tree,[156] which illustrates a passage in Isaiah, might be considered an Old Testament subject. However, the intention of the Jesse Tree was to illustrate the geneaology of Christ and it was used as a prefatory miniature to Matthew as well as Isaiah.[157] Its position at the beginning of Matthew is perfectly understandable since it interprets the opening words of the Gospel which describe the generations of Christ. As in the Gospel, the tree includes the ancestors of Christ as a prelude to the coming of the messiah. The latter tradition apparently governed its inclusion here since the reconstruction of the manuscript outlined in Chapter One and Appendix C indicates that the illustration originally stood at the beginning of the New Testament cycle.

The iconography of the Jesse Tree developed at a relatively late date in the Latin West. The earliest recognizable Western example dates from the eleventh century.[158] In view of the late introduction of the Jesse Tree, it is surprising to discover that a wide variety exists among the representations from the first half of the twelfth century. Among these diverse representations, there is an earlier manuscript which provides an extremely close precedent for the illustration in the Psalter, as noted by Wormald. The Shaftesbury Psalter, fol. 15r (Fig. 81), does possess a Jesse Tree which prefigures the one in the Psalter.[159] The Shaftesbury tree shows Jesse, whose partially naked body is covered by a cloak, lying on the ground asleep. The tree grows from his loins. While his mode of dress differs from the Nero Jesse, the reclining position and especially the way in which he supports his head upon his left arm is similar to the Winchester drawing. Other elements of the illustrations are also comparable. David, the Virgin, Christ and the dove of the Holy Spirit occupy the same prominent positions in the Shaftesbury and Winchester trees. In addition, both illustrations show David crowned and bearded and the Virgin crowned and veiled. As in Nero C.IV, two bearded men stand on the branches of the tree in the Shaftesbury Psalter. Unlike the Winchester Psalter, however, it is possible to identify the two figures beyond the border of the miniature. The figure on the left is Abraham. He holds a scroll inscribed with a verse from Genesis 22:18: 'In semine tuo benedicentur omnes gentes terre.' The figure on the right is Moses, which is already apparent from the golden horns protruding from his head. On his scroll is a verse from Deuteronomy 28:15. The only differences, other than minor details involving pose and gesture, are the identifying inscriptions for the two prophets. In spite of this omission in the Psalter, it is clear that the illustration as a whole is closely patterned after the Shaftesbury model. The other feature which differentiates the two is the elaborate floral forms that adorn the Winchester drawing. The floral ornament which is executed with the utmost refinement and sophistication points to the later date of the Nero C.IV Jesse Tree.

God Sending out the Angel Gabriel for the Annunciation (Fig. 9), *Luke 1:26*

God is seated in a mandorla holding a book propped on his knee. He raises the other hand in a gesture of blessing toward Gabriel who stands before him and solemnly gestures in response. In the margin of the page above the ornamental border is an inscription in Anglo-Norman French: ICI ANVNTIE LI ANGELS A NOSTER DAME NOSTER SALVT.

Sending out the Angel Gabriel was illustrated only infrequently. It is based on the verse from Luke which states that in the sixth month the angel Gabriel was sent from God unto a city of Galilee, named Nazareth. Only three examples of this subject which predate the Psalter are known to exist. Two of them are found in the twelfth-century Byzantine copies of the Homilies of the Monk James.[160] Here the angel stands beneath a long bench where God sits surrounded by a choir of angels.

While the Byzantine precedent for the scene is significant, an English manuscript provides a more striking parallel. As noted by Wormald, in the Shaftesbury Psalter, fol. 12v (Fig. 82), not only is the subject matter identical to the Nero scene but a majority of the iconographic details are also extremely close. In both scenes, God sits enthroned in a double mandorla pointing toward the angel Gabriel who stands on his left. Gabriel responds with the same hand gesture, palm upturned, in each manuscript. In addition, a minor detail shows an affinity between the two scenes. The decorative border on the garment in the Nero Psalter, with its heavy square-cut gems surrounded by smaller rounded stones, is close in design to that in the Shaftesbury Psalter. Only slight differences separate the two illustrations. In the Shaftesbury Psalter, God is crowned, holds an orb and rests his feet on a schematized footstool. The dove of the Holy Spirit hovers above his head. The dove, cross, orb and foot rest are absent from the Winchester Psalter. The only attribute God holds is a closed book.

The Annunciation (Fig. 9), *Luke 1:26–38*

The angel Gabriel stands at the left, holding a palm branch with one hand and raising the other in salutation. The Virgin stands at the right holding a closed book. Above her head appears the dove of the Holy Spirit. In the margin above the architectural frame that surrounds the scene is the inscription: ICI ENTRET LI SAINZ ESPIRS EN LI.

The iconography of the Virgin standing at the moment of the Annunciation is an extremely old and well-established type. The earliest examples date from the sixth century.[161] However, the closest parallels for the particular details in Nero C.IV exist in the manuscripts associated with Echternach, as discussed in Chapter Two.

Two details in the Annunciation scene in the Winchester Psalter cannot be accounted for by the Echternach illustrations. The Virgin holds a closed book and the dove of the Holy Spirit hovers above her head. The book is found exclusively in Western monuments at this date.[162] Among them are several English precedents for the Annunciate represented with a book. The seated Virgin in the St Albans Psalter and two Anglo-Saxon manuscripts, the Benedictional of St Aethelwold, fol. 5v,[163] and a Gospel book in Boulogne, B.M., MS 11, fol. 11r, hold books. A Carolingian precedent for all three scenes exists in the ninth-century ivory casket now in the Brunswick Museum.[164] These three examples differ slightly from the Psalter since the books are open in each case. Several examples do exist where the books are shown closed. One is found on the mid-eleventh century doors of Santa Maria im Kapitol, Cologne,[165] and others include the late eleventh-century Bohemian Coronation Gospels, Prague, University Library, MS XIV.A.13, fol. 20v,[166] and the twelfth-century Cluny Lectionary, Paris, B.N., MS nouv. acq. lat. 2246, fol. 6r.[167] A relationship to the manuscript in Prague is more tenable than to the others. The Bohemian manuscript was discussed by Pächt in relation to the St Albans Psalter[168] because the Albani Annunciation includes both the dove and book. The dove appeared for the first time in the Bohemian manuscript and is found later in the St Albans Psalter. Since the Winchester Annunciation includes the closed book along with the dove, it refers to the eleventh-century model which also influenced its somewhat earlier English contemporary. The Winchester Annunciation scene follows Echternach models, modified by the addition of several details found in England for at least a generation before the Winchester Psalter was produced.

The Visitation (Fig. 9), *Luke 1:39–56*

The Virgin and Elizabeth stand under an arch supported on columns, locked in an embrace. Above the crenellated wall surmounting the arch is the inscription: ICI BAISE SAINTE MARIE ELISABET.

As the Annunciation illustration, the Visitation scene in the Psalter shows a resemblance to Ottonian treatments of the subject. In the *Codex Egberti*, fol. 10v,[169] the sentiment of the moment is expressed with a similar feeling of warmth and tenderness. The faces of both women are shown in three-quarter view, so that their cheeks touch as they embrace. The rendition of the heads is strikingly similar to that in the Psalter where the solemn-faced women place their faces close to one another. The illustration in *Epternacensis* (Fig. 83) provides additional points of comparison. Here the woman on the left wraps her arms around the other woman so that they meet on her cousin's shoulder. The woman on the right passes her arm under that of her companion so that her hand appears below the latter's shoulder. Her other arm is blocked from view but the hand can be seen firmly grasping her cousin on the shoulder. The position of the arms and hands duplicate the gestures of the two women in the Psalter. In the Ottonian Visitation scene, the women stand on the summit of a rock-covered mound. In the Psalter, the women stand on a similar rise composed of what appear to be ovoid rocks, close in shape to those in *Epternacensis*. A last point of comparison, which is not as marked as the previous two, concerns the architectural framing elements surrounding each scene. In *Epternacensis*, two tower-like structures support a crenellated arch which suggests the superstructure in the Psalter. The scene is not illustrated in *Escorialensis*. There is less similarity to the Albani scene where two servants draw back the curtains.[170]

The Nativity (Fig. 9), *Luke 2:1–10*

Mary lies in a bed that is parallel to the picture plane. At her head stands a serving woman who gestures to Joseph seated at the foot of the bed. Joseph inclines his head to the Virgin and returns her salutation. Below the bed, Christ lies in his crib. Columns supporting an arch and exterior architecture frame the scene. Above the scene is the inscription: ICI ENFANTET NOSTER DAME IESV CRIST ICI GIST IES CRIST EN LA CRECHE.

The scene as a whole is based on Anglo-Saxon sources, as discussed in Chapter Two. However, several details of the scene cannot be explained on the basis of Anglo-Saxon illustrations. The architectural framework, curtains, hanging lamps and close proximity of the ox to the infant Christ are not found in these pre-Conquest sources. Similarities for all of these features can be found in the Echternach manuscripts. The Bremen manuscript, fol. 11r, and *Codex Egberti*, fol. 13v,[171] place the scene in an outdoor setting with a walled city acting as a backdrop for the scene. The later Echternach manuscripts include varying types of architectural frames, which offer closer comparisons to the Psalter. The *Codex Aureus Epternacensis* Nativity (Fig. 83) is framed under an arch hung with curtains. More specific comparisons can be made to *Escorialensis*, fol. 96r (Fig. 87). The arch is surmounted by a superstructure close to that in the Winchester Psalter. Curtains hang in the archway and the animals hover directly above the crib. None of these examples include the hanging lamps found in the Psalter. However, in B.L., MS Egerton 809, fol. 1v,[172] two hanging lamps appear. A lamp also hangs in the archway framing the Nativity scene in Brussels, B.R., MS 9428, fol. 7v.[173]

The Annunciation to the Shepherds (Fig. 10), *Luke 2:8–24*

Three angels hover within a semi-circular medallion as they convey their news to the shepherds below. Two of them unfurl scrolls which bear the inscriptions: 'Natus est nobis hodie salvator' (Luke 2:11) and 'Qui est Christus dominus in civitate david' (Luke 2:11). Below them, four shepherds react with varying expressions of reflection and astonishment. In the margin above the decorative border appears the inscription: ICI ANVNCENT LI ANGEL AS PASTURES LA NATIVITE NOSTRE SEIGNVR.

The scene is discussed in Chapter Two. It is interesting to note that although the Annunciation to the Shepherds composition found in the Winchester Psalter cannot be compared to any single earlier composition in every detail, later examples follow the pattern established here. Both the late twelfth-century copy of the Utrecht Psalter, now in Paris, B.N., MS lat. 8846, fol. 2r,[174] and the early fourteenth-century Peterborough Psalter, now in Brussels, B.R., MS. 9961–2, fol. 10v,[175] display strong similarities in arrangement and detail with the composition found in the Winchester Psalter. The shepherd turning into his cloak is also found in Paris, B.N., MS lat. 15675.[176]

The Magi before Herod (Fig. 10), *Matthew 2:7–8*

The three Magi stand before Herod. The king furthest to the left turns slightly away from the assembled company and points upward. His two companions gesture toward Herod who sits enthroned holding a sword and a scroll inscribed: 'Ite et interrogate diligenter de puero' (Matthew 2:8). Above the scene appears the inscription: ICI VIENENT LI TREI REI A HERODE.

The encounter of the kings with Herod was a subject depicted relatively infrequently in the Middle Ages.[177] There are Carolingian examples from the Metz atelier, however, which must have been in possession of an extensive magi cycle.[178] Among them is an ivory casket in the Louvre[179] which bears a certain relation to the Psalter. Herod sits frontally under an arched canopy pointing toward the three magi who stand at the left. The position of Herod on the right and the idea of placing Herod under an architectural frame are echoed in the Winchester illustration.

Closer comparisons are possible with an Anglo-Saxon manuscript heavily dependent on the iconography of the Metz magi cycle. In the Sacramentary of Robert of Jumièges, fol. 36v (Fig. 91), both Herod and the magi bear striking similarities to their Winchester counterparts. Herod sits frontally but turns his head toward the magi so that the face is shown in a three-quarter view. He holds a sceptre in one hand and reaches across his body to gesture to the three kings. In all these respects except for the substitution of the sceptre for a sword in the Psalter, the two manuscripts are quite similar. The attitudes and gestures of the magi also link the Winchester representation closely to the Anglo-Saxon tradition. The two magi closest to Herod relate their experiences to him, aided by gestures, as in the Psalter. The third magi eagerly points to the star seen beyond the picture frame. The king furthest to the left in the Psalter also points straight up but the artist failed to complete the image by including the star, rendering the gesture meaningless. Carelessness is evident again elsewhere. The extraordinarily long sleeve of the white-bearded magi refers to the gesture of the Jumièges magi but again demonstrates his lack of understanding of the Anglo-Saxon model.

The relationship of the Winchester miniature to twelfth-century English illustrations is less striking. In the St Albans Psalter, page 23,[180] Herod is seated holding a book and facing the magi. An armed retainer stands behind him. The three kings, wearing caps instead of crowns, direct their undivided attention to him. The entire scene is set in an architectural frame. While there are general similarities in the arrangement of the two scenes, they are not close enough to suggest that the Winchester artist consulted a model like the Albani illustration. The general affinities between the two scenes are more readily explained on the basis of a common Anglo-Saxon model like the Jumièges miniature. It must be added that the Albani artist took far greater liberties in adapting the model than the Winchester copyist who was more faithful to the Anglo-Saxon original.

The Journey of the Magi (Fig. 11), *Matthew 2:9–10*

The magi appear on horseback against a blank ground which gives no reference to time or place. The two magi furthest to the left point ahead of them while the third turns in his saddle and points back in the direction of his two companions. Above the scene appears the inscription: ICI LVRAREIST LESTEILE KIS MEIN ET EN BETHLEEM.

A limited number of examples of the appearance of the star to the magi[181] survive including several in Echternach manuscripts. Certain similarities do exist between the Winchester scene and both the *Codex Egberti* fol. 17r,[182] and the Bremen Perikope, fol. 14v (Fig. 92). The version in the Bremen Perikope, which deviates from *Egberti*, bears greater similarity to the Winchester Journey. The two kings furthest to the left point up and ahead of them to the star. The third magi glances back at his companions as he points to the star ahead of him. One clear difference between the Ottonian composition and the Psalter is in the attitudes of the kings and the direction in which the backward-glancing magi points. In another obvious respect, the Ottonian scene differs from Nero C.IV. The Ottonian kings are shown bust-length instead of mounted on horses, as in the Psalter. Other examples from Early Christian times onward which have been discussed together with the Ottonian manuscripts[183] fail to explain the Winchester iconography. In these early examples the magi undertake their journey on foot. The most convincing parallels for the magi on horseback are found on a Metz ivory in Frankfurt, and the Jumièges manuscript (Fig. 91). In these examples, magi do approach Bethlehem on horseback, although they are not closely related to the Psalter illustration in any other respect.

While the essential details of the Winchester scene can be found in Ottonian and Anglo-Saxon models, the relationship to them does not appear to be as direct as in some instances. The Albani Journey, page 24 (Fig. 93), is closer to the Winchester scene. The mounted magi are exact precursors of the Winchester kings in arrangement and gesture. The respective ages of the magi, with two mature men and one adolescent, coincides also with the Winchester composition.

The Adoration of the Magi (Fig. 11), *Matthew 2:11*

The Virgin sits enthroned under an architectural frame. She points to the Christ Child sitting in her lap. Christ holds a book and gestures toward the three magi who approach from the left. The first drops to his knee as he offers the Child a circlet. The other two stand behind him. The third magi reaches impatiently past the second with his offering. Above the scene is the inscription: ICI AORENT NOSTRE SEIGNVR E OFRENT LI OR E ENCENS E MIRRE.

The scene shows a certain affinity with Anglo-Saxon models.[184] The closest comparisons for this scene are not with the Sacramentary of Robert of Jumièges, fol. 37r (Fig. 94), which provided comparisons for other scenes from the magi cycle, but rather with the Benedictional of St Aethelwold, fol. 24v (Fig. 95). The Adoration in the Benedictional, like the one in the Rouen Sacramentary is based upon a Carolingian model preserved in several examples from Metz.[185] Interestingly enough, the Benedictional, which can be dated c.975–80, modifies the Carolingian model to a greater extent than does the early eleventh-century Sacramentary. In these innovative respects, the Benedictional is more closely related to the Adoration in the Psalter. In the Benedictional, the Virgin sits frontally under an arch carried by columns. She holds the Child who gestures to the approaching magi. The magi are crowned, as in the Psalter, an innovation not reflected in the Sacramentary and Metz examples.[186] The Benedictional offers an additional comparison for a relatively rare feature in the Psalter. The magi closest to Christ in the Benedictional holds what appears to be three overlapping circlets. These objects have been identified as diadems, a feature found in Early Christian magi scenes, which in turn was derived from the Roman imperial ceremony of the *Aurum Coronarium*.[187] The rarity of the motif and its presence in the Anglo-Saxon manuscript and later in a somewhat reduced and misunderstood rendition in the Psalter, indicates the debt of the Winchester artist to his predecessor. In arrangement and some significant details, then, an Anglo-Saxon model provides analogies for the Winchester Adoration.

While there are enough similarities between the Anglo-Saxon iconography and the Psalter to consider a relationship between the two, the Anglo-Saxon model does not explain all the details found in the Psalter. Extremely close comparisons for these details can be found in the Echternach manuscripts. A number of parallels exist there for the figure group of the Virgin and Child. In the Echternach manuscripts, as in the Psalter, both the Virgin and Child sit frontally. Instead of pointing to the magi, as in the Benedictional, the Virgin either holds the Child, as in the *Codex Egberti*, fol. 17r,[188] Brussels, B.R., MS 9428, fol. 17r,[189] and *Epternacensis*, fol. 19r (Fig. 96), or points to him as in the *Escorialensis*, fol. 24r (Fig. 98). The latter duplicates precisely the gesture of the Virgin in the Psalter who inclines her hand toward the Child. The position and gestures of Christ also find close parallels in the Echternach manuscripts. The Child sits frontally with head, chest and outstretched arm inclined to the left. With his other hand, he holds a book. Both *Epternacensis* and *Escorialensis* offer precedents for these features. The architectural frame and throne in the Psalter are also patterned after models stemming from Echternach. The slender columns carrying an architectural entablature are reminiscent of the one in Paris, B.N.,

MS lat. 18005, fol. 34v,[190] and to a lesser extent to the Escorial copy. The cross-legged stool on which the Winchester Virgin sits is somewhat unusual. The majority of Adoration scenes depict the seat as some sort of sturdy throne or bench.[191] The Psalter is different, depicting the seat as a delicate cross-legged stool. Both B.N. lat. 18005 and *Epternacensis* suggest the source for this rare detail.

The magi in the Psalter are also modelled after the Echternach group in certain respects. The king closest to the Virgin and the Child approaches them on bent knee. Parallels for this exist in the *Codex Egberti*, Bremen and Brussels manuscripts, lat. 18005 and *Escorialensis*. The appearance of the remaining two magi is somewhat more unusual. Only *Epternacensis* and lat. 18005 agree with the Psalter in showing the kings standing erect.[192] The sceptre held by the second king in the Psalter finds a precedent in the Brussels manuscript. The unusual gesture of the third magi who pushes his gift impatiently to the front also has an Ottonian source. This detail does not appear in an Echternach manuscript but it can be found in two closely related works. Both the early eleventh-century Gospels of Otto III in Munich, Staatsbibliothek, Cod. lat. 4453, fol. 29,[193] and the Gospel book in the Herzog-August-Bibliothek in Wolfenbüttel, MS 84.5 Aug. 2,[194] show the third magi pushing his offering in front of the king directly ahead of him. The close affinities between the manuscripts which may come from Reichenau and the Echternach manuscripts have been recognized by several generations of scholars.[195] The influence of the earlier Reichenau group on the Echternach New Testament cycle suggests a plausible explanation for the appearance of the gesture in the context of Ottonian and more specifically Echternach influence on the Psalter. While no single Adoration scene from Echternach corresponds with the Winchester Adoration in every detail, the group taken as a whole shows that one of the sources used by the Winchester artist was Ottonian.

The relationship to the Albani Adoration, page 25, is much less significant. The artist adhered more closely to the Insular tradition represented by the Jumièges illustration and to its Carolingian source.[196] The only link between the Albani Adoration and that in the Psalter is the offering of the first king to Christ. In the Albani Psalter, the king presents Christ with the circlet found in the Winchester Psalter. It is most easily explained by the derivation of the two from an Anglo-Saxon source like the Benedictional. Thus, while Nero C.IV shares a common Anglo-Saxon source with the Albani manuscript, the Winchester artist also drew upon an Ottonian source which he did not share with the earlier work.

The Dream of the Magi (Fig. 12), *Matthew 2:12*

The three magi lie upon a bed supported by a Romanesque arcade. Two of the magi are asleep. The third magi sits upright facing an angel who stands on the right holding a staff. The inscription above the scene reads: ICI LV APAREIST LI ANGELS SIS RVV ET ALER EN LVR CVNTRE PAR AVTRE VEIE.

The Dream of the Magi is relatively rare among even the most extensively illustrated Byzantine and Western cycles. The subject does appear in several examples from the Metz group. Two of these examples, now in the Louvre, Paris,[197] and the Musée des Antiques, Lyon,[198] have a limited resemblance to the dream in the Psalter. In both Carolingian examples and the Psalter, the angel stands at the end of the bed, holding a staff and gesticulating toward the magi. Here the similarity ends for the Carolingian ivories show all three of the magi asleep, unlike the Psalter where one magi sits upright to confront the approaching angel. The Anglo-Saxon tradition followed this Metz formula in every detail. In the Jumièges Sacramentary, fol. 37r (Fig. 94), a standing angel approaches three sleeping magi. It is to this Insular copy of a Carolingian model that the Psalter is most closely related. This Insular formula was revived after the Conquest. In the St Albans Psalter, page 26,[199] an angel stands above the three sleeping kings.

While it is entirely possible that the Winchester artist was influenced by the standing angel, which was an established iconographic feature from Anglo-Saxon times, this does not explain the attitudes of the magi. For this aspect of the illustration, it is necessary to turn to an Ottonian example. Among the large group of heavily illustrated manuscripts from Echternach, only one possesses the scene of the angel appearing to the magi. In *Epternacensis*, fol. 19r (Fig. 96), a flying angel hovers above the beds of the three kings. Although the magi have been arranged somewhat differently in the two works, individual postures and gestures are similar. The magi closest to the picture plane in the Psalter turns his sleeping face away from the angel to rest on a large cushion. The Echternach magi in the centre of the bed reclines in a similar position. The other sleeping magi in the Psalter who lies on his back with upturned face corresponds to the magi closest to the lower border of the Echternach illustration. The most striking comparison between the two compositions is the relationship between the magi sitting upright in each scene. In both cases, one magi is awake and draws himself up to converse with the heavenly messenger. This detail establishes a close link between the two scenes since it sets them apart from the majority of dream scenes where all three magi are shown asleep. It shows that in yet another instance, the Winchester artist did not simply rely upon the established Insular type but consulted additional Ottonian models.

The Dream of Joseph (Fig. 12), *Matthew 2:13*

Joseph sits upright in bed facing an angel who stands on the opposite side of the room. A colonnade and hanging lamp form a backdrop for the interior setting. The inscription above reads: ICI CVMANDET LI ANGELS A JOSEPH KIL MAINT LEMFANT E LA DAME EN EGYPTE.

The appearance of an angel to Joseph in a dream, instructing him to flee into Egypt with the Virgin and Child, is a relatively rare subject. Among the existing examples are two assigned to the Metz atelier and certain similarities appear here. A casket in the Louvre[200] shows an angel standing above the bed where Joseph lies asleep. Both the Carolingian angel and its Romanesque counterpart in Nero C.IV are shown standing on the left, at the foot of Joseph's bed. The comparison between the two cannot be extended further since Joseph is curled up asleep with his face averted from the angel in the Carolingian example. Another Metz example, however, can shed light on the problem. In Paris, B.N., MS lat. 9388, fol. 19r,[201] Joseph sits upright on a chair as the angel approaches him.

The iconography of the Echternach group which explained the appearance of a number of the New Testament scenes in the Psalter bears little relationship to this scene. In the *Codex Egberti*, fol. 12r,[202] and *Epternacensis*, fol. 19v,[203] Joseph lies asleep on his bed. In the Ottonian manuscripts, the angel hovers in the air as he warns Joseph.

There are also precedents in English art for such a figure. One is found in London, B.L., MS. Harley 603, fol. 64v (Fig. 99), and another in Morgan Library MS M. 738.[204] The type was, then, a stock figure in England which might have been selected for inclusion here because it suited the formal design of this particular page. There are a number of correspondences in the design of the Dream of the Magi and Dream of Joseph below it which suggest that the artist intended them to be seen as a unit. Both scenes are framed under an arcade carried on slim columns. Each scene shows an angel standing at the left and gesticulating toward the figure or figures lying in bed. In the magi scene, one of the kings sits up alertly to attend the angel's message. It is possible that the artist used a similar figure below to carry out the compositional balance established by the decorative framing elements and placement of figures in each scene. Whichever explanation for the iconographical derivation of the scene is correct, the Joseph scene remains one of the most unconventional in the New Testament cycle.

The Flight into Egypt (Fig. 13), *Matthew 2:14*

Joseph walks toward a gate representing Egypt. He looks over his shoulder toward the Virgin and Child who ride behind him on a donkey. The beast is just emerging from the city gate of Bethlehem. An angel appears from a cloud censing the path before the Virgin and Child. An inscription above reads: ICI VAIT JOSEPH EN EGYPTE OD LEMFANT E OD LA MERRE.

The Flight into Egypt, limited to a depiction of Mary, Joseph and Christ, was well established in Christian iconography from an early date. One of the oldest examples is on a sixth-century gold medallion in the Archaeological Museum in Istanbul.[205] The positions of the figures and presence of the city gate establish an early precedent for the Winchester scene. Many of these features were adopted by Anglo-Saxon artisans. An illustration resembling the Winchester illustration in many respects is found in the Sacramentary of Robert of Jumièges, fol. 33r (Fig. 88). Here the travellers move toward a city gate much like the one in the Psalter. In both cases, narrow, rounded towers rise above a horizontal roof line and lower brickwork stories. Joseph, carrying provisions for the journey, as in Nero C.IV, leads the donkey. In both examples, the Virgin is seated frontally and looks ahead. These points of comparison link the iconography in the Psalter closely to a type established in England since Anglo-Saxon times which in turn was based on an ancient tradition.

There are, however, certain details which are not found in the Jumièges Flight and require further explanation. In the Psalter, the party emerges from the gate of Bethlehem, something not included in the Anglo-Saxon manuscript. In *Epternacensis*, fol. 19v (Fig. 97), the donkey has just passed through an open gateway to begin the journey. The gesture of Christ in the Ottonian example also echoes that in the Psalter. In contrast to the Jumièges illustration where the Child reaches forward eagerly, the Nuremberg manuscript and Psalter show the Child in a more dignified posture, simply raising a hand in blessing.

Neither the Anglo-Saxon nor the

Echternach source completely explains the derivation of the Winchester scene. In the Psalter, as in the medallion in Istanbul, Joseph turns to look over his shoulder at the Virgin and Child. While this motif does survive into the Middle Ages, its widespread distribution obscures any attempt to determine the direct source used by the Winchester artist.[206]

A last detail of the Flight into Egypt requires an additional word of explanation. The angel flying overhead is rarely included in this scene. Its origins may be traced to the Roman imperial scenes depicting the triumphal progress of an emperor, some of which included a winged figure of victory acting as a *cursor*.[207] Exactly when such a winged *cursor* figure may have been transformed into an angel is unclear; however, it can be established that it was present in the Western tradition by the eleventh century. The closest comparison for the Psalter illustration appears on an eleventh-century Franco-Flemish ivory in the Victoria and Albert Museum.[208] Here the angel flies above the Holy Family, guiding their progress. The *adventus* is also suggested in abbreviated form as a hand in the sky at S.-Benoit-sur-Loire,[209] as a half-length bust among the twelfth-century mosaics in the Capella Palatina, Palermo,[210] and again as a hand on the late twelfth-century altar frontal at Fécamp.[211] This suggests that the motif found in the Psalter could have been derived from a slightly earlier source which in turn was based on the ancient imperial *adventus* iconography.

The Massacre of the Innocents
(Fig. 13), *Matthew 2:16*

Herod is seated at the left flanked by an armed retainer wearing chain mail. Herod holds a sword and gestures toward two soldiers stabbing to death the children of Bethlehem. The bodies of the murdered children are scattered at their feet. At the right, two mothers swoon at the scene of carnage before them. The scene is framed by arches surmounted by an architectural vista. An inscription on one of the arches reads: ICI FAIT HERODE OCIRRE LES INNOCENS.

An extended Massacre scene showing Herod and his soldiers on the left, executioners stabbing their victims in the centre, and the mourning women at the right was an established type in the Western iconographical repertoire from the Ottonian period onward. The appearance of the new type in the Ottonian period has been interpreted as a result of recent Byzantine influence on the Echternach group.[212] The illustration in the Psalter fits into this continuum, resembling the Echternach group in most respects, with occasional references to the Byzantine prototype which stands behind them, a relationship described in Chapter Two.

The Albani scene is not modelled along the same lines as the Winchester scene. The Albani Massacre, page 30,[213] diffuses the action into two separate focuses of attention. On the left, Herod speaks to a soldier about to depart for the slaughter. On the right, the mothers battle with the soldiers to protect their children.

The Presentation in the Temple
(Fig. 14), *Luke 2:22–34*

The Virgin stands to the left of an altar that occupies the centre of the composition. She hands Christ across the altar to Simeon. The Child holds an open book and raises a hand in blessing. On the far left a serving woman holding four doves looks on. The scene is framed under three arches surmounted by architecture. An inscription in the margin reads: ICI

OFFERT LA DAME LEMFANT A SAINT SIMEON AL TEMPLE.

The basic type used for the Winchester Presentation in the Temple is found for the first time in the Drogo Sacramentary, fol. 38r.[214] In the Sacramentary, the Child is being handed from the Virgin to Simeon across an altar. Behind her stand Joseph and a serving woman.[215] The type was assimilated into the Insular repertoire by the late tenth century when it appeared on a slab in Wirksworth, Derbyshire,[216] and the Benedictional of St Aethelwold, fol. 34v (Fig. 101). Here the basic type found in the Metz manuscript is repeated with certain modifications. In addition to the serving woman and Joseph found in the Sacramentary, a second serving woman was added on the left to balance the composition. In the Albani Psalter, page 28 (Fig. 102), the Anglo-Saxon type was accepted with further modifications. Here Joseph was eliminated and both serving women carry a pair of turtle doves. This last detail directly contradicts Mosaic Law which describes the offering as a single pair of doves and has been interpreted as a desire by the artist to create a perfectly symmetrical composition.[217] To emphasize this arrangement, the artist chose an architectural framing device which clarified the placement of the figures. A central arch frames the central group of the Virgin, Christ and Simeon. A cornice surmounted by towers extends on either side to emphasize the placement of the serving women.

In addition to the basic Presentation theme, several accessory features found in Albani and not in the Anglo-Saxon composition are included. The tripartite entablature which compartmentalizes the figures in the Albani composition serves the same function as the triple arch used in the mid-century Psalter. Even the curtains hanging in the archway have been included. The inclusion of a second pair of doves in the hands of the Winchester servant may also be based on the Albani scene. It is highly unlikely that the Winchester artist would have invented the second pair of doves which contradict the text. Since the inclusion of the second pair of doves in Albani is apparently unprecedented, it draws the two English psalters into a closer relationship.

One aspect of the illustration, however, differs from this tradition and indicates that the Winchester artist consulted another source in addition to the Albani model. In the Winchester Presentation, Christ points into an open book as he is handed to Simeon. The book, which is not included in the Drogo Sacramentary or Benedictional, does appear with some frequency from the early eleventh century onward in Presentation scenes which correspond iconographically to the Psalter. It is included in a sacramentary from Liège, Paris, B.N., MS lat. 819, fol. 25v,[218] in the middle of the century at Sta. Maria im Kapitol,[219] and in the later part of the century in the Bohemian Gospel book in Gnesen, Chapter Library, MS I.a, fol. 28v.[220] Here Christ actually points at the book as he is placed in Simeon's arms. It is also found on an early twelfth-century ivory in Trier Cathedral mentioned by Pächt as a source for the Albani Presentation architectural schema. Here Christ actually holds a book as he is handed to Simeon.

Christ among the Doctors (Fig. 14), *Luke 2:46–7*

Christ sits on a raised bench in the centre of the composition. He is framed by an arch. He holds an open book in one hand and points to the doctors with the other. The doctors are squeezed into arched compartments on either side of Christ. They eagerly lurch forward to question the young Child. The inscription in the margin reads: ICI SIET IESUS CHRISTUS EN MI LES MAISTRES DE LA LEI AL TEMPLE.

The idea of setting Christ apart from the doctors to emphasize his importance was established in the iconographical repertoire at an extremely early date. Two Early Christian ivories, one in Milan[221] and another in Berlin (Fig. 103), set precedents for the Winchester scene. The Berlin ivory stands at the beginning of the long tradition from which the Psalter was derived. On the Berlin ivory, Christ sits on a large, sturdy throne which elevates and separates him from the doctors. The heavy chair frame rises into an arch above his head, serving the same function as the arcade in the Psalter. Both isolate him as the central figure in the group. The Berlin Christ, seated frontally with a book in one hand, also parallels the Winchester figure. The exact disposition of the crowd of elders surrounding Christ is also comparable because of the large number included and the excitement they display.

The examples sharing the most striking similarities with the Psalter are two eleventh-century monuments which follow the tradition of the fifth-century ivory. Interestingly enough, the majority of the Echternach examples have little, if any, direct connection with the Psalter. In the *Codex Egberti*, fol. 18v,[222] Bremen Perikope, fol. 15v, Brussels 9428, fol. 18v, and *Epternacensis*, fol. 19v (Fig. 97), Christ sits on a long bench. He is not clearly distinguished from the crowd of men around him. One member of the Echternach group stands apart from the others. The Escorial manuscript, fol. 97v (Fig. 104), shows surprisingly close points of similarity with the Psalter. Christ sits frontally on a low bench. He is framed under a central arch which emphasizes his singular importance. The position of the figure, low bench and the use of the arch agree very closely with the Psalter. The rest of the composition bears a more limited resemblance to the Winchester scene. The doctors are confined to the areas on either side of the central arch. In both cases, the area they occupy is bridged by an architectural framework.

There are certain points on which the *Escorialensis* does not agree with the Psalter. Another eleventh-century monument, mentioned previously in connection with the Flight into Egypt, sheds additional light upon the models available to the Winchester artist. The Flemish ivory in the Victoria and Albert Museum[223] offers striking parallels to Nero C.IV. On the ivory, Christ sits frontally on a low bench and raises his right hand in blessing and holds an open book in the left. Other details also draw the two monuments together. Unlike *Escorialensis*, the Winchester scene includes two large groups of lively, excited elders. Although the arrangement differs slightly on the Victoria and Albert ivory, an analogous spirit is expressed. In both cases, the elders gesture eagerly toward the Child or touch their faces. Like the Psalter, the elaborate architectural frame on the ivory has slender columns decorated in a scroll pattern and terminating in tri-lobed capitals. The gabled roof, surmounted by ball finials and elaborate semi-ovoid shingles, is reminiscent of the more abbreviated superstructure in the Psalter.

Christ with his Parents (Fig. 15), *Luke 2:48*

Christ stands on a raised mound in the centre of the composition. The hand of God appears above his head. He holds a scroll in his left hand and raises the other to his mother. The Virgin stands on the left returning the gesture of her son. Joseph stands to the right of Christ holding a staff. Each of the figures is framed under an arch of a triple arcade. Three of the column capitals are decorated with animal designs. The inscription in the margin reads: ICI LV TRVVAT MARIE JOSEPH.

Christ with his Parents is an extremely rare scene when found in this form. Generally, the parents of Christ are included in the scene of Christ among the Doctors. This type was established in the Insular tradition from an extremely early date. It can be found in the sixth-century Gospels of St Augustine, Cambridge, C.C.C., MS 286, fol. 129v.[224] Closer parallels exist, however, to Byzantine sources which were quite probably incorporated into an Ottonian manuscript, as discussed in Chapter Two.

As in the case of the previous scene, the arrangement can be compared to Mosan sources, the Victoria and Albert ivory and a twelfth-century Mosan miniature, Berlin, Dahlem Prussisches Kulturbesitz Kupferstichkabinett, MS 78.A.6, fol. 9r.[225] In the miniature, the Virgin standing on the left is similar to the corresponding Winchester figure. She is integrated into the scene so that a silent dialogue with Christ is established by the exchange of glances and inscribed scrolls. This effectively sets the two figures apart from the rest. The Virgin, with her veiled, haloed head and upraised hand, brings to mind the Winchester Virgin.

The Baptism (Fig. 15), *Matthew 3:13–7, Mark 1:9–11, Luke 3:21f., John 1:26–36*

Christ stands naked in water that rises to his waist. He steps to the left with arms extended towards the Baptist. John, wearing a hair coat, raises his hands in blessing above Christ's bowed head. The dove of the Holy Spirit appears from a cloud above. On the right stands an angel holding a robe. The inscription above the panel reads: ICI LV BAPTIZAT SAINT JOHANS.

The Winchester Baptism, discussed in Chapter Two, offers more complex problems of interpretation than many of the other New Testament scenes. It does not follow the Anglo-Saxon tradition which was revived in the twelfth century by the Albani artist. Nor does it follow the Echternach group in other than minor details. To further complicate the matter, no other single source reasonably close to the Psalter in time and place duplicates the Winchester Baptism type. Precedents for certain aspects of the scene were established in the Early Christian period. The largest concentration of these features appears later in medieval Mosan monuments. It is to the Mosan sphere of influence that the Baptism miniature in the Winchester Psalter is most closely allied, not only in iconographic type but by the specific patterns for the individual figures. The only clear parallel to the Insular tradition is the robe held by the angel. It is found in the Albani Baptism[226] and British Library leaf.[227]

The Marriage at Cana (Fig. 16), *John 2:1–11*

The Cana scene occupies an entire page. In the upper half of the illustration, the guests are seated at the banquet table. Christ and the Virgin are seated to their right. The inscription above reads: ICI EVT AS NOCES OD ARCHITRICLIN. In the lower half, servants open a cupboard to get water vessels which are filled from a well at the right, then carried up the staircase in the centre. The inscription above reads: ICI FIST DEL EVE VIN.

This unusual scene does not conform to a single formula. The Cana iconography found in the Psalter in this instance bears no relationship to the Echternach type because Christ is seated at the banquet table rather than standing at the side.[228] Examples of Christ seated can be documented from the tenth century when it appears in a Byzantine manuscript now in the Leningrad Public Library, MS 21, fol. 2r.[229] This Middle Byzantine type which concentrated attention upon the feast instead of the miracle by placing Christ at the table, influenced Western iconography from the eleventh century.[230] Several Ottonian examples exist in Fulda manuscripts as well as elsewhere. In the Fulda Sacramentary, Göttingen, theol. fol. 231, fol. 19r,[231] Christ is seated at a sigma table with the guests. As in the Psalter, Christ and the Virgin are seated at the end of the table with the bridal couple and guests beside them. In this respect both the Ottonian and Winchester compositions agree with the Byzantine type found in the Leningrad manuscript and elsewhere. By the twelfth century, this type which made the feast the centre of interest was the rule rather than the exception in Western as well as Byzantine art.[232]

The artist altered this Cana type by using contemporary patterns which find their closest parallels in northern French and Flemish monuments, discussed in Chapter Two. The lower half of the illustration also finds parallels in twelfth-century France. The interest in embroidering upon the biblical narrative with descriptive genre passages became more popular after the middle of the century. The portal of the cathedral at Le Mans, dated before 1158,[233] has an extensive Cana sequence which is spread over no less than five voussoirs. Especially interesting is another Cana scene from northern France, a capital from the cloister of Châlons-sur-Marne-en-Vaux, dated before 1184,[234] which shows the servants fetching the water vessels from a raised shelf. The Châlons capital demonstrates a continuity of cross-Channel influence after the middle of the century.

The Cana scene emerges as one of the most interesting in the New Testament cycle. The artist chose to ignore the Echternach models which he followed so faithfully in a number of instances. That such a model was available in England is made clear by the British Library leaf which copied the Echternach model.[235] Instead, the Winchester artist compiled what emerges as a unique and interesting interpretation of the scene. The emphasis upon the banquet scene rather than the miracle conforms to a widely accepted Romanesque convention. The specific models used indicate that the artist, while following patterns which may stem from Anglo-Saxon conventions, was drawing directly upon a model also in use contemporaneously across the channel in the Franco-Flemish region. The expansion of the scene to include the servants' below stairs preparations had some precedents in Middle Byzantine illustration. Later reflections of the servants' preparations in northern France suggest that the genre aspect of the scene gained increased dissemination in the second half of the century.

The First Temptation of Christ
(Fig. 17), *Matthew 4:3–4*

A furry devil with clawed feet, horns and a tail stands on the left. He wears a brief hooded cape and short skirt. He points to a pile of stones lying at his feet. The inscription above reads: ICI LO RVVAT DEIABLES KE IL FESIST DE PIERES PAIN AL DESERT.

The First Temptation of Christ does not appear among extant Early Christian monuments but a type extremely similar to the Nero Temptation had been developed by the Carolingian period. It is found in works from the Metz atelier, an ivory in the Stadtsbibliothek, Frankfurt,[236] and in the Drogo Sacramentary, fol. 41r (Fig. 113). Both Metz scenes show the stones lying at the feet of the two figures. On the ivory they lie between the two figures, as in the Winchester Psalter. The Sacramentary presents the scene somewhat differently, with the stones lying to the right of both figures. The positioning of a tree to the right of the First Temptation does draw the Drogo iconography into comparison with the Psalter. The ivory, on the other hand, has a tree in the centre of the field, between the protagonists. The type found on the Carolingian ivory was adopted at the Echternach scriptorium in the Ottonian period.[237] In certain respects, the stage of development represented by miniatures of the Echternach group more closely parallels the Winchester illustration than does the Carolingian type. The First Temptation appears in the Bremen Perikope, fol. 25v (Fig. 114), Brussels manuscript, fol. 32v, *Epternacensis*, fol. 20r[238] and *Escorialensis*, fol. 26r.[239] In each case, Christ stands holding a scroll and gestures to the devil with the opposite hand. The devil points to a pile of stones lying between them. The positioning and gestures of the figures show elements of similarity in each case. The depiction of the devil also draws them together. In the Carolingian sources, the devil is shown as a human being. In the Ottonian manuscripts, he is a dark, wingless, furry creature with a tail, bear-like clawed paws and conspicuously protruding tongue. These features reappear in the Winchester devil. The short hood, absent from the Ottonian devil, appears in other twelfth-century devils, as for example, on the tympanum at Le Mans.[240] However, the tree in the Metz illustration has been eliminated in the Echternach Temptation scene. In this minor respect, the Winchester version is closer to the Carolingian source.

The Second Temptation (Fig. 17), *Matthew 4:5–7*

Christ stands on the gable of the temple, pointing to the devil standing on the ground below. The inscription reads: ICI RVVAT DESCENDRE DEL PINNACLE DEL TEMPLE.

The basic iconography of the scene duplicates that in the Drogo Sacramentary. Christ stands atop the gable of a building at the right. The devil, at the left, points upward at him. Even the tree, placed to the left of the devil in the Drogo Sacramentary, is found in exactly the same position in the Psalter. The type was taken over without appreciable change in the Odbert Psalter, fol. 102r,[241] and the British Library leaf.[242] The Second Temptation in the Albani Psalter, page 34, moves further away from this type because two devils appear.[243] One leaps from the roof while a second, behind Christ, shoves the Lord toward the edge.

In the main, the layout of the Echternach Second Temptation scenes differs considerably from the Carolingian version followed in the Winchester Psalter. Instead of calling to Christ from the ground, the devil mounts the roof to tempt him. The position of Christ's arms, placed parallel over one another, also alludes to the presence of an Echternach source.

The Third Temptation (Fig. 17), *Matthew 4:8–10*

The devil, standing at the left, is winged and wears a long gown with knots in the sleeve and hem. He displays to Christ a treasure trove lying between them. The inscription on his scroll reads: 'Hec omnia tibi dabo si adoraveris me'. Christ stands on a mountain unfurling a scroll bearing his reply: 'Vade retro satane non temptabis dominum deum tuam'. In the margin on the right is written in a later hand: 'Ici offert obey se de tute munde. Ihesus sun seigneur commandet ariere'.

Christ standing on the summit of the mountain while the devil tempts him from below was a type established in England before the Conquest. It can be found in Tiberius C.VI, fol. 10v (Fig. 115). Even the treasure scattered at Christ's feet includes some of the same items: rings, drinking vessels and an oliphant. The link to this Anglo-Saxon model becomes increasingly important when Carolingian, Ottonian and other twelfth-century English Temptation scenes are considered. In the Drogo Sacramentary, Christ and the devil stand facing each other on level ground and Satan points to the treasure behind him. In the Ottonian manuscripts, both Christ and the devil stand on the summit with the treasure scattered behind the devil. In a more minor respect, the Ottonian model may have contributed something to the scene. Christ lurches back, arm upraised, in both Nero C.IV and *Escorialensis*.

The appearance of the devil in the Third Temptation raises additional questions. Anglo-Saxon iconography cannot account for the appearance of the devil in the Third Temptation. Unlike his predecessors in the first two Temptation scenes, this devil has a large beak-like nose and clawed feet. The bird-like appearance of the devil in this scene differentiates it from the earlier more animal-like apparitions. Precedents occur for this type in the British Isles and elsewhere. Perhaps the most interesting comparison is to the Bohemian Coronation Gospels, fol. 24v, where a winged, beak-nosed devil with a heavy beard and taloned feet appears.[244] Even more striking is the fact that the devil in this Third Temptation scene is dressed, in contrast to the first two Temptations where he is not. The Bohemian manuscript offers the only precedent for garbing the devil in the Third Temptation. The influence of the Bohemian type is also felt in the Albani Psalter where beaked, taloned devils appear in all three Temptation scenes.

The Raising of Lazarus (Fig. 18), *John 11:38–45*

Christ stands at the left with a scroll that bears the instructions: 'Tollite lapidem'. Behind him stand the apostles, headed by Peter. On the right, a man in a pointed hat, assisted by a crowd, lifts the lid from Lazarus' coffin. Lazarus, wrapped in a winding sheet, sits up. His sisters, Mary and Martha, kneel at Christ's feet.

The closest parallels for this scene are found in the *Codex Egberti*, fol. 51v (Fig. 116) and the *Escorialensis*, fol. 150r (Fig. 117). The Ottonian Lazarus scenes differ somewhat from one another. The Winchester scene preserves elements of both. In the *Codex Egberti*, Christ stands at the right instructing Lazarus to rise from the dead. Immediately behind him are the apostles, headed by Peter. This is extremely close to the arrangement of the onlookers in the Psalter. Also, in *Egberti*, Mary and Martha, overcome by the revivification of their brother, sink to their knees before Christ. In both cases, Mary, overwhelmed with gratitude, clings to Christ's foot. In *Egberti*, Martha, more curious than her sister, turns to look upon her brother. The Winchester artist preserved this idea but moved Martha behind Christ. The right half of the Winchester scene is more closely related to *Escorialensis*. Here Lazarus is wrapped in a winding sheet that crisscrosses on his chest and covers his head, leaving only the face uncovered. As life returns, he begins to sit up in his coffin. A man, looking back at Christ, climbs forward to lift the lid. He is assisted by another man who bends forward to raise the opposite end of the stone slab. In all these respects, the *Escorialensis* provides close parallels for Nero C.IV. The size of the crowd standing behind Lazarus in the Psalter again refers to *Egberti* where a larger group of curious onlookers appears. The close proximity of the Winchester Raising of Lazarus to the two Ottonian manuscripts leaves little doubt about the immediate source for the English illustration.

The relationship to Insular monuments is less direct. The scene does not exist in Albani. The Pembroke leaf follows other sources.[245] The leaf in the Morgan Library is based, in large measure, on the same sources as Nero C.IV but incorporates a different selection of iconographic motifs from them.[246]

The Entry into Jerusalem (Fig. 18), *Matthew 21:1–11, Mark 11:1–10, Luke 19:29–40, John 12:12–19*

Christ rides a donkey toward the city of Jerusalem, seen at the right. He raises a hand in blessing to a crowd emerging from the city. Some stand in the gateway spreading their cloaks or holding palms. Others watch from the windows in the city wall. A second group on the left includes a boy in a tree cutting off its branches.

The earliest extant example of the Nero C.IV type for the Entry into Jerusalem is found in the *Codex Rossanensis*, fol. 1v.[247] The Rossano illustration shares a surprising number of similarities with the Winchester Entry. In both cases, a group of figures stands at the left of the picture field watching Christ's progress. Most notable is the similarity in placement and detail of the boy in the tree. The trees are placed behind Christ and a youth swings from the lower branches as he attempts to cut loose a branch. Christ, although seated sidesaddle in *Rossanensis* in keeping with the Eastern convention, blesses the crowd with the right hand as in the Psalter. The welcoming crowd before the gate of Jerusalem includes both figures on bent knee spreading their cloaks in Christ's path and others standing upright holding palms. They span a wide age group, including youths and older, bearded men. In all these respects, the Psalter follows the Rossano type. The last detail is none the less significant. In the right side of both Entry scenes stands the gate of Jerusalem. People curiously poke their heads through the open windows and eagerly herald Christ's arrival by waving branches. While it would certainly be incorrect to assume that the Winchester artist copied a sixth-century model, it is clear that his source reflected the Rossano type with a high degree of accuracy.

The Benedictional of St Aethelwold, fol. 45v[248] (Fig. 118), provides an intermediary link between the Rossano type and the Winchester Psalter. Here the resemblance is especially striking. The general arrangement and incorporation of details in the Benedictional provides an extremely close precedent for the Psalter. Christ rides astride in the centre of the composition, blessing the awaiting crowd. The people in the crowd hold branches, spread cloaks in the doorway, emerge from arched window openings in the tower and hang from the trees. In addition, the architecture of Jerusalem with horizontal courses in the lower stories and multiple, fenestrated towers above are nearly identical to the Winchester arrangement. The appearance of such a large number of corresponding elements in the Anglo-Saxon manuscript makes it possible to assume that an Insular source, faithfully preserving the Rossano type, was the model for the Winchester artist.

The relationship of the Psalter to the Albani Entry scene is better explained on the basis of a common Anglo-Saxon source than by an interdependence of the contemporary monuments.[249]

The Last Supper (Fig. 19), *Matthew 26:20–30, Mark 14:17–25, Luke 22:14–23, John 13:21–6*

Christ sits behind a long table at the centre of the picture field. He offers the wine chalice to a group of five disciples seated at the right and a loaf of bread to five followers seated on the left. John sits closest to Christ, leaning on his bosom. Judas sits apart from the rest of the group, on the opposite side of the table. He clutches his purse of silver with one hand and points to a dish on the table with the other. The scene is framed by an elaborate architectural setting. Two large arches encompass the groups of apostles and a smaller central arch frames the figure of Christ.

The Last Supper is described by all four evangelists. Their accounts differ somewhat from one another in detail. The elements combined in the Winchester illustration are based on a compilation from several textual sources. The distribution of the bread and wine is mentioned by Matthew, Mark and Luke. Matthew and Mark describe Judas dipping his hand into the dish. John alone relates that the apostle of the same name rested on the breast of Christ.

The distribution of bread and wine described in the first three Gospels was represented relatively infrequently in Western art. Among the existing examples is an Insular precedent,[250] but the immediate source for the Nero C.IV distribution was undoubtedly Ottonian. A Last Supper, strikingly similar to Nero C.IV in design as well as iconography, follows the text of Matthew 26:33 in *Escorialensis*, fol. 52r (Fig. 119).[251] Christ sits in the centre of the composition gazing directly before him. He hands the chalice to the disciple on his right who raises a hand as he receives the cup from Christ. The startled disciples behind him turn to one another gesturing speechlessly. Christ simultaneously hands the loaf to Peter who accepts it quietly. Behind him, the disciples stare attentively at the scene before them. All these details are repeated in Nero C.IV. Even the framing element for the scene is almost identical to the *Escorialensis* setting. Christ is centred under a small arch and the two groups of disciples are framed under larger, flanking arches. Judas is also similarly identified in both cases, clutching his purse of silver. The numerous close comparisons in design and iconography leave little doubt that the Echternach scriptorium provided the model for the distribution of the bread and wine.

A question remains about the source for St John and the placement and action of Judas. That a second Last Supper type was available in the Echternach scriptorium is clear from the *Escorialensis*, fol. 153r,[252] and the Bremen Perikope, fol. 51v. Both illustrations are attached to the text of John who alone of the four evangelists describes the scene. The Bremen Last Supper (Fig. 120) comes slightly closer to the Winchester scene in arrangement and detail than *Escorialensis*. John sits on the right of Christ, leaning over toward him.[253] Judas is also distinguished from the other disciples in the Bremen Last Supper. He reaches toward a shallow, footed bowl containing a fish. The majority of the elements in the Winchester Last Supper appear to have been drawn from an extensive Echternach cycle which illustrated the description of the Last Supper given by both Matthew and John.

Several details cannot be explained adequately on the basis of the Echternach cycle. While these Ottonian works show Judas clutching his purse of silver and reaching into the dish, they depict him behind the table with the other disciples. To show Judas on the opposite side of the table was fairly common in the West from the ninth century when it appeared in the Stuttgart Psalter, fol. 53r.[254] Closer to the Nero C.IV type are illustrations showing Judas in front of the table and reaching into the dish, as recounted by Matthew and Mark. This iconographical type, traditional in Byzantine art from an early date,[255] appears in the West by the first quarter of the eleventh century in the Perikope of Henry II, Munich, Staatsbibliothek, MS Clm 4452, fol. 105r.[256] Whether the motif was derived directly from a Reichenau manuscript or indirectly through a lost Echternach intermediary is unclear. Either source is a logical antecedent for the Winchester scene.

In certain minor respects, the Pembroke 120 Last Supper, fol. 3r (Fig. 121), is similar to the Winchester scene. John, resting on Christ's bosom, comes closer to the Pembroke version than to the Echternach type. In the English examples, John rests the side of his face on his hand. The arm is bent at the elbow and supported by the opposite hand. The posture is slightly different in Bremen–*Escorialensis* where he simply leans forward clasping Christ's chest. Other than in minor details, the English Last Supper scene has little in common with Nero C.IV. The attitudes of the apostles, Judas receiving the sop and lack of framing details in Pembroke 120 exclude it from any close relationship with Nero C.IV and its models. The Albani Psalter Last Supper, page 41, is derived from entirely different sources.[257]

Christ Washing the Feet of the Apostles (Fig. 19), John 13:4–20

Christ kneels at the left, holding Peter's foot over a basin. Peter, seated frontally on a low bench, raises both hands in protest. Behind him sit the other eleven apostles. An attendant stands at the far left holding a length of cloth over his shoulder. An inscription for this scene appears in the scene above. On the upper edge of the table in the Last Supper a scribe has written: ICI LAVAT LES PIEZ AS APOSTLES.

The iconography of the Winchester scene was developed over a long period of time. The reaction of Peter to Christ's intention to wash his apostle's feet is found in some of the earliest representations of the subject. Sarcophagi of the fourth and fifth centuries already show Peter raising his hands in embarrassment and amazement as Christ appears before him.[258] It reappears in Ottonian art, perhaps as the direct result of Early Christian influence.[259] The reluctant Peter type was used in manuscripts of the Reichenau group, and later at Echternach. In the Gospels of Otto III, fol. 237r,[260] *Codex Egberti*, fol. 78r,[261] and the Bremen Perikope, fol. 57v (Fig. 120), this figure of Peter is comparable to the Winchester type. These Ottonian scenes do differ in other respects. Unlike the Winchester depiction, the Ottonian manuscripts show Christ standing, a disciple watches from behind him and a small group of disciples sits on the bench with Peter. The Peter figure is retained in other Echternach compositions while the other elements undergo considerable alteration. The Brussels manuscript, fol. 78v,[262] represents an intermediary stage which comes closer to the Psalter, without offering a precedent for the composition as a whole. Here Peter sits frontally while Christ, on bended knee, grasps his foot. The disciple to the right of Christ has been eliminated. Gradually the rest of the composition was developed into a type later used in the Winchester Psalter. Particularly close to the Winchester scene is one in *Escorialensis*, discussed in Chapter Two.

One detail of the Winchester Washing of the Feet escapes explanation on the basis of the *Escorialensis* iconography. In the Winchester Psalter, an attendant stands behind Christ with a length of cloth. From the tenth century onward, attendants, frequently apostles, assisted Christ by holding water vessels or towels.[263] Several appear in Ottonian monuments including the Gospels of Otto III, a fragment of a sacramentary in Lucca,[264] and also in the Bohemian Coronation Gospels in Prague.[265] Whether the Winchester figure is, as suggested elsewhere, a deacon,[266] or merely based on this widespread Ottonian practice is uncertain.

The Betrayal of Christ (Fig. 20), *Matthew 26:47–56, Mark 14:43–52, Luke 22:47–53, John 18:1–12*

Christ stands in the centre of the composition turning his head back to receive the kiss of Judas, who approaches him from the rear. The Lord is simultaneously led forward by an evil-looking individual who grasps his outstretched, manacled hands. Immediately behind Christ stands Peter who cuts off the ear of Malchus. The central group is surrounded by a large, menacing crowd brandishing weapons.

The Betrayal scene in the Psalter combines three events narrated in the Gospels: Judas' betrayal, Christ's subsequent arrest and Peter's reaction to his master's seizure. All three events were familiar subjects in Western medieval representations. Both the Metz ivories[267] and the Echternach manuscripts[268] illustrate all three events.

The first two episodes depicted in the Winchester Psalter can be documented with an extensive series of comparisons discussed in Chapter Two. The third event, Peter cutting off Malchus' ear, is more puzzling. The scene is included in the majority of examples in Chapter Two but the iconography is consistently different from Nero C.IV. The La Daurade capital exemplifies the type found on the relevant Byzantine and Western monuments. Peter bends over a kneeling figure, grasps him by the head with one hand and wields his knife with the other. In the Psalter, Peter, whose tonsured head leans out from behind Christ, slices off Malchus' ear with an enormous sword. A precedent for the type does exist on an early eleventh-century ivory in the British Museum.[269] Here Peter, similarly shown in a three-quarter view, brings a large sword down on the ear of Malchus, shown in profile, as in the Psalter. Whether the Winchester artist resorted to such a model for the Peter–Malchus group is questionable. The figures in Nero C.IV are squeezed awkwardly into a composition that is complete without them. They draw attention away from the dramatic focus around the Betrayal–Arrest group. The composition of the figure of Malchus is peculiar. The lower half of the body echoes the full front view of the gaoler but Malchus' head is in profile. The connecting torso section is puzzling. It is not clearly identifiable as either a front or side view. This feature, taken together with the unlikely placement of the group as a whole, suggests that the artist may well have inserted the group without consulting a specific model.

The Winchester Betrayal stands apart from earlier English Betrayal scenes. It is derived from an iconographical type which appears to have evolved in the late eleventh century and reached a highly developed form in France by the middle of the twelfth century.

The Flagellation (Fig. 20), *Matthew 27:26, Mark 15:15, John 19:1*

Christ, blindfolded and nude to the waist, is bound to a column in the centre of the picture field. Two scourgers flank Christ. They reel back as they prepare to lash him with their whips. Pilate sits at the far left. A small horned creature is perched on his shoulder and whispers into his ear. Several figures behind Pilate and on the far right jeer at Christ. An inscription above reads: ICI FVT FLAG. . . EST.

The Flagellation of Christ was more frequently depicted in Western art than in the East. The earliest examples are found in the ninth-century Stuttgart Psalter, fol. 43r,[270] and the Utrecht Psalter, fol. 85v.[271] The type found in both manuscripts shows Christ facing away with his back to the viewer. This type reappeared in the St Albans Psalter, page 44 (Fig. 126). A second type was used in the Echternach scriptorium. In the Ottonian type, Christ stands in three-quarter view with his hands bound to a column on his right.[272] The number and placement of the torturers varies from manuscript to manuscript. In *Egberti* and Bremen they stand on either side of Christ, in Brussels both are on the left and in *Epternacensis* one stands on the left. The Echternach artists also dealt differently with Pilate, who was omitted altogether from the Carolingian examples. He stands on the left in *Egberti* and Bremen, sits on the same side in Brussels 9428 and is omitted from *Epternacensis*. Certain elements of the Echternach Flagellation scenes, particularly the placement of Pilate, reappear in the Winchester Psalter. They cannot, however, be considered as the immediate source of the Winchester illustration which is discussed in Chapter Two.

The Crucifixion (Fig. 21), *Matthew 27:35–54, Mark 15:24–39, Luke 23:33–48, John 19:18–37*

The dead Christ hangs from a cross placed in the centre of the composition. The inscription above Christ's head reads: IHC NAZAREN(US) REX IUDEO (RUM). Stephen and Longinus flank the central cross. The thieves hang on smaller crosses to the right and left of Stephen and Longinus. Two men with hammers prepare to break their legs. To either side of them stand the Virgin and John with crowds of people peering out from behind them.

The expanded Crucifixion image of the Psalter was derived from the narrative illustrations found in the Echternach group. In the *Codex Egberti*, the Crucifixion is dealt with in two separate illustrations.[273] The first, on fol. 83v, shows Christ and the thieves still alive on the crosses. Stephen offers Christ the sponge while John and the Virgin, in the company of the two Marys, witness his death. In the succeeding illustration on fol. 84v, Christ and the thieves hang lifelessly from the crosses. Longinus pierces Christ's side with his lance as two men prepare to break the legs of the thieves.

The later Echternach manuscripts do not repeat the elaborate schema of *Egberti*. Instead, they combine various elements of the two scenes in one image.[274] The member of the group that most closely approximates the Psalter is found in *Epternacensis*, fol. 111r (Fig. 127). In *Epternacensis*, Christ is dead on the cross, flanked by Stephen and Longinus. Beyond them stand Mary and John, both of whom are composed and resigned to the death of the Lord. The thieves, on smaller crosses, are still alive and both turn their heads to the right. Two men with mallets are also included on the far edges of the picture field. The Nuremberg illustration, then, shows that the iconographical type found in the Psalter was already a single image in the Ottonian period.

Although the Winchester Crucifixion is closely related to an Echternach model, this was not the only source used by the Winchester illustrator. Several additional details of the Winchester composition are not found in the Echternach illustration or differ from the Ottonian types. The Crucifixion is not represented in the Albani Psalter but the Bury leaf (Fig. 125) already incorporates certain additions and emendations found in the Winchester manuscript. Unlike the Ottonian examples, Christ is bearded and wears a loincloth in both English examples. The crowds of figures behind John and the Virgin in Nero C.IV also appear in Pembroke 120. However, while the Pembroke Crucifixion offers precedents for minor details, the scene as a whole could not have been the model for the Winchester artist. The Pembroke Christ is alive, the thieves are blindfolded and bound with ropes and the men with hammers are absent.

A last detail may also be explained by an English tradition. In the Ottonian manuscripts and Pembroke 120, John expresses his sorrow at the death of Christ by raising one hand to the side of his face in a traditional gesture of mourning. In the Winchester Psalter, John is characterized differently. He holds a writing tablet and stylus, symbolizing his authorship of Holy Scripture. This reference to John's role as an evangelist is clearly precedented in Anglo-Saxon examples.[275] In this additional respect, the Echternach model used by the Winchester artist was tempered by a long-established Insular tradition.

The Deposition (Fig. 21), *Matthew 27:57–60, Mark 15:43–6, Luke 23:50–3, John 19:38*

The dead body of Christ is lowered from the cross by Joseph of Arimathea. The Virgin stands on the left clasping the hand of Christ which has already been detached. Behind her stands a woman in mourning. On the right, Nicodemus prepares to extract the nail from Christ's other hand with a pair of pliers. St John watches from beyond Nicodemus. The inscription above the cross reads: IHC NAZARENUS REX IVDEORU(M).

The Deposition in the Winchester Psalter does not follow the established Insular or Ottonian[276] iconography but a type that originated in the East in the Middle Byzantine period. A scene almost identical to the one in the Psalter is found in a tenth-century Gospel book in Florence, Biblioteca Laurenziana, MS Conv. soppr. 160, fol. 114v.[277] Here Mary and John flank the central group and the Virgin tenderly presses Christ's hand to the side of her face. The earliest Western example appears to be an ivory from the lower Rhine or Meuse area dated c.1000.[278] The influence of Byzantine iconography on the Entombment and Deposition scenes of the ivory is unmistakable. The Mosan Entombment scene can be related to an early stage in the development of the Byzantine *Threnos* scene.[279] This scene, showing the two women at the grave described by Matthew, differentiates it from the Western custom of showing the three women described by Mark. The relationship of the Deposition scene on the ivory to Byzantine sources is equally striking. Christ slumps over Joseph as his mother clasps his hand. Nicodemus works to free the other hand. The same Deposition type is found in northern Spain and southern France where the Winchester Betrayal scene also appeared. It is found on a capital from La Daurade[280] and in the cloister of S. Domingo, Silos,[281] which are dated into the first quarter of the twelfth century.

In England, the Albani artist followed a completely different tradition,[282] but the Bury St Edmunds artist followed the Byzantine type, fol. 4r (Fig. 128). In addition, the Bury artist elaborated upon his model. Several of these details are also found in the Winchester Deposition. The three Marys stand behind the Virgin in Pembroke 120. Their presence is echoed by the grief-stricken women on the left in the Psalter. St John in Nero C.IV is also patterned after the sorrowful figure holding a book in the Bury Psalter. As was the case with other scenes from the Passion cycle, subtle details suggest that the Winchester artist was in close contact with contemporary English models. This also applies to the winding sheet looped around Christ in the Winchester Deposition. A length of cloth, similarly looped around Christ's torso, is found on the Victoria and Albert leaf.[283] While the iconography of the scene as a whole follows the Albani model, the conspicuous presence of this relatively rare detail on the leaf suggests that the Winchester artist consulted twelfth-century English sources.

The Entombment of Christ (Fig. 22), *Matthew 27:60, Mark 15:46, Luke 23:53, John 19:39–42*

Christ lies outstretched on the sepulchre. Three men prepare the body for burial. One supports his head, a second stands at his feet and a third pours oil from a vessel onto the body.

This scene combines two events that followed the Crucifixion, the Entombment and the Anointment of Christ. The Entombment scene, without any reference to the Anointment, was represented in a similar fashion in the Reichenau–Echternach manuscripts. As with a number of scenes from the life of Christ in these Ottonian manuscripts, the compositional elements for the Entombment were reinterpreted individually for each codex, so that the miniatures display subtle degrees of difference from one another. The Entombment scene most closely resembling that in Nero C.IV is found in *Epternacensis*, fol. 111r (Fig. 127).[284] In the Ottonian Entombment, Joseph and Nicodemus, clearly identified by inscriptions, prepare to lower the body into the tomb. Joseph supports Christ's head while Nicodemus stands at the foot of the bier holding Christ's legs. Both men are bearded. The arrangement of Christ's body, tipped at an angle to the picture plane so that both stiff, outstretched arms are visible, is again similar to the Psalter. Other details link the Ottonian miniature to the Psalter. The figures of Joseph and Nicodemus are framed by trees that follow the inward curve of their bodies. To a certain extent, the highly stylized trees in the English manuscript suggest its Ottonian model. The slender hybrids on the far right and left in the Psalter incline toward the bier in the centre of the field.

The relatively simple Ottonian

Entombment scene had only limited acceptance in England during the first half of the twelfth century. The Albani Entombment, page 48, was heavily influenced by Byzantine and Italian models.[285] Only the Pembroke Entombment, fol. 4r (Fig. 128) is indebted to an Ottonian prototype.[286] Two men support Christ's head and feet. A cluster of trees also suggests the *Epternacensis* type. However, a number of alterations place the Bury illustration at a distance from the Ottonian model. The two men hold the body above the sepulchre and two groups of witnesses stand behind them. The similarities between Pembroke 120 and Nero C.IV suggest that the artists may have consulted the same basic type. However, the additions and emendations introduced by the Bury artist make it clear that the Winchester draftsman followed the Echternach type rather than the more nearly contemporary English reinterpretation.

As mentioned above, the Entombment scene in the Psalter was elaborated upon by the addition of a second subject, the Anointment of Christ. The Anointment was a post-Ottonian invention. Modern scholarship on this question credits Byzantine artisans with the invention of the type on visual, historical and liturgical grounds. While the first two theories are not convincing,[287] the third deserves consideration. The Byzantine liturgical Unction ceremony was imported from the East in the twelfth century.[288] This rather indirect liturgical influence may have had an influence since two Western examples of the scene are found on liturgical combs used after the application of holy oil. These twelfth-century Western examples of the scene are discussed in Chapter Two.

The Women at the Sepulchre
(Fig. 22), *Mark 16:1–5*

An angel sits on the open sarcophagus with a group of sleeping soldiers at his feet. The angel gestures to the three Marys who approach in single file from the right carrying censers. The scene is enclosed beneath a triple arcade.

The arrangement of the Winchester scene, including the tomb, angel and soldier, follows the Albani type and is discussed in Chapter Two. The three women were fashioned after other sources. In Albani, Pembroke and their Anglo-Saxon antecedents, the women recoil anxiously into a tight-knit group or fall at the angel's feet, as in the Boulogne Psalter. In the Winchester Psalter, on the other hand, the three women, holding censers, walk in single file toward the angel. A procession of the women to the tomb is found in two Echternach manuscripts.[289] In both the *Epternacensis*, fol. 111v (Fig. 137), and *Escorialensis*, fol. 84r,[290] the women approach the angel in single file. They do not, however, carry censers. On the basis of the Insular precedents for the rest of the scene, another source seems more likely. In a late eleventh-century English manuscript in Oxford, Wadham College, MS A.10.22, fol. 104,[291] the three Marys stand behind one another facing the angel. The woman to the left holds a censer. So both the arrangement of the women and censer find precedents in English art.

The inclusion of three censers in the Psalter is an unusual feature and requires additional explanation. The appearance of the censer, which was a rare occurrence before the millennium, has been explained on liturgical grounds. The *Visitatio* was an extra-liturgical ceremony performed on Easter morning, usually after Matins. A monk, dressed as an angel, would sit on the sepulchre as three other monks, dressed as women, approached swinging censers.[292] That such a ceremony was known in England and could have influenced the iconography of the scene is clear from the text of the *Regularis Concordia*, which is associated with Aethelwold, Bishop of Winchester, in the tenth century. The text of the *Regularis* mentions the three brethren wearing copes and carrying thuribles coming to the tomb.[293] Two twelfth-century ivory combs, as well as the Psalter, show all three women holding censers.[294]

In every respect, the iconography of the Women at the Tomb can be explained on the basis of Insular sources. While precedents exist before the Conquest, the Psalter is most closely allied with twelfth-century English developments of the pictorial theme.

The Harrowing of Hell (Fig. 23)

Christ stands at the left holding a cross staff and drawing Adam from the mouth of Hell. The Hell-mouth, represented as the head of an animal, is filled with representations of the dead. To Christ's left stands an angel who vanquishes the demons lying beneath his feet. The inscription in the upper margin reads: ICI . . . DESCENTE ENFERS.

Christ's visit to Hell to rescue the souls of the dead was not specifically mentioned in the Gospels. Although several biblical passages[295] may be interpreted as alluding to the descent into the inferno, only the apocryphal Gospel of Nicodemus describes the event in detail.[296]

By the Anglo-Saxon period, this scene reached England. It is to these Insular models that one must turn in identifying the immediate sources of the Winchester Harrowing. A fragmentary Anglo-Saxon relief in Bristol Cathedral (Fig. 131) depicts Christ in Hades in a fashion extremely similar to the Nero C.IV illustration.[297] Christ, haloed and bearded, steps forward on bent knee toward the inferno. He stands on the devil, lying in chains under his feet. He simultaneously holds a cross staff, blesses the dead and grasps the uplifted arm of the naked figure before him. In all these respects, the Winchester Harrowing echoes the pre-Conquest stone relief. A number of other features of the Nero illustration not found on the Bristol slab can also be traced to Anglo-Saxon sources. The Harrowing in Tiberius C.VI, fol. 14r, follows another iconographic type for the figure of Christ,[298] but includes a number of details that reappear in the Winchester illustration. Hell is depicted as the mouth of an animal. Although the origins of the type remain partially unexplained,[299] by the Anglo-Saxon period the Hell-mouth is a highly characteristic feature of the Insular tradition. In addition, the Anglo-Saxon drawing agrees with the Nero illustration by personifying the devil in several guises. He is shown both as a furry bear-like creature and as a serpent. The Tiberius Psalter also offers a precedent for the sun found in the upper right-hand corner of the Winchester Harrowing. Although partially destroyed, the rays of the sun can be seen directly above Christ's head in the Anglo-Saxon drawing.

Anglo-Saxon sources were also utilized by other English artists in the twelfth century. Both the Albani, page 49,[300] and the Bury St Edmunds masters incorporated some of the Anglo-Saxon elements used by the Winchester illuminator. The finished products in each case differ to some extent from the models and one another. The Bury illustration, fol. 4v (Fig. 132), is closer to the Psalter than Albani, especially in details and the innovations it incorporates. The Bury

Christ holds a cross staff with a long, flowing banner which is also found in the Winchester Psalter. At Christ's feet lies the devil. As in the Nero Psalter, the devil has a rope around its neck which continues down the chest to confine the hands which are crossed over one another. The feet are bound separately. An angel[301] accompanies Christ into the inferno. In these minor respects, the Bury illustration offers precedents for details not found in the pre-Conquest models.

In fashioning the Harrowing of Hell, the Winchester artist used Insular models. In some respects, the Winchester scene resembles Anglo-Saxon iconographical types and in others those of the twelfth century. He drew selectively upon the Insular heritage to fashion a Harrowing scene that is at once highly characteristic of the English tradition and also unique.

Christ Appears to Mary Magdalene
(Fig. 23), *Mark 16:9, John 20:11–18*

The scene is illustrated twice. On the left, Christ stands holding a palm and gesturing to Mary Magdalene who faces him on the right. Her long hair is plaited into braids and her head is surrounded by a halo. Immediately to the right of this scene is a second subject. Mary, her hair covered by a veil, kneels and grasps Christ's bare foot in her hands. Christ stands facing her on the right side of the composition. He holds a cross staff.

The appearance of the risen Christ to Mary Magdalene is described by both John and Mark. A close inspection of the Winchester drawing reveals that both Gospel passages are illustrated here. In the Gospel of St John, Christ instructs Mary not to touch him. Yet, in the second frame of the drawing Mary clings to Christ's foot with both hands. No illustration of the *Noli me tangere* shows Mary touching Christ. Also, individual details of the two scenes do not correspond. In the first scene, Christ carries a palm and Mary wears long braids. In the second, Mary's head is covered by a veil and Christ holds a cross staff. The differences between the two scenes do not bear out the contention that the scenes illustrate successive events described by St John.[302] Instead, it can be suggested that two different subjects are represented here. The drawings illustrate two different accounts of the meeting of Christ with Mary after the Resurrection, narrated by Mark and John.

The scene to the left follows the text of St John. This more frequently illustrated iconographic type is commonly referred to as the *Noli me tangere*. The iconography found in the Winchester Psalter can most closely be associated with the Reichenau–Echternach school. The scene is found in several manuscripts from the group,[303] but the closest comparisons can be made with the Bremen Perikope, fol. 62v (Fig. 133). In the Ottonian manuscript, Christ stands to one side, gesturing to Mary. The Magdalene responds by genuflexing, head bowed, and extending her arms to Christ. Behind her stands a tree. In all these respects, the Winchester illustration follows the Echternach type with some fidelity. The Winchester artist, did, however, choose to abbreviate the more elaborate Bremen type by eliminating the two angels sitting on the empty tomb. The general arrangement of the Bremen *Noli* scene with the open tomb beside Mary and Christ is comparable to several Carolingian monuments[304] as well as to the extensively illustrated grec 74, fol. 209v (Fig. 134). The similarities between the Byzantine manuscript and Bremen *Noli* are especially striking and have been remarked upon elsewhere.[305]

In the first scene, Mary stands before the tomb. Seated upon it are two angels. The second scene in grec 74 also corresponds to the Bremen *Noli*. Mary encounters Christ in a garden which is suggested by a single tree in the Ottonian illustration. While the figure grouping of Christ and Mary in the two monuments does not correspond exactly, the Byzantine and Western examples appear to be related to one another.

The Ottonian type was employed elsewhere in twelfth-century England. The *Noli me tangere* is omitted from the Albani Psalter but is found in both Pembroke 120 (Fig. 132) and the leaf in the Victoria and Albert Museum.[306] The Pembroke example is nearly identical to the Psalter in its dramatic interchange between Mary and her risen Lord. It was quite probably copied from the Echternach model. The Victoria and Albert example is more extensive, illustrating both the scene of Mary at the empty grave and the *Noli me tangere.*

A second encounter of Mary Magdalene with Christ is pictured to the right of the *Noli me tangere.* The scene of a single woman kneeling and grasping Christ's foot is extremely rare. The only other example of the type is found in grec 74, fol. 101r (Fig. 135). The Byzantine miniature accompanies the text of Mark 16:9, making a definite identification possible. The description in Mark's Gospel is brief, simply mentioning that Christ appeared to Mary Magdalene without describing the encounter in detail. The text does not specifically state Christ prohibited Mary from touching him, as John's description does. In grec 74, Mary's head is covered by a veil and surrounded by a halo. She kneels, bending forward to grasp one of Christ's feet between her hands. The scene in Nero C.IV is extremely similar to grec 74 in these respects.[307]

The Giving of the Keys to Peter
(Fig. 24), *Matthew 16:13–19*

Christ stands on the left holding a scroll. He points toward an open gateway behind him. Before him Peter approaches on bended knee, holding a large key.

The event is not described specifically in the Gospel narrative dealing with the events after the Resurrection. However, the placement of the Giving of the Keys after Christ's appearance to Mary Magdalene is alluded to in St John's Gospel. When the risen Christ was reunited with the apostles, he instructed them to establish his church, as he had done previously when he entrusted the keys to Peter. The inclusion of the subject here emphasizes the parallelism between two mandates of Christ to his apostles.[308]

The iconographical formula employed by the Winchester artist follows a type found earlier in Reichenau and Echternach manuscripts. A number of these manuscripts[309] show Christ standing on the left handing the keys to Peter. Behind Peter stands a group of apostles. In one case, however, a variation appears which is closer to the scene in Nero C.IV. In the Gospels of Otto III, fol. 60v (Fig. 136), the scene is divided into two phases. In the upper register, Christ stands under a roofed enclosure with Peter. The other apostles stand behind Peter following the proceedings with rapt attention. The actual presentation scene places the Reichenau manuscript closer to the Winchester scene than to the other Ottonian manuscripts in the Reichenau–Echternach circle. The proximity of the Reichenau scene to the English manuscript is additionally strengthened by the knowledge that this type of presentation is not employed elsewhere in the tenth and eleventh centuries.[310]

No parallels to twelfth-century English art can be established since neither Albani nor Pembroke 120 include this scene.

The Road to Emmaus (Fig. 24), *Luke 24:3–29*

Christ stands on the left holding a pilgrim's staff. He gestures to two disciples standing on the right. One carries a staff and the other a palm branch. The inscription in the margin above is partially destroyed. The following can be discerned: ICI... EN SEMBLANCE DE PELERIN.

The meeting of Christ with the disciples on the road to Emmaus was represented repeatedly by Carolingian artisans. The ivories and manuscripts from Metz which include the scene offer a variety of different interpretations for the encounter.[311] However, an ivory from the Ada school now in the Aachen Cathedral Treasury[312] more closely approaches the Winchester type than those from Metz. The Aachen ivory shows Christ standing to the left gesturing to two disciples on the right. While the general outline of the Ada composition agrees with that in the Psalter, its reinterpretation by an Echternach artist provides a closer parallel to the Winchester iconography. In the *Codex Epternacensis*,[313] fol. 111v (Fig. 137), Christ approaches the two disciples who stand opposite him. They meet his advance and also point the way to Emmaus which is shown in the scene immediately to the left. The gestures of the disciples were retained by the Winchester artist although the *castellum* Emmaus has been deleted, rendering the gesture relatively meaningless. This type was developed further in the twelfth century, as described in Chapter Two.

The Supper at Emmaus (Fig. 25), *Luke 24:30*

Christ sits at the centre of the composition behind a table. He raises his left hand to bless the bread in front of him on the table. He is flanked on either side by the two disciples, one of whom holds a loaf of bread and the other who pours from a jug.

Since the Supper at Emmaus is closely linked to the previous scene thematically, it is not surprising that the iconography is derived from the same general sources as the previous scene. Interestingly enough, the pattern of specific comparisons does not follow the outline sketched for the Encounter on the Road to Emmaus. The Ottonian sources[314] again suggest the basic outlines of the Winchester scene. The specific points of correspondence, however, are found in a different combination of sources than was the case for the Road to Emmaus scene. Christ sits behind the table in the Winchester Psalter flanked by the two disciples. The *Egberti* manuscript, fol. 88r[315] provides a close parallel for this basic arrangement. In several interesting details, however, the Nero C.IV Supper at Emmaus more closely parallels that in the *Codex Epternacensis* (Fig. 137). In *Epternacensis*, Christ's actions follow Luke 24:30 which describes the Lord blessing the bread he was about to distribute to the apostles. This relatively rare gesture is also found in the Winchester Psalter. Another detail links the two manuscripts. In the Road to Emmaus scene in Nero C.IV both disciples are bearded. In the Supper at Emmaus scene, one is bearded but the second is a clean-shaven youth. The two illustrations do not agree with one another and indicate that two different models were employed. The model for this detail is again *Epternacensis* where one disciple is a youth and the other a wizened, bearded man.[316]

The reshaping of the Emmaus sequence in twelfth-century England was not without influence on the Psalter. In the Albani Psalter[317] and Pembroke 120 (Fig. 132) the general setting is in close agreement with the Winchester scene. In each case, the three figures sit behind a rectangular table. The scenes are framed by an arch carried on columns. The Albani setting is particularly close in type to the Winchester form. The arch carries an architectural superstructure, as in the Psalter. The agreement between the scenes ends here. Albani and Pembroke show Christ offering the divided loaf of bread to the two disciples. The Winchester manuscript differs by showing Christ blessing the bread. Thus, while the general layout of the composition follows the twelfth-century formula, this detail does not. The Winchester artist was heavily influenced by contemporary models but did not copy them in their entirety. His inclination to refer back to the Ottonian source sets his work apart from the fairly standardized type employed during the first half of the century in England.

Christ's Appearance to the Disciples and the Doubting Thomas (Fig. 25), *Mark 16:14–20, Luke 24:36–49, John 20:19–23, John 20:24–9*

Christ stands in the centre of the composition extending his arms to either side. The disciples are gathered around him. Thomas kneels to the left of Christ and touches his wound. The inscription in the margin above reads: ICI APARVT AS APOSTLES ET THOMAS LV MANIAT.

The illustration in the lower register of fol. 26 combines two separate events described by the evangelists. One event mentioned by Luke and John describes Christ's appearance to the disciples. He came into their midst and displayed his wounds to them. Thomas was not present at this gathering and did not believe that his companions had seen the risen Christ. John describes the second visit of Christ to the disciples, this time with Thomas present. Christ instructed Thomas to touch his wounds in order to believe in the Resurrection. The Winchester illustration combines the two visits of Christ to the disciples, the first where he displayed his wounds and the second, eight days later, when he dispelled Thomas' reluctance to believe in the Resurrection.

Christ Displaying his Wounds and the Doubting Thomas were already represented in the Carolingian period in a fashion that is found later in the Winchester Psalter.[318] The Ada ivory in the Aachen Cathedral Treasury depicts the two scenes against an architectural background. This Carolingian type was taken up again in the Reichenau scriptorium. In the Gospels of Otto III, fol. 251r (Fig. 138), the two scenes are placed within the same picture frame. In the first scene, Christ extends his arms to either side. The disciples, equally distributed on either side of him, stand awestruck behind his outstretched arms. The Winchester illustration follows the general outline of the Reichenau scene. It also incorporates two additional details. Christ displays his hands to the disciples but the nail holes described in the text are not present. The Winchester composition also omits them. The Reichenau scene is placed against a neutral background. The Winchester setting, unlike a number of others in the manuscript, is also extremely simple. In the second scene in the Gospels of Otto III, Thomas touches the wound in Christ's side. The scene has little in common with the one in the Winchester Psalter. Only the figure of Thomas, kneeling on the left of Christ, bears comparison. The figure has simply been lifted from this context by the Winchester master and included in the previous scene. The Winchester illustration, then, appears to be a conflation of two scenes found in an Ottonian manuscript from Reichenau.

Whether both scenes were also known at Echternach is a matter of conjecture. Only the second scene, the Doubting Thomas, is found in the extant manuscripts from this school. One example is found in the *Codex Epternacensis* (Fig. 137).[319] In one respect,[320] the iconography employed at Echternach coincides more closely with the English Psalter than does the Gospels of Otto III. Christ's robe in *Epternacensis* is draped over one shoulder, leaving the other side of the body naked to the waist. This is a deviation from the Reichenau type where Christ draws his garment aside to reveal his wound. In this minor respect, the Winchester artist acknowledges his debt to a post-Reichenau invention. Whether he derived it directly from an Echternach source or from an English intermediary such as Pembroke 120 (Fig. 132) is impossible to determine.

The other twelfth-century English manuscripts which depict the Appearance–Doubting Thomas are in some ways comparable to the Winchester scene. Both Pembroke 120 and the Albani Psalter, page 52,[321] illustrate the Appearance to the Disciples with the Doubting Thomas. However, the moments of the narrative illustrated and the models used vary from one another and the Psalter. The Bury illustrator concentrated his attention upon the second scene, the Doubting Thomas. He drew upon the Echternach model which shows Christ half naked to the waist displaying the nail holes in his hands and feet. The Albani artist also combined the two scenes but used the Appearance to the Apostles as the main model, adding the figure of Thomas to it. In spite of the similarities with the Winchester Psalter in choice of subject matter, the models suggested for the Albani composition are not from the Reichenau–Echternach group.[322] The Winchester scene is, then, relatively independent of its twelfth-century contemporaries in its quotation of an Ottonian source.

The Ascension (Fig. 26), *Acts 1:9–11*

An entire folio is devoted to the Ascension. In the upper register, Christ's legs and feet are encircled by a mandorla which disappear into the cloud bank above. Two angels fly down, framing the edges of the mandorla with their wings. The Virgin and the apostles grouped around her witness the Ascension from below. The inscription in the border in the middle of the page reads: ICI LES GARDAT NOSTRE DAME E LI APOSTLES.

Although this scene had been depicted continuously since the Early Christian period, the Winchester Ascension is closely modelled after Insular sources. The unusual motif of the 'disappearing Christ' was a highly characteristic feature of Insular iconography from the beginning of the eleventh century.[323] Not until the mid-twelfth century did the type, distinguished by a view limited to Christ's torso and feet, find general acceptance on the continent.[324] On the basis of the surviving monuments, it appears that the Winchester scene was based on both pre- and post-Conquest English models.

The Winchester Ascension shares a number of points of similarity[325] with the one in the Anglo-Saxon Sacramentary of Robert of Jumièges, fol. 81v (Fig. 139). The general arrangement of the Rouen Ascension portends the Winchester composition.

Christ's feet and the hem of his garment are encircled by a mandorla as they disappear from view. The Lord is flanked by two angels who point toward him. The Virgin stands in the centre of the composition directly under the ascending Christ. Although the disciples are crowded closely around her, a mandorla sets her apart from the group and emphasizes her importance. St Peter stands in a prominent position on the left, pointing to his key. The close correspondence of all these details to the Winchester Ascension make it evident that the composition as a whole follows a model firmly established in the Insular repertoire before the Conquest.

While the Winchester Ascension follows a type established in the Anglo-Saxon period, there are subtle indications that the artist also had access to a twelfth-century interpretation of the subject. Pembroke 120, fol. 5v (Fig. 140), best exemplifies the ways in which the Ascension scene was altered. The angels fly down and inward, pointing at Christ's feet.[326] The Winchester angels are quite similar, although the composition as a whole is more highly structured than that in Pembroke 120. The lower half of the Bury Ascension also varies from the Anglo-Saxon model. A greater sense of clarity and order prevails. The Virgin is still the central focus but it is no longer necessary to encircle her with a mandorla to distinguish her from the others. There is a void separating her from the apostles gathered on either side of her. This spatial division is also found in the Winchester Ascension. The Winchester Ascension could not, however, have been based entirely on the Bury model. Neither the mandorla encircling Christ, the key in Peter's hand nor the wavy ground line are present in the Bury Psalter.

Pentecost (Fig. 27), *Acts 2:1–11*

Peter sits in the centre of the assembled apostles. They look up toward the dove above Peter's head dispensing the gift of tongues. The scene is framed in an architectural setting. The inscription in the upper margin reads: ICI DESCENDIT LI SAINT ESPIRZ SUR LES APOSTLES.

The Pentecost scene is fashioned after sources of the Anglo-Saxon period, discussed in Chapter Two.

Christ in Majesty (Fig. 27)

Christ is seated on a rainbow. His feet rest on a support. He is bearded and holds a closed book on his knee. The figure is inscribed in a quatrefoil which, in turn, is surrounded by the four evangelist symbols in the following positions:

Man	Eagle
Ox	Lion

Inscription: ICI DEVS EN SA MAGESTE.

The scene has no direct connection to those from Echternach[327] or earlier continental examples.[328] Instead, it descends from a type well established in England before the Conquest. One example is found in Tiberius C.VI, fol. 126v (Fig. 144), accompanying Psalm 109. The other appears on an ivory in the Metropolitan Museum (Fig. 145).[329] Although the original quatrefoil frame has been damaged on the ivory, this example is especially important since both the rainbow and footstool found in the Winchester miniature are included here. While these Anglo-Saxon examples offer a clear precedent for most elements of the Winchester Majesty, they do not include the four evangelist symbols. The arrangement of the symbols in the Psalter deviates from the norm by reversing the positions of the lion and ox. This may have been due to the influence of an image based on the description in Ezekiel, since most representations of Ezekiel's vision show the lion and ox in these positions.[330] However, if this was the case, it migrated to this context at an early date and can be found occasionally in Majesty compositions from the eighth century onward.[331]

The Death of the Virgin (Fig. 28)

The Virgin rests on a bier surrounded by the apostles. Christ appears above her holding her soul. Two angels with veiled hands appear in the upper right and left. The hand of God is shown above the head of Christ. There is an open coffin below the bier. Inscription: ICI EST LA SVMTION DE NOSTRE DAME.

The death of the Virgin was celebrated as a major feast in the East before Iconoclasm. The earliest surviving images date from the tenth century.[332] Byzantine examples also made their way to the West at this time, among them the well-known ivory on the cover of the Gospels of Otto III.[333] In spite of their direct dependence upon Byzantine prototypes, most Western depictions soon assumed great variety and individuality.[334] The image in the Psalter deviates from this pattern by adhering with considerable fidelity to the traditional Byzantine feast picture. There are many points of similarity with contemporary Byzantine feast pictures, including the often cited parallel to the mosaic in the Martorana.[335] However, the architectural setting and mourning women included there are absent in the Psalter, precluding any definite connection with this particular example. One detail betrays an awareness of Western tradition. The coffin is never found in Byzantine Koimesis scenes but does appear in Western depictions of the Assumption of the Virgin.[336]

The Virgin Enthroned (Fig. 29)

The Virgin is seated and flanked by two angels carrying *labara.* Inscription: ICI EST FAITE REINE DEL CIEL.

Although the seated Virgin flanked by angels is an image known in the West from the fifth century,[337] this particular type is closely allied to medieval Byzantine examples. While such a connection has long been recognized, the comparisons have been fairly general since they usually drew parallels to the Virgin holding Christ.[338] The focus can be narrowed by considering only examples which depict the Virgin as she appears here, unaccompanied and seated with her hands raised before her. This type occurs far less frequently than the Mother and Child group. The type is relatively rare, even in the East, appearing in the eleventh century in monumental painting and manuscript illumination[339] and in the twelfth century in the Homilies of the Monk James.[340] She appears here several times, including an especially noteworthy depiction on fol. 66v, before whom Adam and Eve kneel, after the Anastasis (Fig. 146). The gestures and position of the standing angels have also been recognized as distinctly Byzantine.

Although there are no Western examples which predate the Winchester scene,[341] there is an indication that there may have been a Western intermediary. The drapery falls over the Virgin's legs in a pattern that is not entirely typical of English or Byzantine painting.[342] A close precedent for the teardrop shapes on the left knee and nested v folds on the right are found in France, as for example, in the Cluny Lectionary.[343]

The Last Judgment: the Dead Rising from their Graves (Fig. 30)

Angels appear blowing trumpets. The dead respond by climbing from coffins, arranged in five tiers. Inscription: ICI EST LA RESVRRECTION COMVNE AL IOR DE IVISE.

Like the New Testament scenes, the Last Judgment group continues to display characteristics most closely paralleled in Ottonian and English monuments. Although this scene is found in both Anglo-Saxon[344] and twelfth-century English monuments,[345] the page is more closely paralleled by one in the Perikope of Henry II.[346]

The Last Judgment: Six Apostles (Fig. 31)

The page is divided into six triangular segments, each of which encloses a seated apostle. Several point toward St Peter who sits in the upper, central section holding a key. Inscription: ICI SIENT LI APOSTLES PVR IVIER.

While the apostles are normally included in Last Judgment representations, they are typically found seated on either side of Christ or directly below him on long benches.[347] The arrangement here is more unusual. It has been suggested that the source was a wall painting or painted altarpiece.[348] While there are no visual examples which support these contentions, there is a precedent for this arrangement in the eleventh-century Grimbald Gospels, London, B.L., MS Add. 34890, fol. 114v (Fig. 149).[349] Here the apostles sit in groups of six in the right and left borders of the page. Christ appears above them flanked by angels. Such a formula could have been adapted to the special problems presented by the extended Last Judgment cycle in the Psalter.

The Last Judgment: Angels (Fig. 32)

Six angels carry symbols of the Passion. The angel in the upper left holds a flag and scourge, the second the crown of thorns, and the third a flag. In the lower segment, the first carries a pail for the vinegar, the second a spear and the angel to the left the nails. Inscription: ICI SVNT LI ANGLE.

The display of the instruments does appear in various forms in the early Middle Ages,[350] including a scene in the Aethelstan Psalter, fol. 21v (Fig. 150).[351] Here the lance and sponge flank Christ. However, the elaborate depiction in the Psalter is more typical of the Romanesque period. In other twelfth-century examples, angels holding instruments are included. At Clayton[352] (Fig. 151) they fly above Christ, in the Bury Gospels, fol. 5v (Fig. 152), they stand on either side of him. There is no precedent, however, for a full-page depiction of this subject or one which incorporates an equal number of references to the instruments of the Passion.

The Last Judgment: the Saved (Fig. 33)

The page is divided into two registers. In the upper half, the heads of men and women appear in seven rows. Some wear crowns or are tonsured. Below stand three bishops followed by three abbots. Inscription: ICIST SERVNT LA DESTREE DEV AL IVISE.

While it is hardly surprising to find this subject included here, the iconography is unusual in several respects. As Wormald observed, the upper portion is paralleled in the Aethelstan Psalter (Fig. 150). However, an important distinction must be drawn. The figures in the Anglo-Saxon manuscript represent choirs of intercessors, not the saved. The earlier image has, as a result, a different meaning for it suggests a visual representation of the litany. The connection with the twelfth-century image would involve the form alone. If such an early model did suggest this particular arrangement to the Winchester artist, it was certainly revised by adding contemporary details, many of which find their closest parallels in Mosan works of the mid-twelfth century.[353] The figures in the lower register are unusual in several respects. Rows of standing figures representing the choirs of the elect are usually led by an angel, as in the Bury Gospels (Fig. 152), at Burgfelden,[354] Clayton (Fig. 151) and Stowe 944.[355] These groups include laymen as well as ecclesiastics. The Winchester group omits any reference to the laity among the standing figures, thereby eliminating the emphasis in the earlier images upon the role of the church in achieving salvation for laymen.

The Last Judgment: Christ Displays his Wounds (Fig. 34)

Christ is seated within a mandorla. His partially undraped torso and open palms reveal the marks of the lance and nails. Inscription: ICI APAREIST DEVS EHVEM EN SA MAIESTE E MVSTRE LA PLAIE DE SVN LAZ.

The Aethelstan Psalter (Fig. 150) offers an Anglo-Saxon precedent for the undraped torso of Christ. This sets it apart from other Insular works or continental examples of the early eleventh century. The undraped torso becomes an increasingly common feature in the Romanesque period.[356] In certain respects, the Winchester figure is particularly close to another twelfth-century monument. In the Clayton wall painting (Fig. 151), Christ raises his hands before his body in a similar position.[357]

The Last Judgment: Angels Flank the Cross (Fig. 34)

An angel stands on either side of the cross which is supported upon a draped base. Inscription: ICI MOSTRENT LI ANGEL LI CRVIZ NOSTRE SEIGNVR.

Although the cross is normally found closely associated with the figure of Christ,[358] there are precedents for the arrangement found in the Psalter. An eleventh-century ivory in Cambridge does show the cross below Christ.[359] While the flying positions of the Cambridge angels differ, angels do stand flanking the cross at Plumpton,[360] Clayton (Fig. 151), and on the seal of Waltham Abbey.[361]

The Last Judgment: Six Apostles (Fig. 35)

Six apostles are shown as on fol. 32. Inscription: ICI SIENT LI AVTRE APOSTLE PVR IVGIER.

The Last Judgment: the Damned (Fig. 36)

The scene follows the arrangement employed for the Saved on fol. 34. Inscription: ICIST SERVNT A LA SENESTRE DAM LE DEV AL IVISE.

The Last Judgment: the Torment of the Damned (Fig. 37)

Devils inflict a variety of punishments on men and women. Inscription: ICI EMMEINENT LI DEIABLE LES DAMNEZ EN ENFERS.

The subject was depicted sporadically in the early Middle Ages but the images only increased in vividness and violence in the eleventh century. It is at this time that the ferocious, animalistic devil becomes a characteristic feature of these scenes. There are examples on the continent (Fig. 114) as well as in Anglo-Saxon England. The examples here follow long-established Insular conventions. Similar creatures appear before the Conquest in the Bury Psalter, Rome, B.A.V., MS Vat. Reg. lat. 12, the Marvels of the East, London, B.L., MSS Tiberius B.V, and Tiberius C.VI.[362] The type continues to appear over the course of the early twelfth century, for example, in the St Albans Psalter and Bury leaves.[363] All of these examples offer general precedents, although the most consistent characteristic of these creatures in Romanesque art is the degree of individuality displayed in the configuration of potentially harmful features like horns, teeth and claws.

Some of the tortures applied to the damned are somewhat more predictable. The punishment for unchastity, showing a woman on the shoulders of a devil and the presence of a biting serpent, are frequently encountered on the continent as well as in Britain.[364] The cauldron is another feature included in earlier depictions.[365] More unusual is the scene in the lower left where two devils chop off the hands of a male victim. This is a punishment which would have rung a chord of response in the twelfth century since it was a sentence encountered in contemporary English law.[366]

The Last Judgment: the Angel Locking the Damned in Hell
(Fig. 38)

The angel stands on the left swinging shut and locking the door at the mouth of Hell. Within, the damned, including kings, queens, laymen and monks, are tormented by devils. Inscription: ICI EST ENFERS E LI ANGELS KI ENFERME LES PORTES.

The representation of Hell as the mouth of an animal is apparently an Insular invention that, as discussed above, can be traced back to the Anglo-Saxon period. The torments of the damned within the confines of Hell is found a century earlier in the Marvels of the East.[367] The motif of the angel locking the door of Hell is found, as Wormald noted, in the Winchester *Liber Vitae*.[368] The motif was more widespread than the single extant visual prototype suggests. It is also encountered in the elaborate descriptions of the Doom in Anglo-Saxon poetry.[369]

Appendix A: Measurements of the Miniatures

The measurements are of the picture space, not including the borders, and are given in centimetres. The first measurement is for the miniature in the upper register. Any measurements that follow are for the middle and/or lower registers, in that order.

Fol. 2	6.8 × 14; 7.6 × 14; 7.8 × 14
Fol. 3	6.8 × 14; 7.6 × 14; 7.8 × 14
Fol. 4	7.7 × 14.2; 7.8 × 14.2; 7.8 × 14.2
Fol. 5	8 × 14.4; 7.9 × 14.4; 7.2 × 14.4
Fol. 6	13.9 × 14.4; 15.3 × 14.4
Fol. 7	11.5 × 13.3; 12.2 × 13.3
Fol. 8	7.8 × 14.8; 8.5 × 14.8; 7.8 × 14.8
Fol. 9	27.2 × 15
Fol. 10	12 × 15.2; 11.8 × 15.2
Fol. 11	10.8 × 14.8; 2.8 × 14.8; 11 × 14.8
Fol. 12	9.6 × 13.7; 2.5 × 13.7; 10 × 13.7
Fol. 13	10.6 × 14.7; 10.9 × 14.7
Fol. 14	12 × 14.2; 12.5 × 14.5
Fol. 15	11 × 15; 2.2 × 15; 11 × 14.9
Fol. 16	12 × 14; 2.5 × 14; 10 × 14
Fol. 17	10 × 14.3; 2.3 × 14.3; 11.2 × 14
Fol. 18	10.9 × 14; 2.5 × 14; 11 × 14
Fol. 19	11.7 × 14; 11.5 × 14
Fol. 20	14.5 × 14.3; 9.5 × 14.1
Fol. 21	12 × 14.2; 11.5 × 14.2
Fol. 22	11.9 × 14.5; 11.5 × 14.5
Fol. 23	11.9 × 14; 12 × 14
Fol. 24	11.9 × 14.5; 11.5 × 14.5
Fol. 25	11.6 × 13.5; 11.5 × 13.5
Fol. 26	11.5 × 13.5; 1.5 × 13.5; 10.1 × 13.5
Fol. 27	11.5 × 13.5; 11.5 × 13.5
Fol. 28	11 × 13; 11 × 13.7
Fol. 29	17.5 × 26.9
Fol. 30	17.5 × 27.5
Fol. 31	17 × 27.9
Fol. 32	12 × 14; 11.8 × 14
Fol. 33	12.2 × 14.5; 12.3 × 14.5
Fol. 34	11.5 × 14; 11.1 × 14
Fol. 35	11 × 14; 11.8 × 14
Fol. 36	11.8 × 13.5; 11.5 × 13.3
Fol. 37	11.5 × 13.5; 11.2 × 13
Fol. 38	11 × 14.5; 11 × 14
Fol. 39	14 × 23.5

Appendix B: Infra-red Analysis of the Inks

The tests on the inks in the Winchester Psalter were performed under a video spectral comparator in the British Library Conservation centre by Anthony Parker, the Conservation Officer. The measurements (given in nanometers) indicate the rate at which the inks in the Winchester Psalter absorb infra-red rays. In testing the black inks, Mr Parker passed light through a LP 1 lamp using the FS 1 infra-red filter bank. For the red inks, he used an LP 1 lamp with a blue-green filter together with the FS 3 filter bank.

The text ink faded at 780 nm and disappeared at 1000 nm.
The Latin inscription ink faded at 780 nm and disappeared at 1000 nm.
The miniature ink faded at 780 nm and disappeared at 1000 nm.
The French inscription ink faded at 830 nm and was still faintly visible at 1000 nm, the highest reading obtainable with this machine.
The ink for large set of Roman numerals faded at 715 nm and was still faintly visible at 1000 nm.
The ink for the smaller set of Roman numerals faded at 630 nm and disappeared at 715 nm.
The ink for the Arabic numerals was still visible at 1000 nm.
The mark on the David miniature (fol. 7) faded at 830 nm and was still faintly visible at 1000 nm.
The red ink used for titles in the text was visible between 455 nm and 570 nm.
The red ink used for the rubric on 142v was visible between 455 nm and 610 nm.

Appendix C: Description of the Verdigris Offsets

The offsets described below are visible only when a fibre-optic lamp is held behind the page in question. The marks are on the back side, not the surface of the vellum.

The arch over Noah (2.5 cm in length) on fol. 3 was imprinted over the angel's wings on fol. 2. The mark here is also 2.5 cm long.

The arch behind Joseph on fol. 5 was imprinted on the Moses page (fol. 4).

The skirt of David on fol. 6 was imprinted on the lion's hind legs on fol. 7.

The decorative border motif on fol. 8 was imprinted on fol. 9.

The .4 cm oval curve on the wing of an angel on fol. 11 was imprinted above the angel in the Sending of the Angel scene on fol. 10. The mark here is also .4 cm in length.

The border pattern from fol. 12 was imprinted on fol. 13.

The border pattern from fol. 15 was imprinted on fol. 14.

A gable and window under it in on fol. 17 were imprinted above the angel on fol. 16.

Three windows and a wall in a building on fol. 19 were imprinted on the leg of the devil in the third Temptation on fol. 18.

The border pattern of fol. 21 was imprinted on fol. 20.

The arms of the cross on fol. 22, 8 cm in length, were imprinted onto fol. 23 beginning on the wing of the angel, and extending 8 cm.

The tree on fol. 24 was imprinted onto fol. 25.

The pattern on the Virgin's robe, fol. 27, was imprinted onto Christ, fol. 26.

The border of fol. 28 was imprinted onto the figure of St Paul, fol. 29.

The border of fol. 31 was imprinted onto the inner margin of fol. 30.

The shield-shaped shading on the leg of an apostle seated in the centre of fol. 32 was imprinted onto fol. 33 between the angel to the left and the one to the centre.

The robe of a bishop on fol. 34 was imprinted onto the ground next to an angel on fol. 35.

Patterns of lines on the apostle to the left on fol. 36 were imprinted on the monk to the right on fol. 37.

The motif from the border of fol. 38 was imprinted onto the border of fol. 39.

Appendix D: Catalogue of the Additions to the Paint Surfaces

Fol. 2: The background of the top panel was originally painted green. It was later overpainted in blue, probably azurite. This pigment and other blue pigments were also used to paint over the grounds of most of the other miniatures and will not be noted separately for each miniature. Red lead was applied to the border and frames surrounding the picture space. White lead was added to the jawbone. Gold was added to the hems of garments, haloes, crowns and the borders of the picture space.

Fol. 3: Red lead was added to Noah's robe. Gold was added to hems, haloes and the borders of the picture space.

Fol. 4: Red lead was added to the borders. Gold was added to hems, haloes, crowns and the borders of the picture space.

Fol. 5: Slate blue and white lead were added to the angel's robes. Gold was added to hems, haloes, crowns and the borders of the picture space.

Fol. 6: Red lead was added to the shield of Goliath in both scenes. Gold was added to cuffs, hems and the borders of the picture space.

Fol. 7: Red lead was added to David's cloak, Jesse's staff, the tree and the borders. Gold was added to hems and the borders of the picture space.

Fol. 8: Red lead was added to a building originally tinted with verdigris. Gold was added to hems and the borders of the picture space.

Fol. 9: Gold was added to hems, crowns and the borders of the picture space.

Fol. 10: Red lead was added to the architecture. Gold was added to haloes, hems and the borders of the picture space.

Fol. 11: Red lead was added to the middle strip. Gold was added to crowns, hems and the borders of the picture space.

Fol. 12: Gold was added to crowns, hems and the borders of the picture space.

Fol. 13: Gold was added to crowns, hems and the borders of the picture space.

Fol. 14: Red lead was added to the architecture. Gold was added to haloes, crowns, hems and the borders of the picture space.

Fol. 15: Red lead was added to the architecture. Gold was added to haloes, hems and the borders of the picture space.

Fol. 16: Red lead was added to the sleeve of the garment held by the angel. Gold was added to haloes, hems and the borders of the picture space.

Fol. 17: Gold was added to hems, drinking vessels and the borders of the picture space.

Fol. 18: Red lead was added to Christ's sleeve. Gold was added to hems and the borders of the picture space.

Fol. 19: Blue, possibly azurite, was added below the coffin. Gold was added to hems and the borders of the picture space.

Fol. 20: Red lead was added to Christ's

sleeve. Gold was added to hems and the borders of the picture space.

Fol. 21: Gold was added to hems, the column and the borders of the picture space.

Fol. 22: White lead and an olive green pigment was added to the faces of the two women. Gold was added to hems and the borders of the picture space.

Fol. 23: Red lead, an olive green pigment, and a purple pigment were added to faces and garments. Gold was added to hems and the borders of the picture space.

Fol. 24: Red lead was added to Christ's garments and staff. Gold was added to hems and the borders of the picture space.

Fol. 25: Red lead was added to the architecture. White lead was added to the faces. Red lead and a lavender pigment were added to the garments. Gold was added to hems and the borders of the picture space.

Fol. 26: Red lead was added to the architecture. Gold was added to hems and the borders of the picture space.

Fol. 27: Purple and green pigments were added to the garments. Gold was added to hems and the borders of the picture space.

Fol. 28: Red lead was added to the architecture. Gold was added to hems and the borders of the picture space.

Fol. 29: There are no additions.

Fol. 30: There are no additions.

Fol. 31: Purple pigment was added to the robes. Gold was added to hems, haloes and the borders of the picture space.

Fol. 32: Red lead was added to the sleeves. Gold was added to hems, haloes and the borders of the picture space.

Fol. 33: Red lead, purple and green pigments were added to the robes. Gold was added to haloes, instruments of the Passion, hems and the borders of the picture space.

Fol. 34: Red lead was added to the sleeves. Gold was added to crowns and the borders of the picture space.

Fol. 35: Red lead, green and purple pigments were added to the robes. Gold was added to haloes, hems and the borders of the picture space.

Fol. 36: Red lead was added to the sleeves. Gold was added to haloes, hems and the borders of the picture space.

Fol. 37: Red lead was added to the ground line. Gold was added to crowns and the borders of the picture space.

Fol. 38: Red lead was added to the flames. Gold was added to the borders of the picture space.

Fol. 39: Red lead was added to the door and flames. Gold was added to hems, door and the borders of the picture space.

Notes

Chapter One: Description of the Manuscript, Reconstruction of the Miniature Cycle

1. The dimensions are given in Appendix A.
2. Wormald, *Winchester*, 87.
3. An analysis of the pigments and inks in the manuscript was made in the British Library conservation centre. The author would like to express her sincere thanks to the conservation officer, Anthony Parker, for patiently undertaking this time-consuming task. A partial description of the pigments was given by A.D. Laurie, *The Pigments and Mediums of the Old Masters* (1914), 86. The results of infra-red analysis of the inks discussed in this chapter are given in Appendix B. A description of the equipment used is given by Victor S. Carter, 'A review of a recently acquired optical examination aid in the British Library', *The Direction Line, 10* (1980), 1–3. For an example of the application of this technique to manuscripts see Lotte Hellinga, *Caxton in Focus* (1982).
4. The author would like to thank Julian Brown for examining the Psalter and offering suggestions on questions concerning the various types of script found throughout the manuscript. She, however, accepts full responsibility for all the opinions expressed here.
5. The author would like to thank Janet Backhouse for pointing out this example. Also see C.E. Wright, 'The dispersal of the libraries in the sixteenth century', in *The English Library before 1700*, ed. F. Wormald and C.E. Wright (1958), 155.
6. A description of the verdigris offsets is given in Appendix C.
7. On the French text see B. Woledge and H.P. Clive, *Répertoire des plus anciens textes en prose française depuis 842 jusqu'aux premières années du XIIIe siècle* (Geneva, 1964), 97–8; Dorothy A. Sneddon, 'The Anglo-Norman psalters: I. a note on the relationship between the Oxford and Arundel Psalters', *Romania, 99* (1978), 396–400; I. Short, 'Liste provisoire de manuscrits du XIIe siècle contenant des textes en langue française', *Romania, 102* (1981), 10.
8. V. Leroquais, *Les psautiers manuscrits dans les bibliothèques publiques de France* (3 vols., Mâcon, 1940–1), I, lxxxix. Also see Wormald, *Winchester*, 93.
9. *Ibid.*, 9–13. In addition to the parallels for the Latin prayers pointed out by Wormald, there are others in a manuscript with a Winchester calendar in Madrid, MS Vit. 23–28. Several prayers are comparable, particularly one addressed to St Faith, fol. 153. See Kauffmann, *Romanesque* (1975), 104–5. On the French prayers see E. Brayer and E.M. Bouly de Lisdain, 'Les prières usuelles annexées aux anciennes traductions françaises du psautier', *Bulletin de l'Institut de recherche et d'histoire des textes, 15* (1967–68), 69–120; Woledge and Clive, *op.cit.*, 80.
10. See Wormald, *Winchester*, figs. 100

and 102. A parallel situation to the one described here is found in the Worms Bible. The scribe drew the initials, then the same individual copied the text. Aliza Cohen-Mushlin, *The Making of a Manuscript: the Worms Bible of 1148* (Wiesbaden, 1983), 75.

11. E.A. Bond and E.M. Thompson, *The Palaeographical Society. Facsimilies of Manuscripts and Inscriptions* (3 vols., 1873–83), III, pl. 124.
12. T.S.R. Boase, *English Art 1100–1216* (1953), 53. On the date also see Andrew Watson, *Catalogue of Dated and Datable Manuscripts c.700–1600 in the Department of Manuscripts, The British Library* (2 vols., 1979), I, 109.
13. Wormald, *Winchester*, 107, 123.
14. Nigel Morgan, 'Notes on the post-Conquest calendar, litany and martyrology of the cathedral priory of Winchester with a consideration of Winchester diocese calendars of the pre-Sarum period', in *The Vanishing Past: Studies in Medieval Art, Liturgy and Metrology Presented to Christopher Hohler*, ed. A. Borg and A. Martindale (1981), 153; K.E. Haney, 'The provenance of the Psalter of Henry of Blois', *Manuscripta, 24* (1980), 40–4.
15. Since the early part of the century it has been suggested by a number of scholars that the Psalter was made for Henry of Blois, bishop of Winchester from 1129 to 1171. J.A. Herbert was the first to raise this possibility in his *Schools of Illumination. Reproductions from Manuscripts in the British Museum. Part II. English 12th and 13th Centuries* (1916), 6. This theory was restated in numerous publications, including that of Wormald, *Winchester*, 107. However, more recently, questions have been raised regarding such a connection, as for example, by M. Kauffmann in *Romanesque* (1984), 118–19. Since there is no documentary evidence to either prove or disprove this theory, the identity of the patron must remain an open question. Whoever this individual was, he had close ties to Winchester, considerable capital and access to the Winchester priory library. While this description may fit Henry, it could equally apply to another, as for example, the prior of Winchester.
16. See Woledge and Clive, *op.cit.*, 94–8. On the use of French in twelfth-century English monasteries see Michael Richter, *Sprache und Gesellschaft im Mittelalter* (Stuttgart, 1979), 92–4. The author would like to thank Ian Short for drawing this reference to her attention.
17. Edward Edwards, *The Lives of the Founders of the British Museum* (1870), 53.
18. Gertrude Rawlings, *The British Museum Library* (1916), 28.
19. Wormald and Wright, *op.cit.*, 151.
20. Wormald, *Winchester*, 69.
21. Mara R. Witzling, 'An archaeological reconstruction of a previous state of the Winchester Psalter', *Gesta, 17* (1978), 29.
22. Wormald, *Winchester*, 69.
23. Witzling, *op. cit.*, 30.
24. Kauffmann, *Romanesque*, 68, 82.
25. *Ibid.*, 106.
26. There are two possible ways in which sheets of vellum can be split. Stretching a skin under tension to produce vellum results in the rearrangement of the fibre bundles of the skin into parallel layers. This makes it possible to tear wet vellum fairly easily into several thinner laminae. Alternatively, a machine can be

employed. Splitting a skin by machine, in other words, subdividing the usable layer, the *stratum corium*, into two or even three thinner sheets was the procedure normally followed in the nineteenth-century preparation of leather. The hides were soaked for up to two weeks. They could then be split with the aid of a band splitting machine, introduced in 1810. The machine consisted essentially of an endless band knife which revolved at considerable speed with its cutting edges close to the sides of a pair of rollers through which the skin was fed and pressed against the knife. There are several considerations which point away from the division of the Winchester leaves in either manner. The clean edges and uniform thickness of all 38 leaves point away from the potential imprecision inherent in manual splitting. A band splitting machine would doubtless have damaged the paint surfaces. Furthermore, neither of these procedures is possible unless the leaves are soaking wet. If the leaves had been soaked for the length of time necessary to render them divisible, virtually all of the water soluble paint would have dissolved. Nor is it likely that a mid-nineteenth-century bookman would have applied such a procedure to a manuscript. Splitting skins by machine did not become a uniformly accepted practice for the preparation of vellum until the end of the last century. See R. Reed, *Ancient Skins Parchments and Leathers* (1972), 46, 120; Daniel Thompson, 'Medieval parchment-making', *The Library, 16* (1935), 115; C. Sirat, 'La paléographie hébraïque médiévale', *Colloques internationaux du Centre national de la recherche scientifique, 547* (1972), 135; Edward Johnston, *Writing and Illuminating, and Lettering* (1906), 140.

27. R. Calkins, *Illuminated Books of the Middle Ages* (Ithaca, 1983), 42; Jean Porcher, *Les manuscrits à peintures en France du viie au xiie siècle* (Paris, 1954), 81; Leroquais, *op.cit.*, I, 16; J. Vezin, *Les scriptoria d'Angers au xie siècle* (Paris, 1974), 233–5; B. Abou-El-Haj, 'Conservation and investiture in the life of Saint Amand, Valenciennes, Bibl. Mun. MS 502', *Art Bulletin, 61* (1979), 342–58; Kauffmann, *Romanesque*, 117; Florens Deuchler, *Der Ingeborgpsalter* (Berlin, 1967).
28. Wormald, *Winchester*, 69.
29. Temple, *Anglo-Saxon Manuscripts*, 115.
30. Carl Nordenfalk, 'Recent publications on illuminated manuscripts', *The Burlington Magazine, 117* (1975), 609.
31. Mara Witzling, 'An archaeological investigation of the Winchester Psalter' (Ph.D. thesis, Cornell University, 1976), 57, 78, 155–8; *idem*, 'The Winchester Psalter: a re-ordering of its prefatory miniatures according to the scriptural sequence', *Gesta, 23* (1984), 17–25.
32. H. Kühn, 'Verdigris and copper resinate', *Studies in Conservation, 15* (1970), 12–36.
33. Witzling, 'An archaeological investigation', *op.cit.*, 62. See Appendix C for a description of the verdigris offsets.
34. Fols. 26–39.
35. Incomplete manuscripts from the twelfth century are not uncommon. A parallel situation is offered by the Winchester Bible. The mid-twelfth-century

artist completed the pen outlines for a number of drawings but only a small number were painted at the beginning of the manuscript. See Kauffmann, *Romanesque*, 110.

36. These figures are found on fols. 5, 23, 28, 30, 34, 35, 36 and 37. See Appendix D for a description of the additions to the paint surfaces.
37. As, for example, in the Lambeth Bible, Lambeth Palace Library, MS 3. Many miniatures are fully painted including the one on fol. 198. Others as on fol. 306 were tinted. See Kauffmann, *Romanesque*, 99.
38. An example on fol. 11 offers the only variant for the letter A.
39. Examples of some of these forms appear in Watson, *op.cit.*, II, pls. 63, 65, 88, 146.
40. *Ibid.*, pls. 79, 93, 115.
41. The author would like to express her sincere thanks to Ian Short for examining the French inscriptions and preparing a statement regarding their date for this publication.

Chapter Two: The Iconography of the Old and New Testament Scenes

1. J. J. Tikkanen, 'Die Genesismosaiken von San Marco in Vendig und ihr Verhältnis zu den Miniaturen der Cottonbibel', *Acta Societatis Scientarium Fennicae, 17* (1889), 205–358; K. Weitzmann, 'Observations on the Cotton Genesis fragments', *Late Classical and Medieval Studies in Honor of Albert Mathias Friend Jr.* (Princeton, 1955), 112–131; *idem*, 'The mosaics of San Marco and the Cotton Genesis', *Venezia e l'europa*, Atti del XVIII congresso internazionale di storia dell'arte (Venice, 1956), 152–3; *idem*, in volume II of Otto Demus recent work, *The Mosaics of San Maraco in Venice* (Chicago, 1984), 50–70; W.R. Lethaby, 'The painted book of Genesis in the British Museum', *Archaeological Journal, 69* (1912), 88; Sahoko Tsuji, 'Un essai d'identification des sujets des miniatures fragmentaires de la Genèse de Cotton', *Bijutsushi, Journal of the Japan Art History Society, 17* (1967), 34–94; *idem*, 'La chaire de Maximien, la Genèse de Cotton et les mosäiques de Saint-Marc à Venise', *Synthronon* (Paris, 1968), 43–51; *idem*, 'Nouvelles observations sur les miniatures fragmentaire de la Genèse de Cotton cycles de Lot, d'Abraham, et de Jacob', *Cahiers Archéologiques, 29* (1970), 29–45; K. Koshi, *Die Genesis-miniaturen in der Wiener 'Histoire Universelle'* (Vienna, 1973); *idem*, 'Der Adam-und-Eva Zyklos in der sogennanten Cotton Genesis-Rezension: ein übersicht über mögliche mitgleider der verzweigten Cotton Genesis Familie', *Bulletin annuel du Musée national d'art occidental, 10* (1975), 48–87. The literature on the relationship of the Cotton group to the Winchester Psalter as well as other theories about its Old Testament cycle has recently been summarized by K.E. Haney, 'Some old testament pictures in the Psalter of Henry of Blois', *Gesta, 24* (1985), 33–45.
2. Koehler, *Die karolingischen*, I(2), 186–212; H. Kessler, *The Illustrated Bibles from Tours* (Princeton, 1977), figs. 1–3.
3. *Ibid.*, fig. 4.
4. See H. Kessler, 'An eleventh-century ivory plaque from South Italy and the Cassinese revival', *Jahrbuch der Berliner Museen, 8* (1966), 80.

5. Hella Voss, *Studien zur illustrierten Millstätter Genesis und Physiologus Handschrift* (Graz, 1967); H. Menhardt, 'Die Bilder der Millstätter Genesis und ihre Verwandten', *Beiträge zur älteren europäischen Kulturgeschichte: Festschrift für Rudolf Egger*, ed. G. Moro (3 vols., Klagenfurt, 1954), III, 248–371; Kracher, *Millstätter.*
6. S. Waetzoldt, *Die Kopien des 17. Jahrhunderts nach Mosaiken und Wandmalereien in Rom* (Munich, 1964), fig. 336. Also see Joseph Garber, *Wirkungen der frühchristlichen Gemäldezyklen der alten Peters- und Pauls- Basiliken in Rom* (Berlin, 1918) and B. Al-Hamdani, 'The iconographical sources for the Genesis frescoes once found in San Paolo fuori le mura', *Atti del IX congresso internazionale de archeologia cristiana* (Vatican City, 1978), 11–35. She compares the scene to that in the Millstatt Genesis.
7. G. Folena and G. Melini, *Bibbia istoriata padovana* (Venice, 1963), pl. 5; G. Henderson, 'The sources of the Genesis cycle at Saint-Savin-sur-Gartempe', *JBAS, 26* (1963), 26, pl. XIII, 6.
8. Bergman, *Salerno*, 22, has interpreted the lack of an altar in this scene as a connection with the Octateuch tradition. Also see Hesseling, *Miniatures*, fig. 24 and Ouspensky, *Octateuque*, fig. 28.
9. It is found in the Roda Bible, discussed below, as well as the fourteenth-century Velislav Bible, Prague, University Library MS XXIII.C.124. See W.O. Hassal, *The Holkham Bible Picture Book* (1954), 25. The author cites Otto Pächt who suggested that the Bible probably follows English models because it contains many parallels with both the Vienna Genesis and Cotton Genesis, assuming that it would be unlikely that there would have been two separate antique models. There are, in fact, a number of similarities between the scenes in the Velislav Bible and Caedmon, including the Creation of Eve, Adam and Eve in the Garden after the Fall, the Calling, Expulsion and Cain and Abel. The connection to the Cotton tradition has also been mentioned recently by H. Kessler, 'Traces of an early illustrated Pentateuch', *Journal of Jewish Art, 8* (1981), n.19. For illustrations of the Velislav Bible see *Velislai Biblia Picta*, ed. Karl Stejskal (Prague, 1970).
10. Bergman, *Salerno*, 25, fig. 17. This can be contrasted to the version in the Octateuchs where the angel is not winged in the combat scene. See Hesseling, *Miniatures*, fig. 111.
11. The figure of Jacob was reversed in the Winchester scene. A similar phenomena occurs at Malmesbury. It has been suggested that this reflects workshop practices for transferring patterns, see J.K. Galbraith, 'The iconography of the biblical scenes at Malmesbury Abbey', *JBAS, 28* (1965), 40.
12. As, for example, in the Octateuchs. See Hesseling, *Miniatures*, fig. 49; Ouspensky, *Octateuque*, fig. 57; Rome, B.A.V., MSS gr. 746, fol. 47; gr. 747, fol. 50.
13. Kracher, *Millstätter*, 38r. (The fol. numbers are the plate references in this publication.)
14. Waetzoldt, *op.cit.*, fig. 345.
15. A. Ferrua, *Le pitture della nuova catacomba di Via Latina* (Rome, 1960); Lieselotte Kötzche-Breitenbruch, *Die Neue Katakombe an der Via Latina in Rom* (Münster, 1976), 67, and K. and U.

Schubert, 'Die Vertreibung aus dem Paradies in der Katacombe der Via Latina in Rom', in *Christianity, Judaism, and Other Greco-Roman Cults: Studies for Morton Smith at Sixty*, ed. J. Leusner (Leiden, 1975), 173–80 who emphasize the relation of elements of the Via Latina catacomb to the Cotton Genesis tradition.

16. Kötszche-Breitenbruch, *op.cit.*, pl. 112b.
17. Wilpert, *I sarcofagi*, II, 5; fig. 117.
18. Volbach, *Spätantike*, 106.
19. According to H. Severin, 'Oströmische Reliefs mit Darstellungen des Abrahamsopfers', *Bulletin du Musée hongrois des beaux-arts*, *36* (1971), 44, the representation of Isaac kneeling on the altar with both knees is a relatively late development appearing in the West at the end of the fourth or early fifth century. Hans-Jürgen Geischer, 'Heidenische Parallelen zum frühchristlichen Bild des Isaakopfers', *Jahrbuch für Antike und Christentum*, *10* (1967), 133, also sees the type as a variant on the older version where Isaac kneels in profile.
20. Examples of the type found in the Psalter are illustrated by Wilpert, *I sarcofagi*, pls. LXXXII, 3; CXXI, 4; CXXVII, 2.
21. Both K. Weitzmann, 'The survival of mythological representations in Early Christian and Byzantine art and their impact on Christian iconography', *Dumbarton Oaks Papers*, *14* (1960), 43–68, and Geischer, *op.cit.*, discussed the possibility that classical prototypes lie behind the iconography for the sacrifice of Isaac. They cited parallels with pagan sacrificial scenes and execution scenes like those on the column of Marcus Aurelius.
22. Charles R. Morey, *The Gold-Glass Collection of the Vatican Library* (Vatican City, 1959), pl. 12.
23. Otto Demus, *Die Mosaiken von San Marco in Vendig 1100–1200* (Baden bei Wien, 1935), fig. 46.
24. Kracher, *Millstätter*, 55r.
25. Folena and Melini, *op.cit.*, pl. 62.
26. The standing type is also found in the Octateuchs. Hesseling, *Miniatures*, fig. 125; Ouspensky, *Octateuque*, fig. 66; Rome, B.A.V., MSS gr. 746, fol. 121v; gr. 747, fol. 60r.
27. Garber, *op.cit.*, 72–5.
28. Hans Gerstinger, *Die Wiener Genesis* (Vienna, 1931); there is also a recent facsimile edited by O. Mazal, *Wiener Genesis* (Frankfurt, 1980). Kötzsche-Breitenbruch, *op.cit.*, 71–3 also ties the Vienna Joseph scenes to those in the Via Latina catacomb.
29. An ivory box in Sens Cathedral parallels the arrangement of the figures in the second scene and includes a scene of Joseph led from prison, although somewhat differently. See the catalogue for a more detailed discussion of these scenes. Gerstinger, *op.cit.*, pl. 36. Although this scene had originally been identified as Joseph interpreting the dream of pharaoh, it has been pointed out by O. Pächt in 'Ephraim illustration, Haggah und Wiener Genesis', *Festschrift Karl M. Swoboda zum 28 Januar 1959* (Vienna, 1959), 219, that since the preceding scene on page 35 clearly represents the dream sequence, the following scene must illustrate the text passage referring to pharaoh honouring Joseph.
30. Similar ideas have been discussed by Koehler, *Die karolingischen* and Bergman, *Salerno*, among others.

31. Israel Gollancz, *The Caedmon Manuscript of Anglo-Saxon Biblical Poetry* (1927); Temple, *Anglo-Saxon Manuscripts*, 76–8, and H. Broderick, 'The iconographic and compositional sources of the drawings in Oxford, Bodleian Library, MS Junius 11' (Ph.D. thesis, Columbia University, 1978).
32. Dodwell and Clemoes, *Hexateuch*, 65–75; Temple, *Anglo-Saxon Manuscripts*, 102–3.
33. Dodwell and Clemoes, *Hexateuch*, 65.
34. For San Marco see S. Bettini, *Mosaici antichi de San Marco a Venezia* (Bergamo, 1955), pl. LVIII; for San Paolo see Waetzoldt, *op.cit.*, fig. 338; for the Millstatt Genesis see Kracher, *Millstätter*, 21r.
35. Bergman, *Salerno*, fig. 8.
36. *Ibid.*, fig. 71.
37. Waetzoldt, *op.cit.*, fig. 339.
38. Bergman, *Salerno*, fig. 8.
39. Kracher, *Millstätter*, 21r.
40. W. Neuss, *Die Katalanische Bibelillustration und die Wende des ersten Jahrtausends und die altspanische Buchmalerei* (Bonn, 1922); Walter Cahn, *Romanesque Bible Illustration* (Ithaca, 1982), 292.
41. See Neuss, *op.cit.*, 18, for a discussion of the common iconographical cycle shared by the two manuscripts. Walter Cook noticed the relationship of the Roda Bible to English works in 'The earliest painted panels of Catalonia', *Art Bulletin*, *5* (1923), 92–105. While Cook linked the Roda Bible to the Caedmon manuscript, the basis of comparison was limited to stylistic details. He concluded that the influence of English illustrations was apparent in the style of the Spanish manuscripts. Additional links between the Roda Bible and English monuments were pointed out by E.W. Tristram, *English Medieval Wall Painting* (1944), 27. He observed that the elders in the wall paintings at Hardham in Sussex closely resembled those in the Roda Bible. More recently, M. Kauffmann, *Romanesque*, 39, observed that the illustrations for the books of prophets in the Lambeth and Winchester Bibles are found in the Roda Bible but do not exist elsewhere.
42. The relationship between the Catalan Bibles and the Cotton Genesis tradition was overlooked by Neuss. It was noticed, however, by Tikkanen, *op.cit.*, 123. Tikkanen cited, among others, the scenes of God moulding the body of Adam and driving the sinners from Paradise. Also see Henderson, *op.cit.*, 16.
43. Buchthal, *Paris Psalter*; Gude Suckale-Redlefsen, 'Die Bilderzyklen zum Davidleben von den Anfangen bis zum Ende des 11 Jahrhunderts' (Ph.D. thesis, Munich, 1972), 48.
44. In 'Prolegomena to a study of the Cyprus plates', *Metropolitan Museum Journal*, *3* (1970), 109, K. Weitzmann gives this identification. A different interpretation was given by Jean Lassus in *L'Illustration byzantine du livre des rois, Vaticanus Graecus 333* (Paris, 1973), 52. He describes the scene as representing I Kings 18:37, where David describes his exploits to Saul, because the illustration is inserted in the text column in the middle of verse 37. There are several objections to his interpretation, however. The relationship of picture to text does not follow a consistent pattern in gr. 333. Some illustrations precede the passage and others follow it, so that the placement is not an

absolute standard for attribution. In addition, there are a number of features in the scene which fit much better with the later scene. David has the shepherd's bag, crook and sling described in verse 40. The figure standing behind him holds the suit of chain mail. Lassus ignored these details, casting doubt upon his interpretation.

45. Anthony Cutler, 'The psalter of Basil II', *Arte Venetia, 30* (1976), 12–13.
46. Buchthal, *op.cit.*, 61; Suckale-Redlefsen, *op.cit.*, 74; J. Gaede, 'The Touronian sources of the Bible of San Paolo fuori le mura in Rome', *Frühmittelalterliche Studien, 5* (1971), 359–400.
47. Temple, *Anglo-Saxon Manuscripts*, 81–2; Kauffmann, *Romanesque*, 96.
48. See J.J.G. Alexander, *Insular Manuscripts 6th to the 9th Century* (1978), 74, for recent opinions on this manuscript. It has been argued that the Corbie Psalter shows Insular influence on Carolingian painting, or just the opposite. Jean Porcher, 'L'Evangéliaire de Charlemagne et le psautier d'Amiens', *La Revue des arts, 7* (1957), 55.
49. Temple, *Anglo-Saxon Manuscripts*, 84–5.
50. Rainer Kahsnitz, *Der Werdener Psalter in Berlin, MS theol. lat. fol. 358* (Düsseldorf, 1979).
51. Suzy Dufrenne, *Les illustrations du psautier d'Utrecht* (Paris, 1978).
52. D.H. Wright, *The Vespasian Psalter* (Copenhagen, 1967); Alexander, *op.cit.*, 55.
53. For the Byzantine type see Millet, *Recherches*, 92.
54. Also see A. Goldschmidt, *Die Elfenbeinskulpturen*, I, figs. 67a and 96a.
55. Temple, *Anglo-Saxon Manuscripts*, 81–2.
56. Frank Stenton, *The Bayeux Tapestry* (1965), fig. 4.
57. Also see Pächt, *St Albans*, pl. 24a.
58. Wormald, *Winchester*, 28.
59. Temple, *Anglo-Saxon Manuscripts*, 72.
60. See Graham D. Caie, *The Judgment Day Theme in Old English Poetry* (Copenhagen, 1976); Milton Gatch, 'Eschatology in the Anonymous Old English Homilies', *Traditio, 21* (1965), 117–165; Joyce Galpern, 'The shape of hell in Anglo-Saxon art' (Ph.D. thesis, University of California, 1977).
61. Kraus, *Die Miniaturen*, pl. IX; Hubert Schiel, *Der Codex Egberti der Stadtbibliothek Trier* (Basel, 1961); Ronig, *Codex*, 29.
62. The major publications on these manuscripts are: S. Beissel, *Das Evangelienbuch Heinrichs III, aus dem Dom zu Goslar in der Bibliothek zu Uppsala* (Düsseldorf, 1900); A. Boeckler, *Das Goldene Evangelienbuch Heinrichs III* (Berlin, 1933); Rainer Kahsnitz, *Das Goldene Evangelienbuch von Echternach* (Frankfurt, 1982); Peter Metz, *Das Goldene Evangelienbuch von Echternach* (Munich, 1956); Carl Nordenfalk, *Codex Caesarius Upsaliensis* (Stockholm, 1971); Joachim Plotzek, 'Das Perikopenbuch Heinrichs III in Bremen und seine Stellung innerhalb der Echternacher Buchmalerei' (Ph.D. thesis, Cologne, 1970).
63. Kraus, *Die Miniaturen*, pl. XIII; Ronig, *Codex*, 37.
64. H. Omont, *Évangile avec peintures byzantines du XIe siècle* (Paris, 1908), pl. 7.
65. A. Boeckler, 'Ikonographische Studien zu den Wunderszenen in der ottonischen Malerei der Reichenau', *Abhandlungen der Bayerischen Akademie der*

Wissenschaften, Phil.-Hist. Abteilung, n.s. *52* (1961).

66. Millet, *Recherches*, 118; J. Leroy, *Les manuscrits coptes et coptes-arabes illustrés* (Paris, 1974).
67. Goldschmidt, *Die Elfenbeinskulpturen*, I, fig. 81; Ottonian: Kraus, *Die Miniaturen*, pl. XVII; Byzantine: London, B.L., MS Add. 39627, fol. 144v; Mt. Athos, Dionysiu MS 587, fol. 135v; Rome, B.A.V., MS Vat. gr. 1156, fol. 283v.
68. K. Weitzmann, 'The narrative and liturgical Gospel illustrations', *Studies in Classical and Byzantine Manuscript Illumination* (Chicago, 1971), 254.
69. Millet, *Recherches*, fig. 656.
70. Another example can be found in a late Byzantine manuscript in the British Library: Add. 39627, fol. 217v.
71. See Pächt, *St Albans*, 57–8; Elizabeth Parker, 'A 12th century cycle of New Testament Drawings from Bury St Edmunds Abbey', *Proceedings of the Suffolk Institute of Archaeology*, *31* (1969), 263–302; Katherine Bateman, 'Pembroke 120 and Morgan 736: a reexamination of the St Albans Bury St Edmunds manuscript dilemma', *Gesta*, *17* (1978), 19–25.
72. T.S.R. Boase, *English Art 1100–1216* (1953), 174.
73. Wormald, *Winchester*, 82.
74. Kauffmann, *Romanesque*, 32.
75. Walter Oakeshott, *The Two Winchester Bibles* (1981), 133.
76. Kauffmann, *Romanesque*, 89; R.M. Thompson, 'The dates of the Pierpont Morgan Vita S. Edmundi and the Bury Bible', *Viator*, *2* (1971), 218–25.
77. Boase, *op.cit.*, 161; Kauffmann, *Romanesque*, 90. Figural scenes: fols. 7, 8, 17. Initials: fols. 45, 57v, 98. E. Parker McLachlan, 'In the wake of the Bury Bible: followers of Master Hugo at Bury St Edmunds', *JWCI*, *42* (1979), 216–24.
78. C.M. Kauffmann, 'The Bury Bible', *JWCI*, *29* (1966), pls. 21–7.
79. E. Parker McLachlan, 'The scriptorium of Bury St Edmunds in the third and fourth decades of the twelfth century: books in three related hands and their decoration', *Medieval Studies*, *40* (1978), 328–48.
80. For further discussion, please consult the catalogue entry.
81. The inspiration for the pilgrim's attire has been discussed by several scholars. See Pächt, *St Albans*, 73, with references to the earlier literature.
82. There is no precedent for blindfolding Christ for the Flagellation, nor is it justified on a textual basis. However, in the Albani Mocking of Christ, Christ is blindfolded. Although the blindfold is mentioned in Luke 22:64, it was not represented visually before it was introduced by the Albani artist. See Pächt, *St Albans*, 90 and pl. 27b.
83. A. Boinet, *La miniature carolingienne* (Paris, 1913), pl. XC; E.G. Millar, *English Illuminated Manuscripts from the Xth to the XIIIth Century* (Paris and Brussels, 1926), pl. 4.
84. The Boulogne illustration is one of the earliest representations where the tomb is represented as a coffin. Early Christian and Carolingian monuments depict the tomb as a free-standing edifice of several stories. See Cook, *op.cit.*, 97.
85. Schiller, *Ikonographie*, III, fig. 32.
86. Boase, *op.cit.*, 174.
87. Pächt, *St Albans*, pl. 33b.
88. Parker, *op.cit.*, pl. XLII.
89. Kauffmann, *Romanesque*, fig. 132.
90. Pächt, *St Albans*, 67, 95.

91. G. Warner, *The Benedictional of St Aethelwold* (1910), fig. 67v.
92. F. Wormald, 'An English 11th century psalter with pictures: British Museum Cotton MS Tiberius C.VI', *Walpole Society, 28* (1960–2), pl. 19.
93. It is entirely possible that this alteration of the older Anglo-Saxon type was due to Ottonian influence. The earliest Western example of the apostles in a straight row with a void between Peter and Paul is found in a Reichenau manuscript: Augsburg, Diözesan-Museum, MS 15a, fol. 73v, S. Selliger, *Pfingsten* (Düsseldorf, 1958), pl. 2.
94. The action of Peter refers to another moment in the narrative, John 13:9, where Peter entreats Christ to wash not only his feet but hands and head as well.
95. Pächt, *St Albans*, pl. 17a and 55.
96. It is found in the Bremen manuscript, fol. 11r. See Plotzek, *op.cit.*, 121.
97. Pächt has established that the Albani composition follows the Benedictional of St Aethelwold type. The leaf is an almost exact copy of the Albani Baptism. See *St Albans*, 86.
98. Volbac, *Spätantike*, nos. 112, 115; Wilpert, *I sarcofagi*, VIII, 4; F. Benoit, *Sarcophages paleochrétiens d'Arles et de Marseille* (Paris, 1954), pl. XXIV.
99. Schiller, *Ikonographie*, I, fig. 351.
100. Goldschmidt, *Die Elfenbeinskulpturen*, I, fig. 5.
101. G. Swarzenski, *Die Regensburger Buchmalerei des X und XI Jahrhunderts* (Leipzig, 1901), pl. XXV, fig. 65;, pl. XXIX, fig. 80.
102. V. Leroquais, *Les psautiers manuscrits latins des bibliothèques publiques de France* (3 vols., Mâcon, 1940–1), I, 137.
103. D. Klos and T. Strommer, *Der Verduner Altar* (Vienna, 1903); F. Röhrig, *Der Verduner Altar*, 3rd edn (Vienna, 1964); H. Buschhausen, 'The Klosterneuberg altar of Nicholas of Verdun, art, theology and politics', *JWCI, 37* (1974), 1–32; *idem, Der Verduner Altar; das Emailwerk des Nikolaus von Verdun* (Vienna, 1980).
104. One minor detail indicates that the Winchester Baptism was based upon an earlier source. There are only four fingers on the left hand of Christ. The artist neglected to include the thumb which is clearly visible in the Mosan example. It seems probable that there was a more complete model earlier than the Psalter which was copied inaccurately by the Winchester artist and more faithfully later by Nicholas. On the availability of Mosan patterns in England see Neil Stratford, 'The Henry of Blois plaques in the British Museum', *Medieval Art and Architecture at Winchester Cathedral* (British Archaeological Association Conference Transactions VI, 1980), 28–37.
105. Josef Strzygowski, *Iconographie der Taufe Christi* (Munich, 1885), figs. 1, 4, 5, 7, 12; G. Restow, *The Baptism of Christ* (Recklinghausen, 1967), 7–13.
106. One of the earliest is a fourth-century fresco in the catacomb of Peter and Marcellinus, Rome, *ibid.*, 16. The later examples are numerous, appearing in almost every example after the Early Christian period.
107. Kraus, *Die Miniaturen*, pl. XVIII; Ronig, *Codex*, 45.
108. Stryzygowski, *op.cit.*, pls. XII, 4; XIII, 7; XIV, 8.
109. Restow, *op.cit.*, pls. 11, 13, 14, 23.
110. *Epternacensis* (fig. 97); G.

Swarzenski, *Die Salzburger Malerei* (Leipzig, 1913), pl. XV, 46.

111. Please refer to the plates cited in notes 105 and 109.
112. Early Christian type: Goldschmidt, *Elfenbeinskulpturen*, I, figs. 5, 66, 67b. Classical–Carolingian type, figs. 27, 74a, 96a, 129.
113. Swarzenski, *Monuments*, 1967, pls. 113, 258, 259.
114. K. Edmondson Haney, 'The Mosan elements in the Psalter of Henry of Blois', *Revue belge d'archéologie et d'histoire de l'art, 51* (1982), 3–15. Observations on Mosan parallels have been recognized elsewhere in English art. For a recent treatment of this subject see P. Lasko, 'Anglo-Saxon or Norman? Observations on some ivory carvings in the English Romanesque exhibition at the Hayward Gallery', *The Burlington Magazine, 126* (1984), 216–24.
115. For the Floreffe Bible see the bibliography in *Rhein und Maas: Kunst und Kultur, 800–1400* (Cologne, 1972), 297.
116. Swarzenski, *Monuments*, fig. 355; F. Masai, *Arts mosans et arts anciens du pays de Liège* (Liège, 1951), 217; Suzanne Collon Gevaert, *Étude sur les miniatures mosans prégothiques: quatre manuscrits mosans de la Bibliothèque nationale à Paris* (Brussels, 1948).
117. The third Winchester guest grips his knife in his right hand. The index finger is extended along the blade and the remaining fingers and thumb are wrapped around the handle. The fourth, fifth, sixth, eighth and ninth guests, from the left to right, extend their hands to grasp food on the table with the same gestures. The woman seated fourth from the left in the Winchester Psalter grasps her drinking vessel with thumb and middle finger. The second, third, fifth, sixth and eighth guests, reading from the left, duplicate this complicated hand movement. The bearded gentleman seated at the centre of the marriage table cradles his drinking horn on an outstretched thumb and index finger while the remaining fingers are coiled below. The first, sixth and eighth banqueters in the Job manuscript use the same gesture to balance their goblets. The face of this same Winchester figure is close in type to the third, fourth and seventh from the left in the Job illustration. The Winchester and Job guests are posed in a three-quarter view. They have drooping moustaches and beards parted in the centre. The hair in all cases is parted in the centre and drawn smoothly along the sides of the head behind the ear to fall down the neck. The implements on the table in the Winchester Cana scene include low, footed bowls, some of which hold fish, oval bowls tipped on their side, and round loaves of bread. All of these items can also be found in the Job banquet scene.
118. There may be a general precedent in English art. Wormald, *Winchester*, fig. 53.
119. *Rhein und Maas, op.cit.*, 292; G. Chapman, 'The Bible of Floreffe: redating of a Romanesque manuscript', *Gesta, 10* (1971), fig. 14.
120. C.R. Dodwell, *Painting in Europe 800–1200* (1970), 162.
121. They are found on fol. 45v in the Harley manuscript and 142v in the Parc Bible. Both examples are unpublished.
122. Compare fol. 31 (Fig. 30).
123. As, for example, on fol. 39 (Fig.

38) and fol. 5 in the Harley manuscript.

124. Goldschmidt, *Elfenbeinskulpturen*, I, fig. 75; *Codex Egberti*, fol. 79, Kraus, *Die Miniaturen*, pl. XLV, Ronig, *Codex*, 93; Metz, *op.cit.*, pl. 83, Boeckler, *Das Goldene*, fig. 87.
125. Goldschmidt, *Elfenbeinskulpturen*, IV, figs. 36–7.
126. *Ibid.*, II, fig. 62.
127. Meyer Schapiro, 'Two Romanesque drawings in Auxerre and some iconographic problems', *Studies in Art and Literature for Belle Da Costa Greene* (Princeton, 1954), 331–49, fig. 254.
128. Adelheid Heimann, 'The capital frieze and pilasters of the Portail Royal, Chartres', *JWCI*, *31* (1968), 84; Ole Naesgard, *Saint-Jacques de Compostelle, et les débuts de la grande sculpture vers 1100* (Aarhus, 1962), 9 dates it c.1105.
129. Marie Lafargue, *Les chapiteaux du cloître de Notre-Dame la Daurade* (Paris, 1940); Kathryn Horste, 'The passion series from La Daurade and problems of narrative composition in the cloister capital', *Gesta*, *21* (1982), 31–62.
130. To find Christ surrounded by a crowd of armed men is by no means exclusive to the La Daurade capital and Psalter. Numerous examples appear in the East, see Millet, *Recherches*, figs. 324–7, 338, 341, 344. In the West, it is found in the *Codex Egberti*, fol. 78, Kraus, *Die Miniaturen*, pl. XLV; Ronig, *Codex*, 45. However, the Winchester and La Daurade examples are particularly close to one another in detail, suggesting the same type of model was employed for both.
131. It appears in the Pamplona cloister, Max Hirmer, *Early Medieval Art in Spain* (1967), pl. 140; and the frescoes of Vic-sur-Saint-Chartrier, Louis Brion-Guerry, *Fresques romanes de France* (Paris, 1958), figs. 51, 53.
132. Chartres frieze: Heimann, *op.cit.*, pl. 37b; west window: Y. Delaport and E. Houvet, *Les vitraux de la cathédrale de Chartres* (Chartres, 1926), pl. II.
133. In Albani and Pembroke 120, for instance, attendants hold small oil jars but are not engaged in anointing the body. See Pächt, *St Albans*, pl. 30a and fig. 128.
134. The Verdun comb was dated into the twelfth century by Goldschmidt, *Elfenbeinskulpturen*, IV, 49. W. Wixom, *Treasures from Medieval France* (Cleveland, 1968), gives an eleventh-century date and Lower Rhenish provenance, 139; Beckwith, *Ivory*, gives a c.1120 date and St Albans provenance, 79. He gives the same date to the other comb, presently in the Victoria and Albert Museum, 76. More recently, a broad dating in the first half of the twelfth century was suggested by Anat Tcherikover, 'Two Romanesque Ivory Combs', *JBAS*, *132* (1979), 7–21.
135. Courtauld Institute negative 393/45(17).
136. P. Pradel, *Sculpture roman des musées de France* (Paris, 1958), fig. 50.
137. There are numerous descriptions of violence done to children during Stephen's reign, for example: Richard, Prior of Hexham, *De Gestis Regis Stephani, et de Bello Standard, The Priory of Hexham, its Chronicles, Endowments, and Annals* (2 vols., 1864), I, 78; Henry of Huntingdon, *The Chronicle of Henry of Huntingdon and Acts of Stephen*, trans. T. Forester (1853), 266. The sort of brutality described here might have influenced the artist. However, it must be noted that this type of

grotesque exaggeration not only characterizes the Massacre scene but many others in the cycle. For this reason, it cannot be determined whether it should be ascribed to historical events or the artist's predilection for caricature.

Chapter Three: The Marian Cycle

1. Wormald, *Winchester*, 17.
2. J. LaFontaine-Dosogne, *Iconographie de l'enfance de la Vierge en l'empire byzantin et en occident* (2 vols., Brussels, 1964), II, 68; also see Fig. 96.
3. This attribution has been accepted by Wormald, *Winchester*, 17; LaFontaine-Dosogne, *op.cit.*, 68; W. Cahn, 'The tympanum of the Portal of Sainte-Anne', *JWCI*, *32* (1969), 64; and C. Nordenfalk, 'Recent publications on illuminated manuscripts', *The Burlington Magazine*, *117* (1975), 609–11. The only exception is M. Witzling, 'An Archaeological Investigation of the Winchester Psalter' (Ph.D. thesis, Cornell University, 1978), 83–9; *idem*, 'The Winchester Psalter: a re-ordering of its prefatory miniatures according to scriptural sequence', *Gesta*, *23* (1984), 17–26. She argues that the inscription which clearly reads 'ioachim' is a scribal error and that the scene actually represents David, based on a comparison to a scene in the Utrecht Psalter (Fig. 78). Such an identification raises numerous objections. As pointed out in Chapter One, the ink used for the Latin inscriptions is identical to that used to draw the figures in this scene. While this does not prove that the scribe and illuminator were one and the same person it, at the very least, suggests the miniature and inscription were the product of close collaboration. This makes it highly unlikely that such a glaring error would have been made. Nor is the visual argument persuasive. She ignores the clear precedent in the Hereford Troper to claim that the Utrecht scene is a mirror image of fol. 4. Such a comparison fails to take into account that in Utrecht David stands with his feet together while in C.IV he steps to the side. The angel in Utrecht flies in the air and holds a wreath while in Nero C.IV he stands and holds a scroll.
4. E. Amann, *Le Protevangile de Jacques et ses remaniements latins* (Paris, 1910), 346; M.R. James, *The Apocryphal New Testament* (1924), 38.
5. Temple, *Anglo-Saxon Manuscripts*, 113–5.
6. They appear in the West before 1160 at Santa Maria Antiqua, Rome, in the Sacramentary of Warmundus in Ivrea, and at San Giovanni a Porta Latina, Lafontaine-Dosogne, *op.cit.*, 22–30.
7. Entries in the calendars at December 8 for 'Conceptio Sanctae Dei Genitricis Mariae' can be found in two Anglo-Saxon Winchester manuscripts and a third from St Mary's Cathedral Priory at Worcester. Cornelius Bauman, 'The Immaculate Conception in the Liturgy', *The Dogma of the Immaculate Conception: History and Significance* (South Bend, 1958), 123–7; F. Wormald, *English Kalendars before A.D. 1100* (1934), 125, 167, 223.
8. *The Leofric Missal*, ed. F.E. Warren (1883), 268.
9. The Canterbury Pontifical, London, B.L., MS Harley 2892, dated after 1023, fol. 161; London, B.L., MS Add. 2888. See X. Le

Bachelet, 'Immaculée Conception', *Dictionnaire de théologie catholique* (16 vols., Paris, 1927), VII, col. 990.

10. M. Levi d'Ancona, *The Iconography of the Immaculate Conception in the Middle Ages and Early Renaissance* (New York, 1957), 15.
11. S.J.P. van Dijk, 'The origin of the Latin Feast of the Conception of the Blessed Virgin Mary', *The Dublin Review, 118* (1954), 253.
12. Francis Mildner, 'The Immaculate Conception in England', *Marianum, 1* (1939), 92.
13. M.R. James, *The Latin Infancy Gospels* (1927), xxxiii; Osbertus de Clara, *The Letters of Osbert of Clare* (1929), 13.
14. van Dijk, *op.cit.*, 264.
15. The annals of Worcester Cathedral record in 1125: 'The Conception of St Mary is celebrated for the first time in England.' The Winchcombe annals of 1126 report: 'This year the solemnity of the Conception of St Mary began first to be celebrated among us.' Similar passages are found in the Gloucester annals of 1113–31, those of St Albans (1119) and Bury St Edmunds (1121–48), *ibid.*, 264.
16. It has been suggested that the re-establishment of the feast was due to a fresh influx of Greek customs in the twelfth century, *ibid.*, 430. The revival and quick popularity of the feast are also identified with the legend of Helsin. This popular tale of a monk relates that he was saved from death in a storm by promising to institute the feast of the Conception at Ramsey where he was abbot. Mildner, *op.cit.*, 98, and R.W. Southern, 'The English origins of the Miracles of the Virgin', *Medieval and Renaissance Studies, 4* (1958), 194–200.
17. *Ibid.*, 177.
18. van Dijk, *op.cit.*, 253.
19. The details of this struggle are found in a letter written by Osbert of Clare to Anselm, bishop of Bury St Edmunds. Osbertus, *op.cit.*, 11.
20. Le Bachelet, *op.cit.*, col. 1006.
21. *Ibid.*
22. Eadmeri Monachi Cantuariensis, *Tractatus De Conceptione Sanctae Mariae*, ed. P. Thurston and T. Slater (Freiburg, 1904).
23. Eadmer tried to explain how the conception of the flesh could be pure before the union of the soul and the body. He distinguished between active and passive conception, that is, between the generative act of the parents of Mary which would be subject to the laws of original sin and the fruit of their generation, the Virgin who was preserved from sin by sanctifying grace. Osbert supported Eadmer's position by adding that since John the Baptist had been sanctified in the womb of his mother, it was likely that the Virgin as the Mother of God received a higher grace. She was therefore sanctified at her conception. Levi d'Ancona, *op.cit.*, 8; Eadmeri, *op.cit.*, 70.
24. Mildner, *op.cit.*, 199.
25. van Dijk, *op.cit.*, 435.
26. On the Lyon controversy also see M. Bernard, *L'Église de Lyon et l'immaculée conception. Essai theologico-historique* (Lyon, 1897); E. Vacanard, 'Saint Bernard et la fête de la conception de la Sainte Vierge', *Science catholique, 7* (1883), 897. Bernard seemed incredulous at the idea that the conception could have been sanctified, arguing that the Virgin had not been conceived by the Holy Ghost. Since active conception involved sin, the Holy Ghost

could have had no part in it. Whereas, if she were conceived by the Holy Ghost, this would lead to the conclusion that Saint Anne was a virgin, a doctrine never heard before. *PL*, CLXXXII, col. 332.

27. A.W. Burridge, 'L'Immaculée conception dans la théologie l'Angleterre médiévale', *Revue d'histoire ecclesiastique*, *32* (1936), 591.
28. *Ibid.*, 588.
29. Francis Mildner, 'The Immaculate Conception in the writings of Nicholas of St Albans', *Marianum*, *2* (1940), 185.
30. *Ibid.*, 187.
31. Burridge, *op.cit.*, 589.
32. E. Harris, 'Mary in the Burning Bush', *JWCI*, *1* (1937), 281–4.
33. Levi d'Ancona, *op.cit.*, 48.
34. *Radii Soli Zeli Seraphici Caeli Veritatis Pro Immaculatae Conceptionis Mysterio Virginis Maria*, ed. P. Alva y Astorga (Louvain, 1666), 618–20.
35. Eadmeri, *op.cit.*, 70, 78.
36. Burridge, *op.cit.*, 580; Eadmeri, *op.cit.*, 15.
37. Mildner, *op.cit.* (1939), 208; Eadmeri, *op.cit.*, 15.
38. C.H. Talbot, 'Nicholas of St Albans and Saint Bernard', *Revue Bénédictine*, *38* (1954), 112.
39. *PL*, CLXXIV, col. 1019; *Virgo Immaculata*, ed. P. Alva y Astorga (Louvain, 1664), col. 452.
40. A. Wilmart, 'Les compositions d'Osbert de Clare en l'honneur de Sainte Anne', *Annales de Bretagne*, *37* (1926), 4.
41. Burridge, *op.cit.*, 580; Eadmeri, *op.cit.*, 15; Talbot, *op.cit.*, 112.
42. Levi d'Ancona, *op.cit.*, 54.
43. Wilmart, *op.cit.*, 17.
44. Eadmeri, *op.cit.*, 7–8; Burridge, *op.cit.*, 580.
45. Levi d'Ancona, *op.cit.*, 44; Eadmeri, *op.cit.*, 24–5.
46. Tolhurst, *Breviary*, IV, fol. 402r.
47. Wormald, *Winchester*, 15.
48. Wilmart, *op.cit.*, 24. This identification was also tentatively proposed by Wormald, *Winchester*, 15.
49. Levi d'Ancona, *op.cit.*, 47; A. Watson, *The Early Iconography of the Tree of Jesse* (1934).
50. Kauffmann, *Romanesque*, 99–100.
51. M. Vloberg, 'The iconography of the Immaculate Conception', *The Dogma of the Immaculate Conception* (South Bend, 1958), 468–512.
52. Although there was no universal formula in the twelfth century, the book and sceptre used interchangeably or together were commonly found associated with David and Solomon. Examples can be found in Paris, B.N., MS lat. 9448, fol. 4; Boulogne, B.M., MS 20, fol. 20; the St Albans Psalter, Pächt, *St Albans*, pl. 73b; Arras, B.M., MS 559, fol. 170r; Paris (formerly) Chambre des Députés, MS 2, fol. 97v; London, B.L., MS Add. 24789, fol. 121; Paris, B.N., MSS lat. 10, fol. 208v; lat. 104, fol. 13v.
53. LaFontaine-Dosogne, *op.cit.*, 68.
54. *Ibid.*, 117–20. The Presentation is not marked in the calendar and was not generally accepted into the feast cycle until the later Middle Ages. However, the event is sometimes referred to in conjunction with the feast of the Nativity. It is also possible that the Presentation had achieved liturgical significance in England before the Conquest. See Sr. M.J. Kishpaugh, 'The Feast of the Presentation of the Virgin Mary in the Temple' (Ph.D. dissertation, Catholic University of America, 1941), 68.
55. Martin Jugie, *La mort et l'assomption de la Sainte Vierge* (Vatican City, 1944; Henri Barré,

'La croyance à l'assumption corporelle en occident de 750 à 1150 environs', *Études Mariales, 7* (1949), 63–123.

56. *Idem*, 'Immaculée conception et assomption en XIIe siècle', *Virgo Immaculata* (17 vols., Rome, 1955), V, 151.
57. *Ibid.*, 175–80.
58. Wormald, *Winchester*, 87.
59. H. Sauerland and A. Haseloff, *Der Psalter des Trierischen Erzbischof Egbert in Cividale* (Trier, 1901), 173.
60. Valeriani Meysztowicz, 'Manuscriptum Gertrudae Filiae Mesconis II Regis Poloniae', *Antemurale, 2* (1955), 151. The author would like to thank Christopher Hohler for pointing out this reference.
61. Hugo Buchthal, *Miniature Painting in the Latin Kingdom of Jerusalem* (1957), 122, pls. 12, 17.
62. *Ibid.*, 123–4.
63. Wormald, *Winchester*, 10–11.
64. Otto Pächt, 'The illustrations of St Anselm's Prayers and Meditations', *JWCI, 19* (1956), 68–83.
65. Walter Delius, *Geschichte der Marienverehrung* (Munich, 1963), 162; H. Barré, 'L'intercession de la vierge aux débuts du moyen âge occidental', *Études Mariales, 23* (1966), 78.
66. Dom B. Cabrol, 'Les témoignages de la liturgie', *Études Mariales, 7* (1949), 54.
67. Barré, *op.cit.* (1966), 36.
68. Schiller, *Ikonographie*, IV, fig. 609.
69. *PL*, CXLI, col. 325.
70. *PL*, CLXXXIII, col. 415.
71. *PL*, CCVIII, col. 665.
72. Barré, *op.cit.* (1949), 103.
73. *BSFRMP* (1927).
74. H. Barré, *Prières anciennes de l'occident à la mère du sauveur* (Paris, 1963), 155.
75. G.G. Meersseman, *Der Hymnos Akathistos im Abendland* (3 vols., Freiburg, 1958–60), II, 177–9.
76. M. Gatch, 'Eschatology in the Anonymous Old English homilies', *Traditio, 21* (1965), 117–65.
77. Temple, *Anglo-Saxon Manuscripts*, 86–7.

Chapter Four: The Pictorial Cycle

1. Pierre Salmon, *Les Tituli Psalmorum des manuscrits latins* (Rome, 1959); also see J.J. Tikkanen, *Psaltarillustration im Mittelalter, Acta Societatis Scientarium Fennicae, 31* (1903).
2. Salmon, *op.cit.*, 29.
3. Donatian De Bruyne, *Préfaces de la Bible latine* (Namur, 1920), 62.
4. *PL*, CLVIII, cols. 876–7.
5. Pierre Salmon, *L'Office divin* (Paris, 1959), 99–120.
6. *PL*, CI, cols. 465–6.
7. E. Bishop, 'On the origin of the prymer', *Liturgica Historica* (1918), 211–37.
8. A.B. Kuypers, *The Book of Cerne* (1902); N.R. Ker, *Catalogue of Manuscripts Containing Anglo-Saxon* (1957), 39–40; Lilli Gjerlow, *Adoratio Crucis. The Regularis Concordia and The Decreta Lanfranci* (Oslo, 1961), 16; *idem*, 'Notes on the Book of Cerne and on MS Uppsala C 222', *Nordisk Tidskrift för Bok-och Biblioteksväsen, 47* (1960), 2–3.
9. Kuypers, *op.cit.*, 201–25.
10. Walter de Gray Birch, *An Ancient Manuscript of the Eighth or Ninth Century: formerly belonging to St Mary's Abbey or Nunnaminster, Winchester* (1889).
11. The texts of the prayers in Arundel 155, Tiberius C.VI and Nero C.IV are based directly on the manuscripts. The orthography and punctuation have been

modernized and a few minor textual errors have been silently corrected. The author would like to express her sincere thanks to Julian Brown for his assistance in preparing these texts for publication.

12. Temple, *Anglo-Saxon Manuscripts*, 36–7; J.J. Alexander and C.M. Kauffmann, *English Illuminated Manuscripts* (Brussels, 1973), 20–2. Dr E. Parker McLachlan is currently preparing a more detailed study of the miniature cycle of this manuscript. On the possibility of continental precedents see F. Wormald, 'Continental influence on English illumination', *Transactions of the Fourth International Congress of Bibliophiles* (1967), 10; J. Porcher, *Les manuscrits à peintures en France*, 2nd edn (Paris, 1954), 11.
13. Rainer Kahsnitz, *Der Werdener Psalter in Berlin Ms. theol. lat. fol. 358* (Düsseldorf, 1979), 154.
14. Temple, *Anglo-Saxon Manuscripts*, 98; F. Wormald, 'Late Anglo-Saxon art: some questions and suggestions', *Romanesque and Gothic Art* (Princeton, 1963), 19–26.
15. Tolhurst, *Breviary*.
16. Suibert Bäumer, *Histoire du brévaire* (2 vols., Paris, 1905), I, 355–415; Salmon, *Office, op.cit.*; Christopher Wordsworth and Henry Littlehales, *The Old Service-Books of the English Church* (1904); Cyrille Vogel, *Introduction aux sources de l'histoire du culte chrétien du moyen âge* (Spoleto, 1966); Klaus Gamber, *Codices latini liturgici antiquiores* (2 vols., Freiburg, 1968); Victor Leroquais, *Les brévaires manuscrits des bibliothèques publiques de France* (6 vols., Paris, 1934).
17. Tolhurst, *Breviary*, I, fol. 3.
18. *Ibid.*, fol. 3.
19. *Ibid.*, fols. 16–20.
20. *Ibid.*, fols. 25v–9.
21. *Ibid.*, fol. 38v.
22. *Ibid.*, fols. 39v–40.
23. *The Missal of the New Minster, Winchester (Le Havre, B.M. MS 330)*, ed. D. Turner (1962), 69.
24. Tolhurst, *Breviary*, I, fols. 43–4.
25. *Ibid.*, fol. 43v.
26. *Ibid.*, fol. 48; also see René Laurentin, *Jésus au temple, mystère de Pâques et foi de Marie* (Paris,1966).
27. Salmon, *Office, op.cit.*, 138; also see Abbot Guéranger, *The Liturgical Year, Septuagesima* (1909).
28. Tolhurst, *Breviary*, I, fol. 61v.
29. *Ibid.*
30. *Ibid.*, fols. 63v–4.
31. *Ibid.*, fol. 66.
32. *Ibid.*, fols. 74v–5.
33. *The Hereford Breviary*, ed. Walter H. Frere (2 vols., 1904), I, 281.
34. Tolhurst, *Breviary*, fol. 78v.
35. *Ibid.*, fol. 81v.
36. *Ibid.*, fol. 82v.
37. *Ibid.*, fols. 84, 92.
38. *The Bec Missal*, ed. Dom Anselm Hughes (1963), fols. 93–7.
39. Tolhurst, *Breviary*, fols. 112, 123v.
40. Hughes, *op.cit.*, 22.
41. Tolhurst, *Breviary*, fol. 105v.
42. *Ibid.*, fols. 125, 127.
43. *The Blickling Homilies*, ed. R. Morris (1880), 82.
44. M. Gatch, 'Eschatology in the anonymous Old English homilies', *Traditio, 21* (1965), 131; *idem, Preaching and Theology in Anglo-Saxon England: Aelfric and Wulfstan* (Toronto, 1977).
45. A collation of the first quire revealed that it is intact and the text for the Easter sermon follows the illustration without interruption. Also see Temple, *Anglo-Saxon Manuscripts*, 74, and M.R. James, *The Western Manuscripts in the Library of Trinity College* (4 vols., 1900–4), I, no. 369.
46. Tolhurst, *Breviary*, I, fols. 109v–110.

47. *Ibid.*, fols. 72v, 115. On this subject see Allen J. Frantzen, *The Literature of Penance in Anglo-Saxon England* (New Brunswick, 1983); A.C. Mortimer, *The Origins of Private Penance in the Western Church* (1939); P. Anciaux, *La théologie du sacrament de penitence au XIIe siècle* (Louvain, 1949); O.B. Hardison, *Christian Rite and Christian Drama in the Middle Ages* (Baltimore, 1965), 8–138; O.D. Watkins, *A History of Penance* (2 vols., 1920).
48. A. Wilmart, *Auteurs spirituels et textes dévots au moyen âge latin* (Paris, 1932); J. Leclercq, 'Culte liturgique et prière intime dans le monachism au moyen âge', *La Maison dieu, 69* (1962), 40–55. The author would like to thank Nigel Morgan for pointing out this reference. There is also an account of a Flemish monk, Goscelin, in England c.1080, who recommended to Eva that she meditate upon Christ's sufferings during the canonical hours of the day and night. See James Marrow, *Passion Iconography in Northern Europe of the Late Middle Ages and Early Renaissance* (Kortrijk, 1979), 9.
49. *PL*, LXXXXIV, cols. 561–8; L.M.F. Daniëls, 'Van den Seven Ghetijden der Passien onses Heren', *On Feestelijk Erf, 16* (1942), 186–235; J. Stadlhuber, 'Zur Entwicklung des Laienstundengebetes in Altertum', *Zeitschrift für katholische Theologie, 71* (1949), 129–83.
50. *The Antiphonary of Bangor*, ed. F.E. Warren (1895), 59, n. 19.
51. J. Stadelhuber, 'Das Laienstudengebet von Leiden Christi in seinem Mittelalterlichen Fortleben', *Zeitschrift für katholische Theologie, 72* (1950), 282–325.
52. *PL*, CLXXVII, cols. 340–5.
53. *PL*, CLXX, cols. 13–16.
54. A. Wilmart, 'Prières médiévales pour l'adoration de la croix', *Ephemerides Liturgicae, 46* (1932), 37; E. Bishop, 'On the origin of the prymer', *Liturgica Historica* (1918), 224.
55. *The Stowe Missal*, ed. G. Warner (2 vols., 1915), II, fol. 12; E. Bishop, 'The litany of the saints in the Stowe Missal', *Liturgica Historica*, 137–40.
56. Fol. 132r.
57. Fol. 142r.
58. Fol. 133r.
59. A. Wilmart, 'Le manuel de prières de Saint Jean Gualbert', *Revue Bénédictine, 48* (1936), 283–5; P. Salmon, 'Livrets de prières de l'époque carolingienne', *Revue Bénédictine, 86* (1976), 218–34.
60. A. Wilmart, *Precum Libelli Quattuor Aevi Karolini* (Rome, 1940); *idem, Auteur spirituels, op.cit.*; Salmon, 'Livrets', *op.cit.*
61. Wilmart, 'Le manuel', *op.cit.*, 264; R. Southern, *Saint Anselm and his Biographer* (1966), 40.
62. Salmon, 'Livrets', *op.cit.*, 277.
63. *Ibid.*
64. Wormald, *Winchester*, 13.
65. Kuypers, *op.cit.*, 110–11.
66. *Ibid.*, 114–17.
67. *Ibid.*, 89, 94, 112–17, 127, 148, 152–3.
68. *Bangor Antiphonary*, *op.cit.*, II, 86; Kuypers, *op.cit.*, 215.
69. *Ibid.*, 214, 217.
70. Fols. 143r–144r. London, B.L., MS Arundel 155, fols. 172r–v.
71. Fols. 22r–22v.
72. Fol. 177v; T. Bestul, 'St Anselm and the continuity of Anglo-Saxon devotional traditions', *Annuale Mediaevale, 18* (1978), 20–41, esp. 25.
73. Southern, *op.cit.*; *PL*, CLVIII, cols. 876–7; fol. 137r.
74. Henri Barré, *Prières anciennes de l'occident à la mère du sauveur* (Paris, 1963).
75. *Ibid.*, 140–2.

76. G.G. Meersseman, *Der Hymnos Akathistos im Abendland* (3 vols., Freiburg, 1958–60), II, 34–5.
77. The identification of the scene as *Regina Angelorum* does not rest on the inscription, which was added. The iconography of the scene establishes the identification, see F. Rademacher, *Regina Angelorum in der Kunst des frühen Mittellters* (Düsseldorf, 1972).
78. Fol. 135v.
79. On the French rubric see B. Woledge and H.P. Clive, *Répertoire des plus anciens textes en prose française depuis 842 jusqu'aux premières années du XIIe siècle* (Geneva, 1964), 80. Also see Appendix B. The red ink used for this inscription is not the same as the red ink used elsewhere in the manuscript.
80. See C.H. Talbot, 'Some notes on the dating of the Ancrene Riwle', *Neophilologus*, *40* (1956), 38–50; E.J. Dobson, *The Origins of Ancrene Wisse* (1976); R.W. Ackerman, 'The liturgical day in Ancrene Riwle', *Speculum*, *53* (1978), 734–44; on various editions see E.J. Dobson, 'The affiliations of the manuscripts of Ancrene Wisse', *English and Medieval Studies Presented to J.R.R. Tolkien on the Occasion of his Seventieth Birthday* (1962), 128–163; *The Ancrene Riwle (Corpus MS Ancrene Wisse)*, trans. M.B. Salu (1955), 8.
81. N. Morgan, *Early Gothic Manuscripts (I) 1190–1250* (1982), 119–20.

Catalogue of Miniatures

1. Israel Gollancz, *The Caedmon Manuscript of Anglo-Saxon Biblical Poetry* (1927), 45r. (The fol. numbers are the plate references in this publication.)
2. The flaming sword and gate of Paradise are also found in Aelfric, Dodwell and Clemoes, *Hexateuch*, 8r. (The fol. numbers are the plate references in this publication.)
3. Trees are included on fols. 3r and 7v. See Dodwell and Clemoes, *Hexateuch*, 118, and Pamela Blum, 'The cryptic creation cycle in MS Junius xi', *Gesta*, *15* (1976), 220.
4. The angel also looks back and Eve touches her chin in the Octateuchs. However, there are essential differences. The angel pushes Adam out with two hands and does not carry the flaming sword. See Hesseling, *Miniatures*, fig. 23 and Ouspensky, *Octateuque*, fig. 26; Rome, B.A.V., MSS Vat. gr. 746, fol. 44r; Vat. gr. 747, fol. 25r.
5. R. Charles, *The Apocrypha and Pseudoepigrapha of the Old Testament in English* (1913).
6. *Ibid.*, 138. The Latin text can be found in Wilhelm Meyer, *Vita Adae et Evae*, *Abhandlungen der Philosophisch-Philologischen Classe der Königlichen Bayerischen Akademie der Wissenschaften*, XIV (1878), 228.
7. George Zarnecki, *Later English Romanesque Sculpture* (1953), 16.
8. The relationship of Sigena to English art was first noticed by Esther Lewittes, 'The Old Testament representations in the chapter house of the convent of Sigena' (M.A. thesis, New York University, 1938). Also see Otto Pächt, 'A cycle of English frescoes in Spain', *Burlington Magazine*, *10* (1961), 166, and Walter Oakeshott, *Sigena* (1972).
9. Hénri Omont, *Miniatures des plus anciens manuscrits grecs de la Bibliothèque Nationale* (Paris, 1929), pl. XXXVII. Wormald drew attention to this comparison, *Winchester*, 69–70, concluding that

it should be interpreted as an indication of Byzantine influence in the Psalter.

10. S. Bettini, *Mosaici antichi de San Marco a Venezia* (Bergamo, 1955), pl. C.
11. Herrad of Hohenbourg, *Hortus Deliciarum*, with a text by Rosalie Green *et al.* (2 vols., 1979), II, pl. 13.
12. This can be contrasted to the tradition represented in the Octateuchs where Adam and Eve are shown seated next to a plough. See Hesseling, *Miniatures*, fig. 23; Ouspensky, *Octateuque*, fig. 26; Rome, B.A.V., MS Vat. gr. 746, fol. 43r.
13. J.K. Galbraith, 'The iconography of the biblical scenes at Malmesbury Abbey', *JBAS*, *28* (1965), 42.
14. Lawrence Stone, *Sculpture in Britain* (Baltimore, 1972), 83–4; F. Saxl, *English Sculptures of the Twelfth Century* (1954), 64, and Galbraith, *op.cit.*, 39. This can be contrasted to the only Byzantine representation in the ninth-century Homilies of Gregory Nazianzus, Paris, B.N., MS grec 510, fol. 52v: Omont, *op.cit.*, pl. XXIV. Also see Wormald, *Winchester*, 70.
15. Galbraith, *op.cit.*, 40.
16. *Ibid.*, 42; Lewettes, *op.cit.*, 50. Concerning the influence of apocryphal sources on the Cotton cycle see H. Kessler, *The Illustrated Bibles from Tours* (Princeton, 1977), 20; for the Caedmon manuscript see Rosemary Woolf, 'The fall of man in Genesis B and the Mystère d'Adam', *Studies in Old English Literature in Honor of Arthur G. Brodeur*, ed. Stanley B. Greenfield (Eugene, Oregon, 1963), 187–99.
17. Kessler, *op.cit.*, figs. 1–4.
18. The child is also found in the Octateuchs where Adam and Eve are shown seated in attitudes of despondency instead of at labour. Hesseling, *Miniatures*, fig. 23; Ouspensky, *Octateuque*, fig. 26; Rome, B.A.V., MS Vat. gr. 746, fol. 43v.
19. Bettini, *op.cit.*, pl. C.
20. Green, *op.cit.*, II, pl. 13.
21. G. Folena and G. Melini, *Bibbia istoriata padovana* (Venice, 1963), pl. 5.
22. G. Henderson, 'The sources of the Genesis Cycle at Saint-Savin-sur-Gartempe', *JBAS*, *26* (1963), 26, pl. XIII, 6.
23. For the belt around Cain's waist see George Zarnecki, 'A Romanesque bronze candlestick in Oslo and the problems of the "belts of strength" ', *Saertrykk Av Arbok*, *26* (1963–4), 45–66.
24. W.O. Hassall, *The Holkham Bible Picture Book* (1954), 25.
25. Hesseling, *Miniatures*, fig. 24; Ouspensky, *Octateuque*, fig. 28; Rome, B.A.V., MSS Vat. gr. 746, fol. 45v; Vat. gr. 747, fol. 25v.
26. The version in San Marco, Caedmon and Aelfric shows Cain raising a club above his head while Abel lies on the ground below him. Otto Demus, *Die Mosaiken von San Marco in Vendig 1100–1200* (Baden bei Wien, 1935), pl. 27; Caedmon (Fig. 48); Aelfric, Dodwell and Clemoes, *Hexateuch*, 8v.
27. In the representations discussed in n. 26, Abel is depicted as either resisting Cain's attack by raising a hand to protect himself or slipping to the ground as a result of the blow.
28. Abraham and Isaac were long used as models for the sacrifice of Christ. By the second century, Isaac's sacrifice was viewed in connection with the Crucifixion by Melito, bishop of Sardes. By the

fourth century, the section of the canon of the Mass in which the sacrifices of Abel, Abraham and Melchisedech are included came into use. Here the parallel of the sacrifices of Abel and Isaac to Christ occurs. See Isabel S. Van Woerden, 'The iconography of the sacrifice of Abraham', *Vigiliae Christianae, 15* (1961), 214–55. The typological relationship was also represented visually: F. Gerke, *Der Sarkophag des Junius Bassus* (Berlin, 1936), pls. 13; 121/4; F.W. Deichmann, *Frühchristliche Bauten und Mosaiken von Ravenna* (Baden, 1958), pls. 327, 407; *Reallexikon zur deutschen Kunstgeschichte* (5 vols., Stuttgart, 1937), I, fig. 3.

29. Hesseling, *Miniatures*, figs. 32–3; Ouspensky, *Octateuque*, fig. 38; Rome, B.A.V., MSS Vat. gr. 746, fols. 54r, 55v; Vat. gr. 747, fols. 29v, 30r.
30. Gollancz, *op.cit.* (1927), 66–73.
31. Milton Gatch, 'Noah's raven in Genesis A and the illustrated Old English Hexateuch', *Gesta, 14* (1975), 8; R. Bergman, *Salerno*, 24.
32. K. Weitzmann, *The Joshua Roll* (Princeton, 1948), pl. XXXIX, figs. 127–8. Hesseling, *Miniatures*, fig. 49; Rome, B.A.V., MSS Vat. gr. 746, fol. 81v; Vat. gr. 747, fol. 43r.
33. Wilpert, *I sarcofagi*, I, pls. CCIII, 1; CLXXX, 4; CLXXXIII, 24.
34. K. Weitzmann, *Illustrations in Roll and Codex* (Princeton, 1947), pl. XXXIX, fig. 128.
35. On this point see K. Weitzmann, 'The mosaics of San Marco and the Cotton Genesis', *Venezia e l'europa* (Venice, 1956), 152–3.
36. Bergman, *Salerno*, fig. 16.
37. Dodwell and Clemoes, *Hexateuch*, 38r.
38. Wilpert, *I sarcofagi*, II, fig. 117.
39. Volbach, *Spätantike*, 78.
40. R. Stettinger, *Prudentius Handschriften* (Leyden, 1905), pl. 85(1).
41. Swarzenski, *Monuments*, fig. 290.
42. Saxl, *op.cit.*, pl. LXXIII.
43. See Van Woerden, *op.cit.*, and Hans-Jürgen Geischer, 'Heidnische Parallelen zum frühchristlichen Bild des Isaakopfers', *Jahrbuch für Antike und Christentum, 10* (1967), 127–44.
44. According to H. Severin, 'Oströmische Reliefs mit Darstellungen des Abrahamsopfers', *Bulletin du Musée hongrois des beaux-arts, 36* (1971), 44, the representation of Isaac kneeling on the altar with both knees is a relatively late development, appearing in the West in the late fourth or fifth century. Geischer, *op.cit.*, 133, also sees the type as a variant on the older version where Isaac kneels in profile. Examples of the type found in Nero C.IV are illustrated by Wilpert, *I sarcofagi*, pls. LXXXII, 3; CXXI, 4; and CXXVII, 2.
45. The relationship of S. Bertin and England in the eleventh and twelfth centuries has been discussed by Claire Kelleher, 'Illumination at Saint-Bertin at Saint Omer under the abbacy of Odbert' (Ph.D. thesis, University of London, 1968); R.M. Harris, 'The marginal drawings of the Bury St Edmunds Psalter (Rome, Vatican Library MS Reg. lat. 12)' (Ph.D. thesis, Princeton University, 1960); C.R. Dodwell, *The Canterbury School of Illumination* (1954), 55.
46. Hesseling, *Miniatures*, fig. 156; Ouspensky, *Octateuque*, fig. 97; Rome, B.A.V., MS Vat. gr. 746, fol. 157r.
47. Joachim E. Gaede, 'Carolingian interpretations of an Early Christian picture cycle to the

Octateuchs in the Bible of San Paolo fuori le mura', *Frühmittelalterliche Studien*, *8* (1974), 351–384.

48. Dodwell and Clemoes, *Hexateuch*, fol. 78v.
49. *BSFRMP*, *18* (1931–3), pl. II; Buchthal, *Paris Psalter*, 70.
50. On the leaves see Kauffmann, *Romanesque*, 95, with earlier bibliography.
51. Dodwell and Clemoes, *Hexateuch*, 78r–85v.
52. Cosimo Stornajolo, *Miniature delle omilie di Giacomo monaco* (Rome, 1910), pl. 21 and Hénri Omont, 'Miniatures des homélies sur la Vierge du moine Jacques', *BSFRMP*, *11* (1927), pl. X.
53. Adelheid Heimann, 'The last copy of the Utrecht Psalter', *The Year 1200: A Symposium*, ed. J. Hoffeld (New York, 1975), 328; *idem*, 'Moses-Darstellungen', *Kunst als Bedeutungsträger, Gedankschrift für Gunter Bandmann* (Berlin, 1978), 10–7.
54. Louis Grodecki, 'Les vitraux allégoriques de Saint-Denis', *Art de France*, *1* (1961), 19; *idem*, *Vitraux de Saint-Denis: étude sur le vitrail au xii*[e] *siècle* (Paris, 1976); K. Hoffmann, 'Suger's "Anagogisches Fenster" in St-Denis', *Wallraf-Richartz Jahrbuch*, *30* (1968), 90.
55. Kauffmann, *Romanesque*, 90 and fig. 161.
56. Galbraith, *op.cit.*, pl. XIX, fig. 1.
57. Gretel Chapman, 'The Floreffe Bible, the redating of a Romanesque manuscript', *Gesta*, *10* (1971), 49–62, fig. 17. Kauffmann, *Romanesque*, 123.
58. C. Kraeling, *The Excavations at Dura Europas Final Report: The Synagogue* (8 vols., New Haven, 1956), VIII/I, fig. 60.
59. It occurs on an ivory pyxis at Dumbarton Oaks, in grec 510, the Octateuchs, and a number of psalters. For plate references see *Dumbarton Oaks Papers*, *14* (1960), 68, fig. 29; Omont, *op.cit.*, pl. XXIV; Hesseling, *Miniatures*, fig. 187; Ouspensky, *Octateuque*, fig. 132; Buchthal, *Paris Psalter*, pls. X, XXV, fig. 73.
60. One type found in the West from an early date is Moses standing flatfooted and raising his arms to receive the law. It occurs on several Early Christian sarcophagi: see Wilpert, *I sarcofagi*, pls. XIV, 3; XXXIX, 1. The type can also be found in several Carolingian monuments: E. DeWald, *The Stuttgart Psalter* (Princeton, 1930), fol. 39r; *Der Stuttgarter Bilderpsalter, Bibl. Fol. 23, Wüttembergische Landesbibliothek* (2 vols., Stuttgart, 1965–8) and the Grandval and Vivian Bibles, H. Kessler, *The Illustrated Bibles from Tours* (Princeton, 1977), figs. 1–4. It also occurs in the Chuldolv Psalter, fol. 108v, where Moses raises his arms, partially covering his face, as he does in the Winchester Psalter.
61. It appears on several Early Christian sarcophagi, as well as on the fifth-century doors of Santa Sabina in Rome. Wilpert, *I sarcofagi*, pls. LXXXII, 2; CXXII, 3; CXXVII, 3; Buchthal, *Paris Psalter*, pl. XXII, fig. 60.
62. J. Gaede, 'The painters of the Carolingian Bible of San Paolo fuori le mura in Rome' (Ph.D. thesis, New York University, 1963); *idem*, 'The Touronian sources of the Bible of San Paolo fuori le mura in Rome', *Frühmittelalterliche Studien*, *5* (1971), 359–400.
63. Ruth Mellinkoff, *The Horned Moses in Medieval Art and Thought* (Berkeley, 1970), 61.
64. E. Amann, *Le protoevangile de Jacques et ses remaniements latins* (Paris, 1910), 289, 346; M.R.

James, *The Apocryphal New Testament* (1924), 38–49, 79–80.

65. Eastern representations of the scene include a sculpted scene on a column supporting a ciborium at San Marco which has been variously dated from the sixth to the thirteenth centuries. There is also a fresco in the ninth/eleventh century Cappadocian church of Kizil-Tchoukour, see J. LaFontaine-Dosogne, *Iconographie de l'enfance de la Vierge, l'empire byzantin et en occident* (2 vols., Brussels, 1964), I, 76. Western representations include a ninth-century fresco in the church of Maria Gradellis, Rome, a twelfth-century capital at Autun, and a scene on the frieze at Chartres. For these examples see II, 75.
66. Temple, *Anglo-Saxon Manuscripts*, 113–5; H. Swarzenski, 'Der Stil der Bibel Carilefs von Durham', *Form und Inhalt Otto Schmitt zum 60. Geburtstag am 13. December 1950* (Stuttgart, 1950), 89–95.
67. *BSFRMP* (1927), pl. X.
68. Omont, *op.cit.*, pl. XXXVII.
69. Hesseling, *Miniatures*, fig. 111.
70. *Ibid.*, fig. 49; Ouspensky, *Octateuque*, fig. 57.
71. T.S.R. Boase, *English Art 1100–1216* (1953), pl. 58.
72. Demus, *op.cit.*, 54.
73. Hans Gerstinger, *Die Wiener Genesis* (2 vols., Vienna, 1931), I, 111, discusses this point, listing 38 Joseph scenes in S. Marco, 22 in the Cotton Genesis, 14 in the Ashburnham Pentateuch, 29 in the Vatican Octateuchs, 32 in the Smyrna Octateuch, 19 in the Seraglio Octateuch, 9 in Vat. Barb. lat. 4406, 5 in Santa Maria Antiqua, as well as other groups in grec 510, Byzantine ivories and the Millstatt Genesis.
74. J. and O. Pächt, 'Ephraimillustration, Haggah und Wiener Genesis', *Festschrift Karl M. Swoboda zum 28 January 1959* (Vienna, 1959), 45; Gerstinger, *op.cit.*, 112; J.J. Tikkanen, 'Die Genesismosaiken von San Marco in Vendig und ihr Verhältnis zu den miniaturen der Cottonbible', *Acta Societatis Scientarium Fennicae*, XVII (1889), 65; W. Grüneisen, *Sainte Marie Antique* (Rome, 1911), 44. For the relationship of the Vienna Genesis to the Octateuchs see Gerstinger, *op.cit.*, 112; J.J. Tikkanen, 'Die Genesismosaiken von San Marco in Vendig und ihr Verhältnis zu den miniaturen der Cottonbible', *Acta Societatis Scientarium Fennicae*, XVII (1889), 65; W. Grüneisen, *Sainte Marie Antique* (Rome, 1911), 44. For the relationship of the Vienna Genesis to the Octateuchs see Gerstinger, *op.cit.*, 112. Also Gary Vikan, 'Joseph iconography on Coptic textiles', *Gesta, 18* (1979), 99–109.
75. Hesseling, *Miniatures*, fig. 125; Ouspensky, *Octateuque*, fig. 66.
76. Demus, *op.cit.*, fig. 46..
77. Grüneisen, *op.cit.*, 44.
78. Gerstinger, *op.cit.*, pl. 32.
79. Hesseling, *Miniatures*, fig. 20; Rome, B.A.V., MS Vat. gr. 746, fol. 122v.
80. Goldschmidt, *Die byzantinischen*, I,64.
81. K. Weitzmann, *The Miniatures of the Sacra Parallela, Parisinus Graecus 923* (Princeton, 1979), 47.
82. Goldschmidt, *Die byzantinischen*, pl. LXXIV.
83. Rome, B.A.V., MS Vat. grec. 1927, fol. 191v. Ernest DeWald, *The Illustrations of the Manuscripts of the Septuagint III, Psalms and Odes Part 1: Vaticanus Graecus 1927* (Princeton, 1941), pl. XLV.
84. Dodwell and Clemoes, *Hexateuch*, 60r.
85. Type one: San Marco, Sens, Aelfric; type two: Vienna Genesis, Octateuchs.

86. Gerstinger, *op.cit.*, pl. 36.
87. Pächt, 'Ephraimillustrationen'; Gerstinger, *op.cit.*, pl. 35.
88. Dodwell and Clemoes, *Hexateuch*, 60r.
89. Gude Suckale-Redlefsen, 'Die Bilderzyklen zum David Leben von den Anfangen bis zum Ende des 11 Jahrhunderts' (Ph.D. thesis, University of Munich, 1972), 48.
90. Erica C. Dodd, *Byzantine Silver Stamps* (Washington, 1961), pl. 61.
91. Adolph Goldschmidt, *Die Kirchentür des hl. Ambrosius in Mailand* (Strasbourg, 1901), pl. IV.
92. Jean Clédat, 'Le monastère et la nécropole de Baouît', *Memoires publiés par les membres de l'Institut français d'archéologie orientale du Caire, 12* (1904), pl. XVI. Also see Buchthal, *Paris Psalter*, 17, and S.H. Wander, 'The Cyprus plates, the story of David and Goliath', *Metropolitan Museum Journal, 8* (1973), 90–104.
93. Weitzmann, *Sacra Parallela, op.cit.*, fig. 118.
94. The Souvigny Bible, Moulins, B.M., MS 1, fol. 93, C.R. Dodwell, *Painting in Europe* (1971), pl. 238; Walter Cahn, *Romanesque Bible Illumination* (Ithaca, 1982), 273.
95. This scene is represented in a late twelfth-century English psalter in Paris, B.N., MS lat. 8846 where it is clearly identified by the inscription: 'Saul David sumens arma ad expugnandum Golyani', Hénri Omont, *Psautier illustré (xiiie siècle)* (Paris, 1906), pl. IV.
96. Jean Lassus, *L'Illustration byzantine du livre des rois, Vaticanus Graecus 333* (Paris, 1973), fig. 42.
97. Dodd, *op.cit.*, 58.
98. For a discussion of the relationship of the psalters, see Buchthal, *Paris Psalter*, 16, figs. 4, 26; Lassus, *op.cit.*, 22; K. Weitzmann, 'Prolegomena to a study of the Cyprus plates', *Metropolitan Museum Journal, 3* (1970), figs. 4, 8, 9.
99. Anthony Cutler, 'A psalter from Mar Saba and the evolution of the Byzantine David cycle', *Journal of Jewish Art, 6* (1979), 39–63.
100. *Idem*, 'The aristocratic psalter: the state of research', *Rapport au XVe congrès international d'études byzantines* (Athens, 1976), 423–47.
101. Silver plate, top register, Dodd, *op.cit.*, pl. 58.
102. For illustrations, see n. 98.
103. Raffaele Garrucci, *Storia della arte cristiana nei primi otto secoli della chiesa* (6 vols., Prato, 1879), V, pl. 341; Paul Bauer, 'David and Goliath on an Early Christian lamp', *Yale Classical Studies, 1* (1928), 43–51.
104. The erect, unmoving Goliath can be found in the Marciana Psalter (Fig. 72) and Tiberius C.VI, Temple, *Anglo-Saxon Manuscripts*, fig. 308.
105. The Bible of Stephen Harding, Dijon, B.M., MS 14, fol. 13, C. Oursel, *La miniature du XIIe siècle. L'abbaye de Cîteaux d'après les manuscrits de la bibliothèque de Dijon* (Dijon, 1926), pl. V; the Souvigny Bible, Dodwell, *Painting, op.cit.*, pl. 238; Cahn, *op.cit.*, 273.
106. Dodwell, *Canterbury*, *op.cit.*, pl. 55, fig. a.
107. Lassus, *op.cit.*, fig. 43.
108. It is also found on a twelfth-century capital at Vézelay and the Mosan Bible from Parc Abbey, London, B.L., MS Add. 41789, fol. 10r. For Vézelay, see A.K. Porter, *Romanesque Sculpture of the Pilgrimage Roads* (10 vols., Boston, 1923), II, fig. 131.
109. Cahn, *op.cit.*, 270, fig. 95.
110. Temple, *Anglo-Saxon Manuscripts*, figs. 307–8.

111. *Ibid.*, 84.
112. Dodwell, *Canterbury*, *op.cit.*, pl. 55, fig. a.
113. Rainer Kahsnitz, *Der Werdener Psalter in Berlin Ms. theol. lat. fol. 358* (Düsseldorf, 1979), 192.
114. Buchthal, *Paris Psalter*, fig. 31.
115. *Ibid.*, fig. 4.
116. *Ibid.*, fig. 26.
117. Ernest DeWald, *The Illustrations of the Manuscripts of the Septuagint Vol. III Psalms and Odes Part 2 Vaticanus Graecus 752* (Princeton, 1942), pl. LIII.
118. Goldschmidt, *Die byzantinischen*, I, fig. 123.
119. Garrucci, *op.cit.*, V, pl. 341.
120. A.K. Porter, *The Crosses and Culture of Ireland* (New Haven, 1931), fig. 238.
121. Kahsnitz, *op.cit.*, fig. 132.
122. Vézelay, Autun, Saint-Aubin, Angers, Saint-Maurice, Vienne: Suckale-Redlefsen, *op.cit.*, 74; Gaede, *op.cit.*, 359.
123. See nn. 94–5 for the plate reference.
124. See n. 92 for the plate reference.
125. See n. 93 for the plate reference.
126. Buchthal, *Paris Psalter*, 13; Lassus, *op.cit.*, 22.
127. The scene appears in the Chuldov Psalter, fol. 24r; the Theodore Psalter, fol. 28r and the Barbarini Psalter, fol. 44v. See S. Der Nessessian, *L'illustration des psautiers grecs du moyen âge II. Londres Add. 19.352* (Paris, 1970), fig. 49. Also see Suzy Dufrenne, *L'illustration des psautiers grecs du moyen âge* (Paris, 1966).
128. DeWald, *The Stuttgart Psalter*, *op.cit.*, fol. 158v.
129. Goldschmidt called the plaque Carolingian and grouped it with the Liuthar ivories and assigned a date of ninth–tenth century. Goldschmidt, *Die Elfenbeinskulpturen*, I, 67f. Weitzmann ascribed it to a Fulda workshop and assigned it to the tenth century. See 'Eine Fuldaer Elfenbeingruppe', *Festschrift zum 70. Geburtstag Adolph Goldschmidt* (Berlin, 1935), 14. More recently, Weitzmann offered another opinion, assigning it to the ninth century. See 'The Heracles plaques of St Peter's cathedra', *AB*, *15* (1973). Another study by Hermann Fillitz assigns it to the fourth quarter of the ninth century and ascribes the work to the north Italian workshop that he feels produced the Milan diptych and Magdeburg antependium group. See 'Die David-Platte einer Basler Privatsammlung', *Festschrift für Hanns Swarzenski zum 70. Geburtstag am 30. August 1972* (Berlin, 1973), 223–6.
130. Wilpert, *I sarcofagi*, pls. XLIX, 5, 8; LXXIV, 5; CXVIII, 2, 3; CCCXXXVIII, 3.
131. Buchthal, *Paris Psalter*, pl. 11.
132. Der Nessessian, *op.cit.*, fig. 295.
133. The life of David was apparently a popular subject in early Insular art. A variety of other types for David fighting the lion exist. See Helen Roe, 'The David cycle in early Irish art', *Journal of the Royal Society of Antiquaries*, *69* (1949), 39–59 Suckale-Redlefsen, *op.cit.*, 35.
134. David Wright, *The Vespasian Psalter, British Museum Cotton Vespasian A.I* (Copenhagen, 1967).
135. Lassus, *op.cit.*, fig. 40; Buchthal, *Paris Psalter*, fig. 3. The close analogies of the Anointment scene in the Psalter with the Book of Kings–aristocratic psalter representations gains in importance when it becomes evident that this type can be differentiated from the one found in the marginal psalters. In this group, represented by examples in the Chuldov Psalter, the

Pantocrator Psalter, Mt Athos, Pantocrator MS 61 and the Theodore Psalter, the Anointment takes place near David's flock without the presence of Jesse and David's brother. Dufrenne, *op.cit.*, pl. 19; Der Nessessian, *op.cit.*, fig. 297.

136. Buchthal, *Paris Psalter*, fig. 27.
137. *Ibid.*, 18.
138. Omont, *op.cit.*, pl. XXXVII.
139. Wander, *op.cit.*, 99; Cahn, *op.cit.*, fig. 98.
140. Dodwell, *Canterbury*, *op.cit.*, pl. 55, fig. a.
141. This detail has been used to distinguish between Eastern and Western representations of the scene. See Walter Cahn, 'The Souvigny Bible: A study in Romanesque manuscript illumination' (Ph.D. thesis, Institute of Fine Arts, New York University, 1967), 295.
142. Gertrud Schiller, *Ikonographie*, IV/2, 44; J.G. LaFontaine-Dosogne, *op.cit.*, II, 22.
143. Schiller, *Ikonographie*, IV/2, 59.
144. LaFontaine-Dosogne, *op.cit.*, 67.
145. Wormald, *Winchester*, 17; Schiller, *Ikonographie*, IV/2, 59; LaFontaine-Dosogne, *op.cit.*, 68.
146. Schiller, *Ikonographie*, 61.
147. LaFontaine-Dosogne, *op.cit.*, 79.
148. Frank Stenton, *The Bayeux Tapestry* (1965), fig. 19.
149. Schiller, *Ikonographie*, IV/2, 63.
150. Wormald, *Winchester*, 17; LaFontaine-Dosogne, *op.cit.*, 86.
151. Kauffmann, *Romanesque*, 210.
152. Schiller, *Ikonographie*, IV/2, 67, fig. 527.
153. LaFontaine-Dosogne, *op.cit.*, 23–4; Schiller, *Ikonographie*, 67.
154. Wormald, *Winchester*, 17.
155. Swarzenski, *Monuments*, figs. 2–5.
156. See Arthur Watson, *The Early Iconography ofthe Tree of Jesse* (1934); J.E. Snyder, 'Geertgen schildert de voorouders van Christus', *Bulletin van het Rijksmuseum*, *5* (1957), 85–94.
157. According to Watson, *op.cit.*, 144, the subject occurs with great frequency in illustrations at the beginning of Matthew. The examples he cites are: Prague, University Library, Vysehrad MS XIV.A.13; Trier, Cathedral MS 142.A.124; Dijon, B.M., MS 2; Paris, B.N., MS 16746; Paris, B. de Saint-Geneviève, MS 10.
158. R. Ligtenberg, 'De Genealogie van Christus in de Beeldende Kunst der Middeleeuwen, Voornamelikj van het Westen', *Oudheidkundig Jaarboek*, *9* (1929), 3; Watson, *op.cit.*, 78.
159. M.A. Farley and F. Wormald, 'Three related English Romanesque Mss', *AB*, *22* (1940), 157–60; H. Swarzenski (review of Farley–Wormald), *AB*, *24* (1942), 295; Boase, *op.cit.*, 135, 147; Kauffmann, *Romanesque*, 82.
160. Rome, B.A.V., MS Vat. gr. 1162, fol. 113v: Stornajolo, *op.cit.*, pl. XIX; Paris, B.N., MS grec 1204, fol. 153v: Omont, *op.cit.*, pl. XIX.
161. Millet, *Recherches*, 69 for a discussion of this type and its distribution.
162. Pächt, *St Albans*, pl. 117c.
163. *Ibid.*, pl. 118f.
164. *Ibid.*, pl. 118e.
165. Richard Hamann, *Die Holztür der Pfarrkirche zu St. Maria im Kapitol* (Marburg, 1926), pl. III.
166. Pächt, *St Albans*, pl. 117c.
167. *Ibid.*, pl. 118c.
168. *Ibid.*, 66.
169. Kraus, *Die Miniaturen*, pl. X; Ronig, *Codex*, 31.
170. Pächt, *St Albans*, pl. 16a.
171. Ronig, *Codex*, 35. The columns, curtains and hanging lamp can also be found in a Carolingian example, Goldschmidt, *Die Elfenbeinskulpturen*, I, fig. 53, but

closer comparisons exist to the Echternach group.

172. Pächt, *St Albans*, pl. 102c.
173. Camille Gaspar and Frédéric Lyna, *Les principaux manuscrits à peintures de la Bibliothèque royale de Belgique* (Paris, 1937), 39–43.
174. Omont, *Psautier illustré*, *op.cit.*, pl. 3.
175. Lucy Freeman Sandler, *The Peterborough Psalter in Brussels and other Fenland Manuscripts* (New York, 1974), fig. 18.
176. Swarzenski, *Monuments*, fig. 355.
177. The majority of the examples are Byzantine. For instance, Paris, B.N., MS grec 74; Rome, B.A.V., MS gr. 1156; Florence, Laurentiana, MS VI, 23. See Millet, *Recherches*, 55.
178. Pächt, *St Albans*, 55. Drogo Sacramentary: Koehler, *Die karolingische Miniaturen* (7 vols., Berlin, 1931–71), III, pl. 82c; *idem*, *Drogo-Sakramentar, Manuscrit Latin 9428, B.N. Paris* (Graz, 1974); Frank Unterkircher, *Zur Ikonographie und Liturgie des Drogo-Sakramentars* (Graz, 1977).
179. Goldschmidt, *Die Elfenbeinskulpturen*, I, pl. XLIIe.
180. Pächt, *St Albans*, pl. 17.
181. Hugo Kehrer, *Die heiligen drei Könige in Literatur und Kunst* (2 vols., Leipzig, 1908), II, 27.
182. Kraus, *Die Miniaturen*, pl. XV; Ronig, *Codex*, 39.
183. Kehrer, *op.cit.*, 26.
184. For a discussion of the Byzantine types see Kehrer, *op.cit.*, 30.
185. *Ibid.*, 103, fig. 125.
186. O. Homburger, *Die Anfänge der Malschule von Winchester im X. Jahrhundert* (Leipzig, 1912), 16, first noted that the Adoration in the Benedictional is one of the first representing the kings wearing crowns. On the possible significance of representing the magi as kings see Robert Deshman, 'The iconography of the full-page miniatures of the Benedictional of St Aethelwold' (Ph.D. thesis, Princeton University, 1970); *idem*, 'Christus rex et magi reges. Kingship and christology in Ottonian and Anglo-Saxon art', *Frühmittelalterliche Studien, 10* (1976), 367–405. The sacramentary and Carolingian Adorations show the Virgin and Child sitting in profile while the magi approach them wearing caps.
187. Deshman, *op.cit.*, 'The iconography', 131, n. 86. On the Roman ceremony see T. Klauser, 'Aurum coronarium', *Mitteilungen des Deutschen Archaeologischen Instituts, Römische Abteilung, 59* (1944), 129–53; K. Wessel, 'Aurum coronarium und oblaticium', *Reallexikon zur byzantinischen Kunst* (4 vols., Munich), I, 448–451. For Early Christian examples of the magi presenting crowns see *Repertorium der christlich-antiken Sarkophage*, ed. F. Deichmann (2 vols., Wiesbaden, 1967), I, no. 5; Volbach, *op.cit.*, pl. 12.
188. Kraus, *Die Miniaturen*, pl. XV; Ronig, *Codex*, 39.
189. Kehrer, *op.cit.*, fig. 22.
190. *Ibid.*, fig. 115.
191. Please consult the plates in the Kehrer publication. Of the approximately 50 examples from the Early Christian period through the twelfth century, only four have cross-legged stools.
192. The other manuscripts show them kneeling (*Codex Egberti*, Bremen Perikope) or walking (*Epternacensis*, *Escorialensis*).
193. Kehrer, *op.cit.*, fig. 112.
194. *Ibid.*, fig. 113.
195. Hans Jantzen, *Ottonische Kunst* (Munich, 1947), 90; Florentine

Mütherich, 'Ottonian art, changing aspects', in *Romanesque and Gothic Art* (Princeton, 1962), 27; A. Boeckler, *Abendländische Miniaturen* (Berlin, 1930), 44.

196. Pächt, *St Albans*, 55, pl. 18b.
197. Goldschmidt, *Die Elfenbeinskulpturen*, I, fig. 95.
198. *Ibid.*, fig. 68.
199. Pächt, *St Albans*, pl. 19a.
200. Goldschmidt, *Die Elfenbeinskulpturen*, I, fig. 95h. Other examples, including a standing angel, which predate the Winchester example are found in the Boulogne Psalter, Boulogne, B.M., MS 20, fol. 59, and an eleventh-century ivory in the Victoria and Albert Museum, *ibid.*, II, fig. 65.
201. Koehler, *Die karolingische*, III, pl. 71a.
202. Kraus, *Die Miniaturen*, pl. XI; Ronig, *Codex*, 33.
203. Metz, *Golden Gospels*, pl. 31.
204. Barbara Abou-el Haj, 'Bury St Edmunds abbey between 1070 and 1124: a history of property, privilege and monastic art production', *Art History*, *6* (1983), fig. 12.
205. D.V. Ainalov, *The Hellenistic Origins of Byzantine Art* (New Brunswick, 1961), 148; David T. Rice, *Kunst aus Byzanz* (Munich, 1959), 51, n. 66.
206. An especially close parallel appears in a Regensburg manuscript. See G. Swarzenski, *Die Regensburger Buchmalerei* (2 vols., Leipzig, 1901), II, fig. 153. The type is also found on an altar frontal at Fécamp, F. Avril, *Trésors des abbayes normandes* (Rouen, 1979), 219–21; Jean Vallery-Radot, 'Cinq tombeaux d'abbés à la Trinité de Fécamp', *Revue de l'art ancien et moderne*, *53* (1928), 111; Berlin MS 78.A.6, E. Klemm, *Ein Romanischer Miniaturenzyklus aus dem Maasgebiet* (Vienna, 1973), pl. 14.
207. A. Grabar, *L'Empereur dans l'art byzantin* (Paris, 1936), 234; E. Kantorowitz, 'The king's advent and the enigmatic panels in the doors of Santa Sabina', *AB*, *25* (1944), 207f.; E. Kitzinger, 'The mosaics of the Cappella Palatina in Palermo', *AB*, *31* (1949), 279.
208. Goldschmidt, *Die Elfenbeinskulpturen*, II, fig. 65.
209. *St Benoît-sur-Loire* (Dijon, 1965), pls. 25–6.
210. Kitzinger, *op.cit.*, fig. 7.
211. See n. 209 for plate references.
212. J. Plotzek, 'Das Perikopenbuch Heinrichs III in Bremen und seine Stellung innerhalb der Echternacher Buchmalerei' (Ph.D. thesis, Cologne University, 1970), 127.
213. Pächt, *St Albans*, pl. 21a.
214. D. Shorr, 'The iconographic development of the Presentation in the Temple', *AB*, *28* (1946), 23 and fig. 13.
215. The indoor setting and presence of the altar distinguishes the scene from Byzantine compositions which follow a different tradition. The Byzantine scenes were designed to celebrate the meeting of Simeon and Christ which was celebrated in the East as the Hypapante. In these representations, Simeon meets Christ outside the temple. In the West, the emphasis changed. Here the purification of the Virgin was honoured, *ibid*, 17.
216. The slab in Wirksworth, which has certain analogies with Early Christian sarcophagi has been variously dated. Suggestions range from an early dating in the eighth century to the late tenth century. See B. Kurth, 'The iconography of the Wirksworth slab', *Burlington Magazine*, *86* (1945), 114.

217. Pächt, *St Albans*, 84 and pl. 20a. Leviticus 12:2–8 and Luke 2:24. The law states that the offering should be a lamb and young turtle dove. If the family could not bring a lamb, two doves might be offered in its place.
218. M. Schott, *Zwei Lütticher Sacramentare* (Strasbourg, 1931), 83 and Swarzenski, *Monuments*, 53.
219. Hamann, *op.cit.*, pl. XVII.
220. Stanislava Sawicka, 'La bibliothèque du chapitre de Gniezno', *BSFRMP*, *19* (1938), pl. XXXVIII.
221. Volbach, *Spätantike*, fig. 119.
222. Kraus, *Die Miniaturen*, pl. XVII; Ronig, *Codex*, 43.
223. Goldschmidt, *Die Elfenbeinskulpturen*, II, fig. 65.
224. F. Wormald, *The Miniatures of the Gospels of St Augustine* (1954), fig. 14.
225. Klemm, *op.cit.*, fig. 17.
226. Pächt, *St Albans*, pl. 22a.
227. Kauffmann, *Romanesque*, fig. 175.
228. *Codex Egberti*, fol. 20v: Kraus, *Die Miniaturen*, pl. XIX; Ronig, *Codex*, 47; Bremen Perikope, fol. 16v; *Epternacensis*, fol. 52v: Metz, *Golden Gospels*, pl. 49; *Escorialensis*, Boeckler, *Das Goldene*, fig. 139.
229. H.H. Arnason, 'Early Christian silver of North Italy and Gaul', *AB*, *20* (1938), fig. 10.
230. Ursula Nilgen, 'Hochzeit zu Kana', *Lexikon der christlichen Ikonographie* (4 vols., Herder, 1970), II, 299–306.
231. E. Heinrich Zimmermann, 'Die Fuldaer Buchmalerei in karolingischer und ottonischen Zeit', *Kunstgeschichtlicher Jahrbuch der K.K. Zentralkommission für Kunst- und Historische Denkmale* IV (1910), 1–104.
232 Nilgen, *op.cit.*, 302.
233. W. Säuerlander, *Gotische Skulptur in Frankreich, 1140–1270* (Munich, 1970), 70 and pls. 16–17.
234. *Ibid.*, 54 and pl. 53 shows the other side of the capital where the guests are seated at the table. The subject has been identified by Säuerlander as a Marriage at Cana.
235. Kauffmann, *Romanesque*, fig. 176.
236. Goldschmidt, *Die Elfenbeinskulpturen*, I, fig. 75.
237. Plotzek, *op.cit.*, 168.
238. Metz, *Golden Gospels*, 32.
239. Boeckler, *Das Goldene*, pl. 44.
240. Säuerlander, *op.cit.*, pls. 16–17.
241. Pächt, *St Albans*, pl. 107d.
242. Kauffmann, *Romanesque*, fig. 176.
243. *Ibid.*, 60, 86, 198, pl. 23a.
244. This bearded type may have had a minor influence upon the appearance of the devil in the first two Temptation scenes.
245. Elizabeth Parker, 'A 12th century cycle of New Testament drawings from Bury St Edmunds Abbey', *Proceedings of the Suffolk Institute of Archaeology*, *31* (1969), 274 and pl. XXXIII.
246. Kauffmann, *Romanesque*, fig. 175.
247. Schiller, *Ikonographie*, II, fig. 34.
248. Also see Deshman, 'The iconography', *op.cit.*, 139.
249. Pächt, *St Albans*, pl. 25b.
250. Wormald, *The Gospels*, *op.cit.*, pl. IV.
251. Two other Ottonian manuscripts, one in Maihingen and Berlin, theol. lat. fol. 134 depict the same scene. But the table in these cases is oval, placing them further from the Nero C.IV than *Escorialensis*, Plotzek, *op.cit.*, 189.
252. Boeckler, *Das Goldene*, fig. 150.
253. On the iconography of this group see Betty Kurth, 'Zur Christus-Johannes-Gruppe', *Zeitschrift für Kunstgeschichte*, *2* (1933); Reiner Hausherr, 'Christus-Johannes-Gruppen in der Bible Moralisée', *Zeitschrift für Kunstgeschichte*, *27* (1964), 133–52.
254. DeWald, *Stuttgart*, *op.cit.*, fol. 53.

This example and a succession of others show Judas receiving the sop from the hand of Christ, an event described by John.
255. Millet, *Recherches*, 266.
256. Schiller, *Ikonographie*, II, pl. 84.
257. Pächt, *St Albans*, 59 and pl. 26b.
258. E. Kantorowicz, 'The Baptism of the Apostles', *Dumbarton Oaks Papers*, IX-X (1955–6), 205–52; Hildegard Giess, *Die Darstellung der Fusswaschung Christi in den Kunstwerken des 4.–12. Jahrhunderts* (Rome, 1962), 45; H. Schnitzler, 'Ein frühchristliche Sarkophagszene und die Reichenauer Buchmalerei', *Festschrift Friederich Gerke* (Baden-Baden, 1962), 93–102.
259. Schnitzler, *op.cit.*, 93–8.
260. Giess, *op.cit.*, fig. 34.
261. Kraus, *Die Miniaturen*, pl. XLIV; Ronig, *Codex*, 91.
262. Giess, *op.cit.*, fig. 39.
263. The oldest example is found in a fresco in S. Sebastiano al Palatino, Rome. J. Wilpert, *Die römischen Mosaiken und Malereien der kirchlichen Bauten vom IV. bis VIII. Jahrhundert* (4 vols., Freiburg, 1916), II, pl. 379; Giess, *op.cit.*, 31.
264. Lucca, Biblioteca Governativa, MS 1275, *ibid.*, fig. 37.
265. *Ibid.*, fig. 43.
266. *Ibid.*, 70.
267. Goldschmidt, *Die Elfenbeinskulpturen*, I, fig. 75.
268. *Codex Egberti*, fol. 97, Ronig, *Codex*, 93; Metz, *Golden Gospels*, pl. 83; Boeckler, *Das Goldene*, fig. 87.
269. Goldschmidt, *Die Elfenbeinskulpturen*, I, fig. 133a.
270. DeWald, *Stuttgart*, *op.cit.*, fol. 43.
271. *Idem*, *The Utrecht Psalter* (Princeton, 1932), pl. CXXXV. Also see Schiller, *Ikonographie*, II, 76, on Byzantine types.
272. *Codex Egberti*, fol. 79, Kraus, *Die Miniaturen*, pl. XLVI; Ronig, *Codex*, 1023; Bremen Perikope, fol. 49v; Brussels 9428: Schiller, *Iconographie*, II, fig. 228; *Epternacensis*, fol. 110v, Metz, *Golden Gospels*, pl. 83.
273. Kraus, *Die Miniaturen*, pls. XLIV, L; Ronig, *Codex*, 103, 103.
274. *Codex Egberti*, fol. 89, Kraus, *Die Miniaturen*, pl. LI; Bremen Perikope, fol. 58v; *Epternacensis*, fol. 111, Metz, *Golden Gospels*, pl. 84.
275. See for example, London, B.L., MSS Harley 2904, fol. 3v; Stowe 944, fol. 6; Arundel 60, fol. 12v; Cambridge, C.C.C., MS 157, fol. 77v, Rickert, *op.cit.*, pls. 30, 37b, 43, 52, 60.
276. *Codex Egberti*, fol. 39, Kraus, *op.cit.*, pl. LI; Bremen Perikope, fol. 58v; *Epternacensis*, fol. 111, Metz, *op.cit.*, pl. 84. H.A. Wilson, *The Missal of Robert of Jumièges* (1896), pl. VII.
277. Schiller, *Ikonographie*, II, 165; Millet, *Recherches*, 471.
278. Goldschmidt, *Die Elfenbeinskulpturen*, I, 45. He places the ivory stylistically in the Meuse–Lower Rhine region around 1000.
279. K. Weitzmann, 'The origin of the Threnos', *De Artibus Opuscula XL. Essays in Honor of Erwin Panofsky*, ed. M. Meiss (2 vols., New York, 1961), I, 475–90.
280. Marie Lafargue, *Les chapiteaux du cloître de Notre-Dame la Daurade* (Paris, 1940), pl. XIV, fig. 3.
281. Schiller, *Ikonographie*, II, fig. 556. Also see W.S. Cook, 'The earliest painted panels of Catalonia', *AB*, *5* (1927), 153–204, where Cook illustrates two additional examples: Huesca, S. Pedro el Viego, and Tarragona Cathedral, figs. 70–1.
282. Pächt, *St Albans*, 70 and pl. 29b.
283. Elizabeth Parker, *The Descent from the Cross: Its Relation to the Extra*

Liturgical Deposition Drama (New York, 1978). She has explained the cloth as the sindon in which Christ was wrapped. The sindon had liturgical significnce because it was symbolized in the medieval Mass by the sub-deacon, 78–9; Kauffmann, *Romanesque*, fig. 179.

284. The entombment is also found in the Bamberg Apocalypse, Bamberg Cathedral, H. Wöflin, *Die Bamberger Apokalypse* (Munich, 1921), pl. 54; *Codex Egberti*, fol. 82, Kraus, *Die Miniaturen*, pl. LI; Ronig, *Codex*, 103; Perikope, fol. 58v.
285. Pächt, *St Albans*, 62, 72; pl. 30a.
286. Parker, 'Bury', *op.cit.*, 289 and pl. XXXVIII.
287. M. Graeve, 'The stone of unction in Caravaggio's painting for Chiesa Nova', *AB*, *40* (1958), 230.
288. Adelheid Heimann, 'The capital frieze and pilasters of the Portail Royal, Chartres', *JWCI*, *31* (1968), 87.
289. Carolingian precedents for the three women standing behind one another exist but they are not as close in type to the Winchester Psalter as are the Ottonian examples. For the Carolingian examples see Goldschmidt, *Die Elfenbeinskulpturen*, I, figs. 41, 84, 144.
290. Boeckler, *Das Goldene*, fig. 93.
291. D.T. Rice, *English Art 871–1100* (1952), 200, 209; J.J.G. Alexander, *Anglo-Saxon Illumination in Oxford Libraries* (1970), 12; Kauffmann, *Romanesque*, fig. 18.
292. Cook, *AB*, *10*, *op.cit.*, 356.
293. Karl Young, *The Drama of the Medieval Church* (1933), 29–40.
294. Beckwith, *Ivory* (1972), fig. 130.
295. I Peter 3:19; I Corinthians 15:55.
296. C. Tischendorf, *Evangelia Apocrypha* (Leipzig, 1876), 389.
297. M.Q. Smith, 'The Harrowing of Hell relief in Bristol Cathedral', *Transactions of the Bristol and Gloucestershire Archaeological Society*, *94* (1976), 101–6.
298. The type is found earlier in the Utrecht Psalter, Psalm xv (16), DeWald, *Utrecht*, *op.cit.*, pl. XIII.
299. The earliest example of Hell represented as the mouth of an animal is found on a ninth-century ivory in the Victoria and Albert Museum. The provenance is a matter of dispute. Both England and Tours have been suggested. See Beckwith, *Ivory*, figs. 1, 16. Also see M. Bauer, 'Die Ikonographie der Höllenfahrt Christi von ihren Anfägen bis zum XVI Jahrhundert' (Ph.D. thesis, Göttingen, 1948), 165.
300. Pächt, *St Albans*, pl. 30b.
301. According to Schiller, *Ikonographie*, III, 49, the angel is a common feature in Western Harrowing scenes. It is found, for example, in the Carolingian fresco at Müstair and in the Reichenau manuscript in Hildesheim, MS 688, fol. 57r.
302. Wormald, *Winchester*, 25.
303. The *Noli me tangere* is also illustrated in the Gospels of Otto III, G. Leidinger, *Das sogenannte Evangeliarium Kaiser Ottos III* (Munich, 1912), pl. 51; *Codex Egberti*, fol. 91, Kraus, *Die Miniaturen*, pl. LVI; Ronig, *Codex*, 115; *Epternacensis*, fol. 111v, Metz, *Golden Gospels*, pl. 85.
304. Drogo Sacramentary; Brussels 9428, Schiller, *Ikonographie*, III, fig. 277; Goldschmidt, *Die Elfenbeinskulpturen*, I, fig. 27.
305. Plotzek, *op.cit.*, 225.
306. Kauffmann, *Romanesque*, fig. 180.
307. The only detail found in the Winchester Psalter that does not appear in grec 74 is the cross staff carried by Christ. This can be found in other Western *Noli me tangere* scenes. For example, on Bernward's doors at Hildesheim,

R. Wesenberg, *Bernwardische Plastik* (Berlin, 1955), and an eleventh-century Frankish ivory, Goldschmidt, *Die Elfenbein-skulpturen*, II, fig. 150.

308. Wormald alludes to this passage without elaborating, *Winchester*, 25. Schiller, *Ikonographie*, III, 178, discusses the problem in greater detail.

309. Among them are Munich Clm. 4452, fol. 152v, G. Leidinger, *Das Perikopenbuch Heinrichs II* (Munich, 1914), pl. 31; Bremen Perikope, fol. 111r; Brussels 9428, fol. 153v; *Escorialensis*, fol. 40, Boeckler, *Das Goldene*, fig. 54. The scene also occurs in a mid-eleventh century manuscript, possibly from lower Saxony, with a strong dependence on Reichenau. The scene is found on fols. fv–g. Peter leads a procession of disciples on fol. fv. Christ sits enthroned on fol. g holding the keys in Hannover Niedersächsisches Landesmuseum Hs. XXIa, nr. 34; W. Vöge, 'Ein deutsche Malerschule um die Wende des ersten Jahrtausends', *Westdeutsche Zeitschrift Erg.-H.*, *7* (1891), 146–7.

310. Plotzek, *op.cit.*, 165.

311. Among them, the Drogo Sacramentary, Schiller, *Ikonographie*, III, fig. 304 and several ivories, *ibid.*, fig. 308 and Goldschmidt, *Die Elfenbeinskulpturen*, I, fig. 184.

312. *Ibid.*, I, fig. 122.

313. The scene is also found in the *Codex Egberti* but is represented differently. Christ stands between the two disciples, fol. 88. Kraus, *Die Miniaturen*, pl. LIII; Ronig, *Codex*, 109.

314. In this instance, the Carolingian sources discussed above are not repeated in the Ottonian works. The Ottonian scene has earlier precedents, as, for example, the ninth-century silver reliquary in the Vatican, Schiller, *Ikonographie*, III, fig. 305.

315. Kraus, *Die Miniaturen*, pl. LIII; Ronig, *Codex* 109.

316. The Albani Psalter, 70, Pächt, *St Albans*, pl. 37, also shows both a youthful and bearded disciple.

317. *Ibid.*, 73, pls. 38–40.

318. The Doubting Thomas type found on Carolingian monuments can be traced back to an Early Christian prototype preserved on the fifth-century sarcophagus in S. Celso, Milan. Wilpert, *I sarcofagi*, II, pl. CCXL, 6; Schnitzler, *op.cit.*, 101.

319. The scene is also found in the Bremen Perikope, fol. 66r, and Brussels 9428, fol. 97v.

320. In other respects, the Echternach examples do not agree with the Winchester scene. Christ displays the nail holes in his hands and the scene takes place within an architectural setting.

321. Pächt, *St Albans*, pl. 32a.

322. Pächt cited south Italian and Byzantine sources, *ibid.*, 94. Another possibility, not considered by Pächt, is the tenth-century Basilewsky situla in the Victoria and Albert Museum. Here Christ stands with his arms upraised instead of extended to the side. The disciples are arranged in two groups on either side of Christ instead of behind him. See J. Beckwith, *The Basilewsky Situla* (1963), pl. 14.

323. M. Schapiro, 'The image of the disappearing Christ: the Ascension in English art around the year 1000', *Gazette des beaux-arts*, *85* (1943), 135–52.

324. There are two continental examples from the eleventh century, the Boulogne Gospels, Morgan Library, MS 333, and the Gospel book of Bernward of

Hildesheim, A. Goldschmidt, *Die deutsche Buchmalerei* (2 vols., Florence, Munich, 1928), pl. C, both of which are discussed by Schapiro, *op.cit.* Some examples from after the mid-twelfth century include a Mosan enamel, Swarzenski, *Monuments*, fig. 400 and the relief at Fécamp.

325. The Rouen type is also found in Rome, B.A.V., MS Vat. Reg. lat. 12; London, B.L., MS Cotton Caligula A.XIV, and Morgan Library, MS 333, Schapiro, *op.cit.*, figs. 3, 6, 7.

326. The Albani angels, p. 54, are similarly disposed. Pächt, *St Albans*, pl. 33a. In general, however, the Albani Ascension is not as close to the Winchester scene as the one in Pembroke 120.

327. See Carl Nordenfalk, *Codex Caesareus Upsaliensis* (Stockholm, 1971), 104.

328. On the *Maiestas Domini* in general, see Robert Berger, *Die Darstellung des thronenden Christus in der romanischen Kunst* (Reutlingen, 1926); Franz Rademacher, *Der thronende Christus der Chorschranken aus Gustorf* (Cologne, 1964); Schiller, *Ikonographie*, III, 234; F. van der Meer, *Maiestas Domini, théophanes de l'apocalypse dans l'art chrétien* (Rome, Paris, 1938).

329. Beckwith, *Ivory*, 123.

330. Schiller, *Ikonographie*, III, 241.

331. *Ibid.*, figs. 679, 696.

332. Martin Jugie, *La Mort et l'assomption de la Sainte Vierge* (Vatican City, 1944); Henri Barré, 'La croyance à l'assomption corporelle en occident de 750 à 1150 environs, *Études Mariales*, *7* (1949), 63–123; Schiller, *Ikonographie*, IV/2, 92.

333. *Ibid.*, fig. 587.

334. *Ibid.*, 96–106.

335. Wormald, *Winchester*, 27.

336. Schiller, *Ikonographie*, IV/2, figs. 608, 620, 622.

337. Franz Rademacher, *Die Regina Angelorum in der Kunst des frühen Mittelalters* (Düsseldorf, 1972), 22; G.A. Wellen, *Theotokos* (Antwerp, 1960).

338. Otto Demus, *Byzantine Art and the West* (New York, 1970), 161; Wormald, *Winchester*, 85.

339. Rademacher, *op.cit.*, 41, 56; fig. 28.

340. *Ibid.*, 54–6; Schiller, *Ikonographie*, IV/2, 30; Ernst Guldan, *Eva und Maria* (Cologne, 1966), 36–8; Rademacher, *op.cit.*, 86, 119.

341. From the late twelfth century, the doors in Pisa; A. Boeckler, *Die Bronzetüren des Bonnus von Pisa und des Barisanus von Trani* (Berlin, 1953), 17, figs. 1, 29, 30; Lavadieu, in O. Demus, *Romanesque Mural Painting* (1970), fig. 187.

342. For a recent critique of Wormald's discussion of the 'English' icon, *Winchester*, 87, see Robert S. Nelson, 'An icon at Mt Sinai and Christian painting in Muslim Egypt during the thirteenth and fourteenth centuries', *AB*, *65* (1983), 201–18.

343. Demus, *Byzantine Art*, *op.cit.*, fig. 115.

344. Beckwith, *Ivory*, fig. 1; London, B.L., MS Harley 603, fol. 71.

345. On Clayton, see Demus, *Mural Painting*, *op.cit.*, 507, and Clive Bell, *Twelfth-Century Paintings at Hardham and Clayton* (1947), pl. 12; for Plumpton see E.W. Tristram, *English Medieval Wall Painting* (1944), 143.

346. On the possible presence of a Reichenau apocalypse manuscript at Echternach see Nordenfalk, *Codex*, *op.cit.*, 108 and Beat Brenk, *Tradition und Neuerung in der christliche Kunst der ersten Jahrtausends, Studien zur Geschichte*

des Weltgerichtsbildes (Vienna, 1966), 47.
347. Both Ottonian and English parallels can be cited. See Brenk, *op.cit.*, figs. 45–9; Beckwith, *Ivory*, 121, fig. 41; Clayton, in Bell, *op.cit.*, pl. 20; Kauffmann, *Romanesque*, fig. 102.
348. Wormald, *Winchester*, 72–3; G. Scharf, 'Observations on a picture in Gloucester Cathedral, and some other representations of the Last Judgment', *Archaeologia*, *36* (1855), 1–28.
349. Temple, *Anglo-Saxon Manuscripts*, 86.
350. Brenk, *op.cit.*, 58; Wormald, *Winchester*, 72–3.
351. R. Deshman, 'Anglo-Saxon Art after Alfred', *AB*, *61* (1974), 176–200.
352. Brenk, *op.cit.*, fig. 49; Bell, *op.cit.*, pl. 20.
353. Haney, 'Mosan', *op.cit.*.
354. Burgfelden, in Demus, *Mural Painting*, *op.cit.*, fig. 43; Brenk, *op.cit.*, 144.
355. Temple, *Anglo-Saxon Manuscripts*, figs. 247–8.
356. Brenk, *op.cit.*, 136.
357. Bell, *op.cit.*, pl. 22.
358. Brenk, *op.cit.*, 135.
359. Beckwith, *Ivory*, fig. 41.
360. E.W. Tristram, *English Medieval Wall Painting* (1944), 143.
361. T.A. Heslop, 'English seals from the mid-ninth century to 1100', *JBAS*, *133* (1980), pl. 12 D.
362. Bury Psalter, fols. 11, s, u; M.R. James, *Marvels of the East* (1929), pl. XV.
363. Pächt, *St Albans*, pl. 23b.
364. M.F. Hearn, *Romanesque Sculpture* (Ithaca, 1981), fig. 130; Saxl, *op.cit.*, fig. 40.
365. Hearn, *op.cit.*, fig. 136.
366. B. Thrope, *Ancient Laws and Institutes of England* (3 vols., 1840), I, 206–7; Felix Liebermann, *Die Gesetze der Angelsachsen* (3 vols., Halle, 1903–16).
367. James, *op.cit.*, pl. XV.
368. Wormald, *Winchester*, 73.
369. George Kennedy, *The Caedmon Poems* (1916), 53.

Bibliography

Appleby, John T., *The Troubled Reign of King Stephen* (1969)

Alexander, J. J.G., *Insular Manuscripts: Sixth to the Ninth Century* (1978)

Barré, H., *Prières anciens de l'occident à la Mère du Sauveur* (Paris, 1963)

Bäumer, Suitbert, *Geschichte des Breviars* (2 vols., Freiburg, 1895)

Beckwith, John, *Ivory Carvings in Early Medieval England* (1972)

Beissel, S., *Geschichte der Verehrung Marias in Deutschland während des Mittelalters* (Freiburg, 1901)

Bergman, Robert, *The Salerno Ivories* (Cambridge, MA, 1980)

Bishop, Edmund, *Liturgica Historica* (1918)

Bose, T.S.R., *English Art 1100–1215* (1953)

Boeckler, A., *Abendländische Miniaturen bis zum Ausgang der romanischen Zeit* (Berlin, 1930)

— *Das Goldene Evangelienbuch Heinrichs III* (Berlin, 1933)

Bond, E.A. and Thompson, E.M., *The Palaeographical Society. Facsimilies of Manuscripts and Inscriptions* (1873–83)

Brayer, E. and Bouly de Lisdain, E.M., 'Les prières usuelles annexées aux anciennes traductions français es du psautier', *Bulletin de l'Institut de Recherche et d'Histoire des Textes, 15* (1967–8), 68–120

Buchthal, Hugo, *The Paris Psalter* (1938)

Cahn, Walter, *Romanesque Bible Illustration* (Ithaca, 1982)

Crown, Carol, 'The Winchester Psalter: iconographic sources and themes of the Virgin Mary, kingship and law' (Ph.D. thesis, Washington University, 1976)

Cutler, Anthony, 'The psalter of Basil II', *Arte Venetia, 30* (1976), 12–13

De Bruyne, D., *Préfaces de la Bible Latine* (Namur, 1920)

Delius, W., *Geschichte der Marienverehrung* (Munich, 1963)

Deshman, R., ' "Christus rex et magi reges": kingship and christology in Ottonian and Anglo-Saxon art', *Frühmittelalterliche Studien, 10* (1976), 367–405

Dodwell, C.R., *The Canterbury School of Illumination, 1066–1200* (1954)

Dodwell, C.R. and Clemoes, P., *The Old English Illustrated Hexateuch, British Museum Cotton Claudius B.IV* (Baltimore, 1974)

Dressler, Fridolin, Mütherich, F., and Beauman, H., *Das Evangeliar Ottos III* (Frankfurt, 1973)

Dufrenne, Suzy, *Les illustrations du Psautier d'Utrecht: Problèmes des sources et de l'apport carolingien* (Paris, 1978)

Edmondson, Kristine, 'The Psalter of Henry of Blois, A Study in Romanesque manuscript illumination' (Ph.D. thesis, Institute of Fine Arts, New York University, 1978)

Farley, Mary Ann and Wormald, Francis, 'Three related English Romanesque manuscripts', *AB, 22* (1940), 157–61

Galbraith, K.J., 'The iconography of the biblical scenes at Malmesbury Abbey', *JBAS, 28* (1965), 39–56

Goldschmidt, A. and Weitzmann, K., *Die byzantinischen Elfenbeinskulpturen des X.–XIII. Jahrhunderts* (2 vols., Berlin, 1930–4)

Goldschmidt, A., *Die Elfenbeinskulpturen aus der Zeit der karolingischen und sächsischen Kaiser, VIII.–XI. Jahrhundert* (4 vols., Berlin, 1914–26)

Gollancz, Israel, *The Caedmon Manuscript of Anglo-Saxon Biblical Poetry* (1927)

James, M.R., 'Four leaves of an English psalter of the 12th century and an English picture-book of the late 13th century', *The Walpole Society, 25* (1936–7), 1–32

Haney, Kristine E., 'The Mosan elements in the Psalter of Henry of Blois', *Revue Belge d'Archéologie et d'Histoire de l'Art, 51* (1982), 3–15

— 'The provenance of the Psalter of Henry of Blois', *Manuscripta, 24* (1980), 40–4

— 'The paint surfaces in the Psalter of Henry of Blois', *British Library of Journal, 7* (1973), 149–57

Harris, Robert, 'The marginal drawings of the Bury St Edmunds psalter' (Ph.D. thesis, Princeton University, 1960)

Heimann, Adelheid, 'The capital frieze and pilasters of the Portail Royal, Chartres', *JWCI, 31* (1968), 73–102

Henderson, George, 'Cain's jaw-bone', *JWCI, 24* (1961), 108–14

— 'The sources of the Genesis Cycle at Saint-Savin-sur-Gartempe', *JBAS, 26* (1963), 11–26

Homburger, Otto, *Die Anfänge der Maleschule von Winchester im X. Jahrhundert* (Leipzig, 1912)

Kahsnitz, Rainer, *Der Werdener Psalter in Berlin, Ms. theol. lat. fol. 358, Eine Untersuchung zu Problemen mittelalterlicher Psalterillustration* (Düsseldorf, 1979)

Kahsnitz, Rainer and Rücker, E., *Das Goldene Evangelienbuch von Echternach* (Frankfurt, 1982)

Kauffmann, C.M., 'The Bury Bible', *JWCI, 29* (1966), 60–81

— *Romanesque Manuscripts 1066–1190* (1975)

Ker, N.R., *English Manuscripts in the Century after the Norman Conquest* (1960)

Knowles, David, *The Monastic Order in England* (1965)

Koehler, W., *Die karolingischen Miniaturen* (7 vols., Berlin, 1930–71)

Kracher, A., *Die Millstätter Genesis und Physiologus Handschrift* (2 vols., Graz, 1967)

Kraus, F., *Die Miniaturen des Codex Egberti* (Freiburg, 1884)

Kuypers, A.B., *The Book of Cerne* (1902)

LaFontaine-Dosogne, J., *Iconographie de l'Enfance de la Vierge dans l'empire byzantin et en occident* (2 vols., Brussels, 1965)

Leroquais, Victor, *Les bréviaires manuscrits des bibliothèques publiques de France* (5 vols., Paris, 1934)

— *Les livres d'heures manuscrits de la Bibliothèque Nationale* (3 vols., Paris, 1927–43)

— *Les psautiers manuscrits latins des bibliothèques publiques de France* (3 vols., 1940–1)

McLaughlan, E. Parker, 'In the wake of the Bury Bible: followers of Master Hugo at Bury St Edmunds', *JWCI, 42* (1979), 216–24

Metz, P., *The Golden Gospels of Echternach, Codex Aureus Epternacensis* (New York, 1957)

Millar, E.G., *English Illuminated Manuscripts from the Xth to the XIIIth Century* (Paris, 1926)

Millet, G., *Recherches sur l'iconographie de l'évangile* (Paris, 1916)

Morgan, Nigel, 'Notes on the post-Conquest calendar, litany and martyrology of the cathedral priory of Winchester with a consideration of Winchester diocese calendars of the pre-Sarum period', in *The Vanishing Past: Studies in Medieval Art, Liturgy and Metrology Presented to Christopher Hohler*, ed. A. Borg and A. Martindale (1981), 131–58

Mütherich, Florentine, 'Die verschiedenen Bedeutungsschichten in der frühmittelalterlichen Psalterillustration', *Frühmittelalterliche Studien, 6* (1972), 232–44

Nordenfalk, Carl, *Codex Caesarius Upsaliensis* (Stockholm, 1971)

— 'Recent publications on illuminated

manuscripts', *The Burlington Magazine*, *117* (1975), 609–11

Oakeshott, Walter, *The Artists of the Winchester Bible* (1945)

— *The Two Winchester Bibles* (1982)

Ouspensky, T., *L'Octateuque de la bibliothèque du Serail à Constantinople* (Sofia, 1907)

Pächt, Otto, 'A Giottesque episode in English medieval art', *JWCI*, *6* (1943), 51–69

— 'Hugo Pictor', *The Bodleian Library Record*, *3* (1950–1), 96–103

— 'The illustrations of St Anselm's Prayers and Meditations', *JWCI*, *19* (1956), 68–83

— *The Rise of the Pictorial Narrative in Twelfth-Century England* (1962)

Pächt, Otto, Wormald, F., and Dodwell, C.R., *The St Albans Psalter (The Albani Psalter)* (1960)

Parker, Elizabeth, 'The scriptorium of Bury St Edmunds in the twelfth century' (Ph.D. thesis, University of London, 1965)

— 'A 12th century cycle of New Testament drawings from Bury St Edmunds Abbey', *Proceedings of the Suffolk Institute of Archaeology*, *31* (1969), 263–302

Plotzek, Joachim, 'Das Perikopenbuch Heinrichs III in Bremen und seine Stellung innerhalb der Echternacher Buchmalerei' (Ph.D. thesis, Cologne University, 1970)

Plummer, John, *Liturgical Manuscripts for the Mass and Divine Office* (New York, 1964)

Rickert, Margaret, *Painting in Britain, the Middle Ages* (Baltimore, 1965)

Ronig, F., *Codex Egberti* (Trier, 1970)

Salmon, Pierre, *Les manuscrits liturgiques latins de la Bibliothèque Vaticane, Bd. 1: Psautiers, antiponaires, hymnaires, collectaires, brévaires* (Vatican City, 1968)

Saxl, F., *English Sculptures of the Twelfth Century* (1954)

Schapiro, Meyer, ' "Cain's jaw-bone that did the first murder" ', *AB*, *24* (1942), 205–12

— 'The image of the disappearing Christ, the Ascension in English art around the year 1000', *Gazette des Beaux-Arts*, *85* (1943), 135–52

Schiller, G., *Ikonographie der christlichen Kunst* (4 vols., Gütersloh, 1966–80)

Southern, R.W., *Saint Anselm and his Biographer* (1966)

Stratford, Neil, 'The Henry of Blois plaques in the British Museum', *Medieval Art and Architecture at Winchester Cathedral* (British Archaeological Association Conference Transactions VI, 1980), 2837

Swarzenski, Hanns, *Monuments of Romanesque Art*, 2nd edn (Chicago, 1967)

Temple, Elzbieta, *Anglo-Saxon Manuscripts 900–1066* (1976)

Thomson, Rodney, 'Early Romanesque book-illustration in England: the dates of the Pierpont Morgan *Vitae Sancti Edmundi* and the Bury Bible', *Viator*, *2* (1971), 211–26

Tolhurst, J.B.L., *The Monastic Breviary of Hyde Abbey, Winchester* (6 vols., 1933–42)

Volbach, W.F., *Die Elfenbeinskulpturen der Spätantike und des frühen Mittelalters*, 3rd edn (Mainz, 1976)

Warner, George, *Illuminated Manuscripts in the British Museum* (1903)

Weitzmann, K., 'Observations on the Cotton Genesis fragments', *Late Classical and Mediaeval Studies in Honor of Albert Matthias Friend, Jr.* (Princeton, 1955), 112–30

Wilmart, A., *Auteurs spirituels et textes dévotes du moyen âge latin* (Paris, 1932)

Wilpert, G., *I sarcofagi cristiana antichi* (5 vols., Rome, 1918–32)

Witzling, Mara, 'An archaeological reconstruction of a previous state of the Winchester Psalter', *Gesta*, *17* (1978), 28–35

— 'An archaeological investigation of the Winchester Psalter' (Ph.D. thesis, Cornell University, 1978)

— 'The Winchester Psalter: a re-

ordering of its prefataory miniatures according to the scriptural sequence', *Gesta, 23* (1984), 17–25
Woledge, B. and Clive, H.P., *Répertoire des plus anciens textes en prose française depuis 842 jusqu'aux premières années du XIIIe siècle* (Geneva, 1964)
Wormald, Francis, 'Continental influence on English illumination', *Transactions of the Fourth International Congress of Bibliophiles* (1967), 4–16
— 'The development of English illumination in the 12th century', *JBAS, 8* (1943), 31–49
— *English Drawings of the Tenth and Eleventh Centuries* (1952)
— 'An English 11th century psalter with pictures: British Museum Cotton MS Tiberius C.VI', *The Walpole Society, 38* (1960–1), 1–14
— 'The survival of Anglo-Saxon illumination after the Norman Conquest', *Proceedings of the British Academy, 30* (1944), 1–19
— 'The Sherborn "Chartulary" ', *Fritz Saxl 1890–1948, A Volume of Memorial Essays from his Friends in England* (1957), 101–19
— *The Winchester Psalter* (1973)
Wright, David, *The Vespasian Psalter (British Museum Cotton MS Vespasian A.I)* (Copenhagen, 1967)

Index of Manuscripts

General Index

The Illustrations

[*The miniatures from the Winchester Psalter (B.L. Cotton Nero C.IV) are reproduced at a standard reduction of approximately 70%. The remaining illustrations are at variable reductions.*]

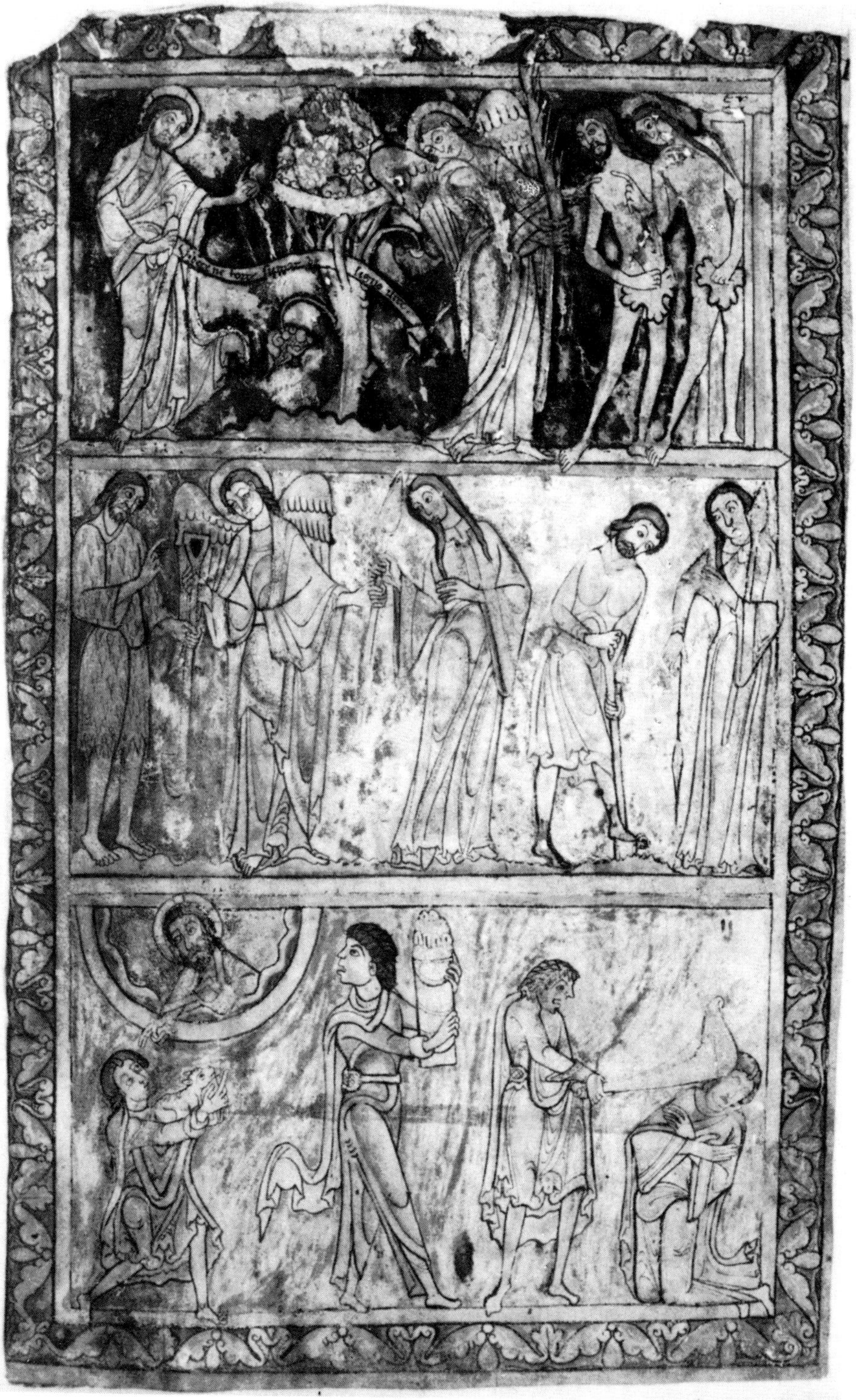

1 London, B.L., MS Cotton Nero C.IV, fol.2, the Expulsion from Paradise, Giving of the Labours, Labours of Adam and Eve, Offerings of Cain and Abel, Murder of Abel

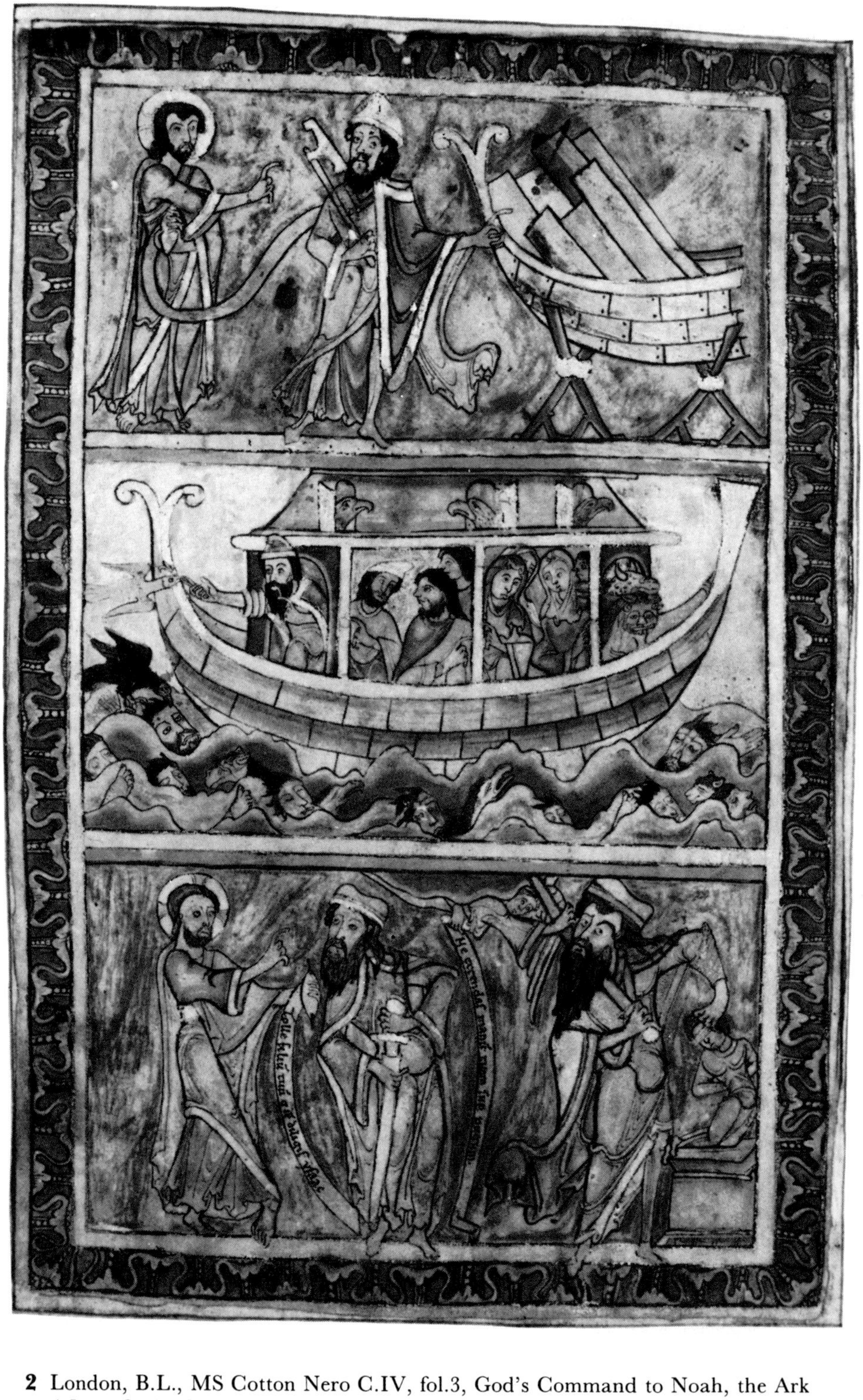

2 London, B.L., MS Cotton Nero C.IV, fol.3, God's Command to Noah, the Ark Afloat, God's Command to Abraham, the Sacrifice of Isaac

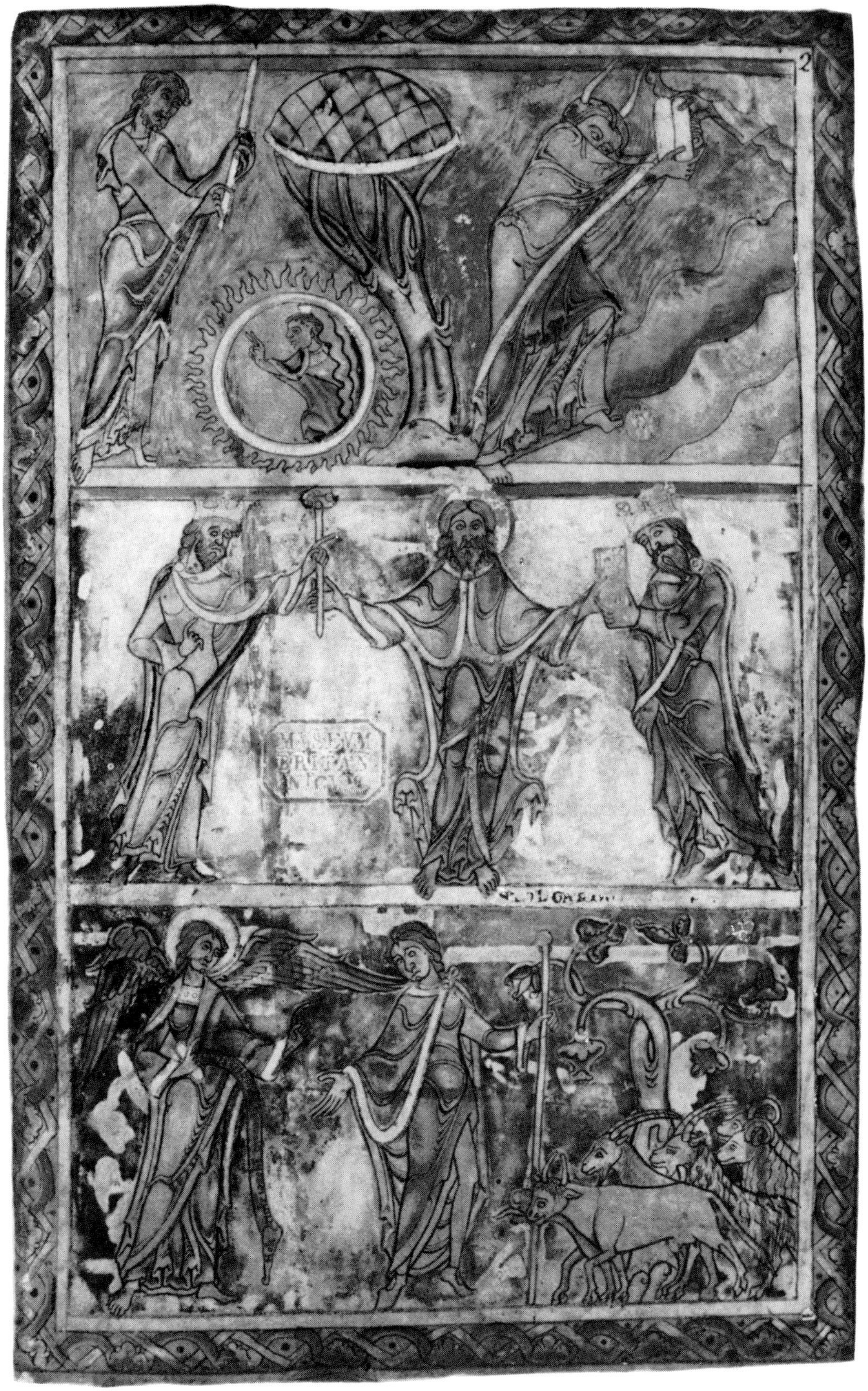

3 London, B.L., MS Cotton Nero C.IV, fol.4, Moses before the Burning Bush, Moses Receiving the Law, David and Solomon with the Lord (?), the Annunciation to Joachim

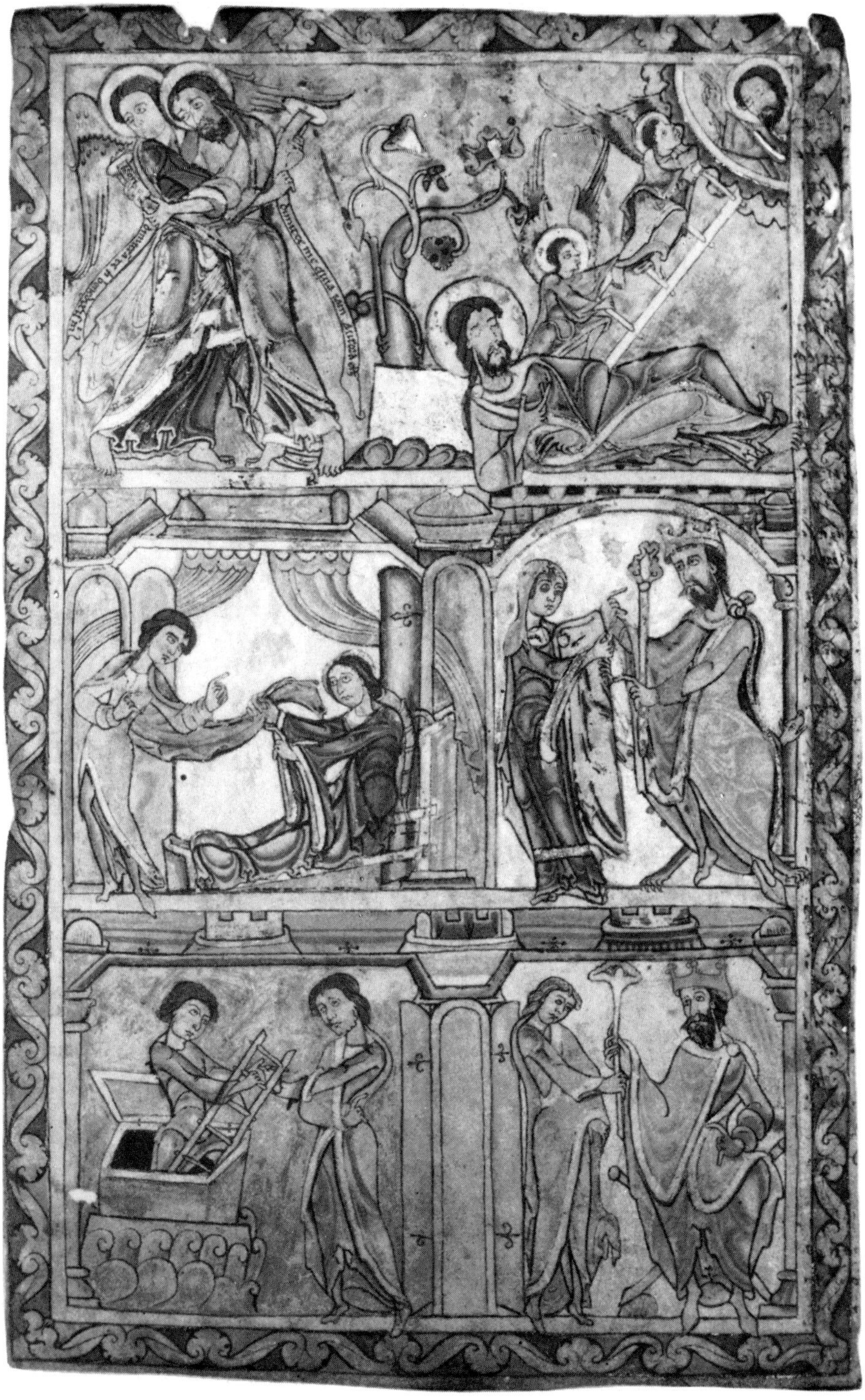

4 London, B.L., MS Cotton Nero C.IV, fol.5, Jacob Wrestling with the Angel, Jacob's Dream, Joseph and Potiphar's Wife, Potiphar with his Wife, Joseph Released from Prison, Joseph before Pharaoh

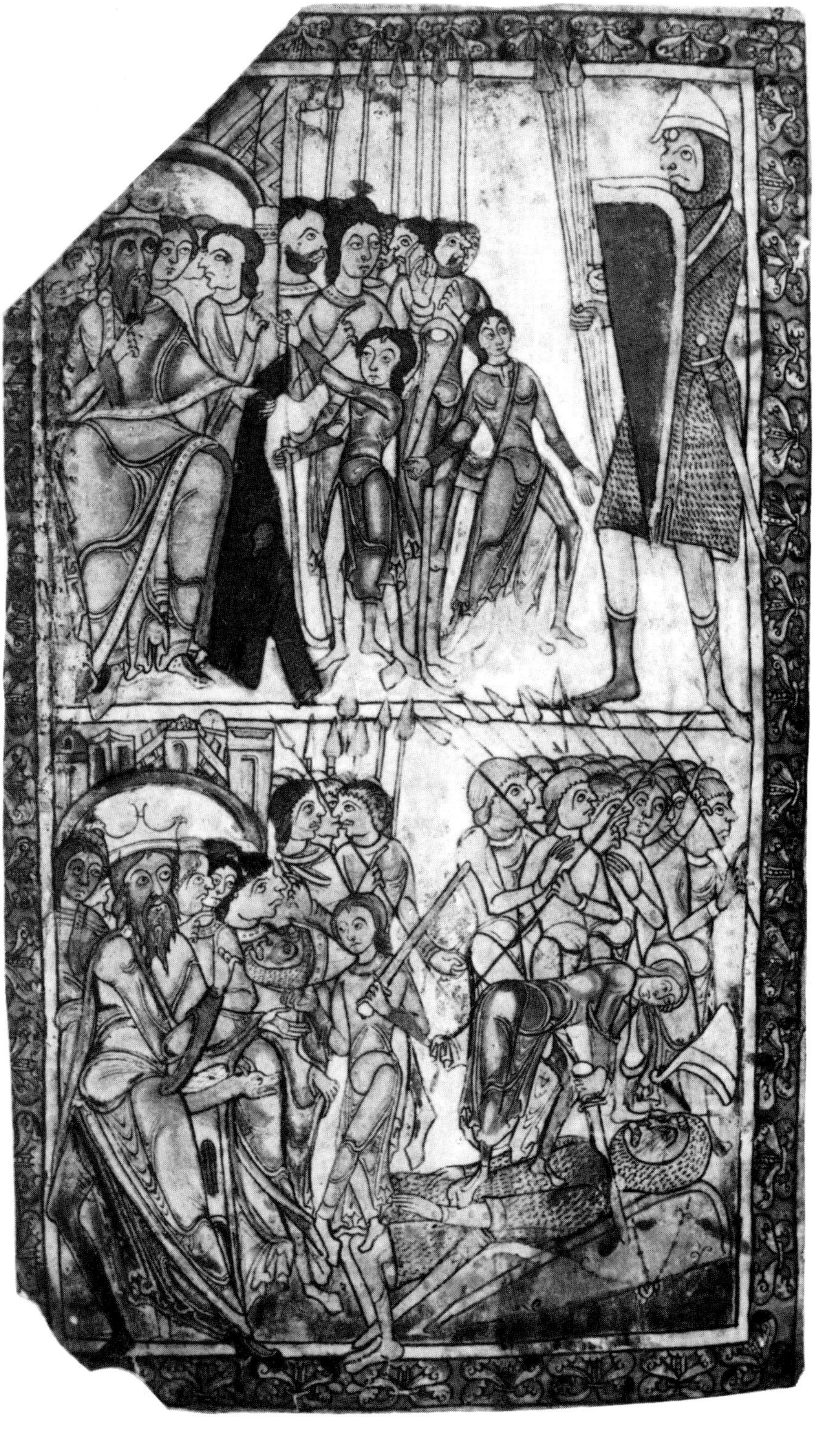

5 London, B.L., MS Cotton Nero C.IV, fol.6, David and Goliath

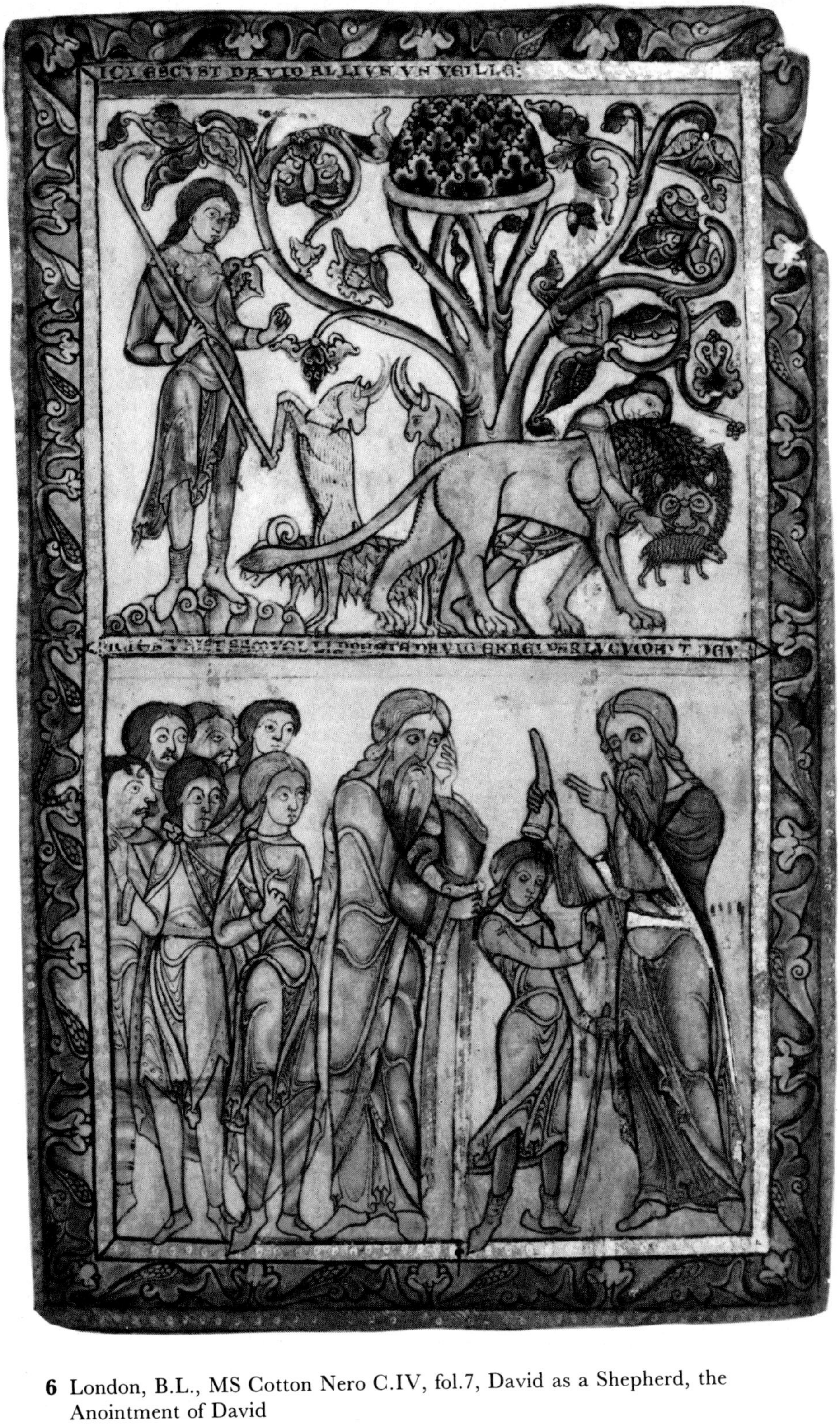

6 London, B.L., MS Cotton Nero C.IV, fol.7, David as a Shepherd, the Anointment of David

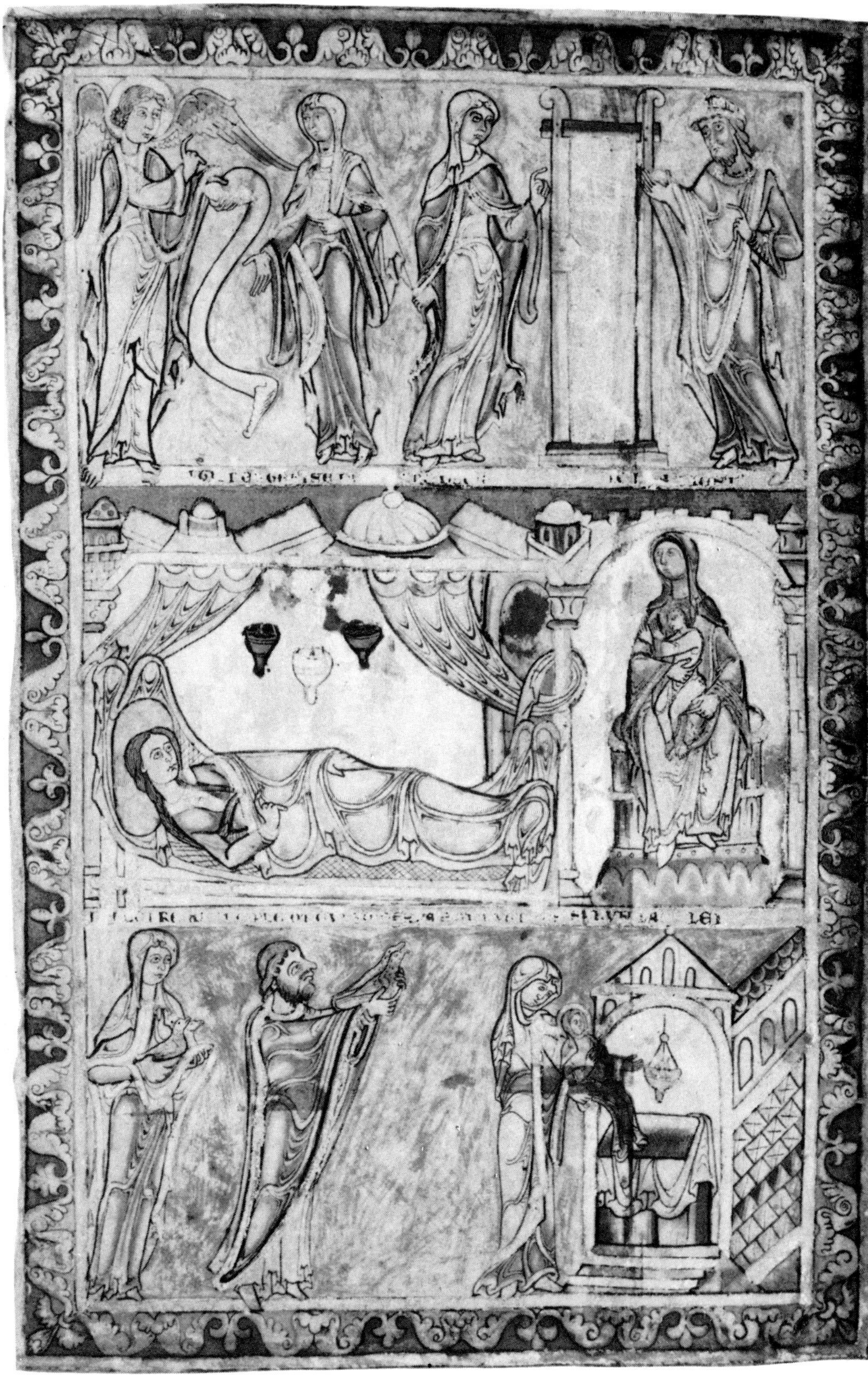

7 London, B.L., MS Cotton Nero C.IV, fol.8, the Annunciation to Anna, the meeting of Joachim and Anna at the Golden Gate, Birth of the Virgin, the Presentation of the Virgin in the Temple

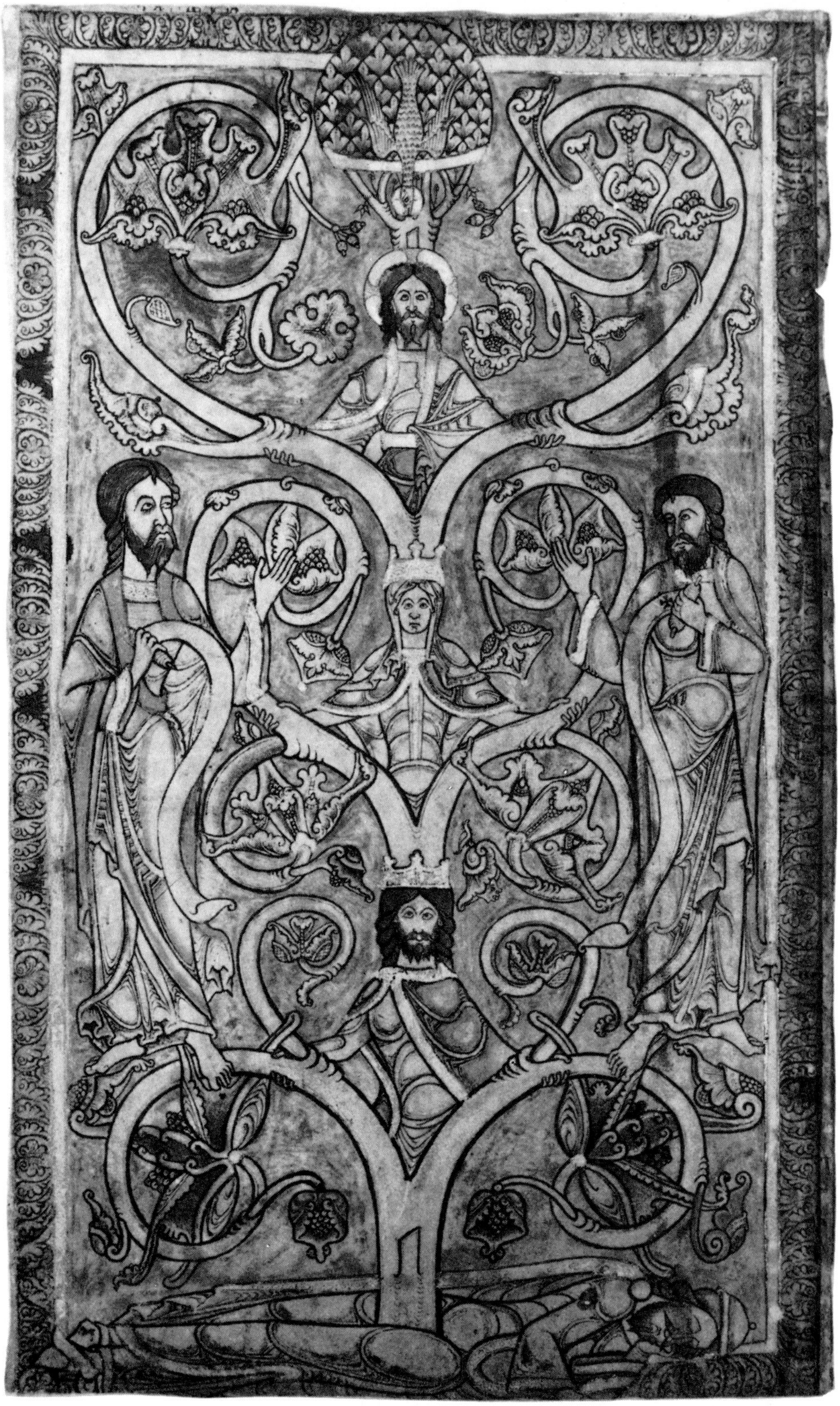

8 London, B.L., MS Cotton Nero C.IV, fol.9, the Jesse Tree

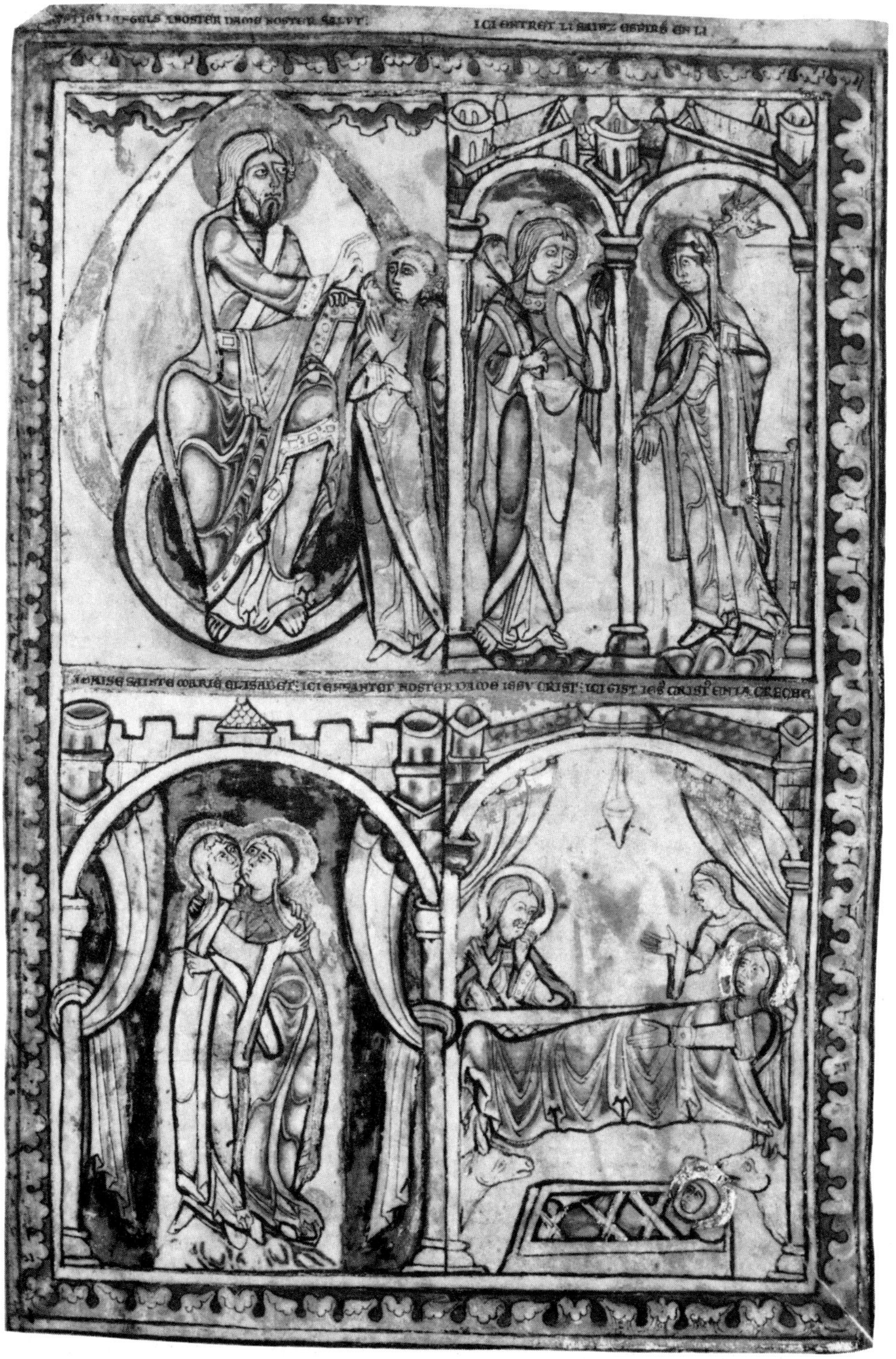

9 London, B.L., MS Cotton Nero C.IV, fol.10, God Sending the Angel, the Annunciation, Visitation, Nativity

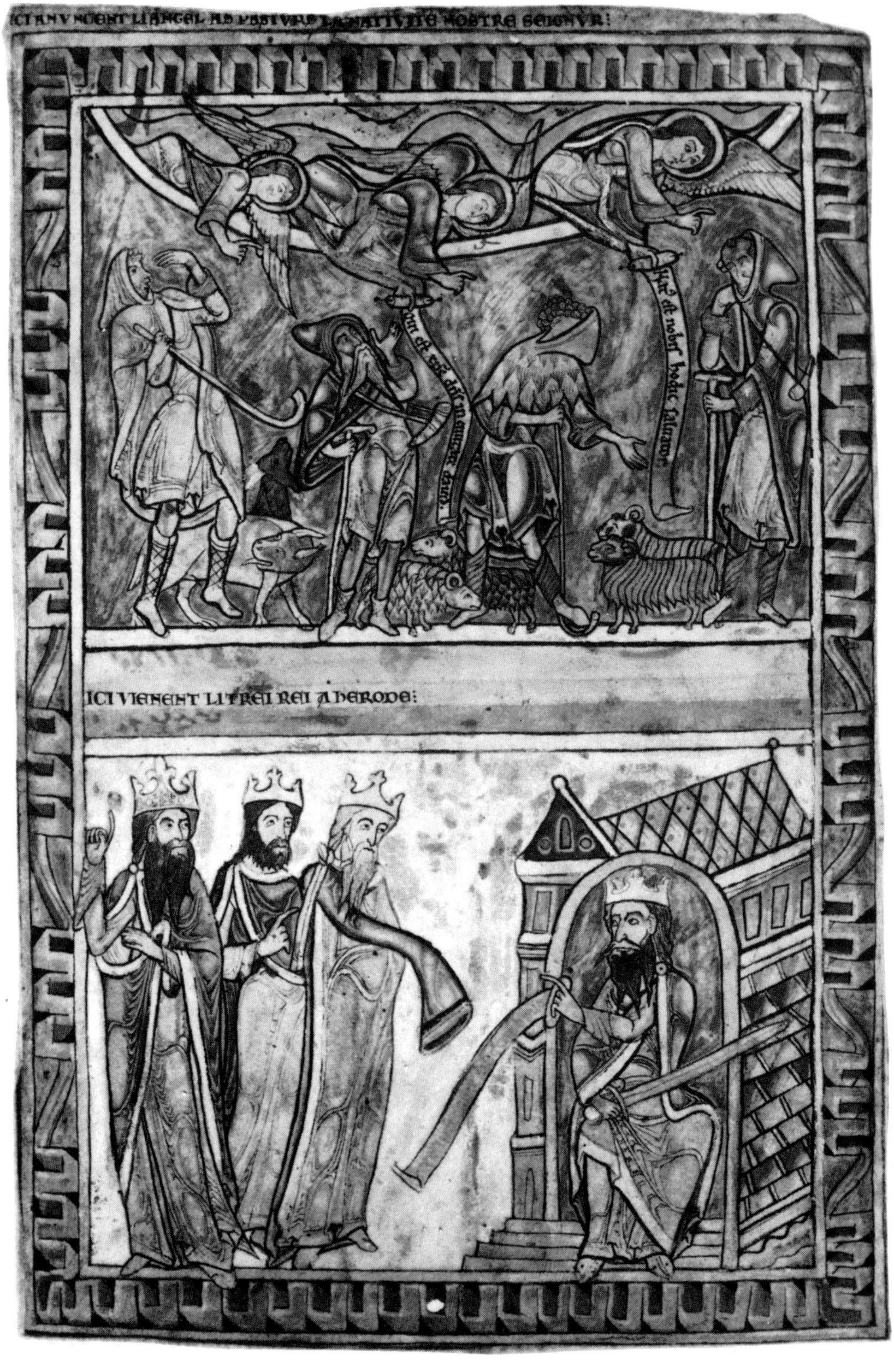

10 London, B.L., MS Cotton Nero C.IV, fol.11, the Annunciation to the Shepherds, the Magi before Herod

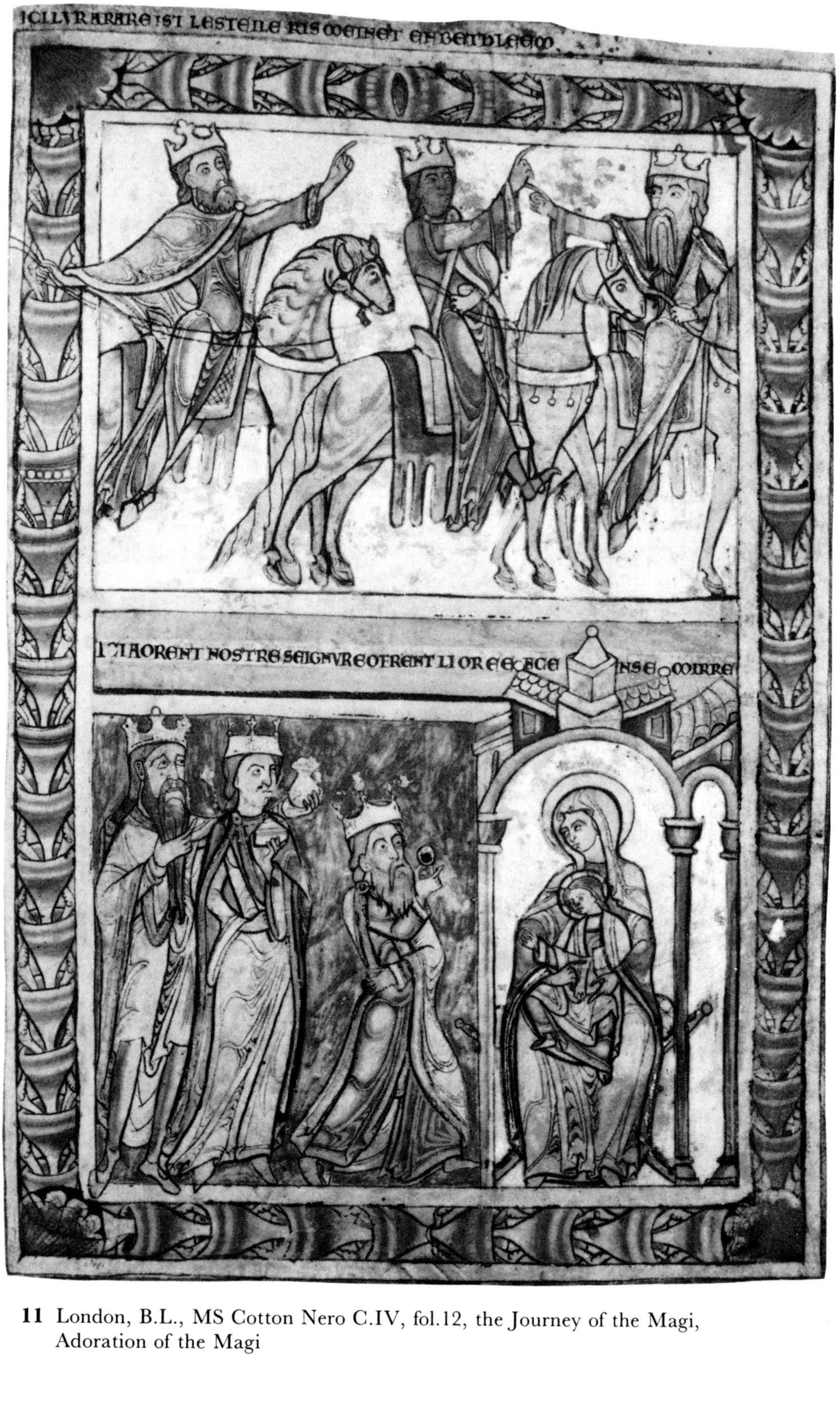

11 London, B.L., MS Cotton Nero C.IV, fol.12, the Journey of the Magi, Adoration of the Magi

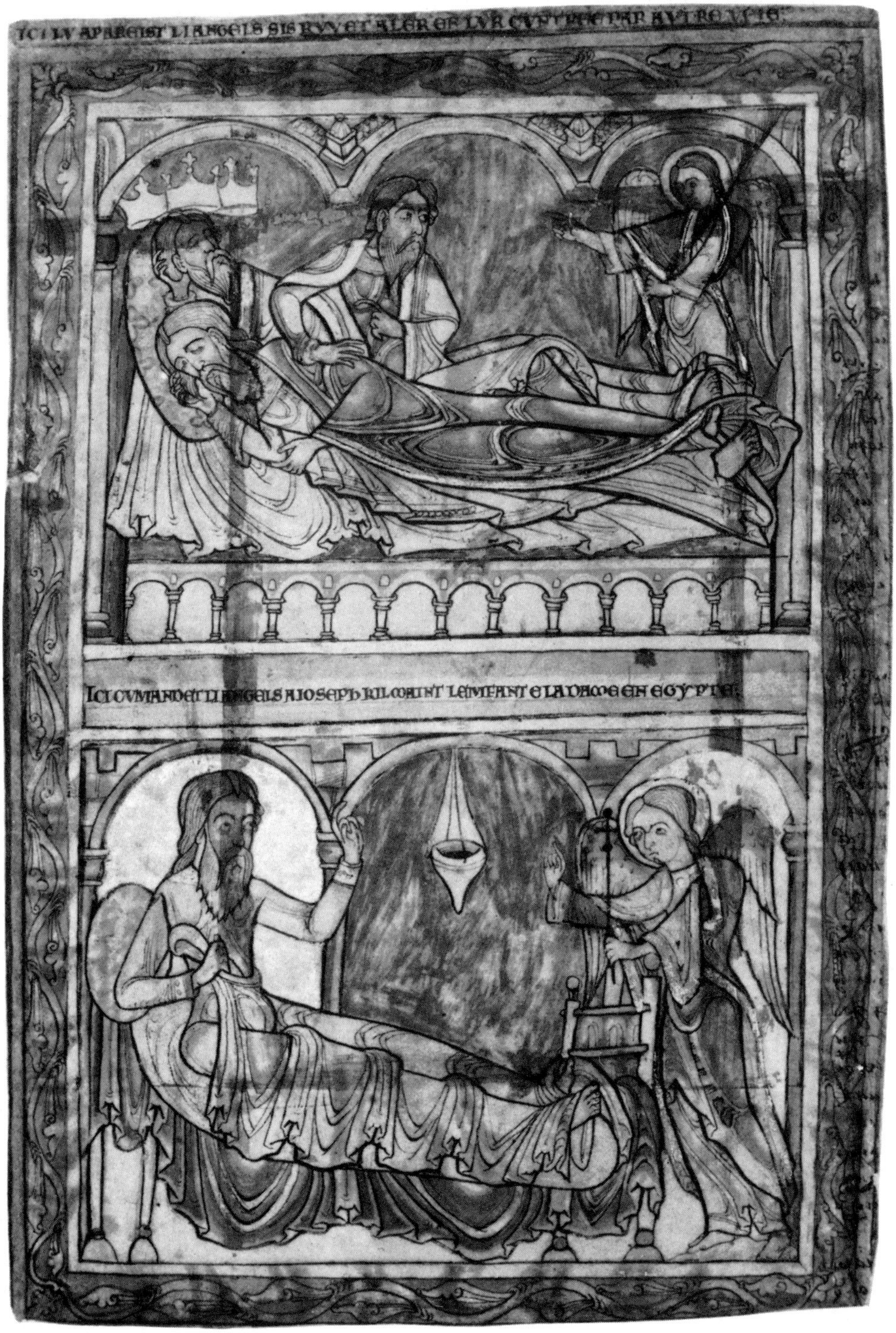

12 London, B.L., MS Cotton Nero C.IV, fol.13, the Dream of the Magi, Dream of Joseph

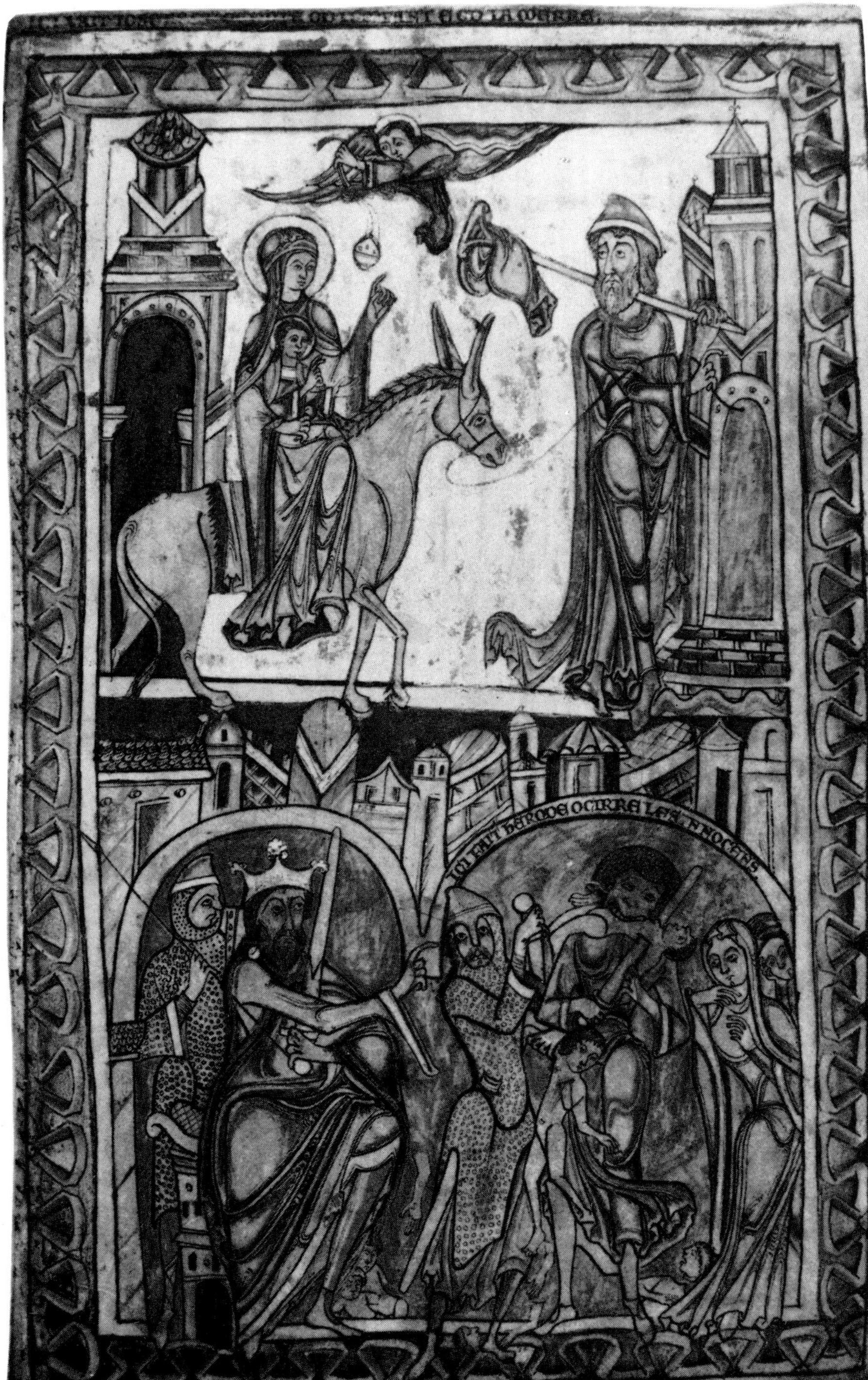

13 London, B.L., MS Cotton Nero C.IV, fol.14, the Flight into Egypt, Massacre of the Innocents

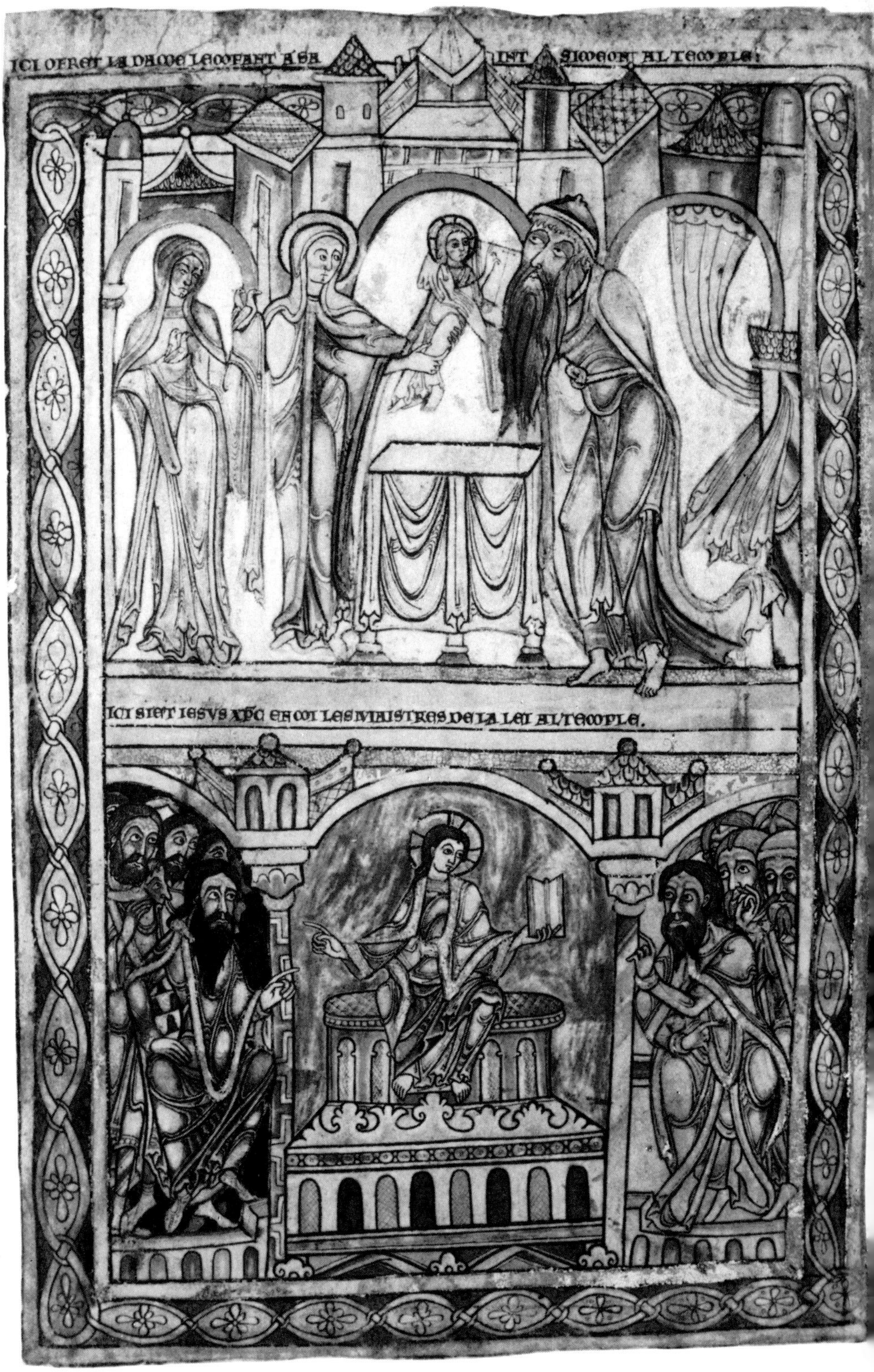

14 London, B.L., MS Cotton Nero C.IV, fol.15, the Presentation in the Temple, Christ Among the Doctors

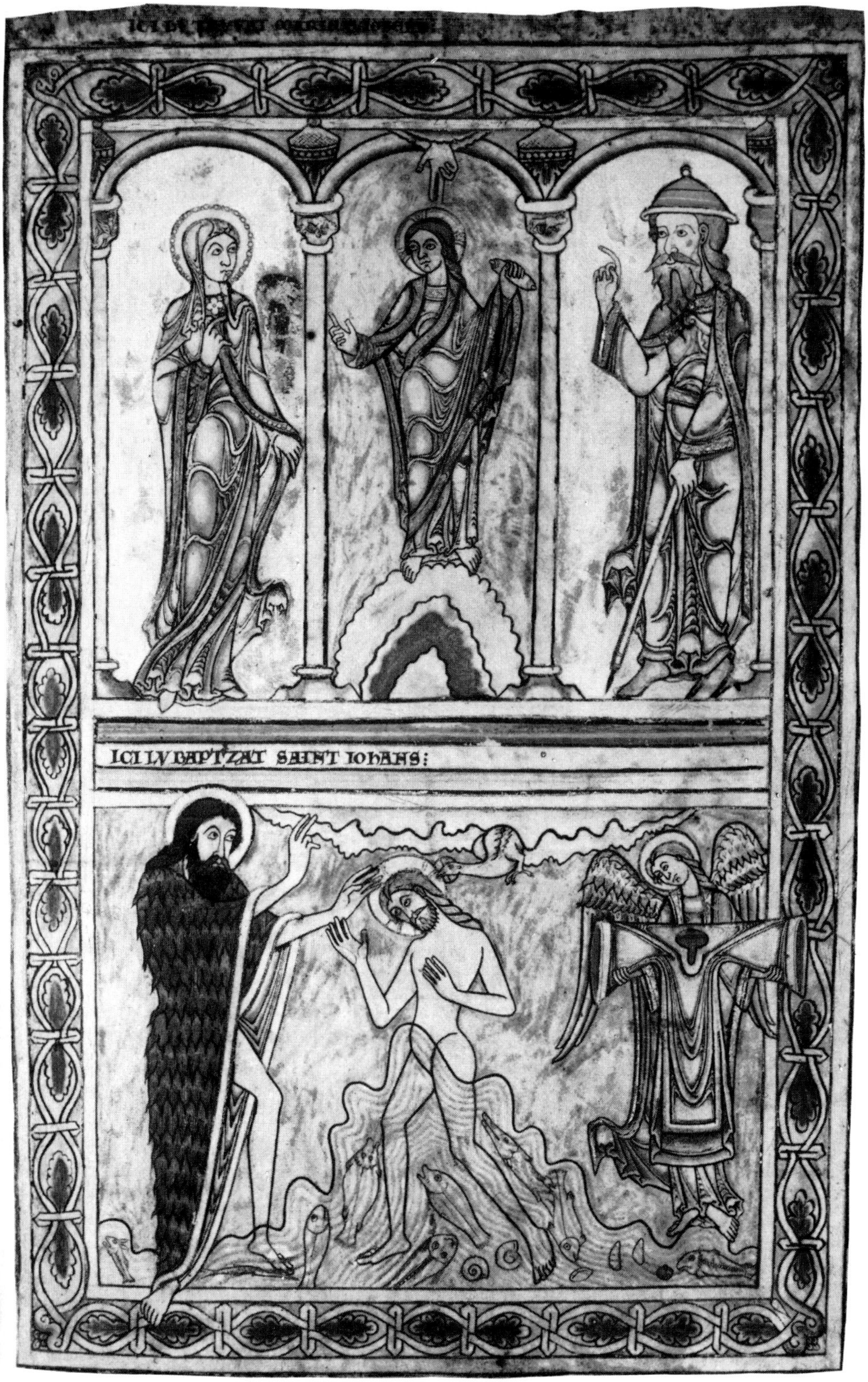

15 London, B.L., MS Cotton Nero C.IV, fol.16, Christ with his Parents, the Baptism of Christ

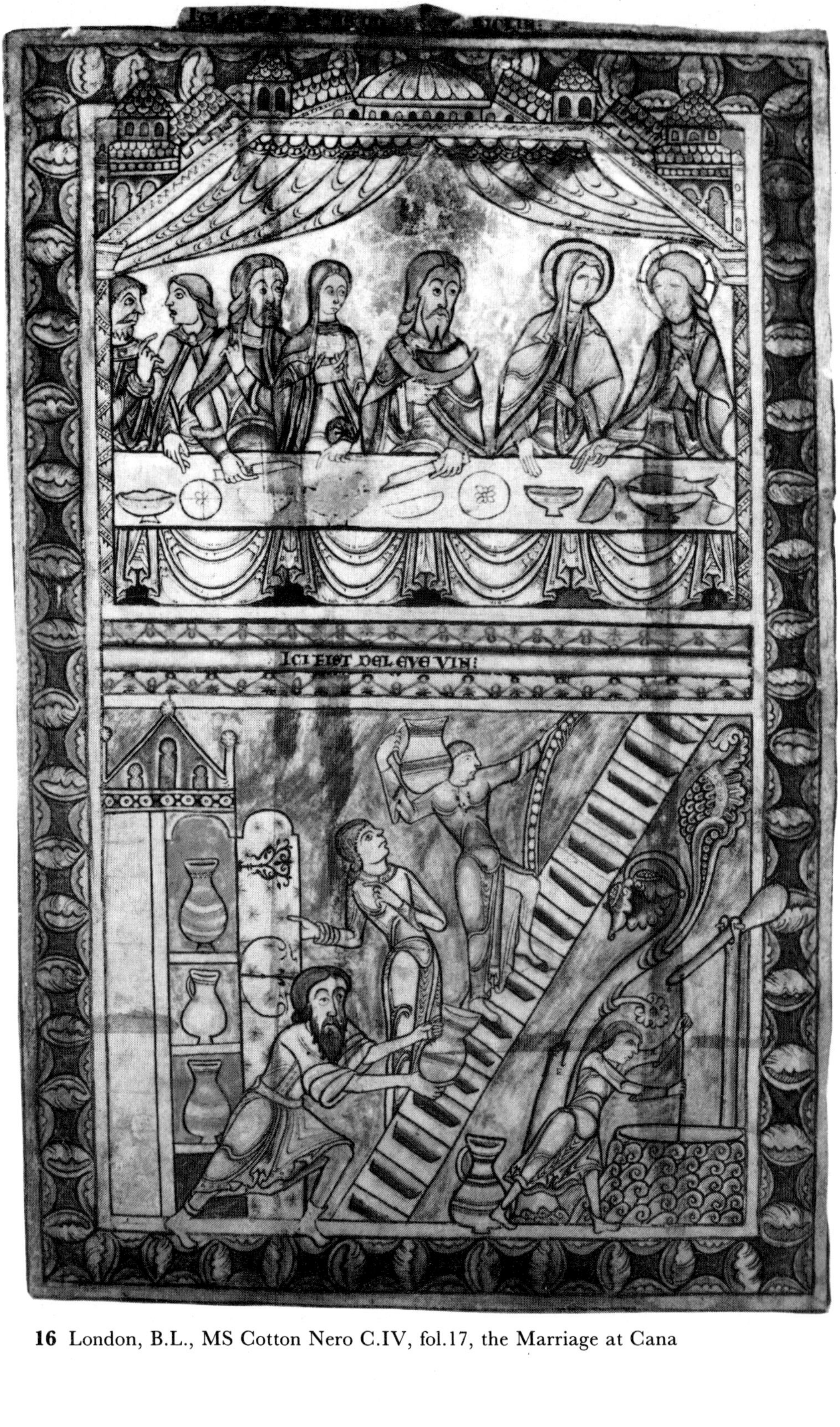

16 London, B.L., MS Cotton Nero C.IV, fol.17, the Marriage at Cana

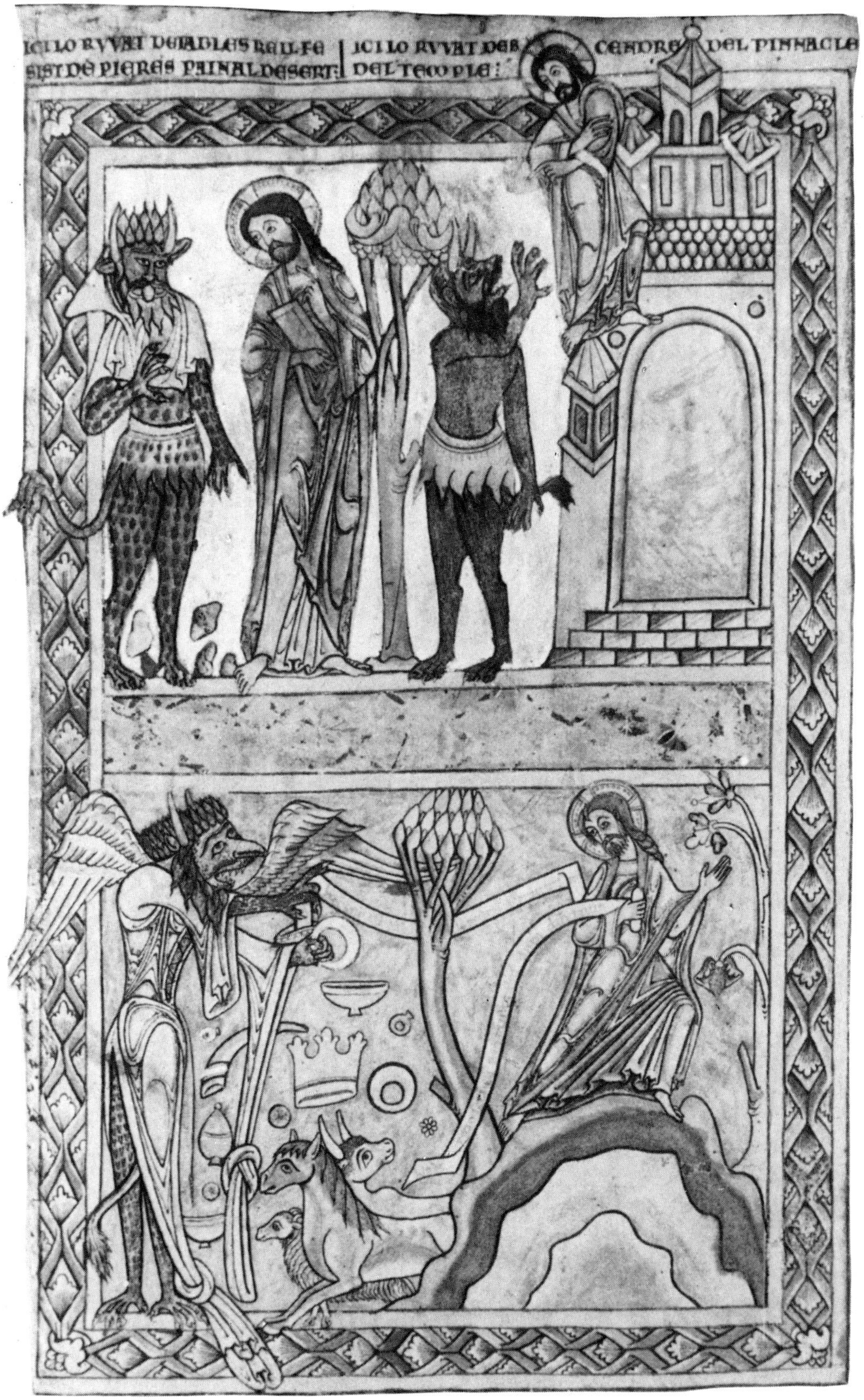

17 London, B.L., MS Cotton Nero C.IV, fol.18, the Temptations of Christ

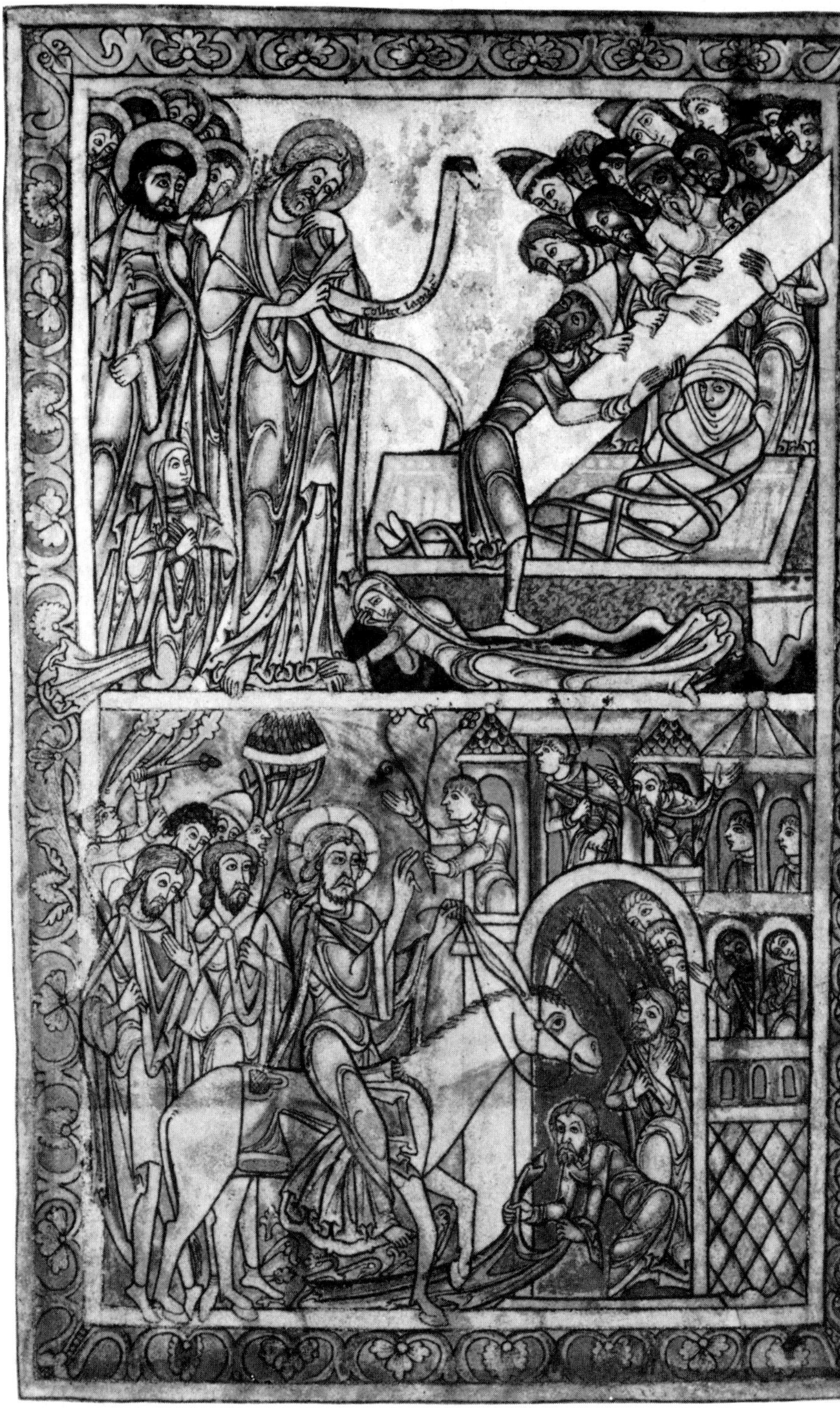

18 London, B.L., MS Cotton Nero C.IV, fol.19, the Raising of Lazarus, Entry into Jerusalem

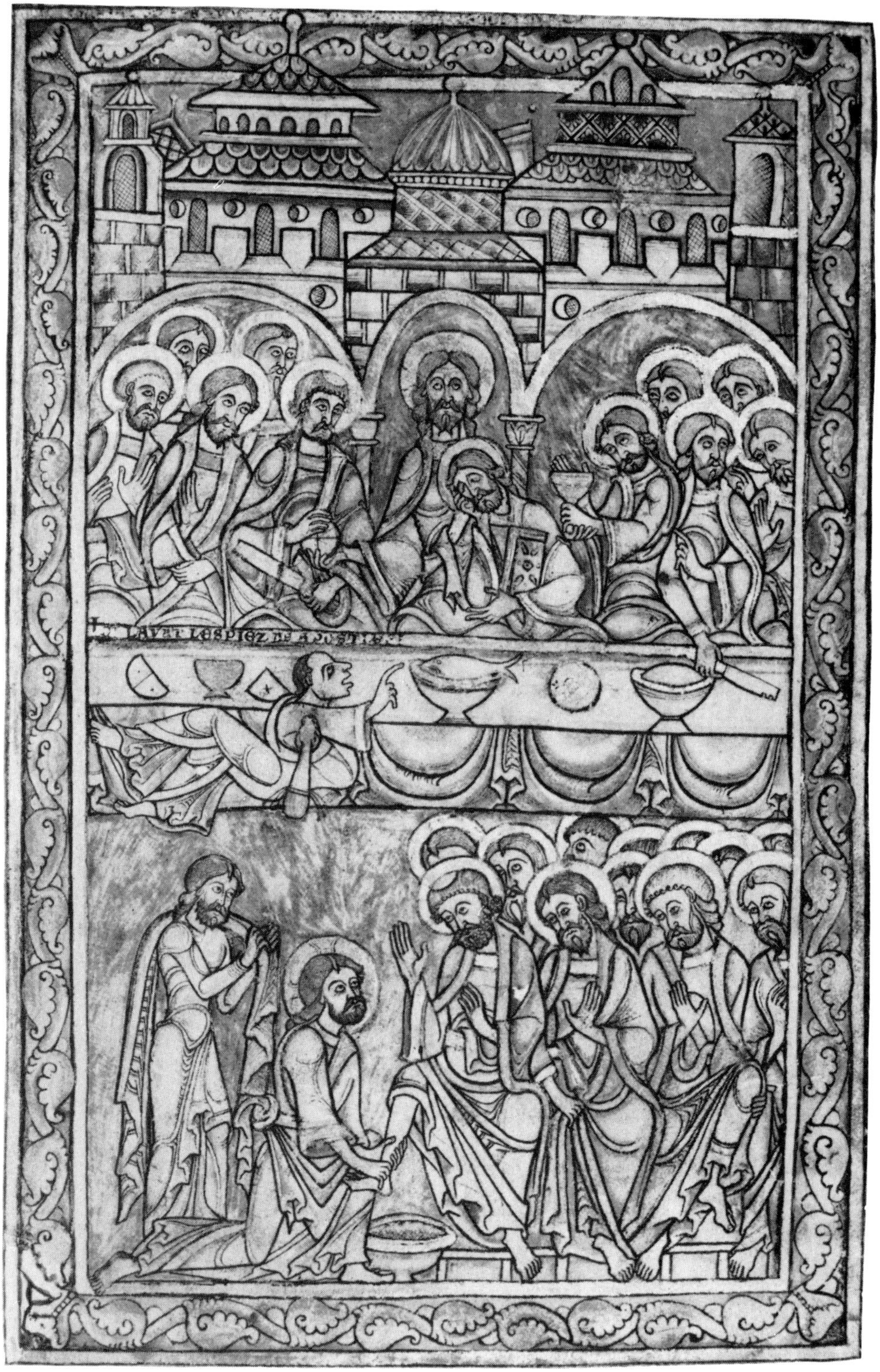

19 London, B.L., MS Cotton Nero C.IV, fol.20, the Last Supper, Christ Washing the Feet of the Apostles

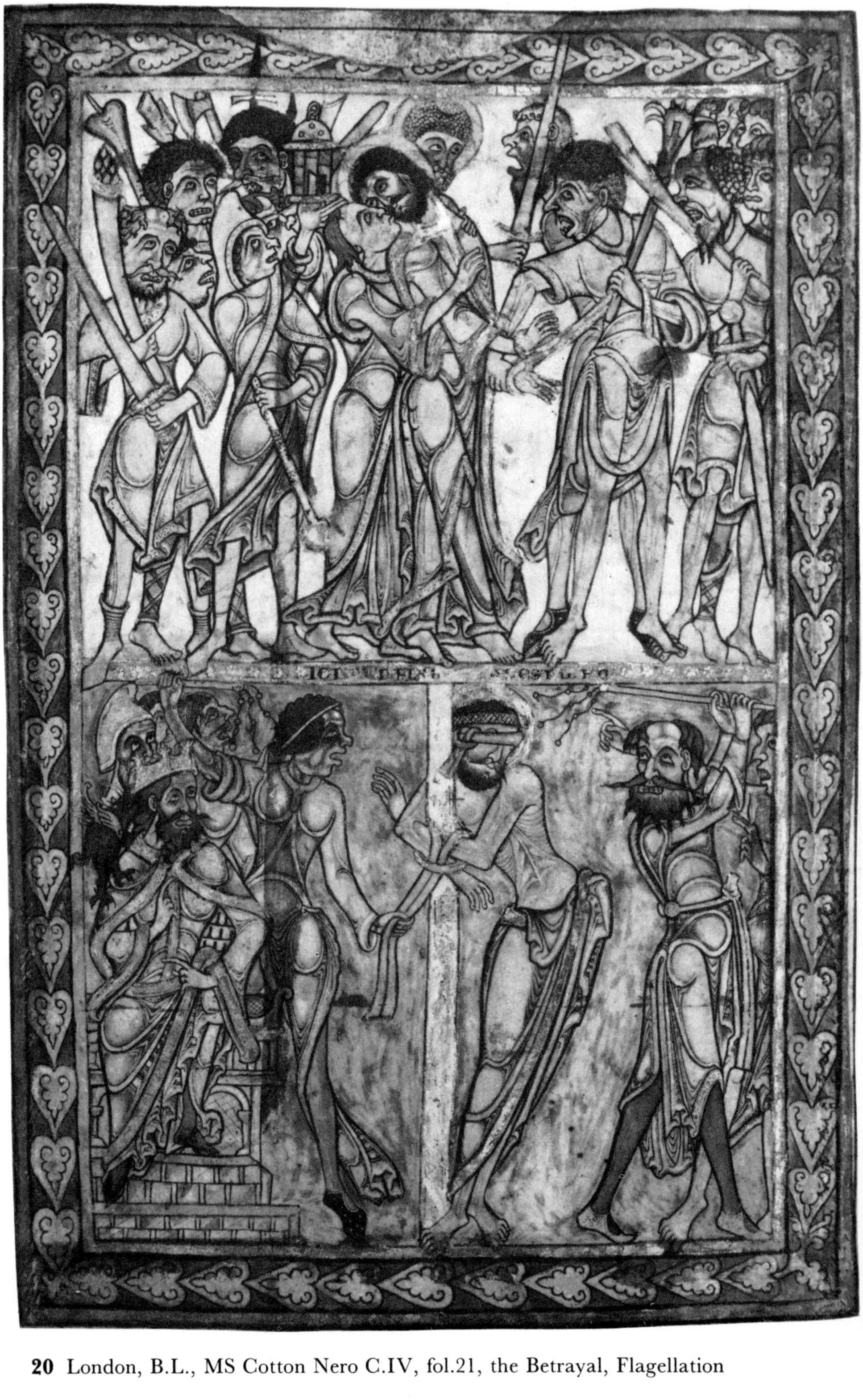

20 London, B.L., MS Cotton Nero C.IV, fol.21, the Betrayal, Flagellation

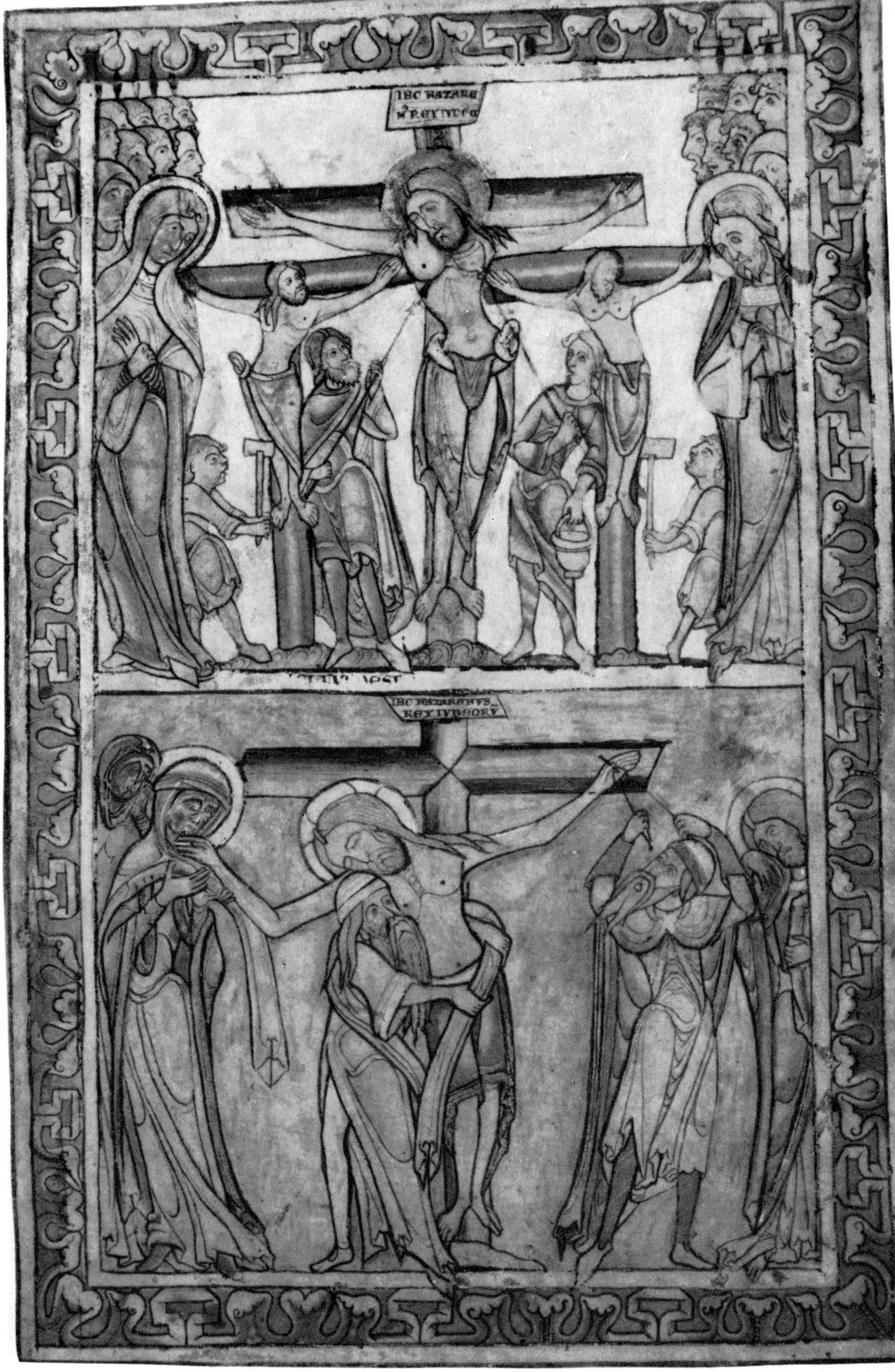

21 London, B.L., MS Cotton Nero C.IV, fol.22, the Crucifixion, Deposition

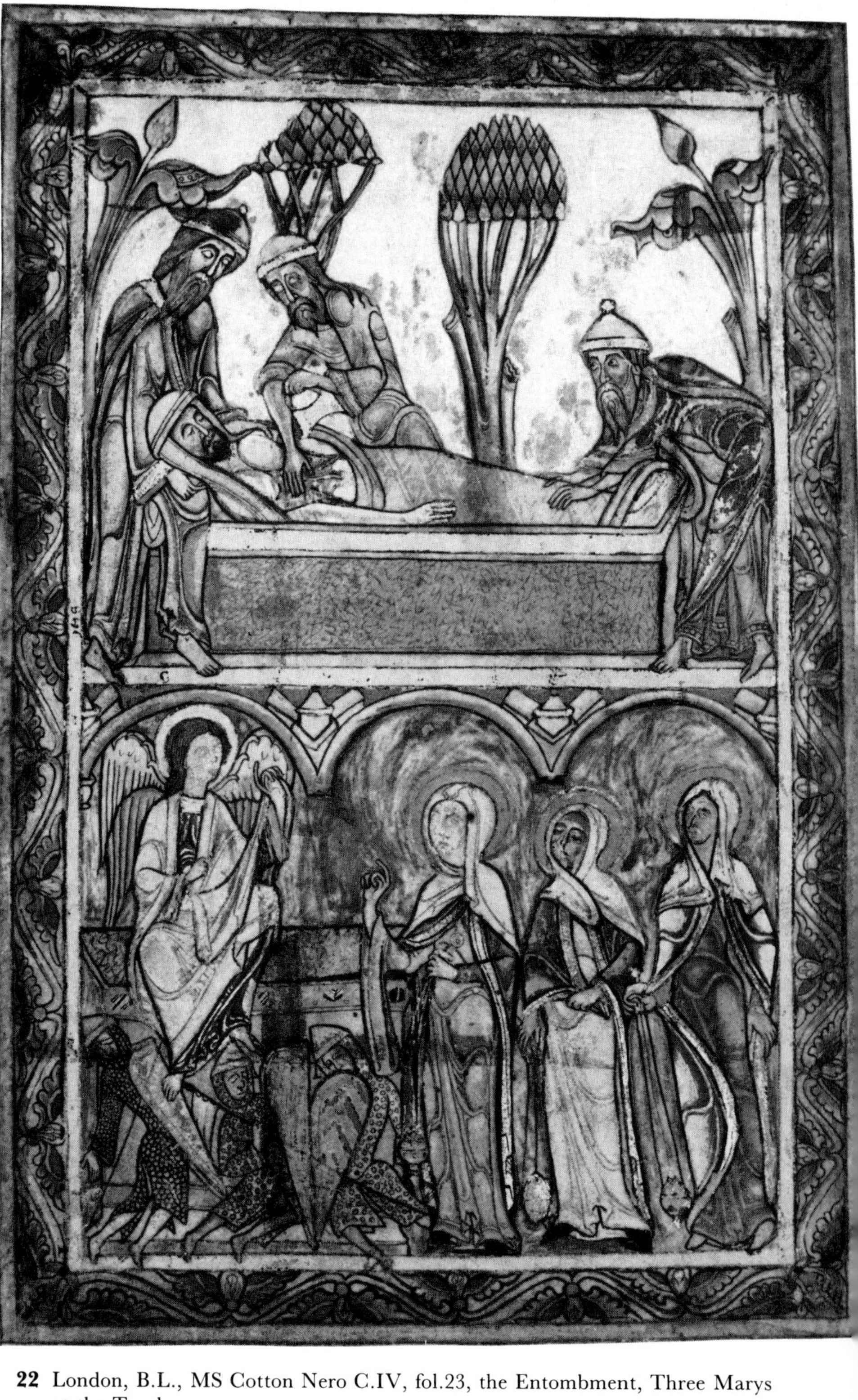

22 London, B.L., MS Cotton Nero C.IV, fol.23, the Entombment, Three Marys at the Tomb

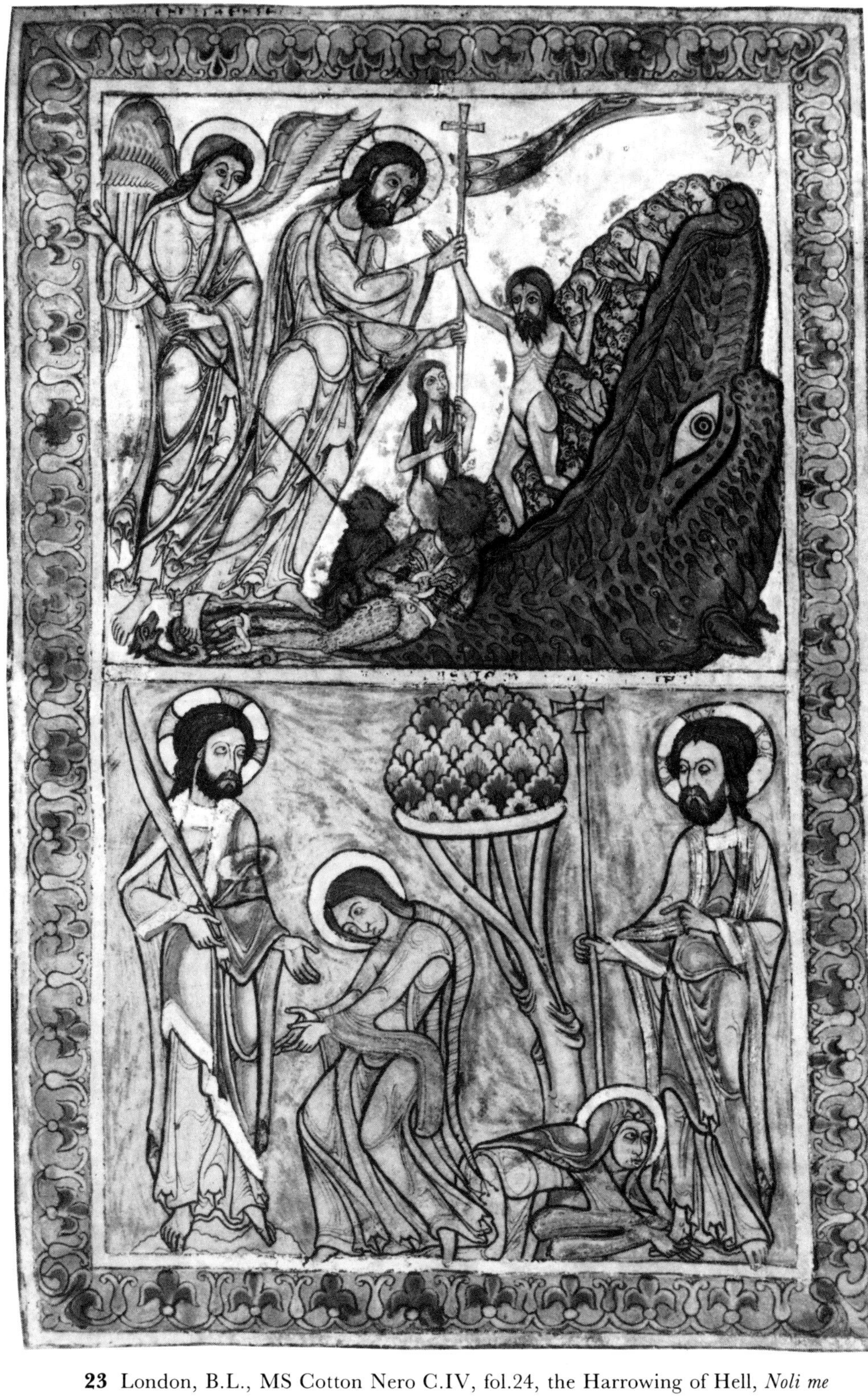

23 London, B.L., MS Cotton Nero C.IV, fol.24, the Harrowing of Hell, *Noli me tangere*

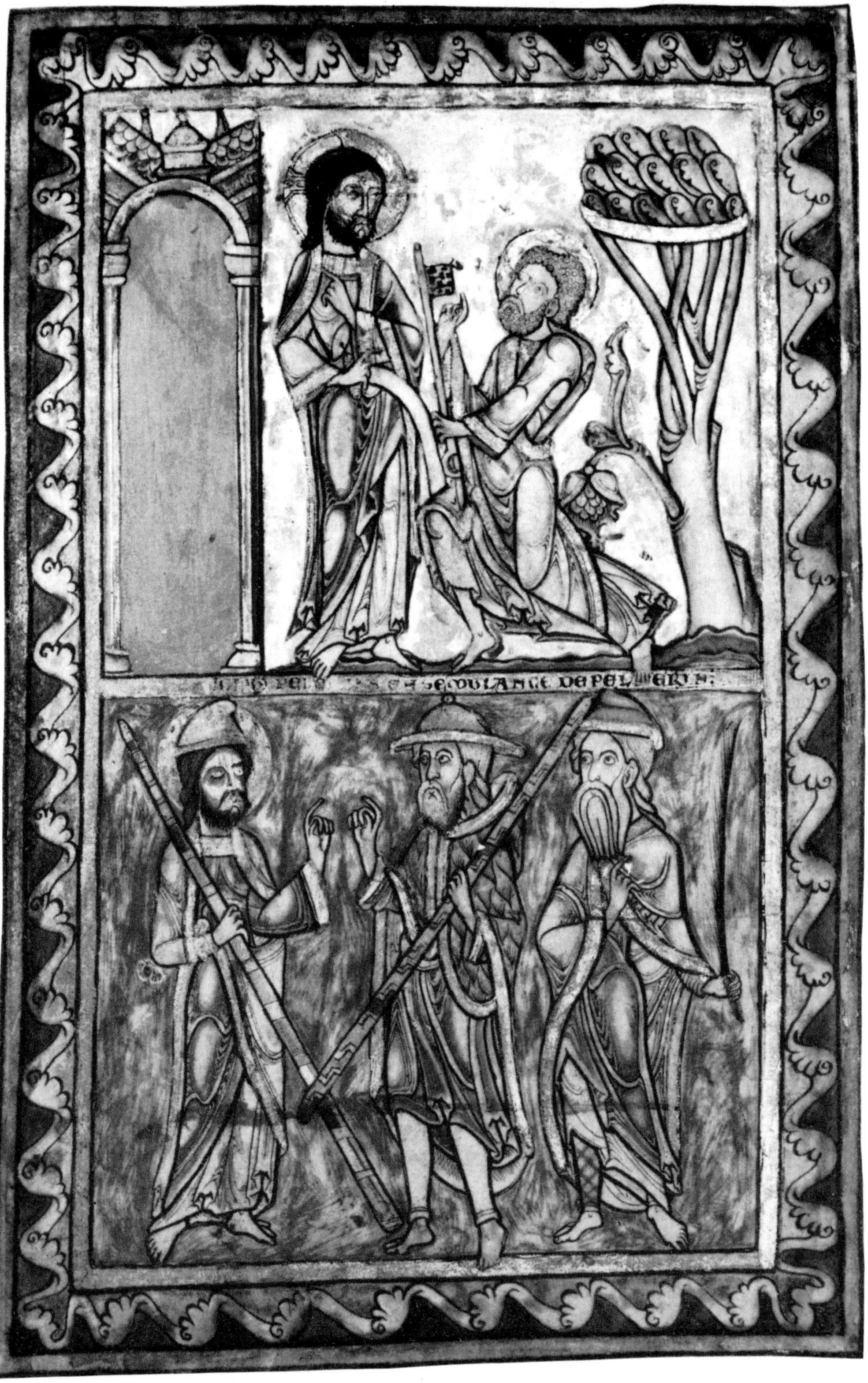

24 London, B.L., MS Cotton Nero C.IV, fol.25, Christ Giving the Keys to Peter, Road to Emmaus

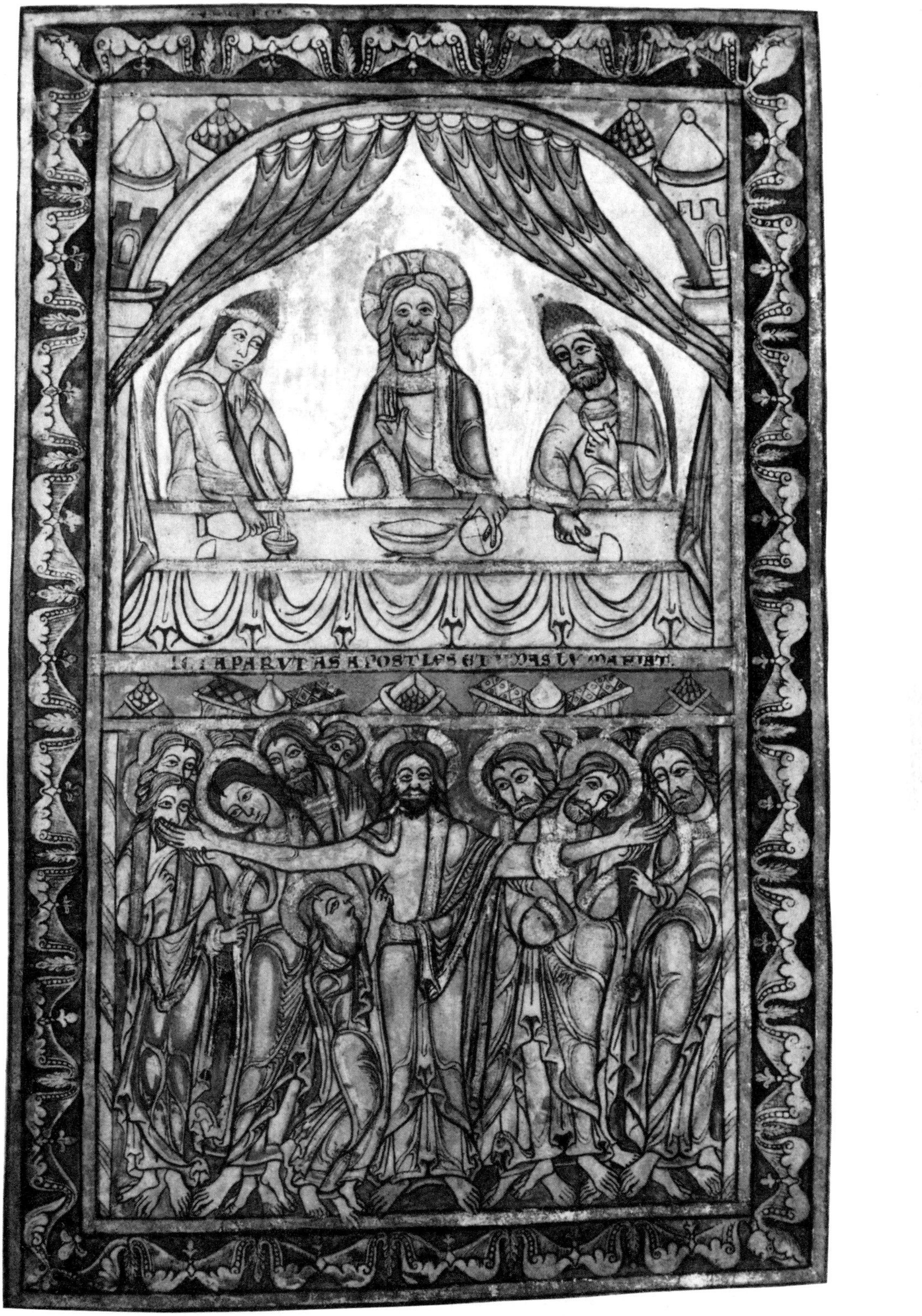

25 London, B.L., MS Cotton Nero C.IV, fol.26, the Supper at Emmaus, Doubting Thomas

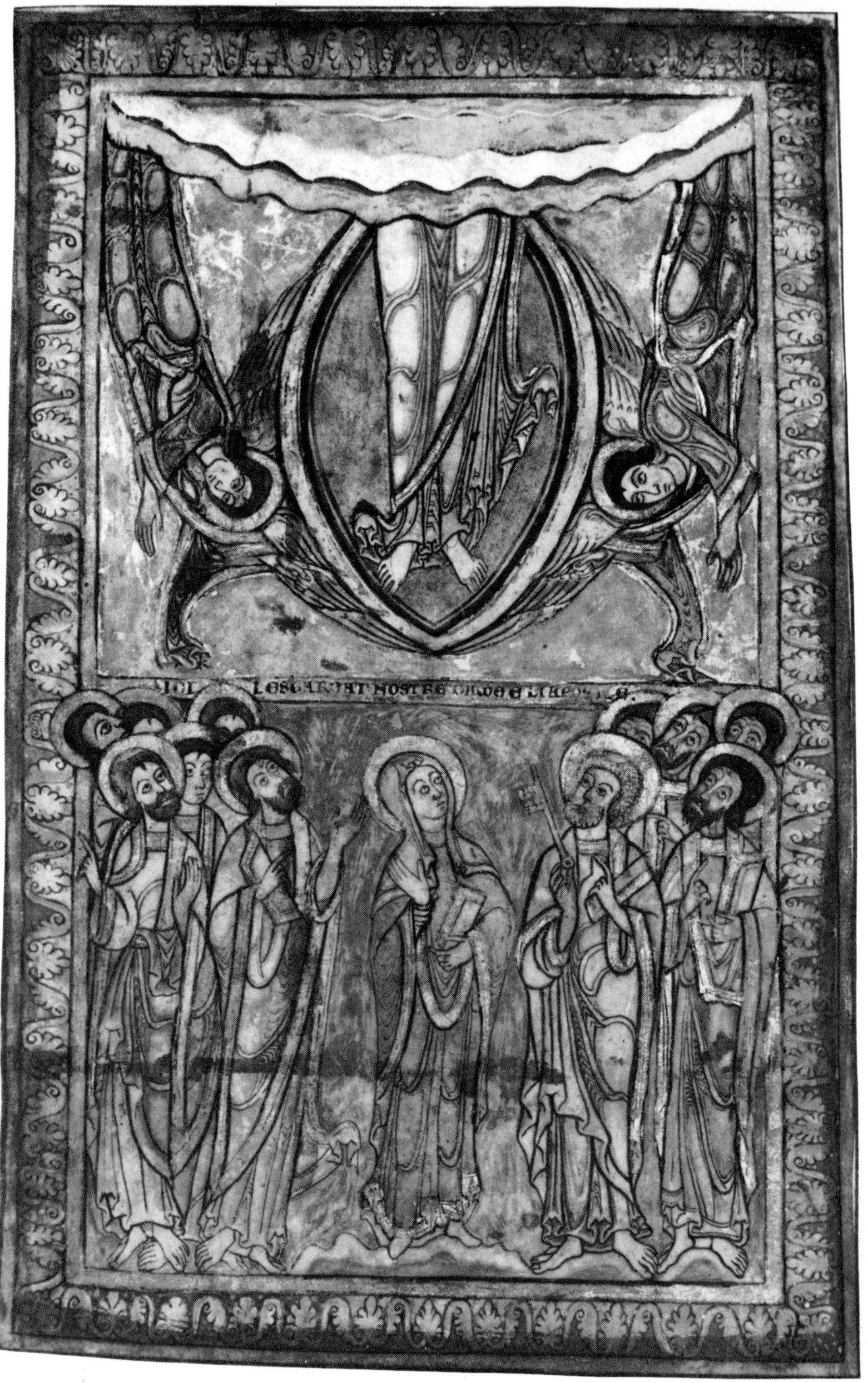

26 London, B.L., MS Cotton Nero C.IV, fol.27, the Ascension

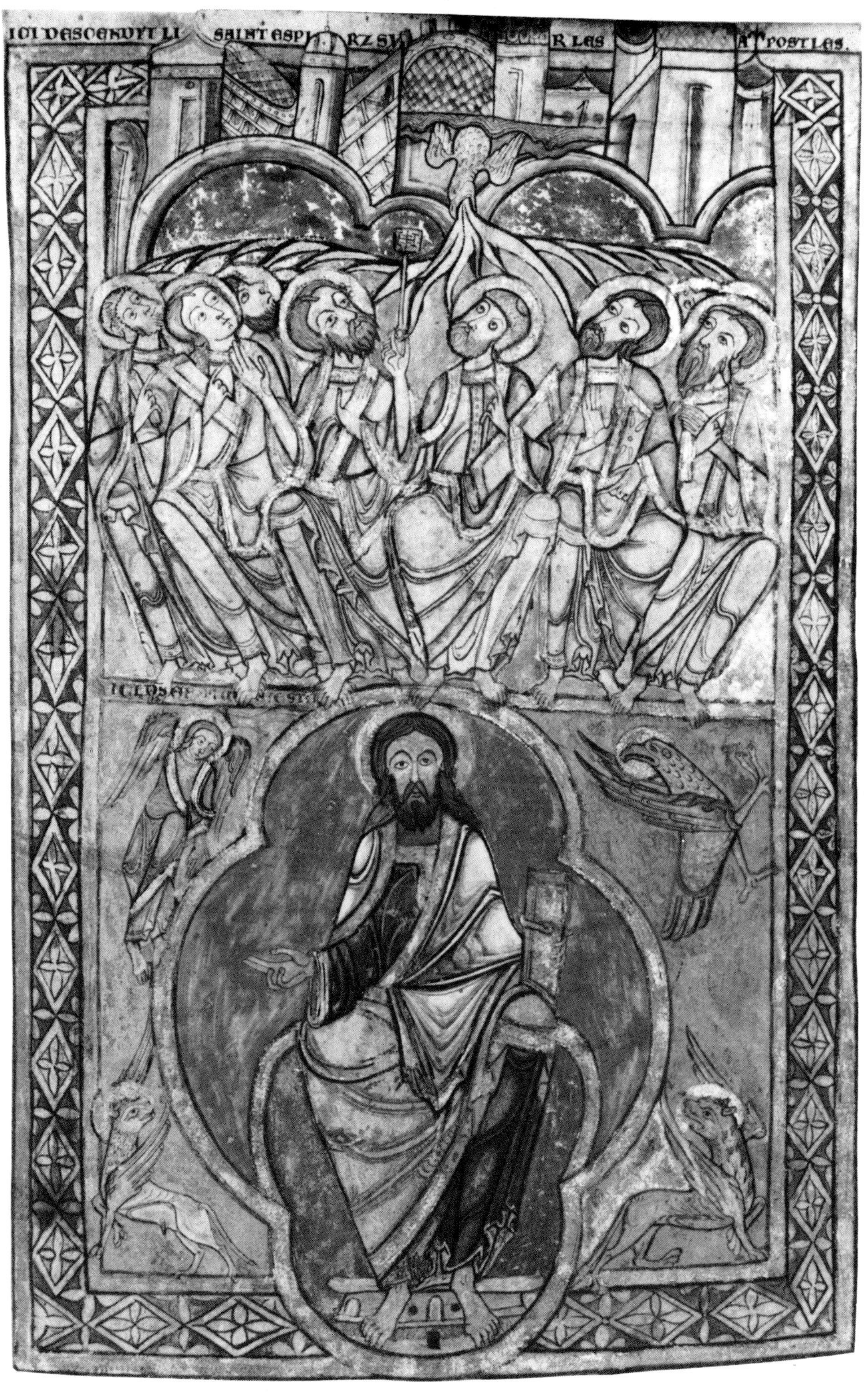

27 London, B.L., MS Cotton Nero C.IV, fol.28, Pentecost, Christ in Majesty

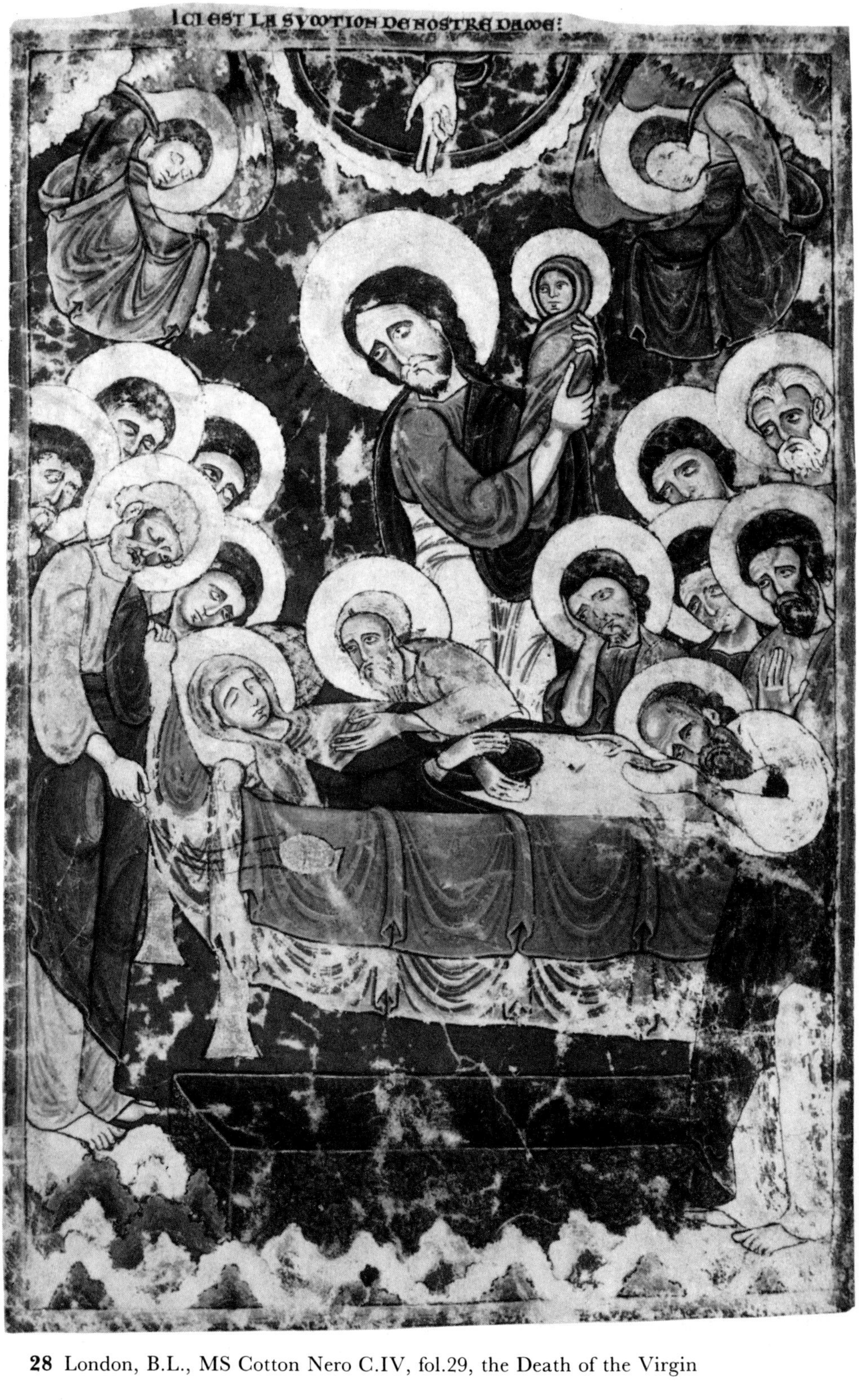

28 London, B.L., MS Cotton Nero C.IV, fol.29, the Death of the Virgin

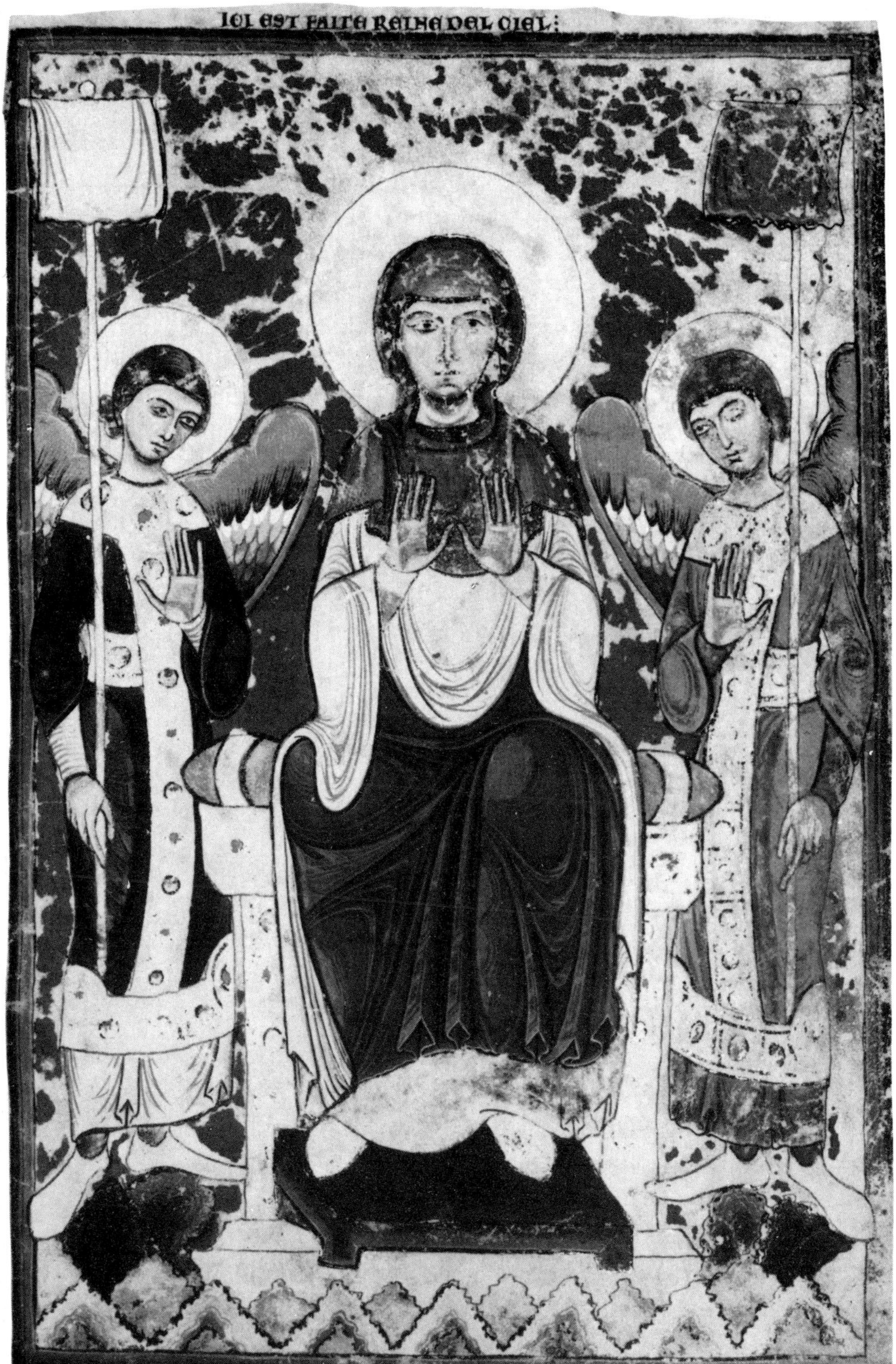

29 London, B.L., MS Cotton Nero C.IV, fol.30, *Maria, Regina Angelorum*

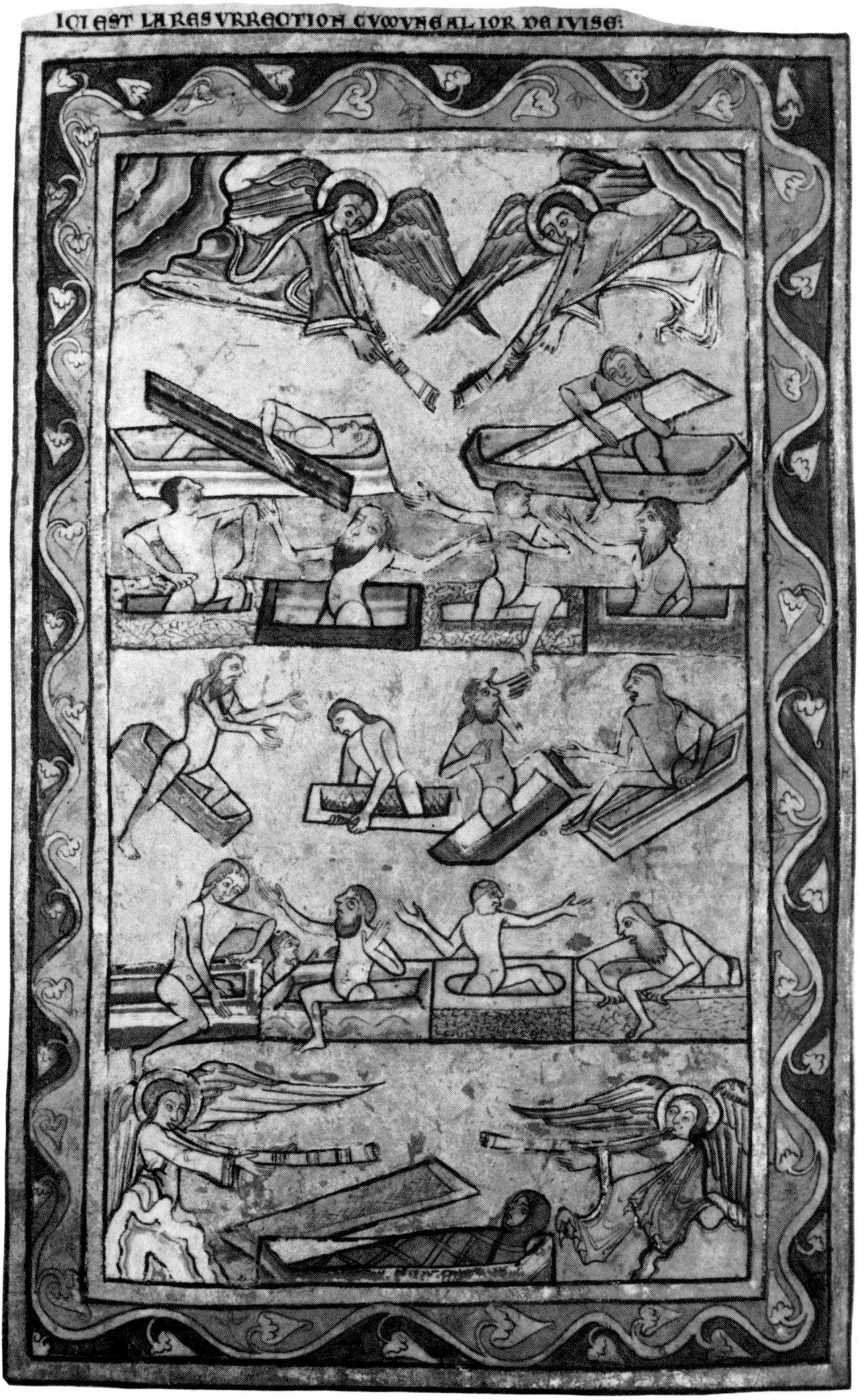

30 London, B.L., MS Cotton Nero C.IV, fol.31, the Dead Arising

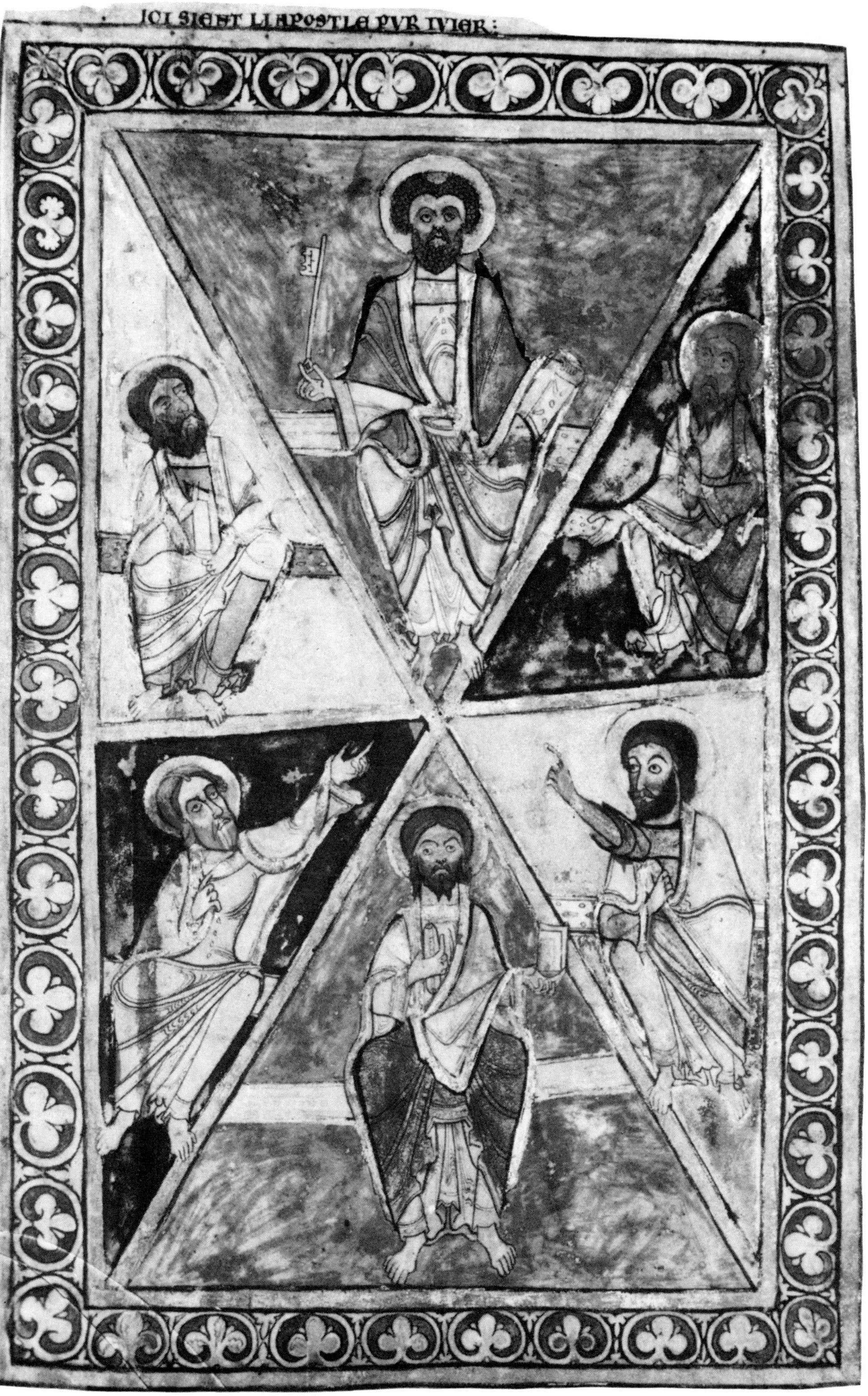

31 London, B.L., MS Cotton Nero C.IV, fol.32, Six Apostles

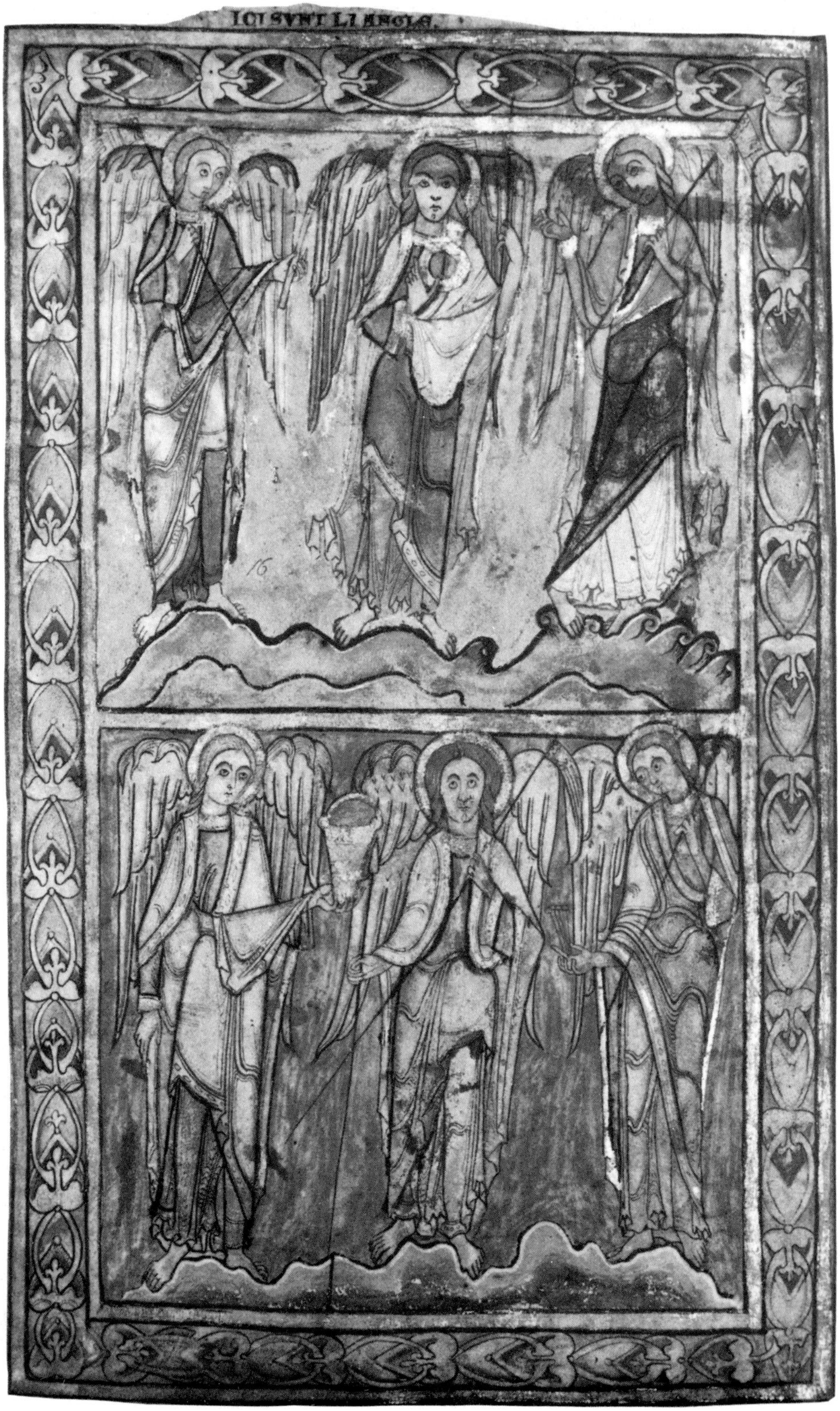

32 London, B.L., MS Cotton Nero C.IV, fol.33, Six Angels

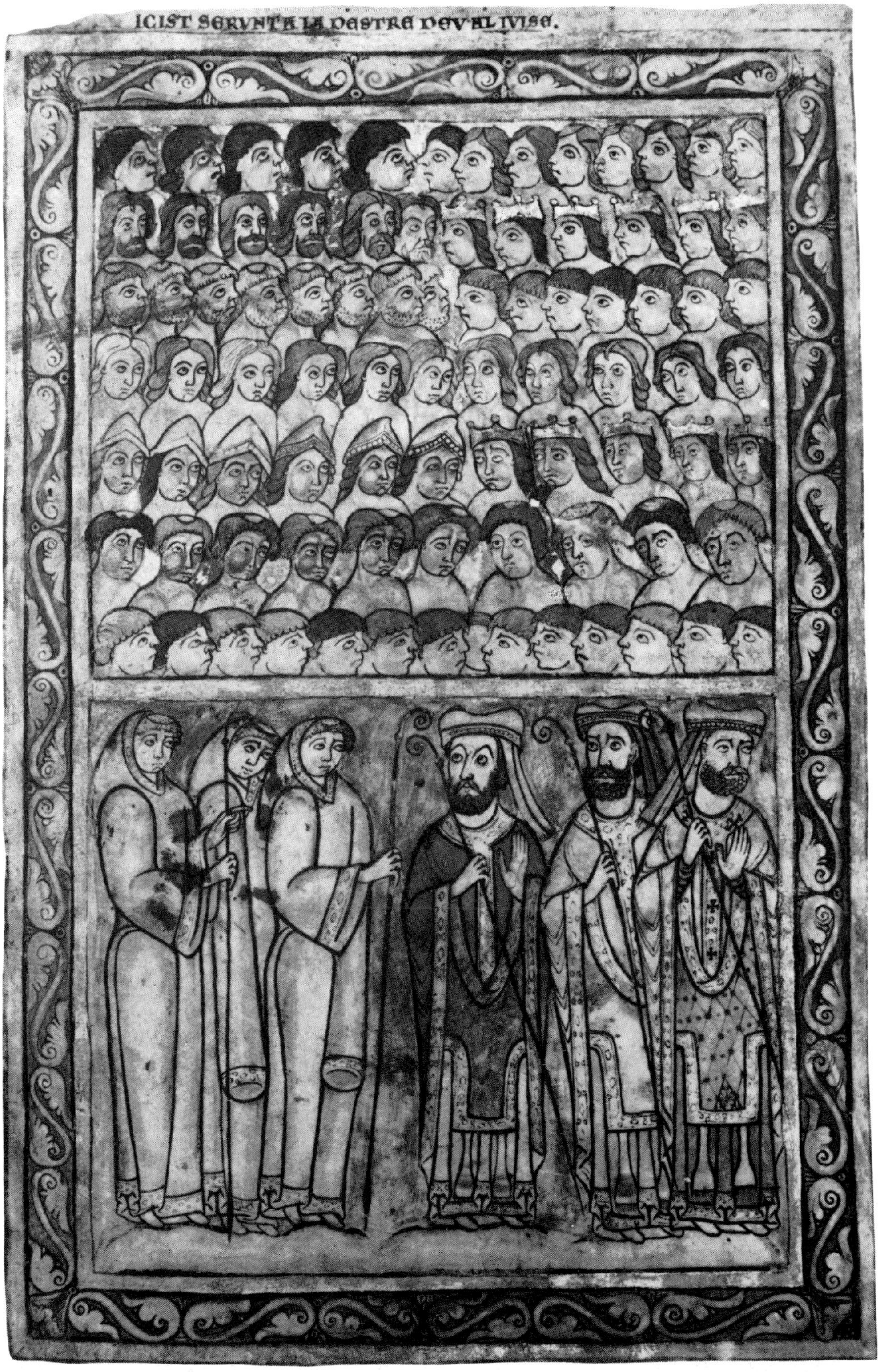

33 London, B.L., MS Cotton Nero C.IV, fol.34, the Saved

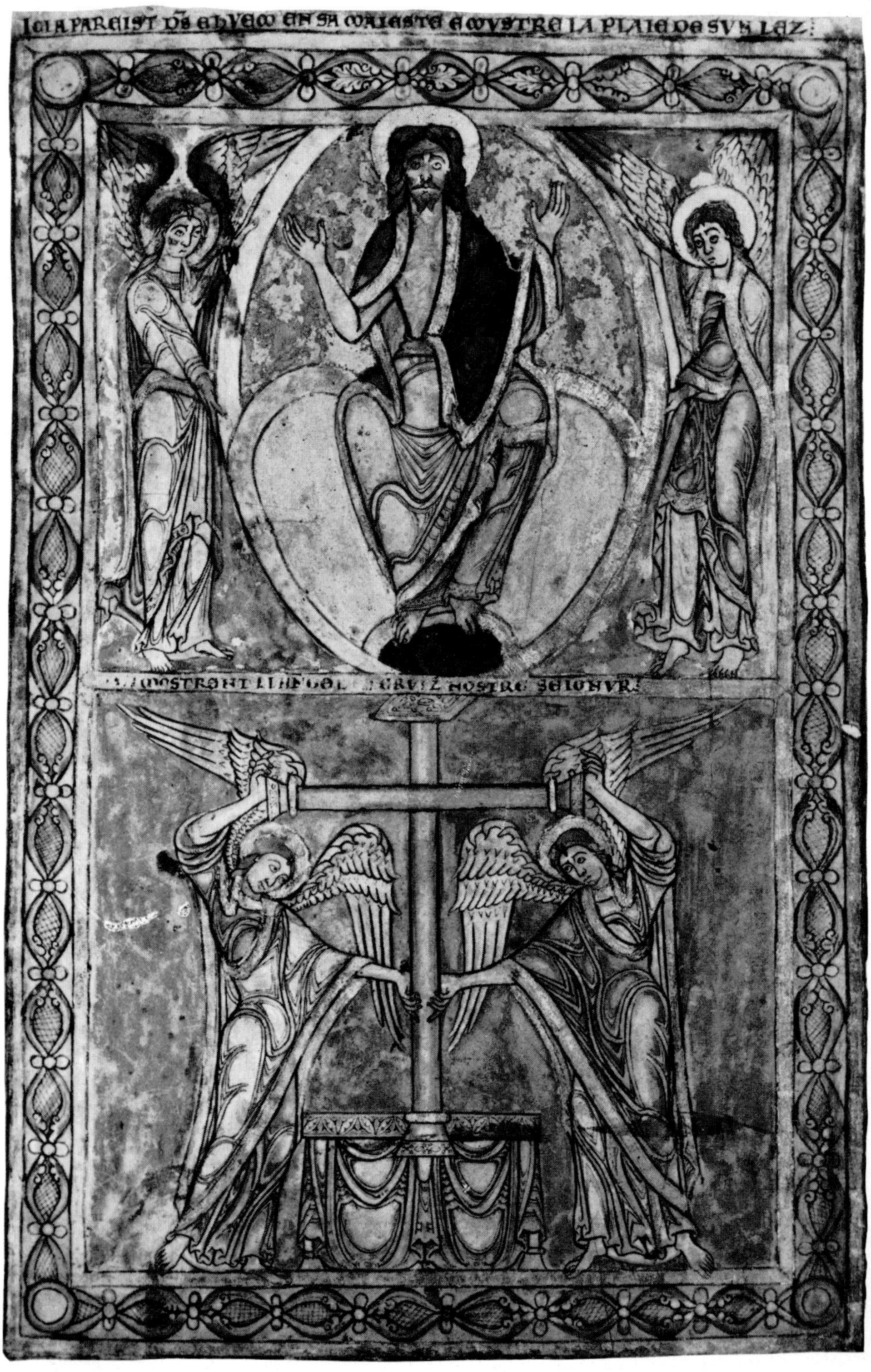

34 London, B.L., MS Cotton Nero C.IV, fol.35, Christ Displaying his Wounds, Angels Flanking the Cross

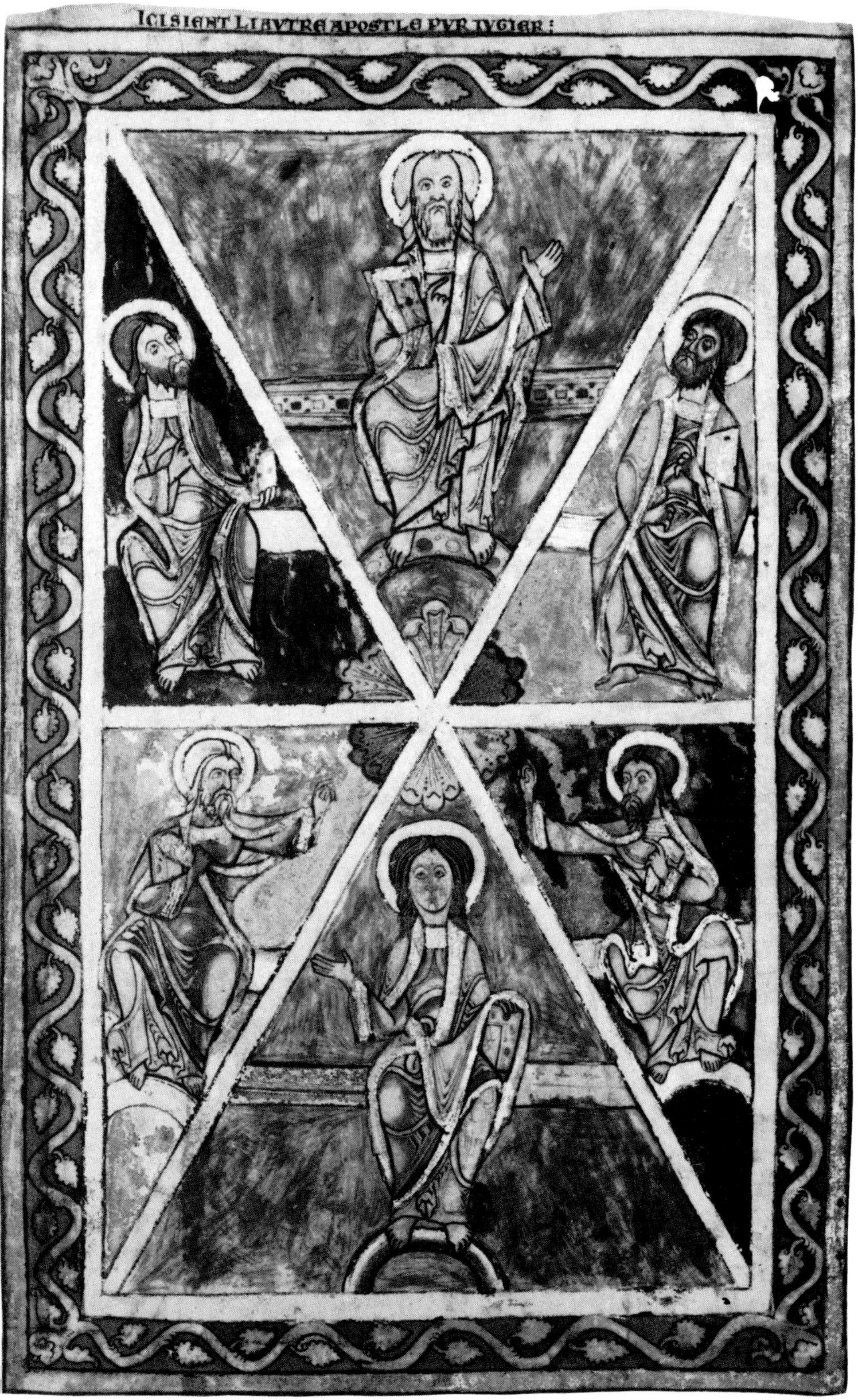

35 London, B.L., MS Cotton Nero C.IV, fol.36, Six Apostles

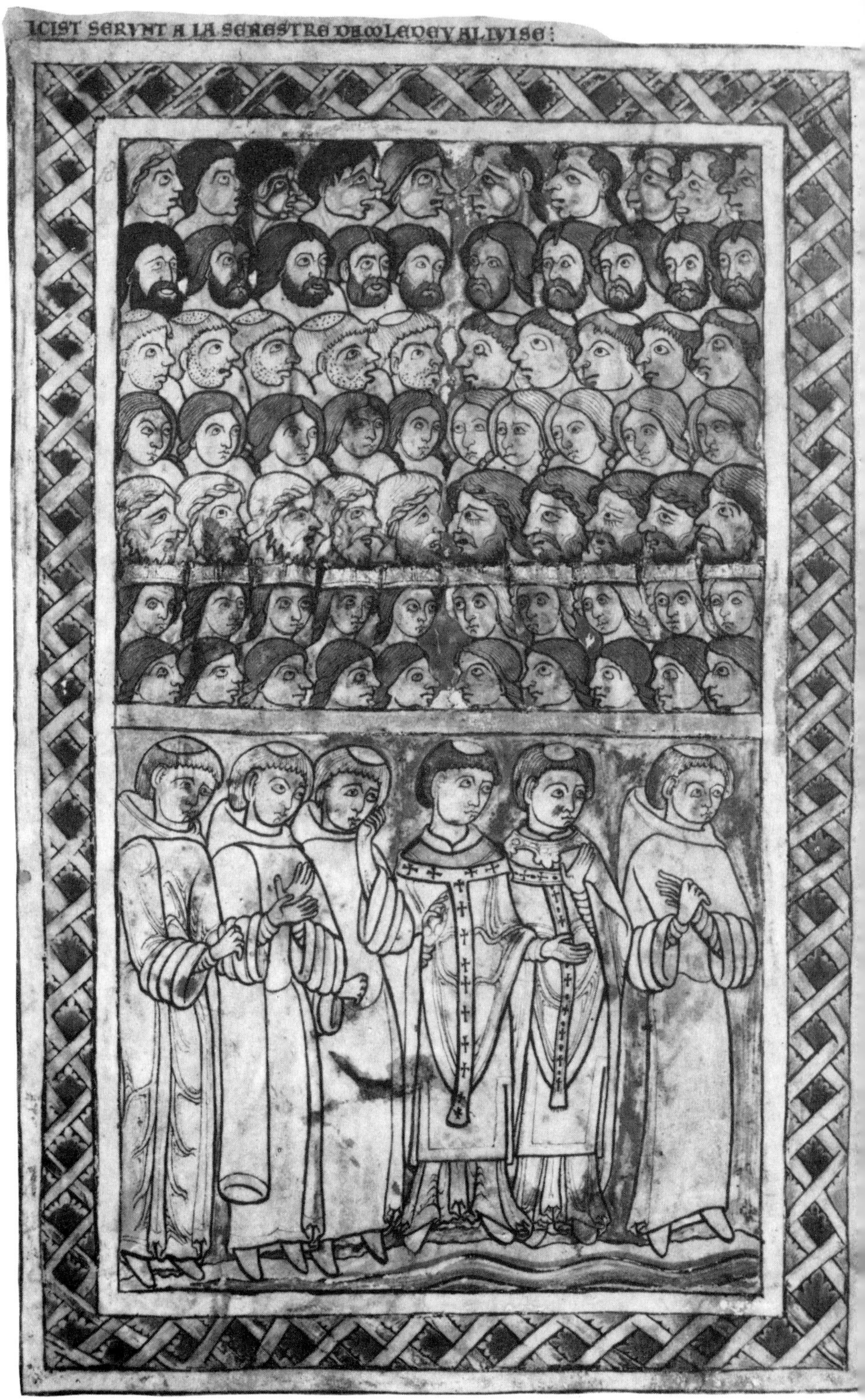

36 London, B.L., MS Cotton Nero C.IV, fol.37, the Damned

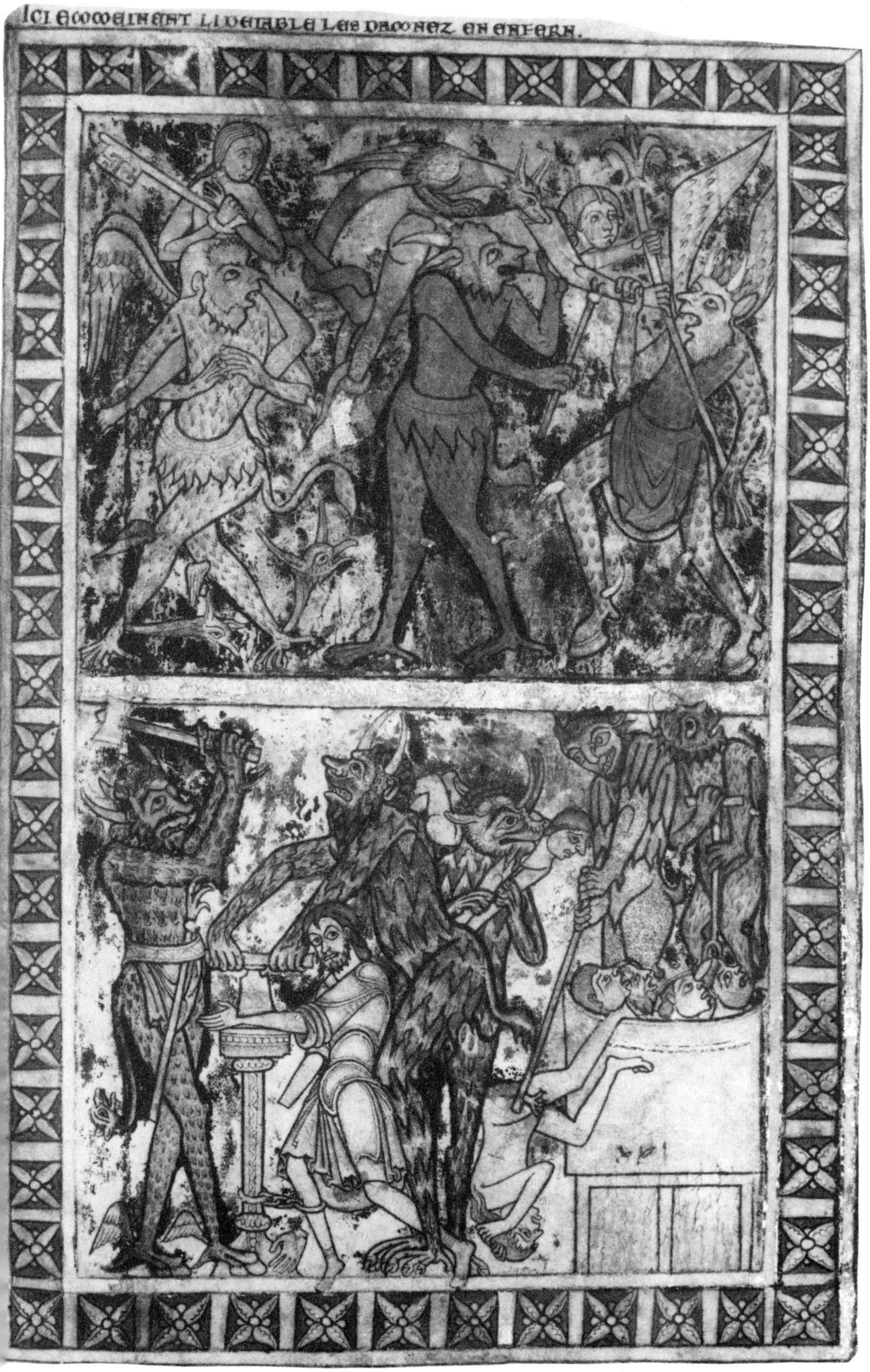

37 London, B.L., MS Cotton Nero C.IV, fol.38, the Torment of the Damned

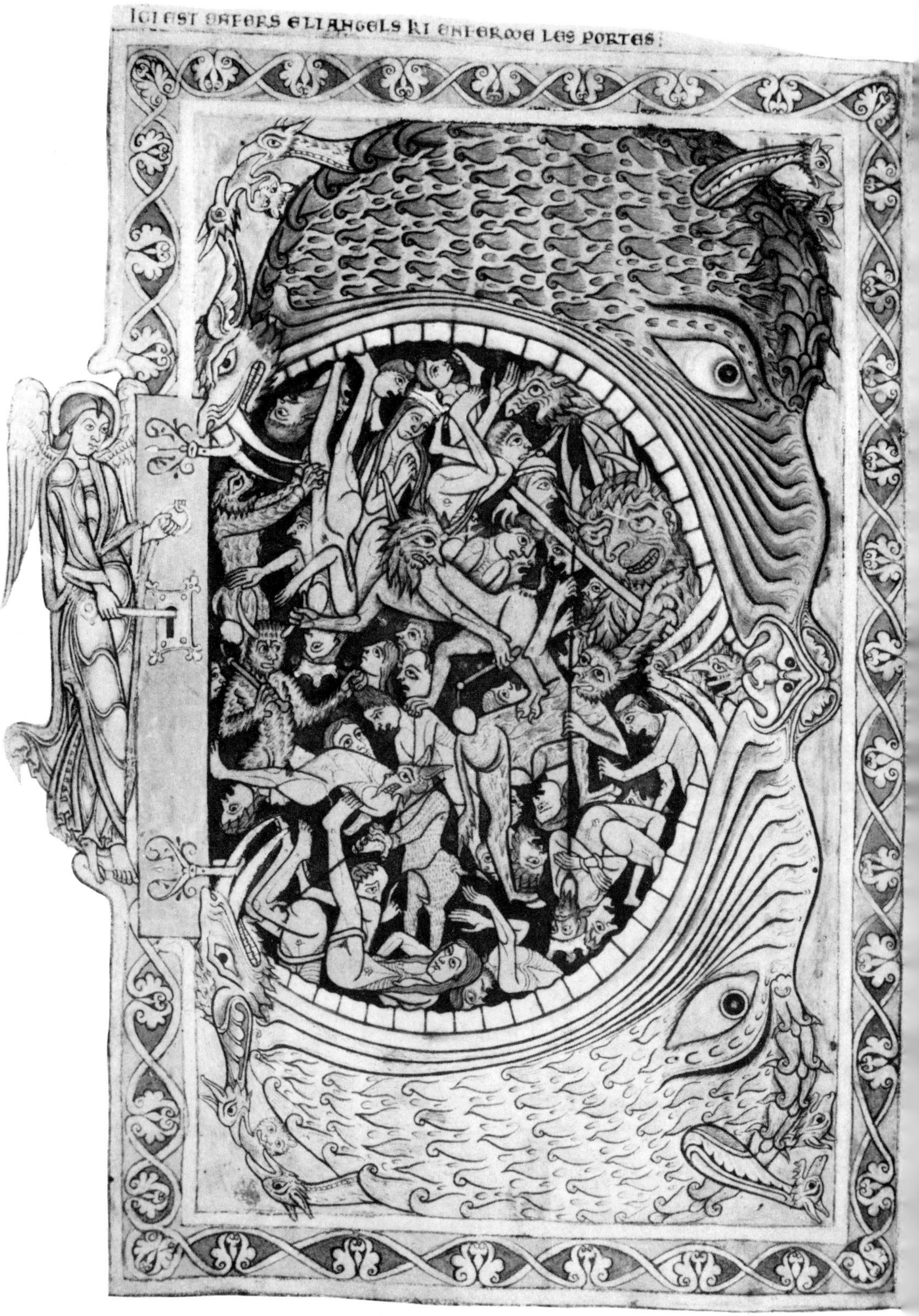

38 London, B.L., MS Cotton Nero C.IV, fol.39, the Angel Locking the Damned in Hell

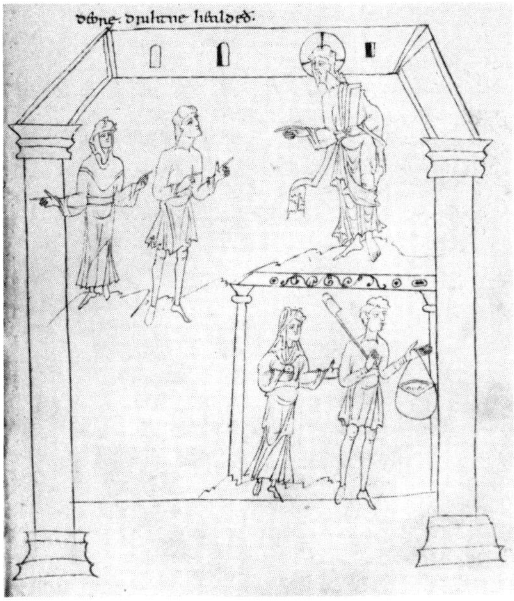

39 (above) Oxford, Bodl., MS Junius 11, p. 45, God's Reprimand

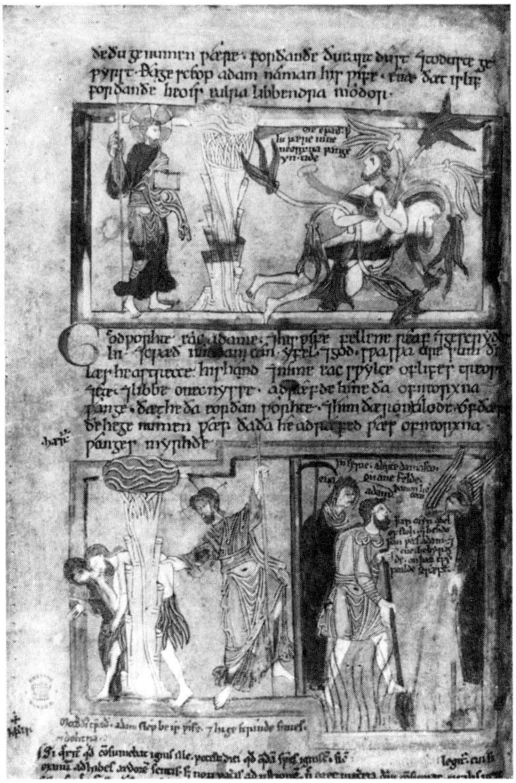

40 (right) London, B.L., MS Cotton Claudius B.IV, fol.7v, the Expulsion, Angel Instructing Adam and Eve

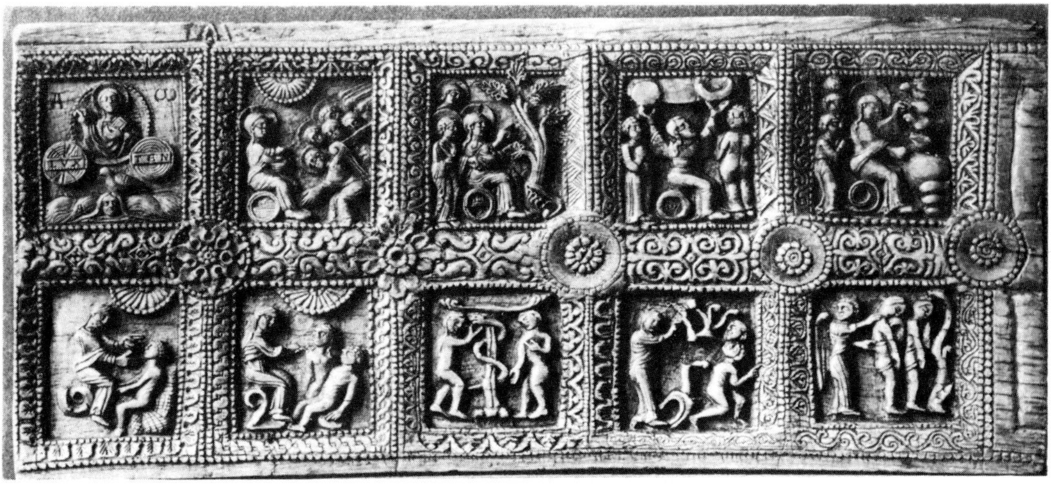

41 Berlin, Dahlem, Staatliche Museen, Skulpturenabteilung, ivory box, the Expulsion

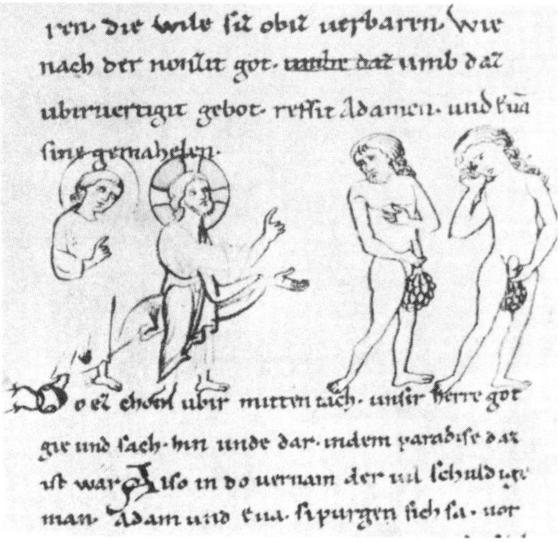

42 (above) Klagenfurt, Mus. Cod. VI, fol.12r, the Expulsion

43 (below) Malmesbury Abbey, Wiltshire, archivolt, the Angel Giving the Labours to Adam and Eve

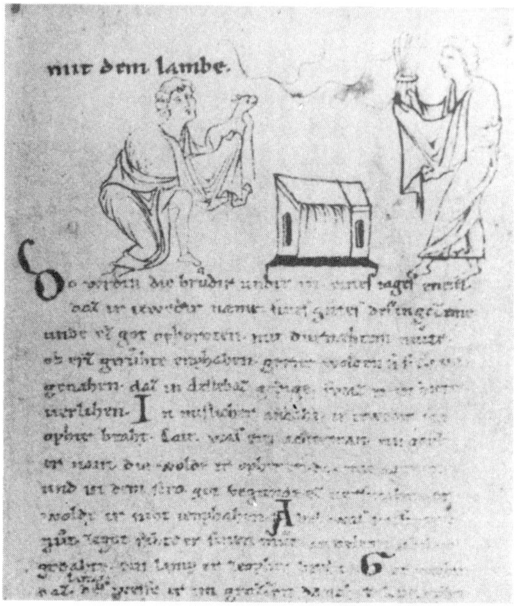

44 (above) Klagenfurt, Mus. Cod. VI, 19, fol.19r, the Offerings of Cain and Abel

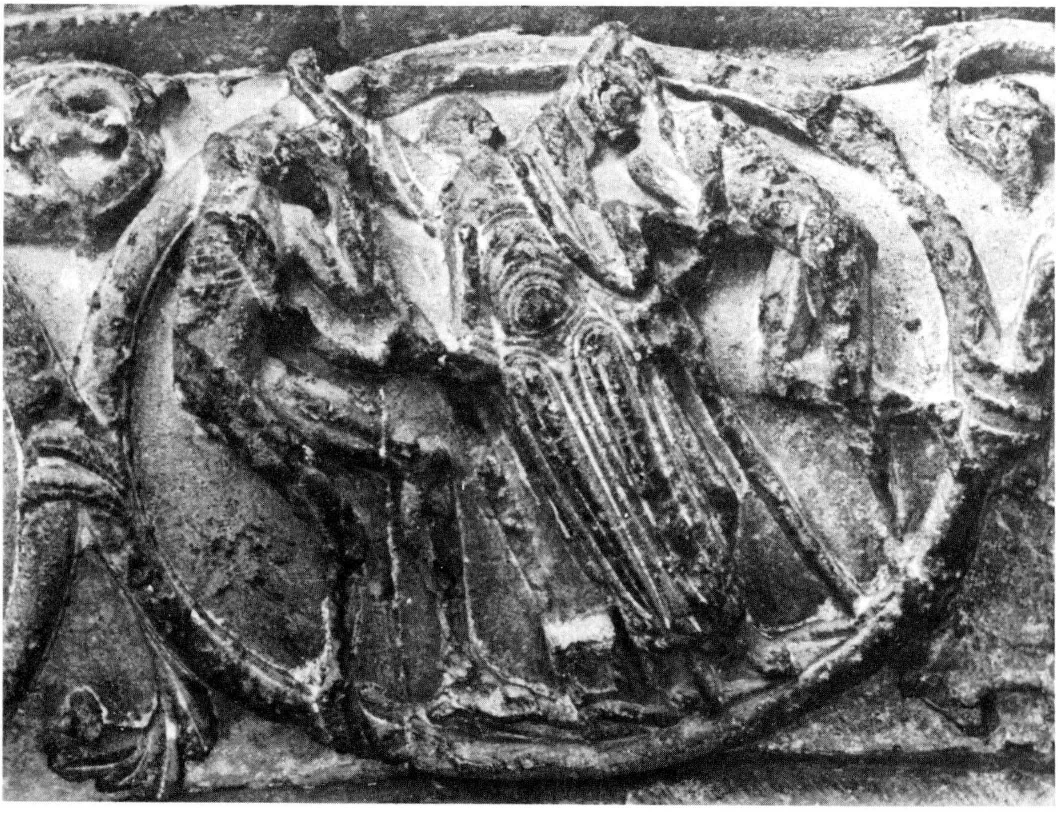

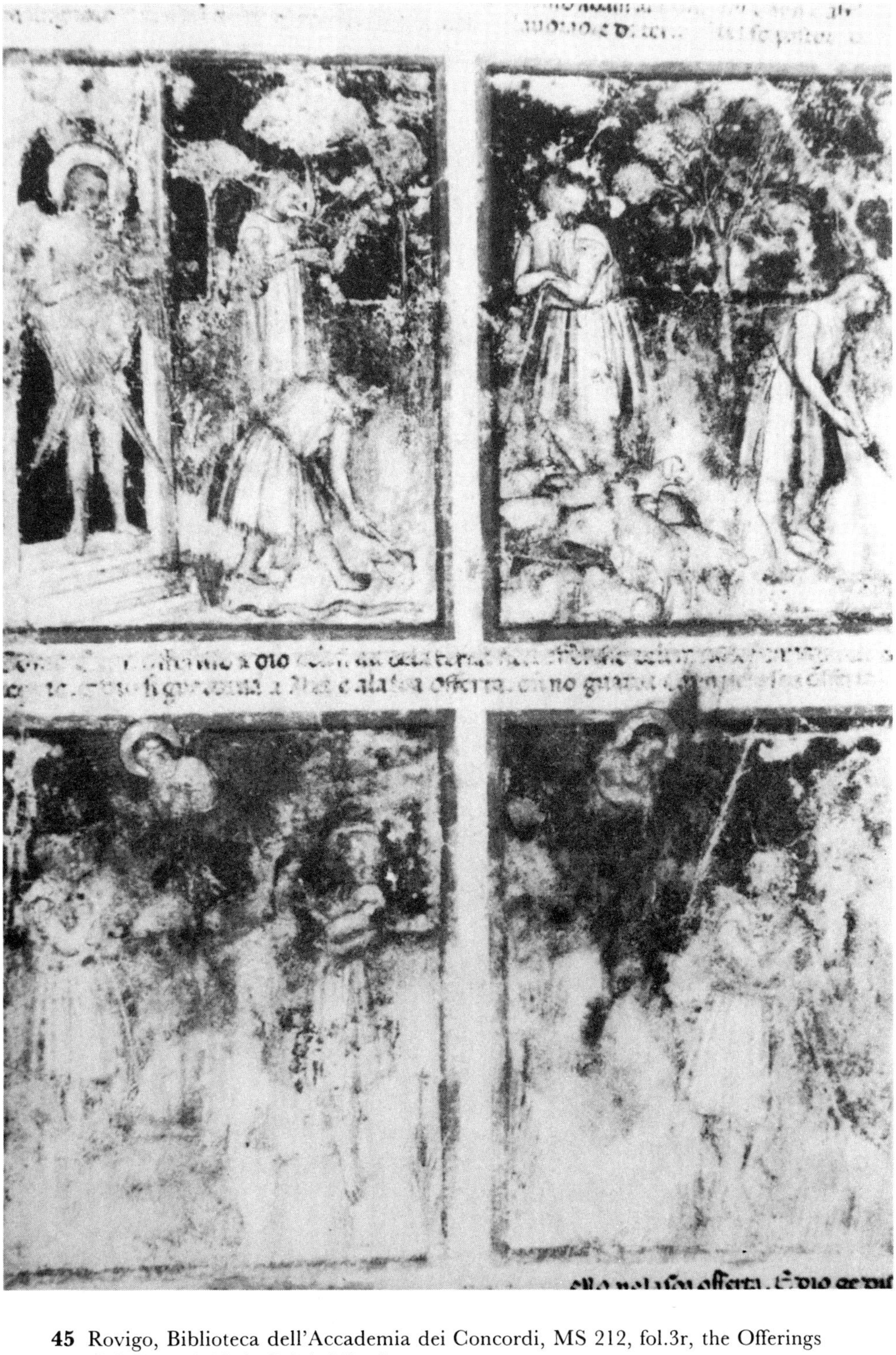

45 Rovigo, Biblioteca dell'Accademia dei Concordi, MS 212, fol.3r, the Offerings of Cain and Abel, Cain's Wrath

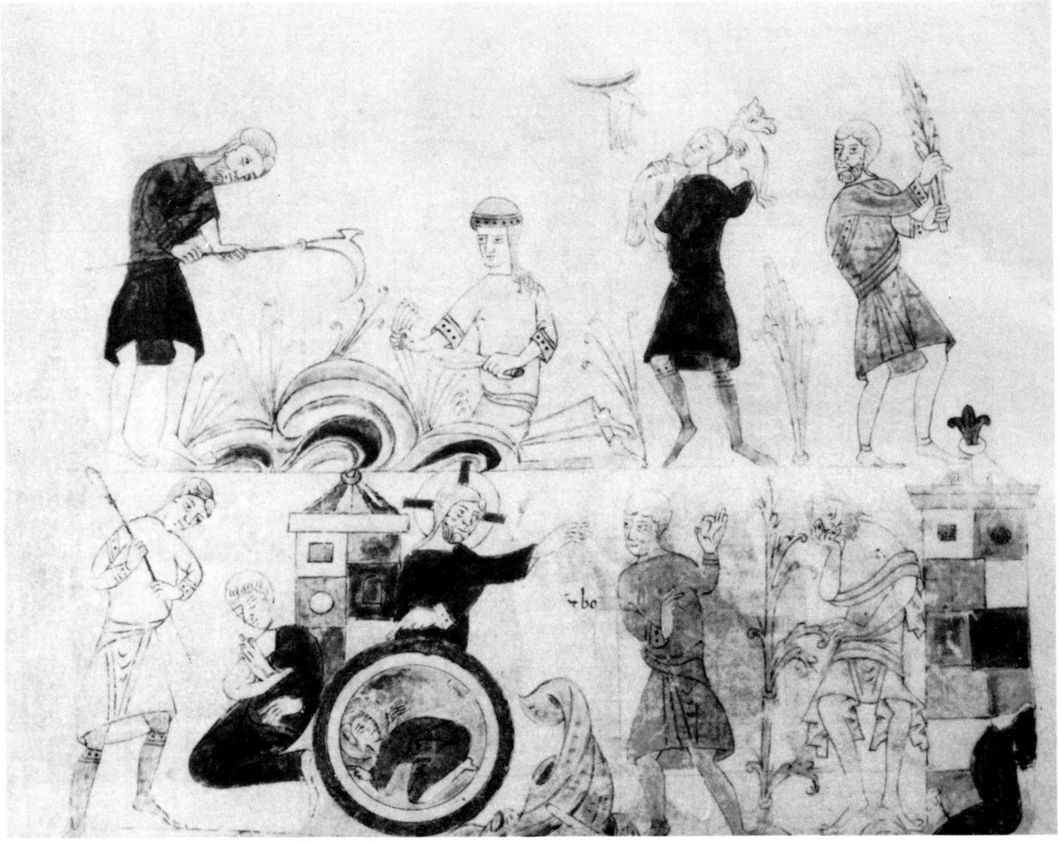

46 Rome, B.A.V., MS Vat. lat. 5729, fol.6r the Offerings of Cain and Abel

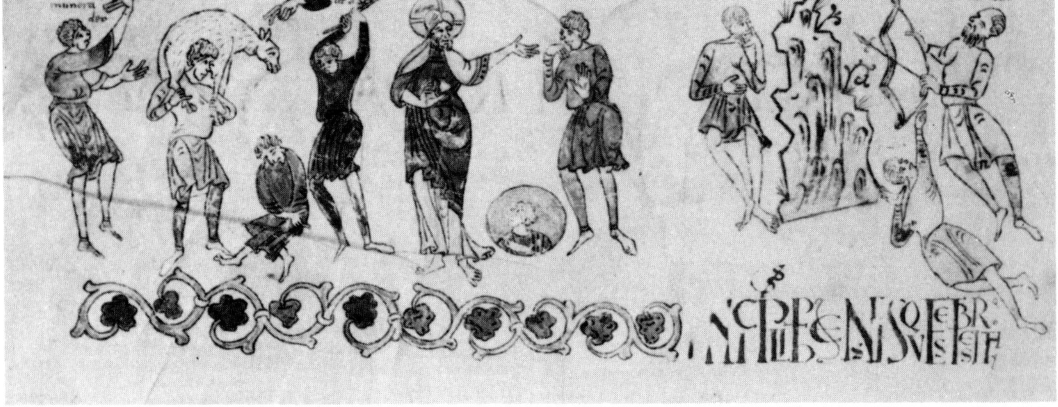

47 Paris, B.N., MS lat. 6, fol.6r, the Offerings of Cain and Abel

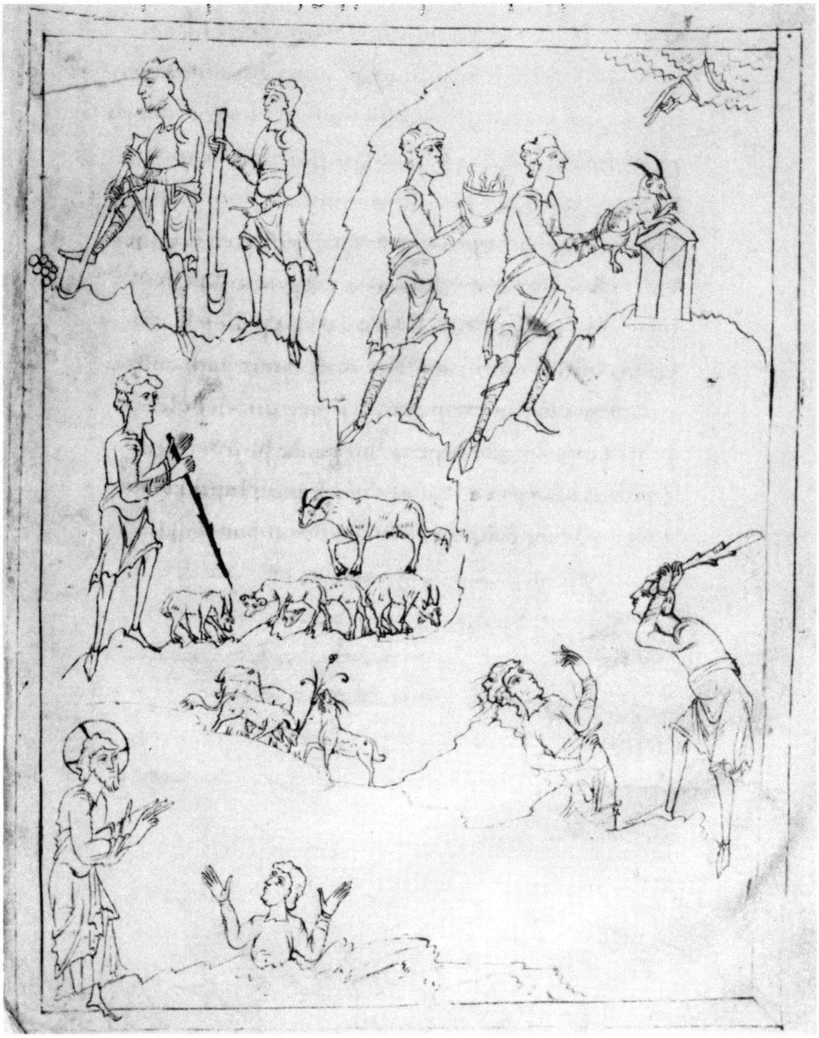

48 Oxford, Bodl., MS Junius 11, p. 49, the Offerings of Cain and Abel

49 Rochester Cathedral, tympanum, the Sacrifice of Isaac

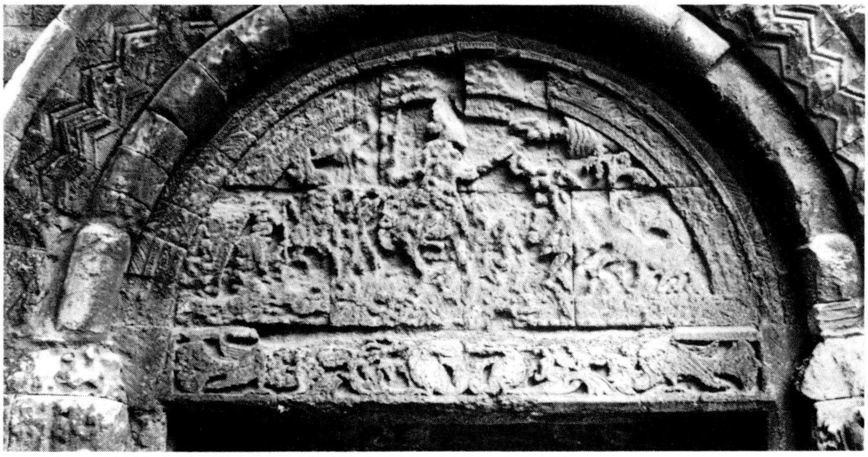

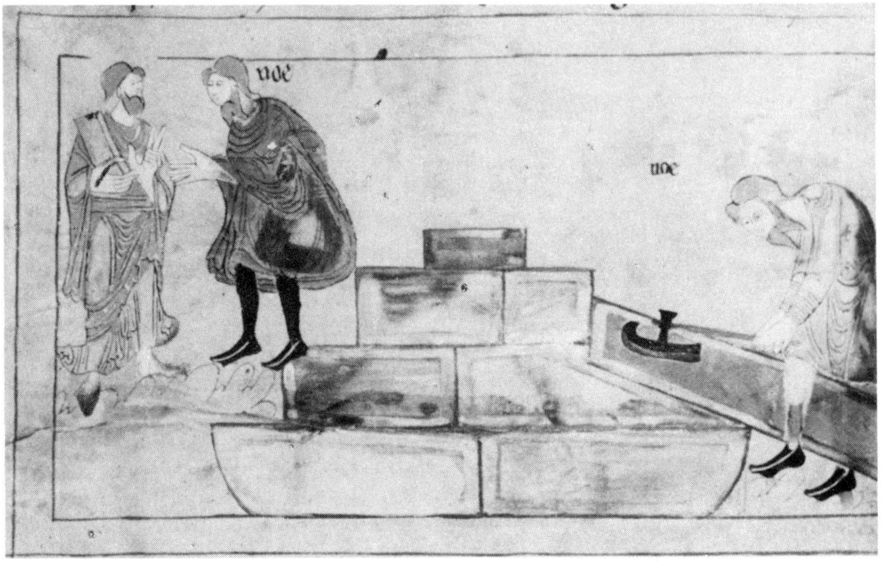

50 London, B.L., MS Cotton Claudius B.IV, fol.13v, Noah Commanded to Build the Ark

51 Oxford, Bodl., MS Junius 11, p. 65, Noah Commanded to Build the Ark

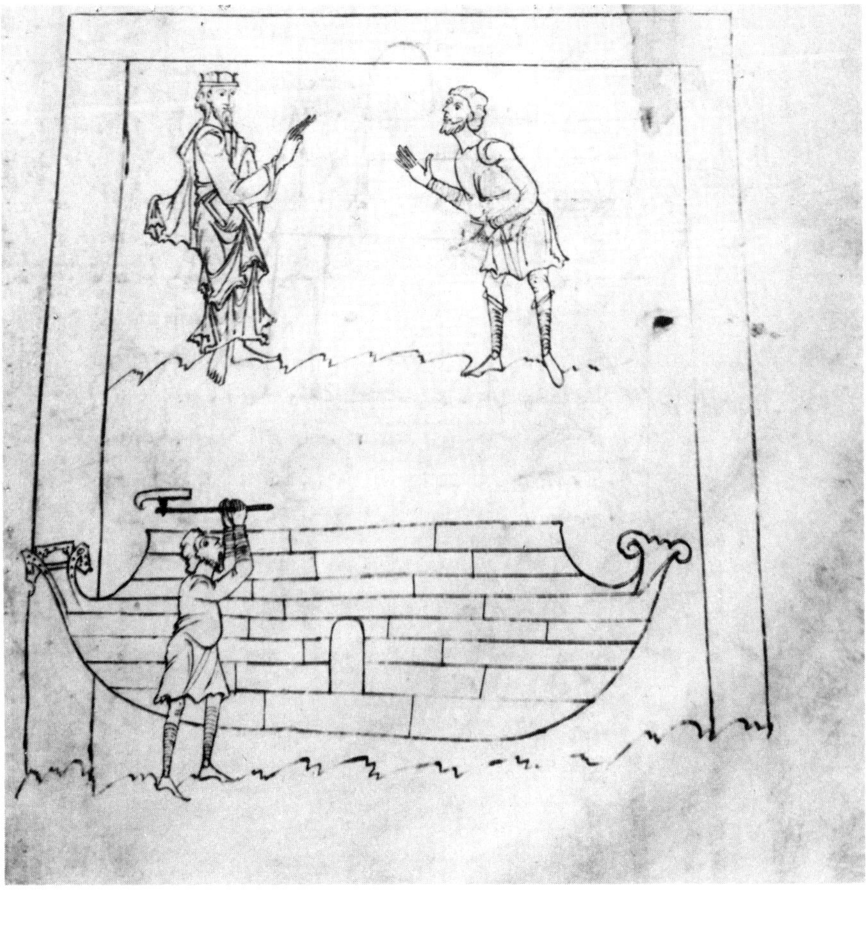

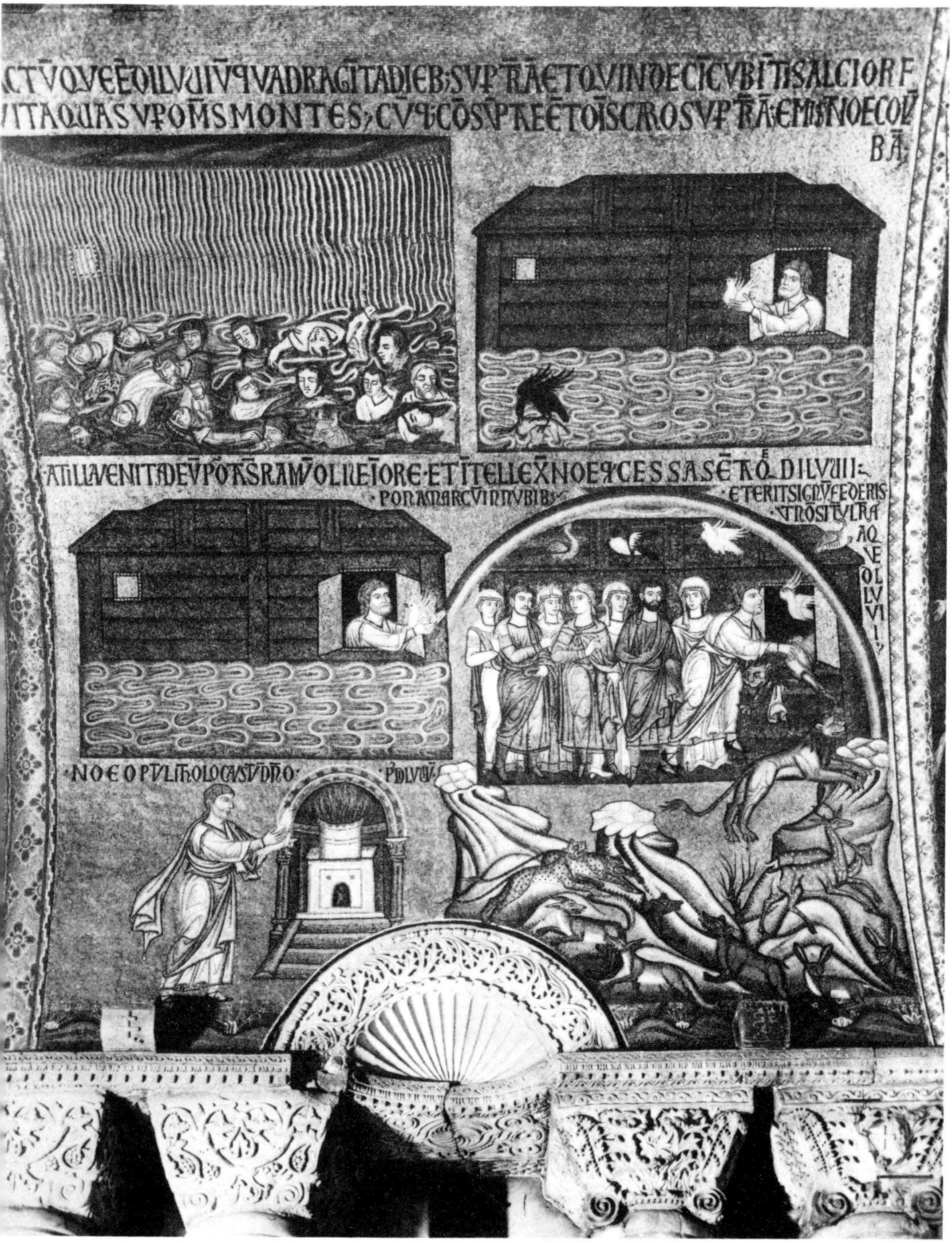

52 Venice, San Marco, narthex mosaic, the Flood

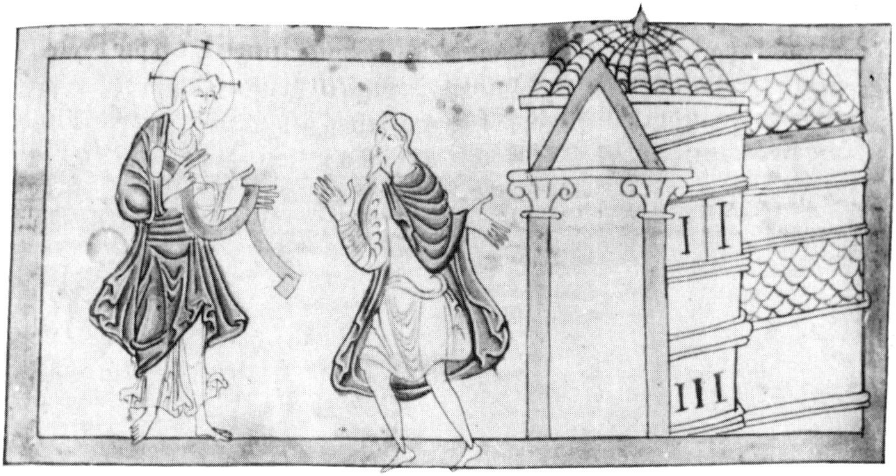

53 London, B.L., MS Cotton Claudius B.IV, fol.37v, Abraham Commanded to Sacrifice Isaac

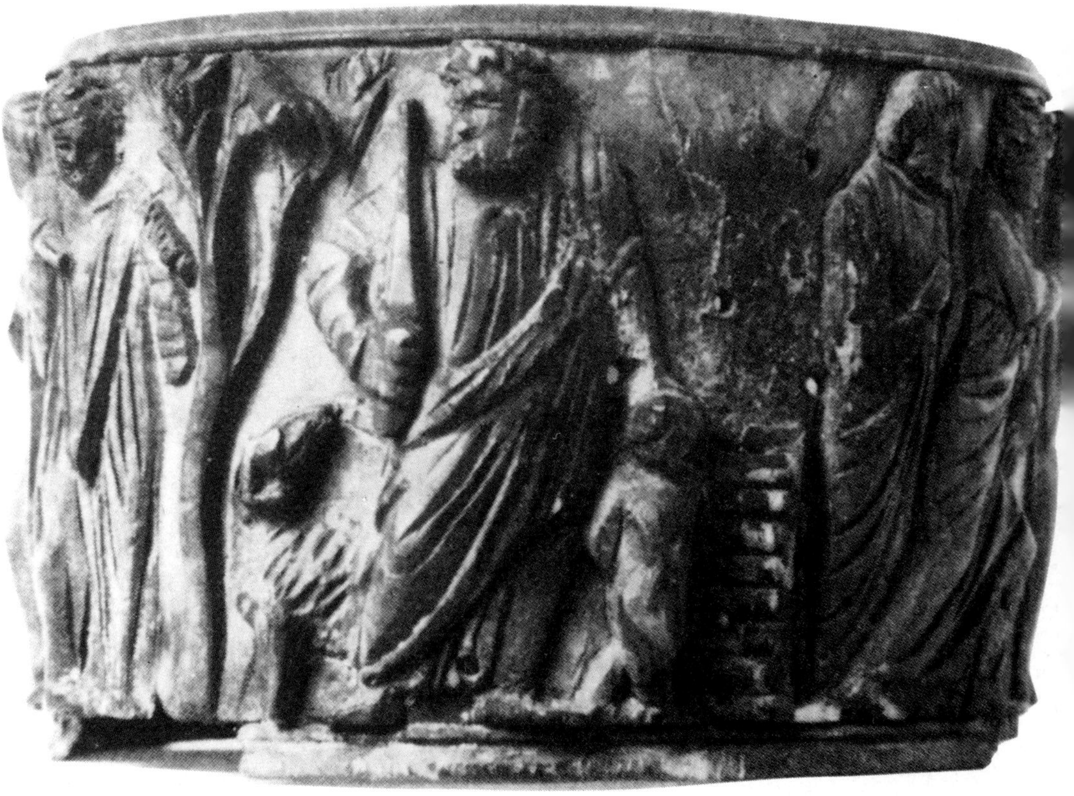

54 Bologna, Museo Civico, ivory pyxis, the Sacrifice of Isaac

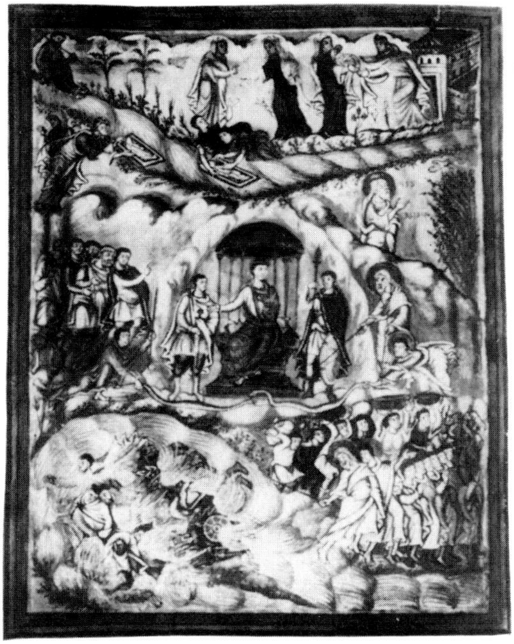

55 Rome, San Paolo fuori le mura, Bible, fol.20v, Moses before the Burning Bush

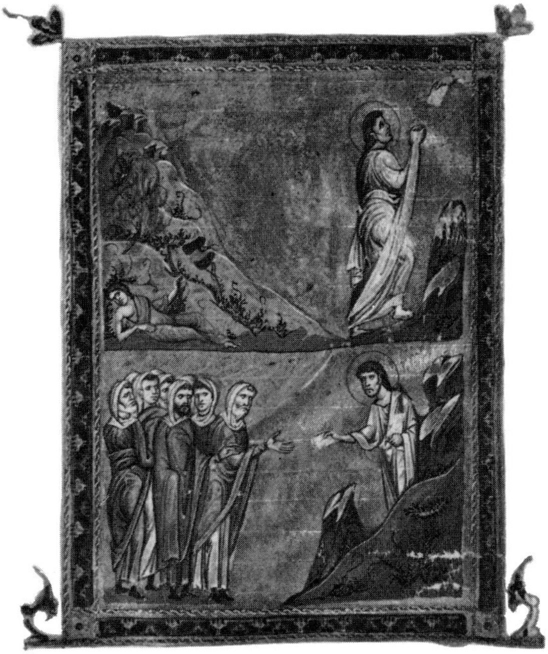

56 Rome, B.A.V., MS Vat. gr. 342, fol.133v, Moses Receiving the Law

57 London, B.L., MS Cotton Caligula A.XIV, fol.26v, the Annunciation to Joachim

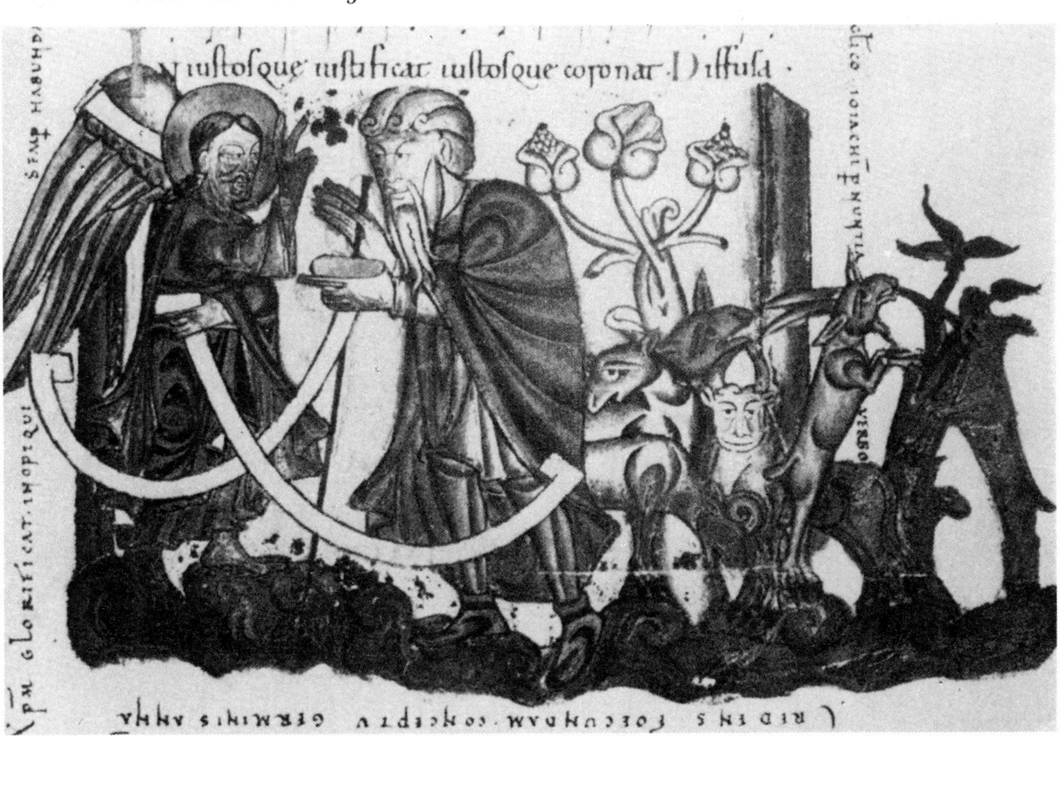

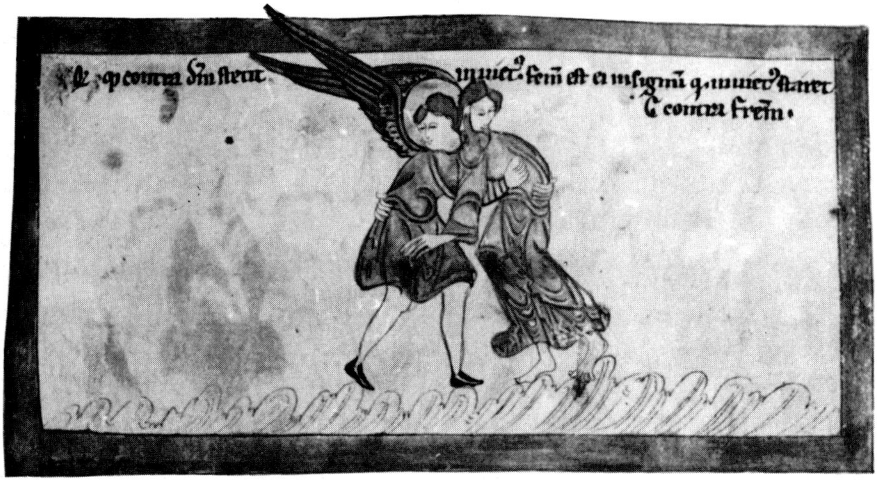

58 London, B.L., MS Cotton Claudius B.IV, fol.50r, Jacob Wrestling with the Angel

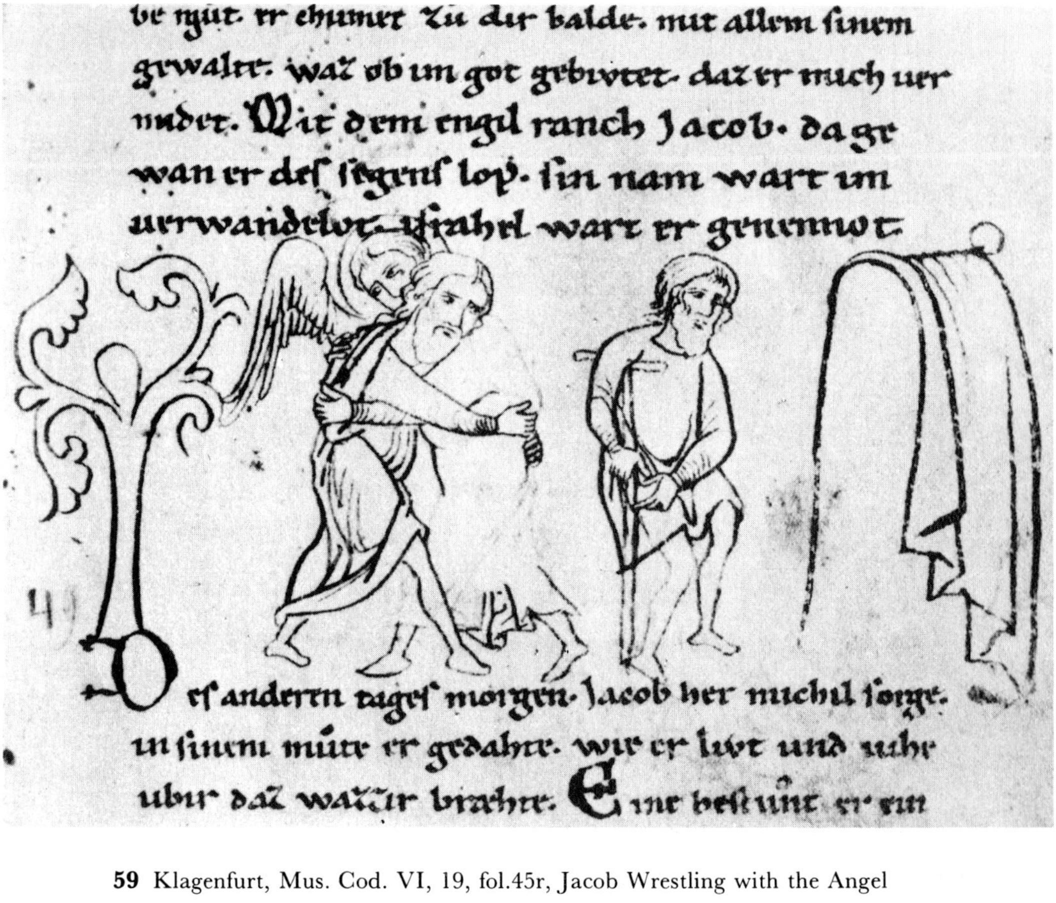

59 Klagenfurt, Mus. Cod. VI, 19, fol.45r, Jacob Wrestling with the Angel

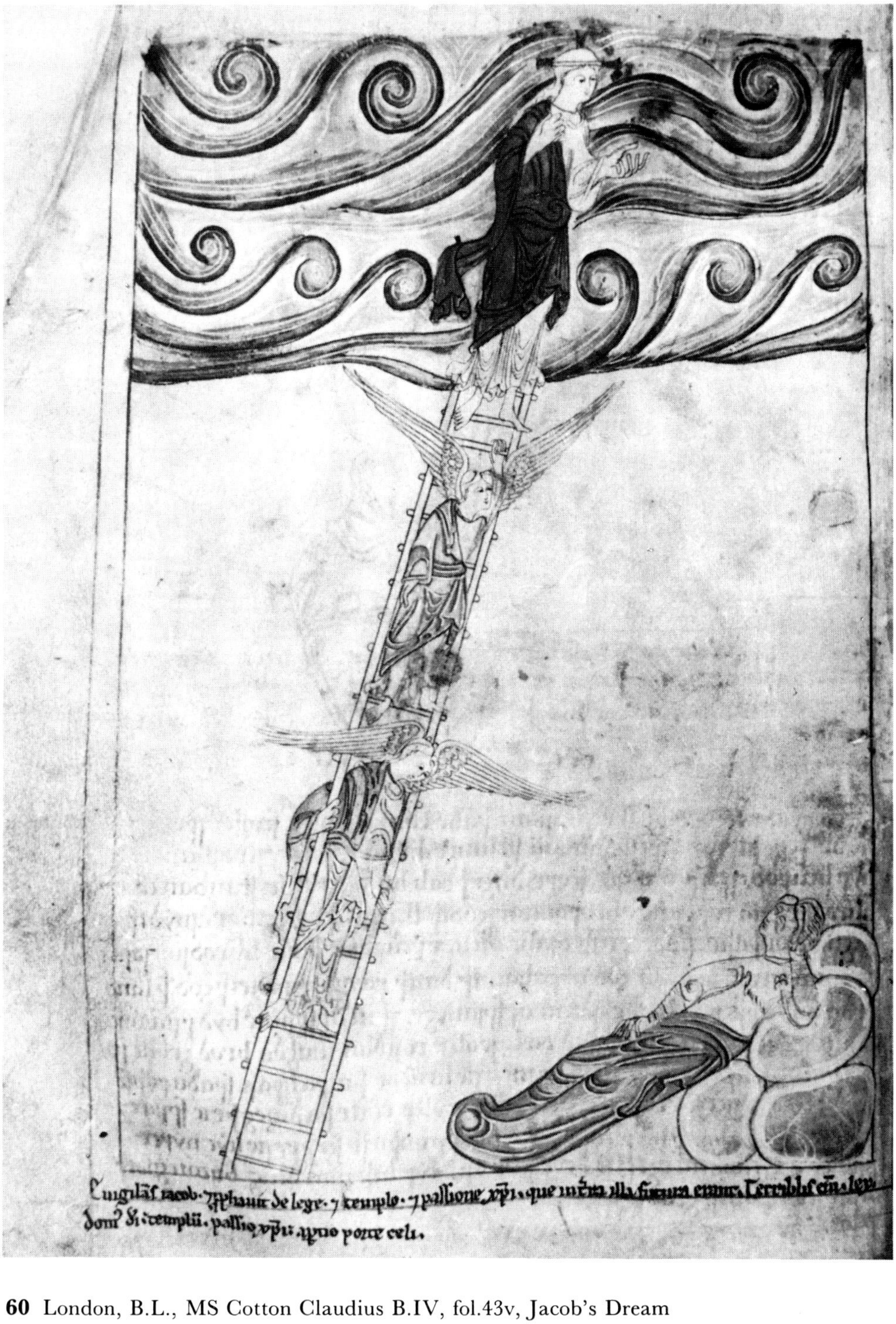

60 London, B.L., MS Cotton Claudius B.IV, fol.43v, Jacob's Dream

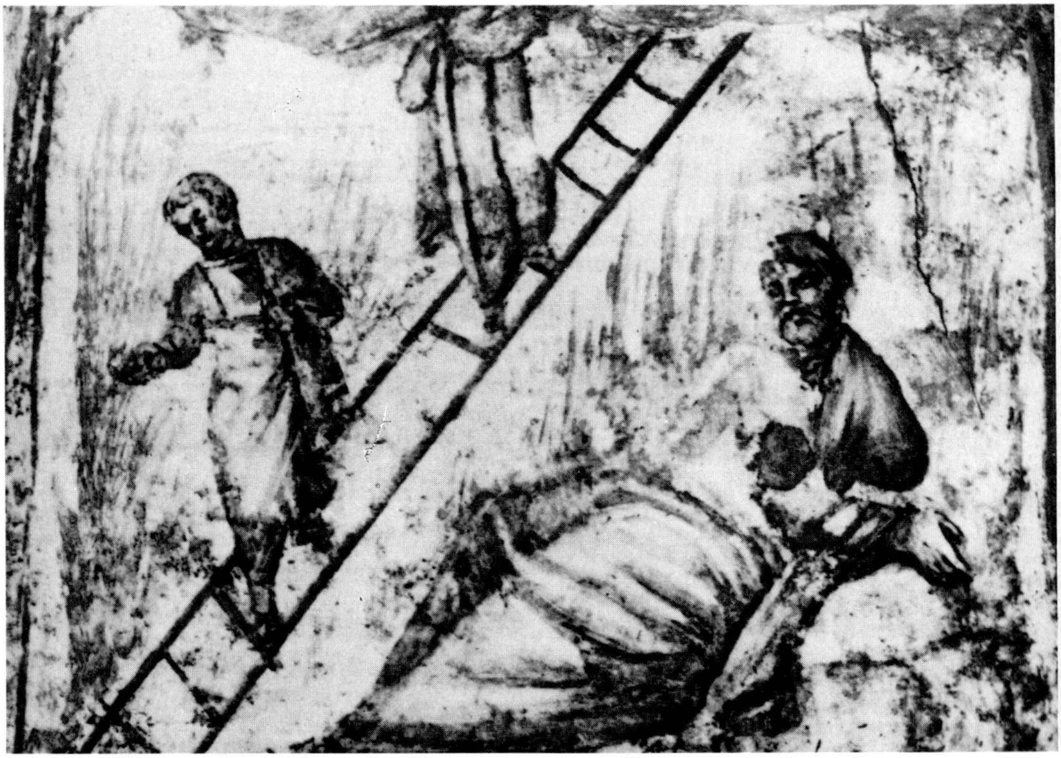

61 Rome, Via Latina catacomb, wall painting, Jacob's Dream

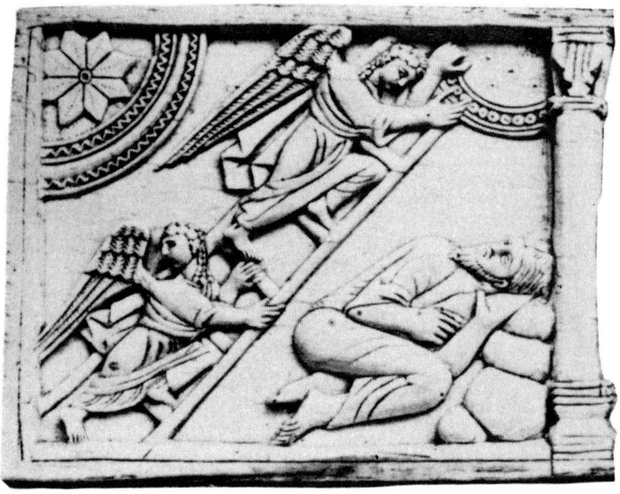

62 Salerno, Museo del Duomo, ivory, Jacob's Dream

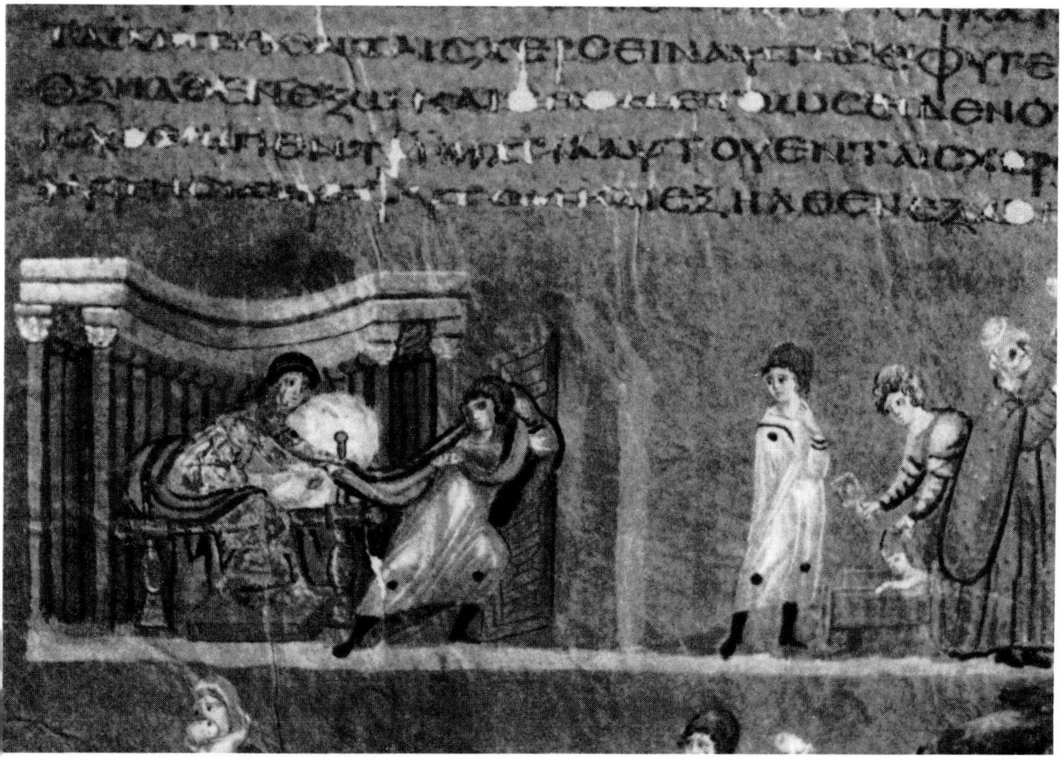

63 Vienna, Nationalbibliothek, Cod. Vindob. Theol. Graec. 31, p. 31, Joseph and Potiphar's Wife

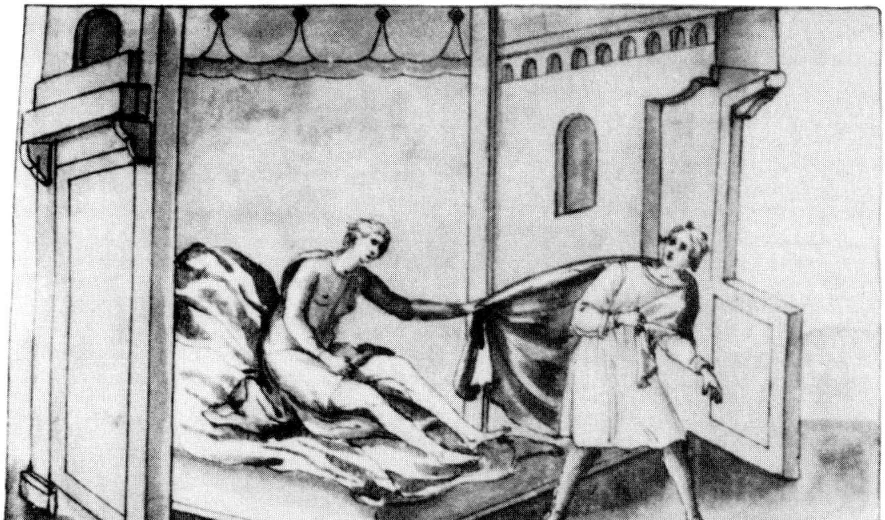

64 Rome, San Paolo fuori le mura, wall painting (formerly), Joseph and Potiphar's Wife

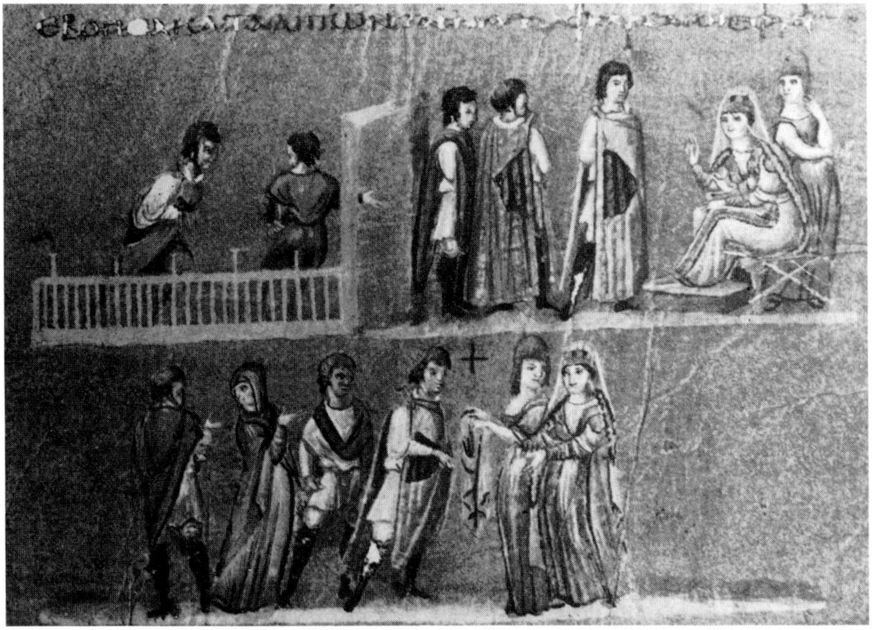

65 Vienna, Nationalbibliothek, Cod. Vindob. Theol. Graec. 31, p. 32, Potiphar's Wife Displaying the Cloak of Joseph to Potiphar

66 Sens, Trésor de la Cathédrale, ivory, Potiphar's Wife Displaying the Cloak of Joseph to Potiphar

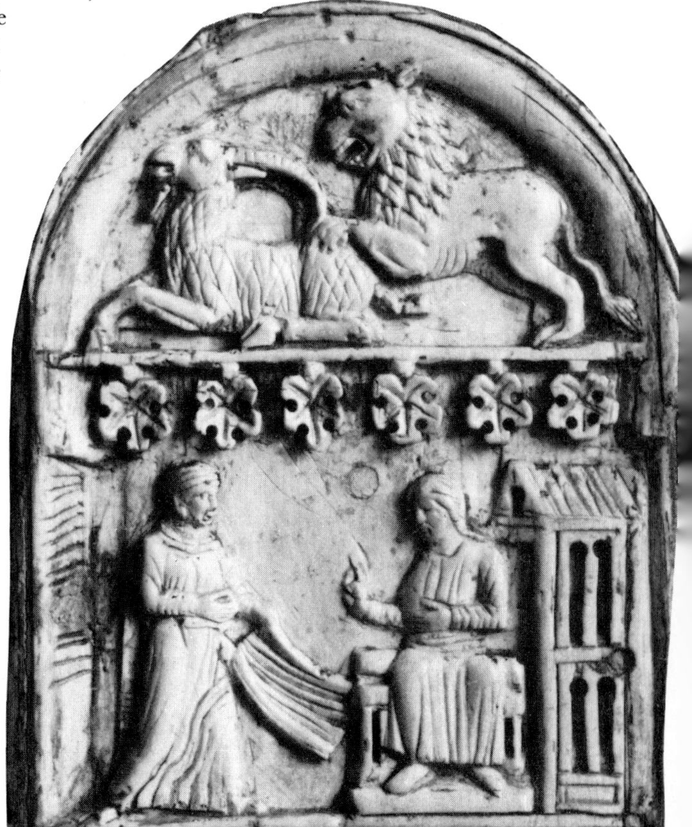

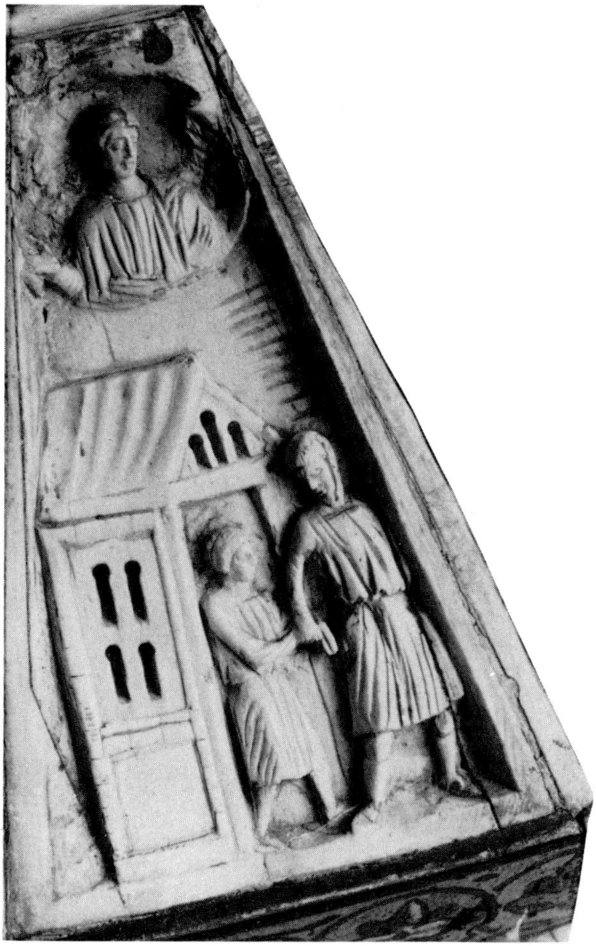

67 Sens, Trésor de la Cathédrale, ivory, Joseph Led from Prison

68 Vienna, Nationalbibliothek, Cod. Vindob. Theol. Graec. 31, p. 36, Joseph before Pharaoh

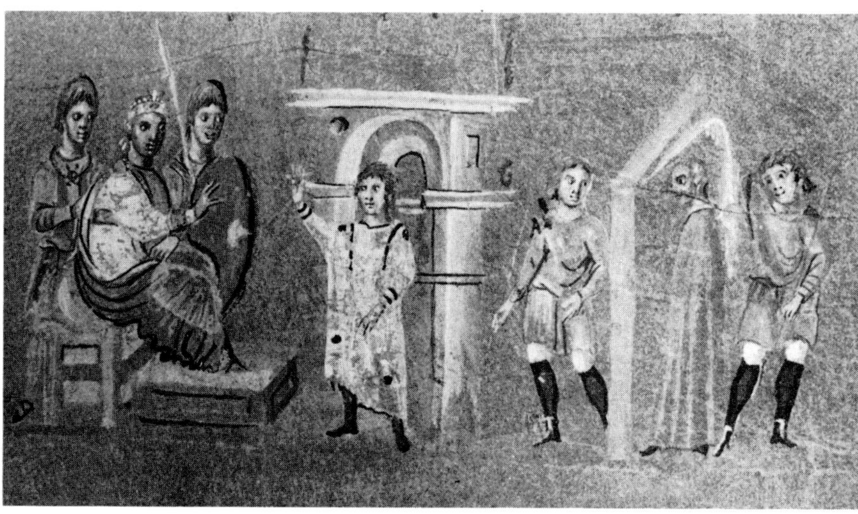

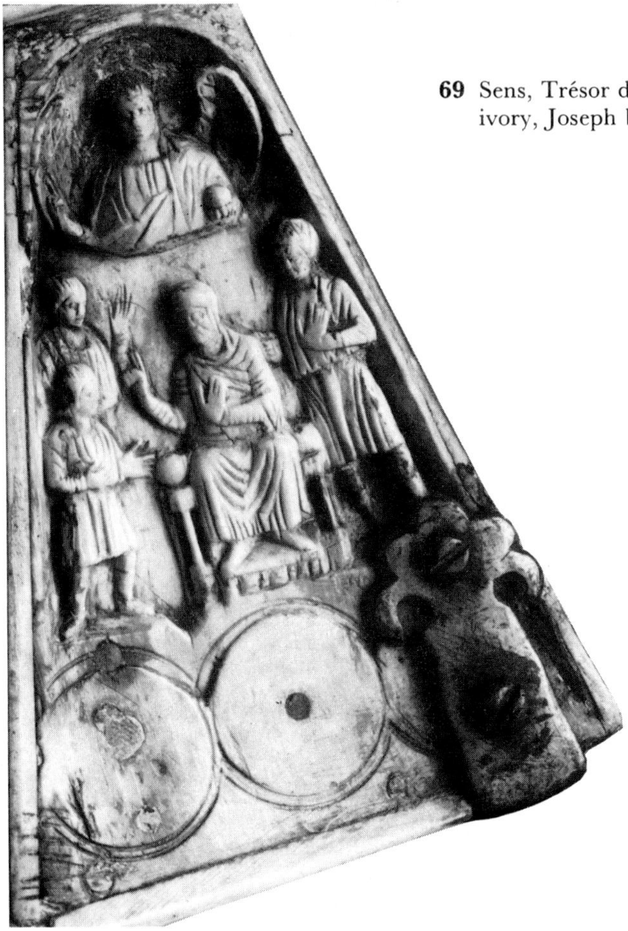

69 Sens, Trésor de la Cathédrale, ivory, Joseph before Pharaoh

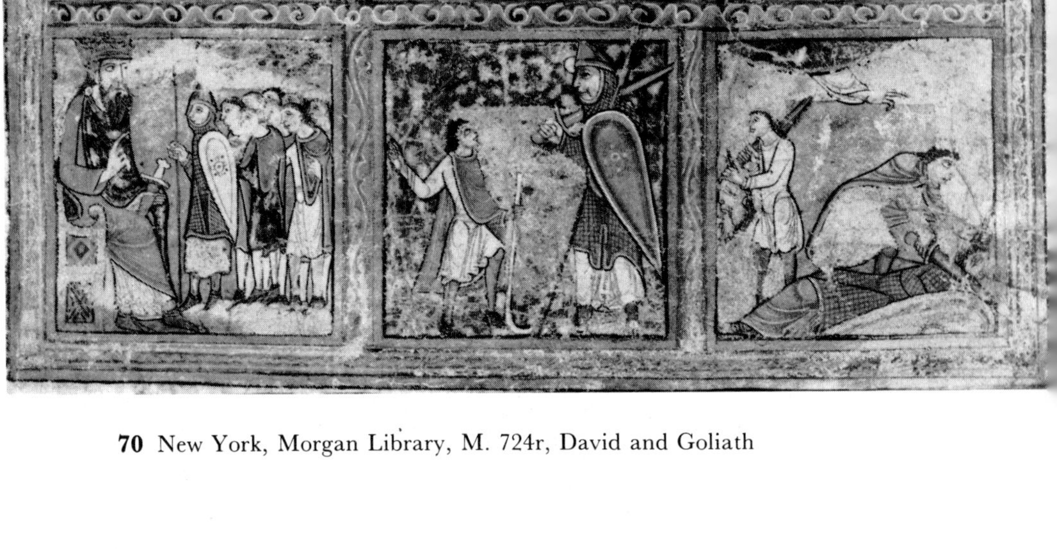

70 New York, Morgan Library, M. 724r, David and Goliath

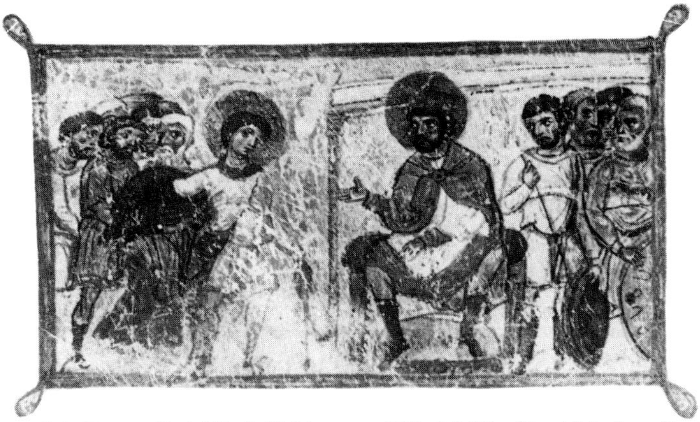

71 Rome, B.A.V., MS Vat. gr. 333, fol.23r, David before Saul

72 Venice, Biblioteca Marciana, MS 17, fol.1v, David and Goliath

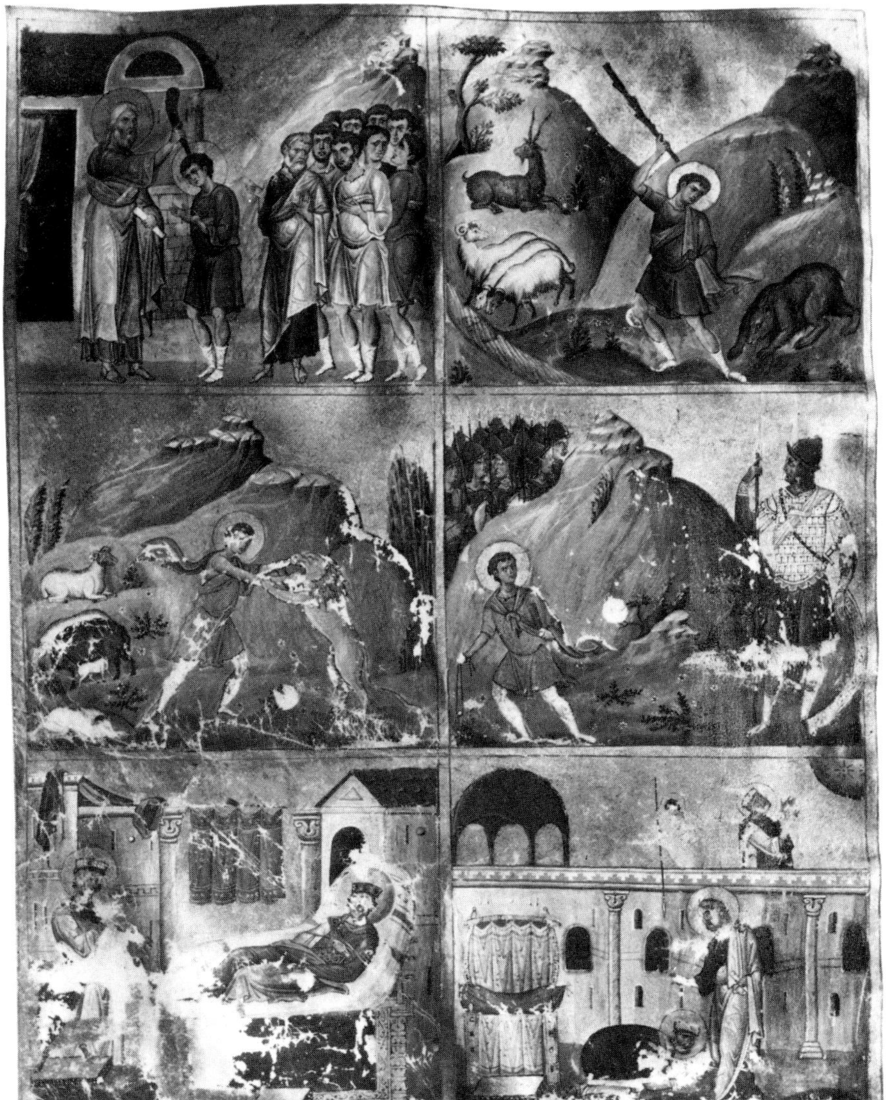

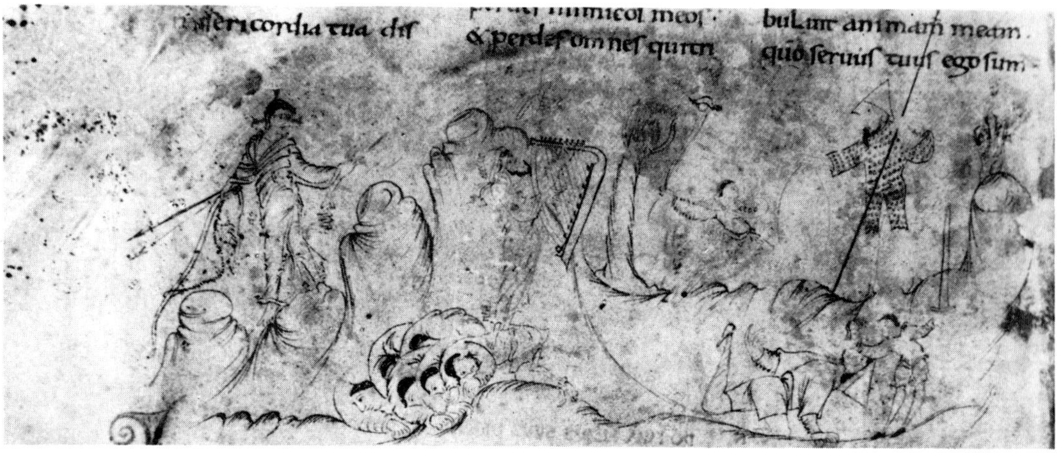

73 London, B.L., MS Harley 603, fol.73v, David and Goliath

74 Amiens, B.M., MS 18, fol.123v, David and Goliath

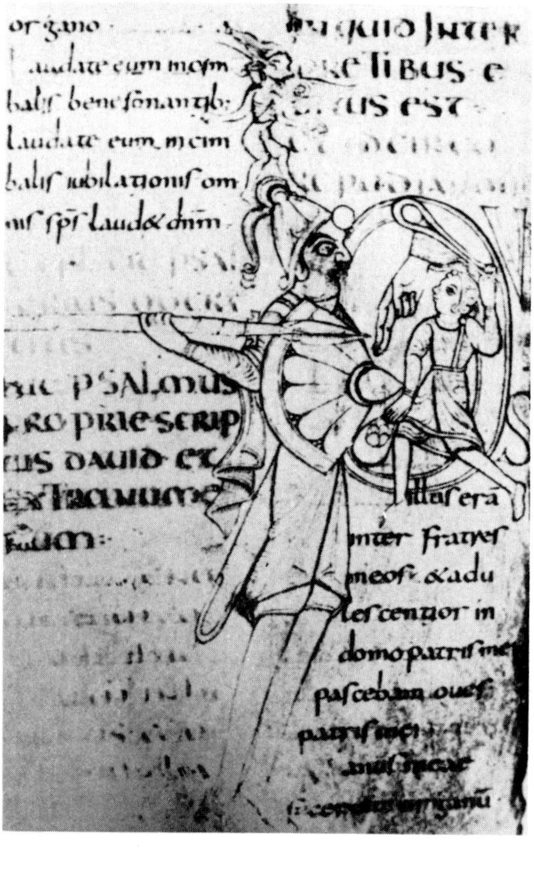

75 London, B.L., MS Arundel 155, fol.93r, David Beheads Goliath

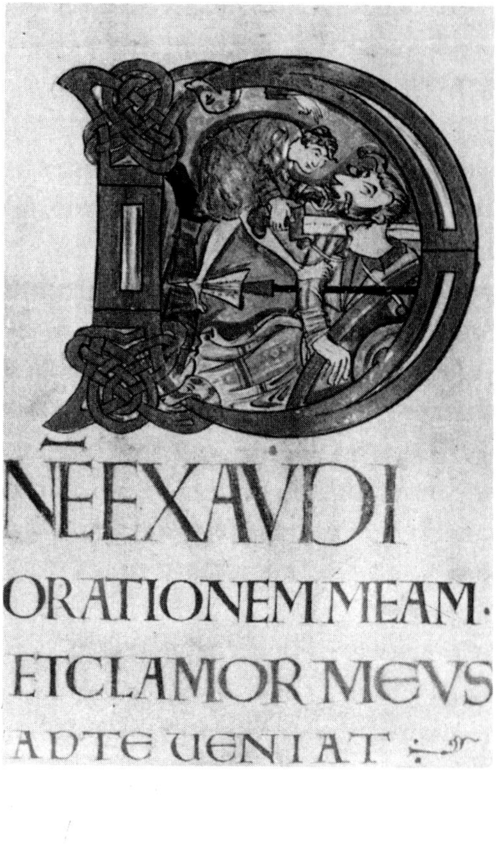

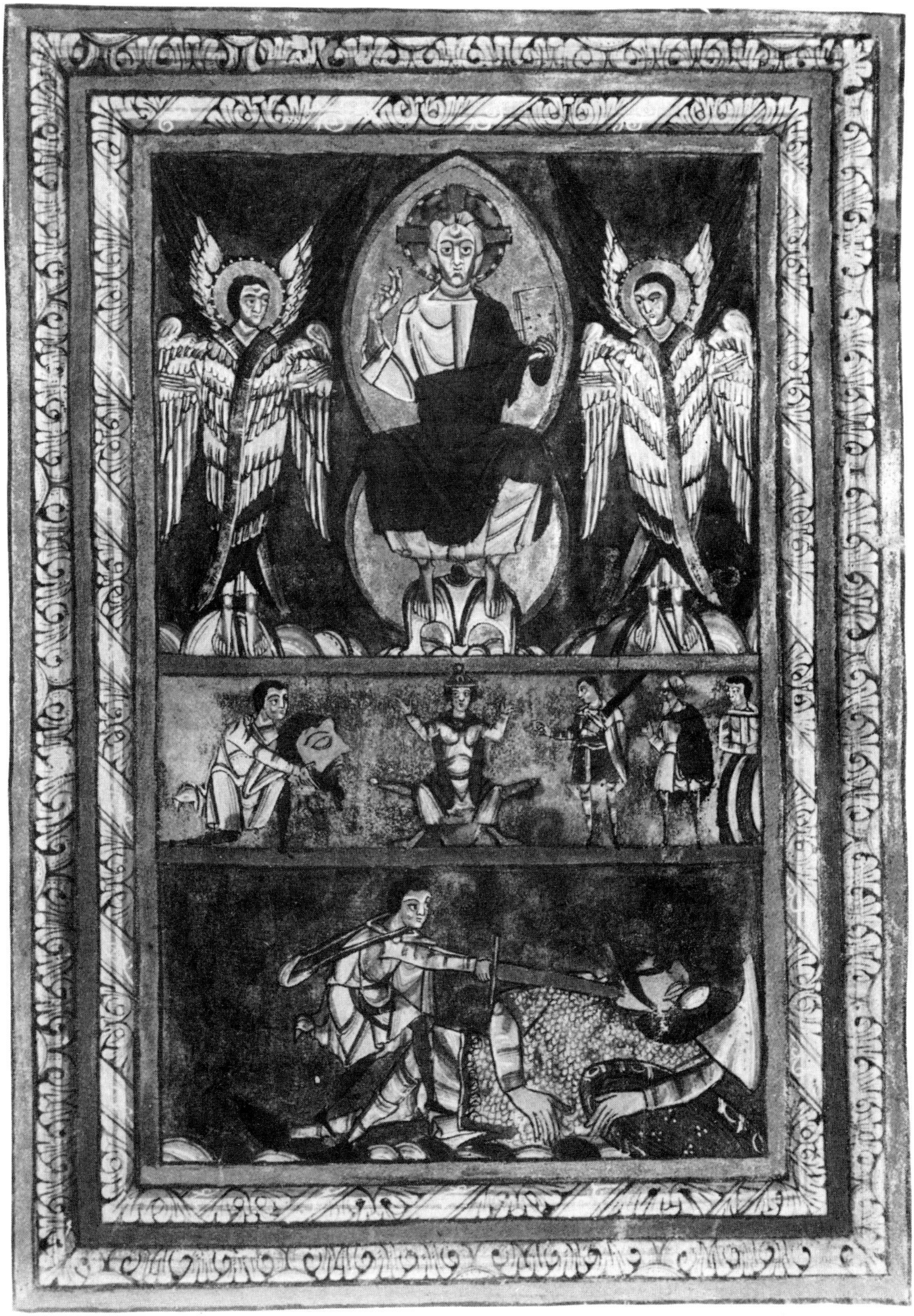

76 Berlin, Staatsbibliothek, Preuss. Kulturbesitz, MS theol. lat. fol. 358, fol.74r, David and Goliath

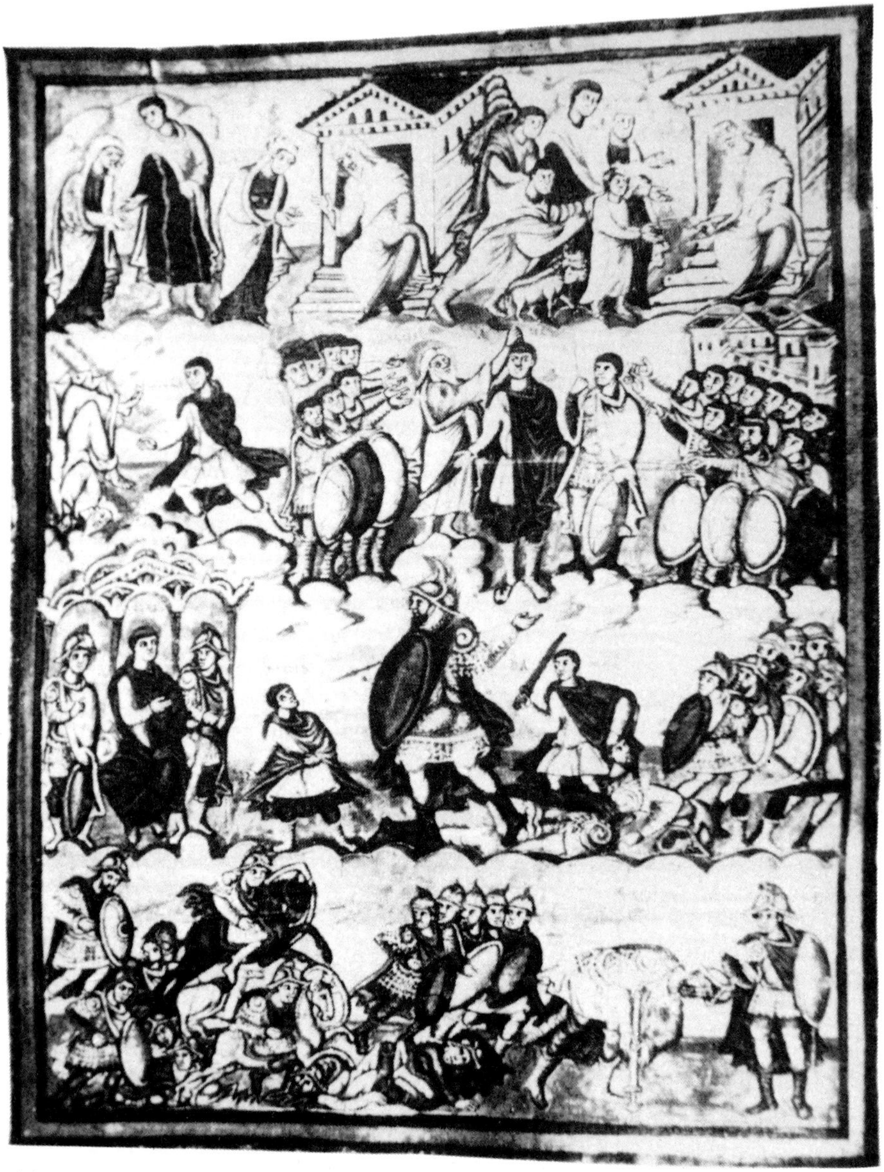

77 Rome, San Paolo fuori le mura, Bible, fol.81r, David and Goliath

78 Utrecht, Univ. Bibl., MS 32, Psalm 151, fol.91v, David as a Shepherd, David Presenting the Head of Goliath to Saul

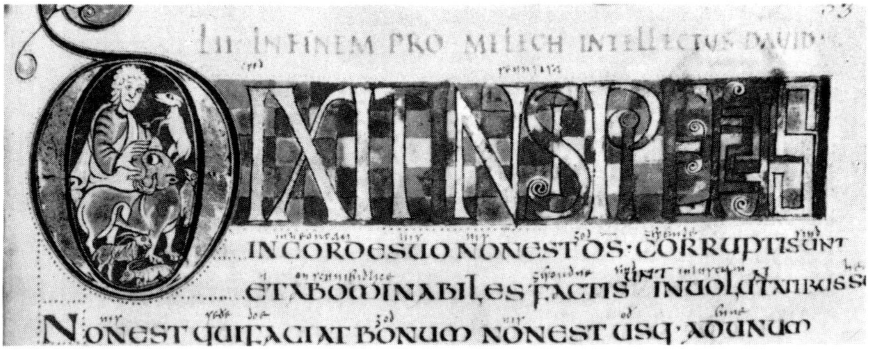

79 London, B.L., MS Vespasian A.I., fol.53r, David and the Lion

80 London, B.L., MS Tiberius C.VI, fol.9v, the Anointment of David

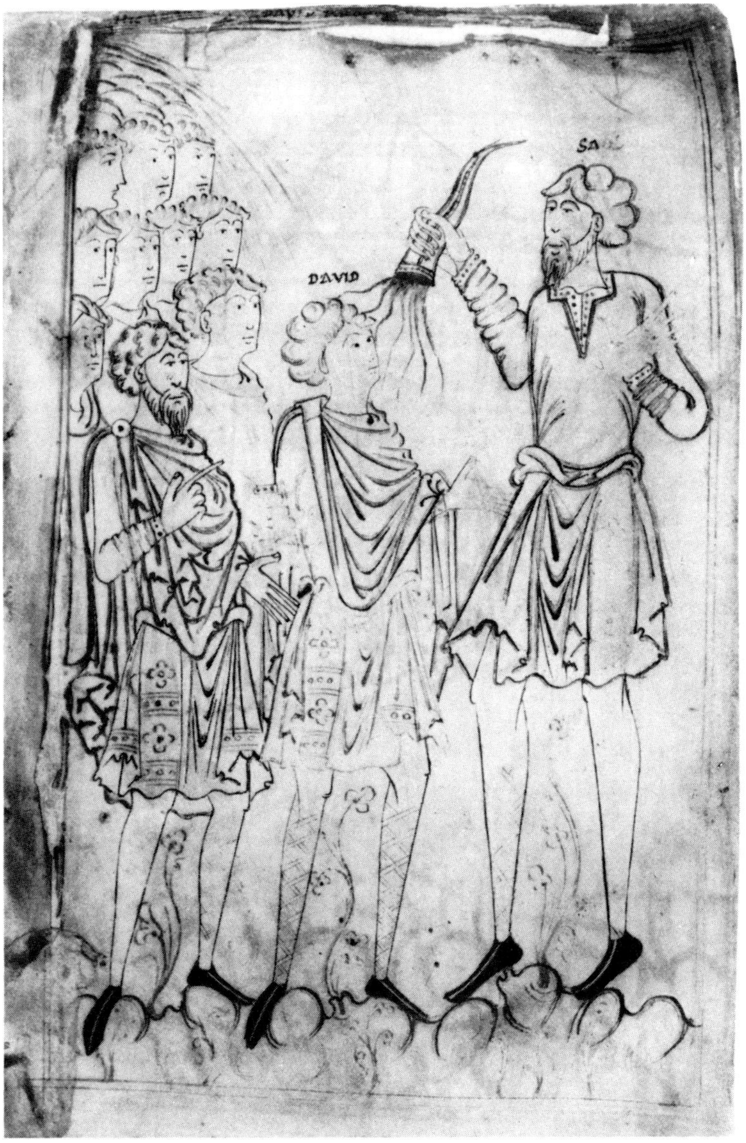

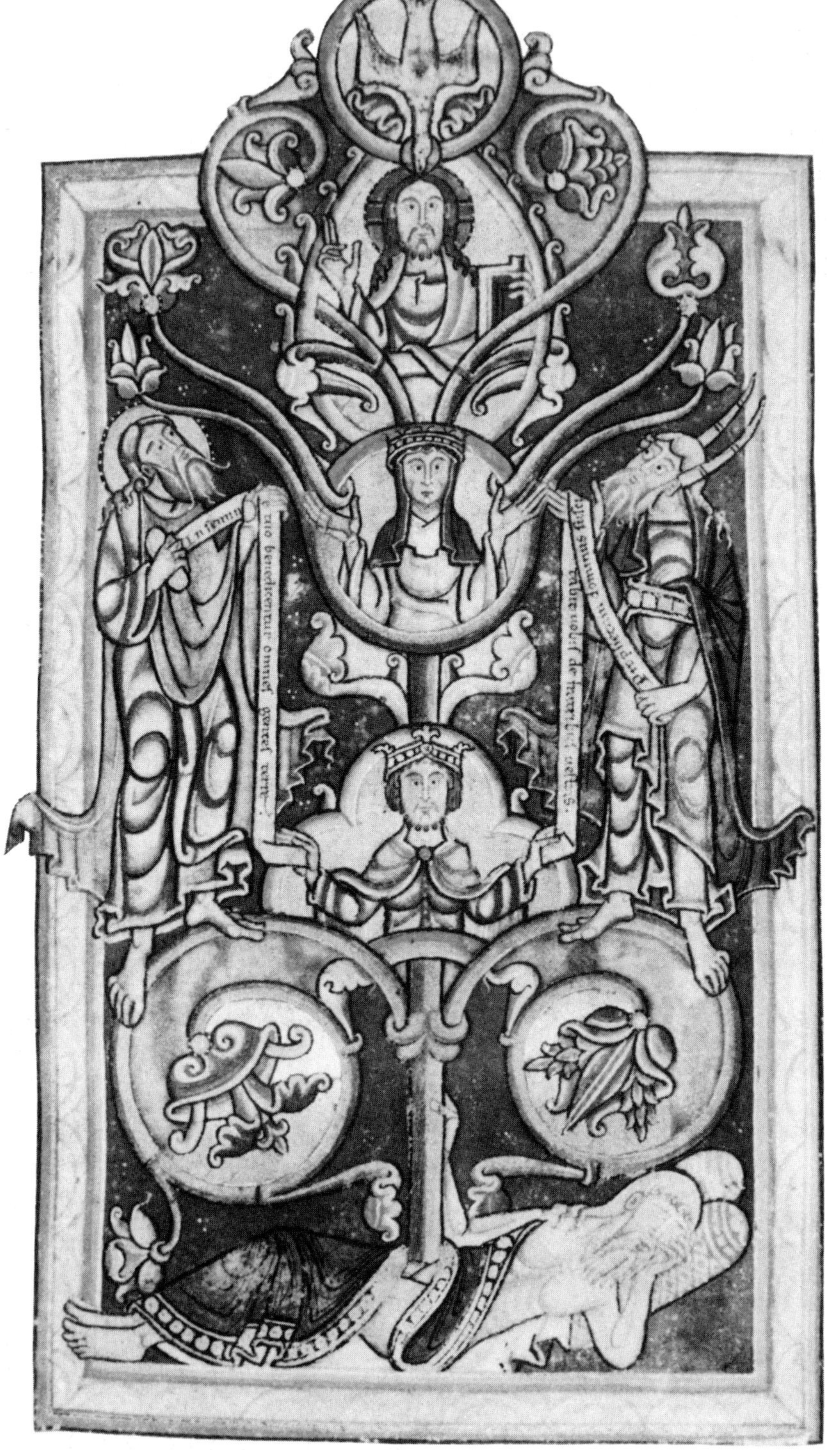

81 London, B.L., MS Lansdowne 383, fol.15r, the Jesse Tree

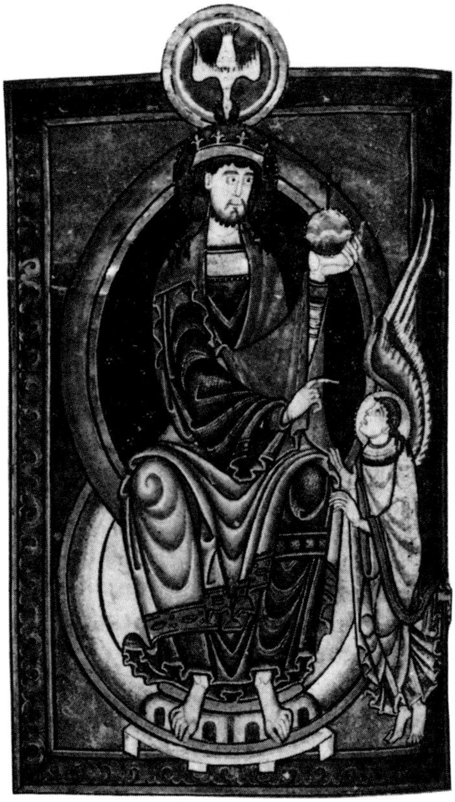

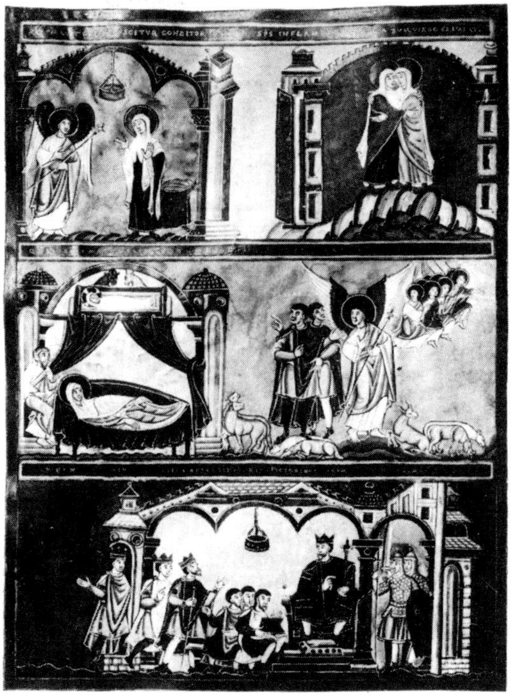

82 London, B.L., MS Lansdowne 383, fol.12v, God Sending the Angel

83 Nuremberg, Germanisches-Nationalmuseum, MS 156142, fol.18v, the Annunciation, Visitation, Nativity, Magi before Herod

84 Escorial, Codex Vitrinas 17, fol.94v, the Annunciation

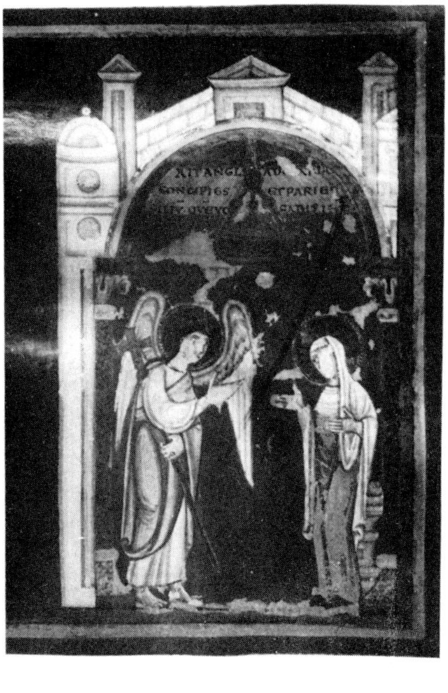

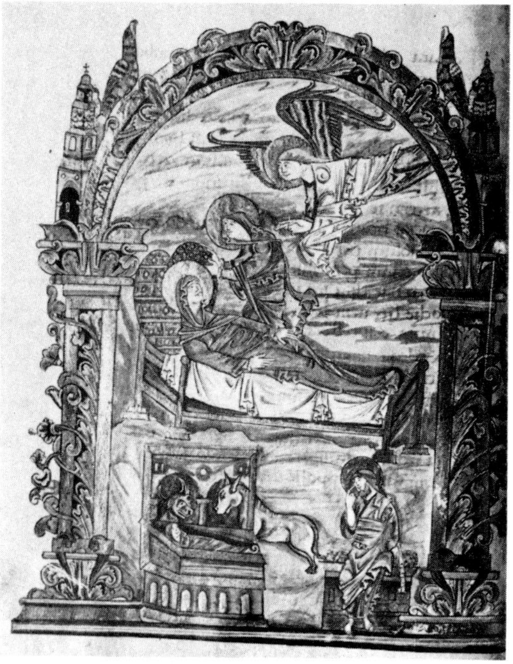

85 Rouen, B.M., MS Y.6, fol.32v, the Nativity

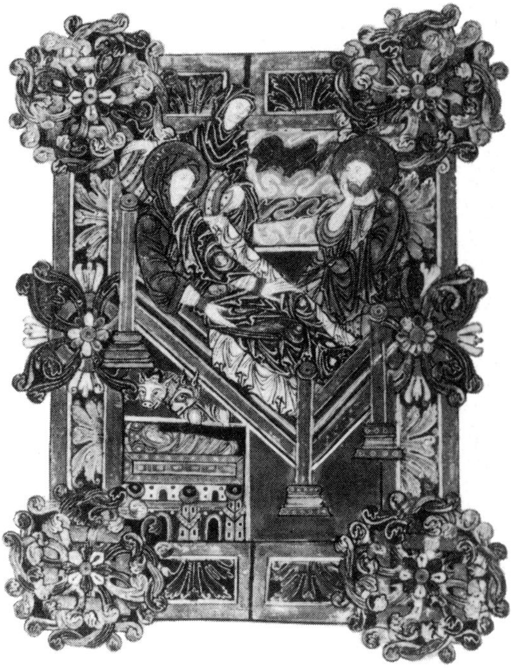

86 London, B.L., MS Add. 49598, fol.15v, the Nativity

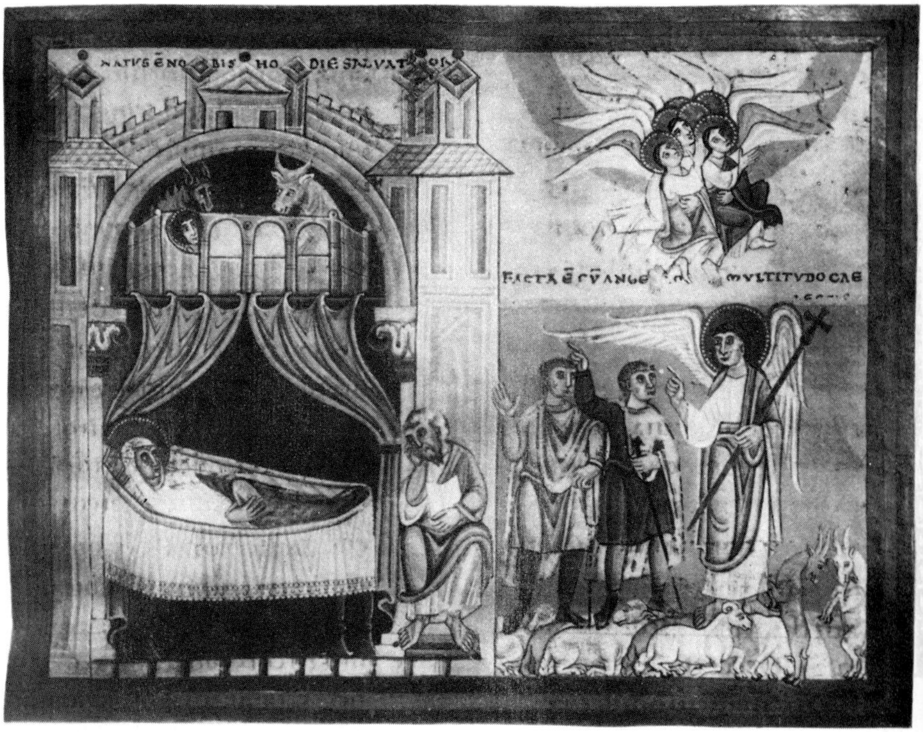

87 Escorial, Codex Vitrinas 17, fol.96r, the Nativity, Annunciation to the Shepherds

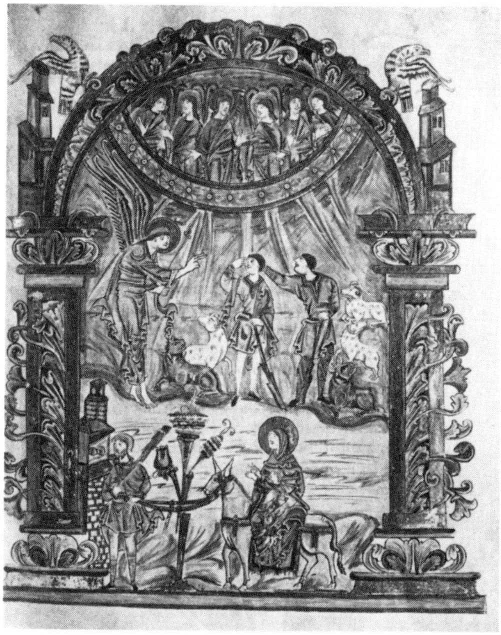

88 Rouen, B.M., MS Y.6, fol.33r, the Annunciation to the Shepherds

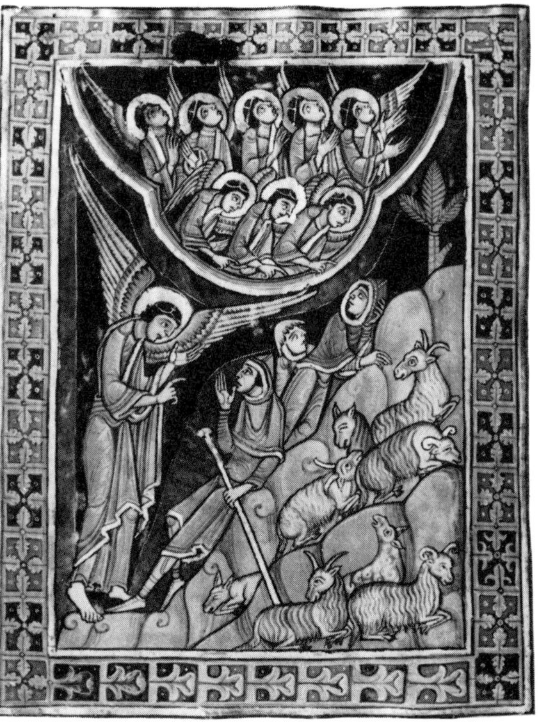

89 Hildesheim, St Godehard, p. 22, the Annunciation to the Shepherds

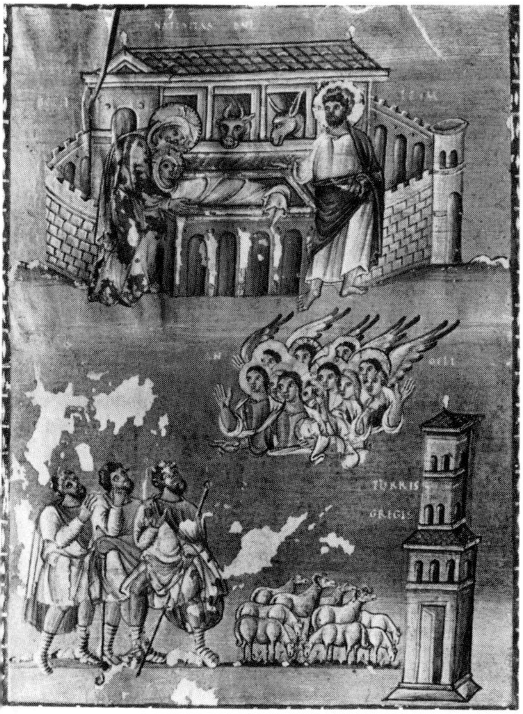

90 Trier, Stadtsbibliothek, MS 24, fol.13v, the Annunciation to the Shepherds

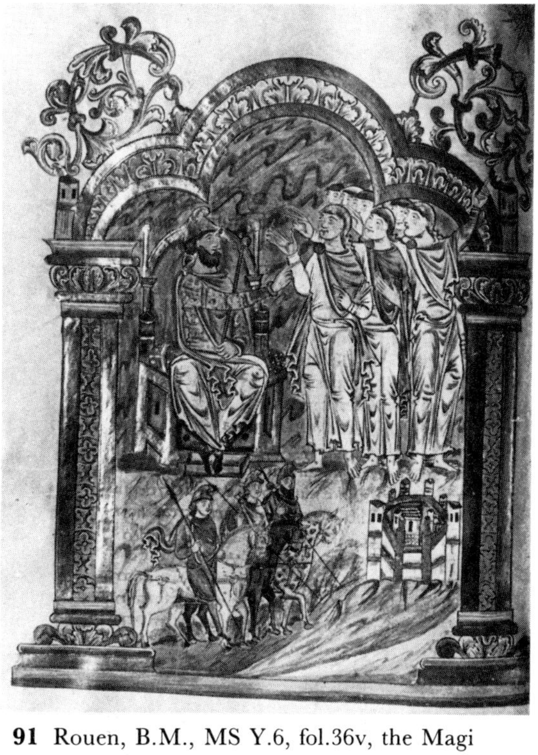

91 Rouen, B.M., MS Y.6, fol.36v, the Magi before Herod, Journey of the Magi

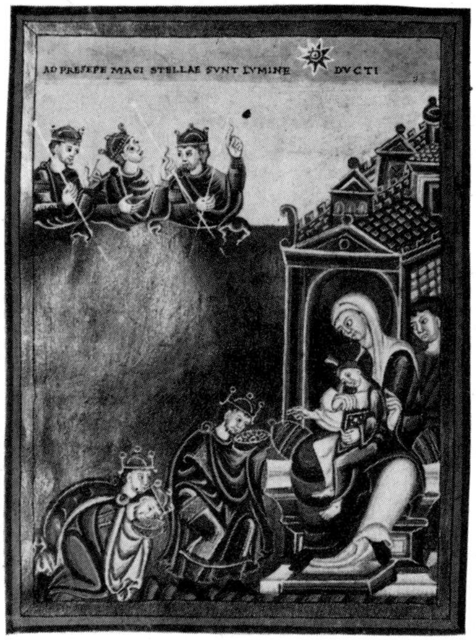

92 Bremen, Universitätsbibliothek, MS b.21, fol.14v, the Journey of the Magi, Adoration of the Magi

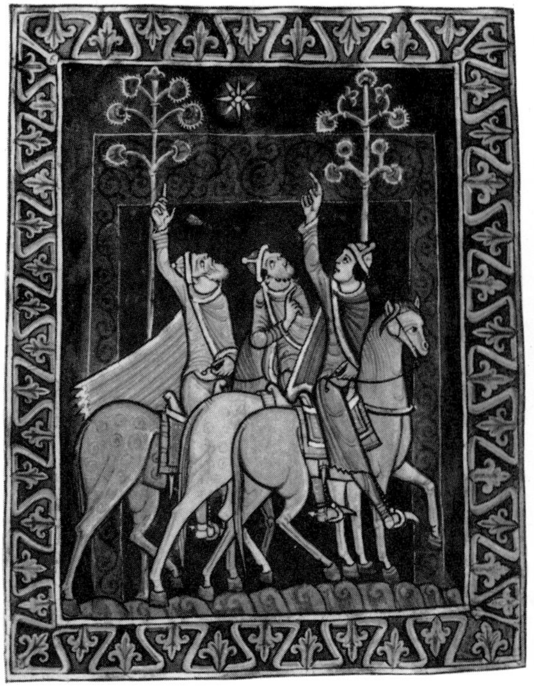

93 Hildesheim, St Godehard, p. 24, the Journey of the Magi

94 Rouen, B.M. MS Y.6, fol.37r, the Adoration of the Magi, Dream of the Magi

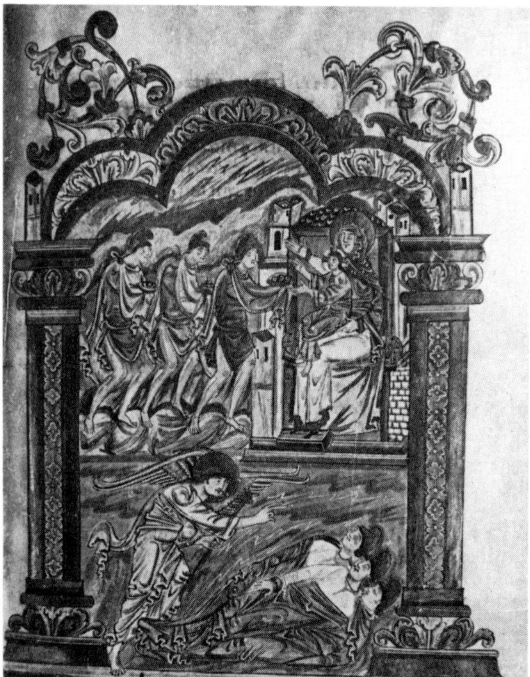

95 London, B.L., MS Add. 49598, fol.24v, the Adoration of the Magi

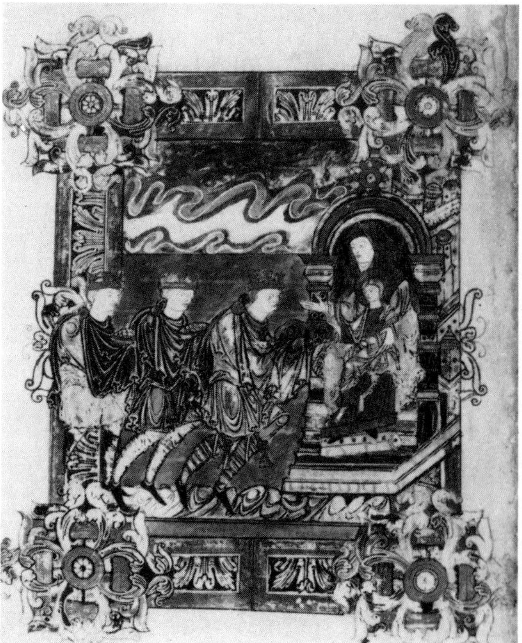

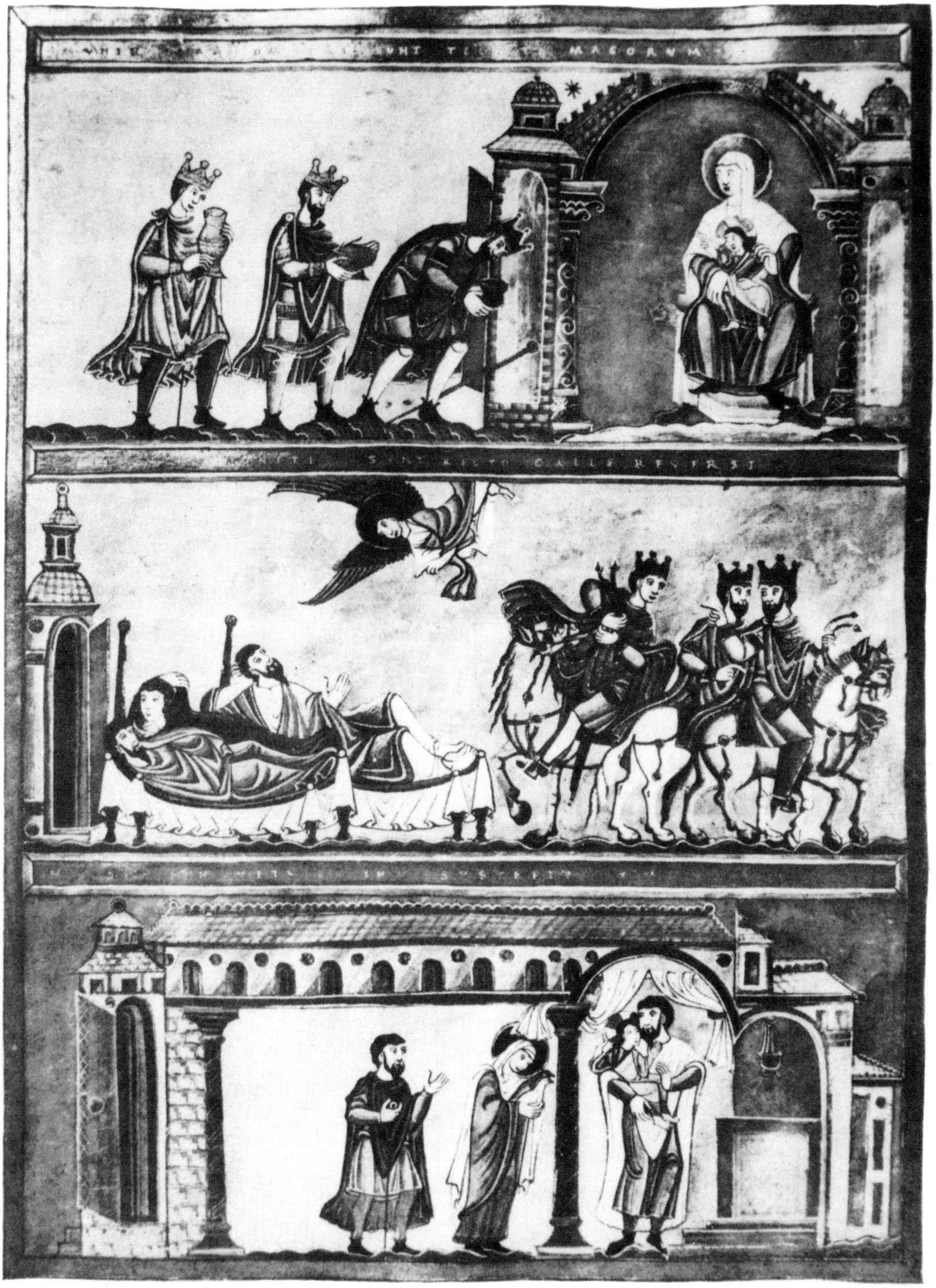

96 Nuremberg, Germanisches-Nationalmuseum, MS 156142, fol.19r, the Adoration of the Magi, Dream of the Magi, Journey of the Magi, Presentation in the Temple

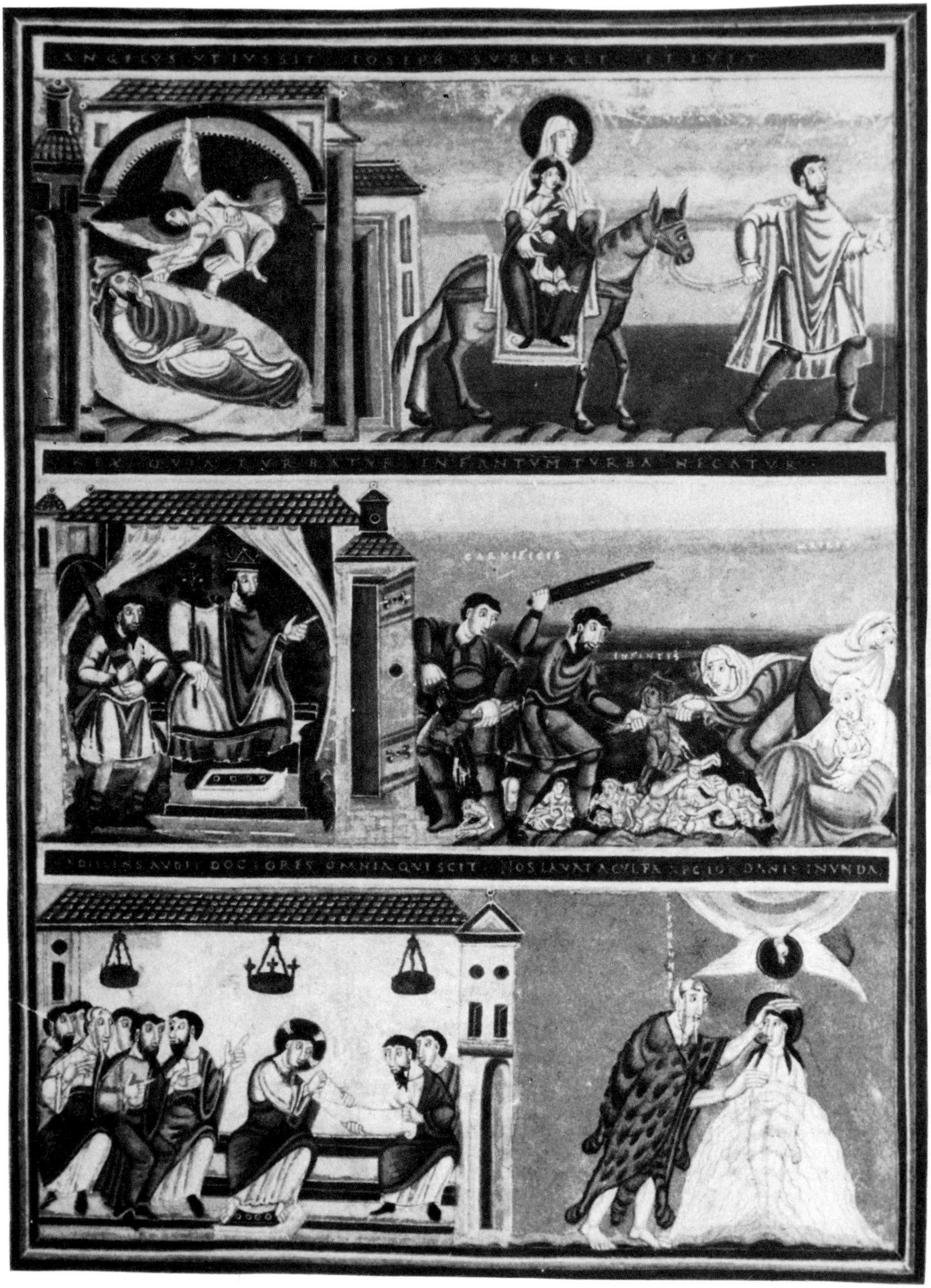

97 Nuremberg, Germanisches-Nationalmuseum, MS 156142, fol.19v, the Dream of Joseph, Flight into Egypt, Massacre of the Innocents, Christ in the Temple, Baptism of Christ

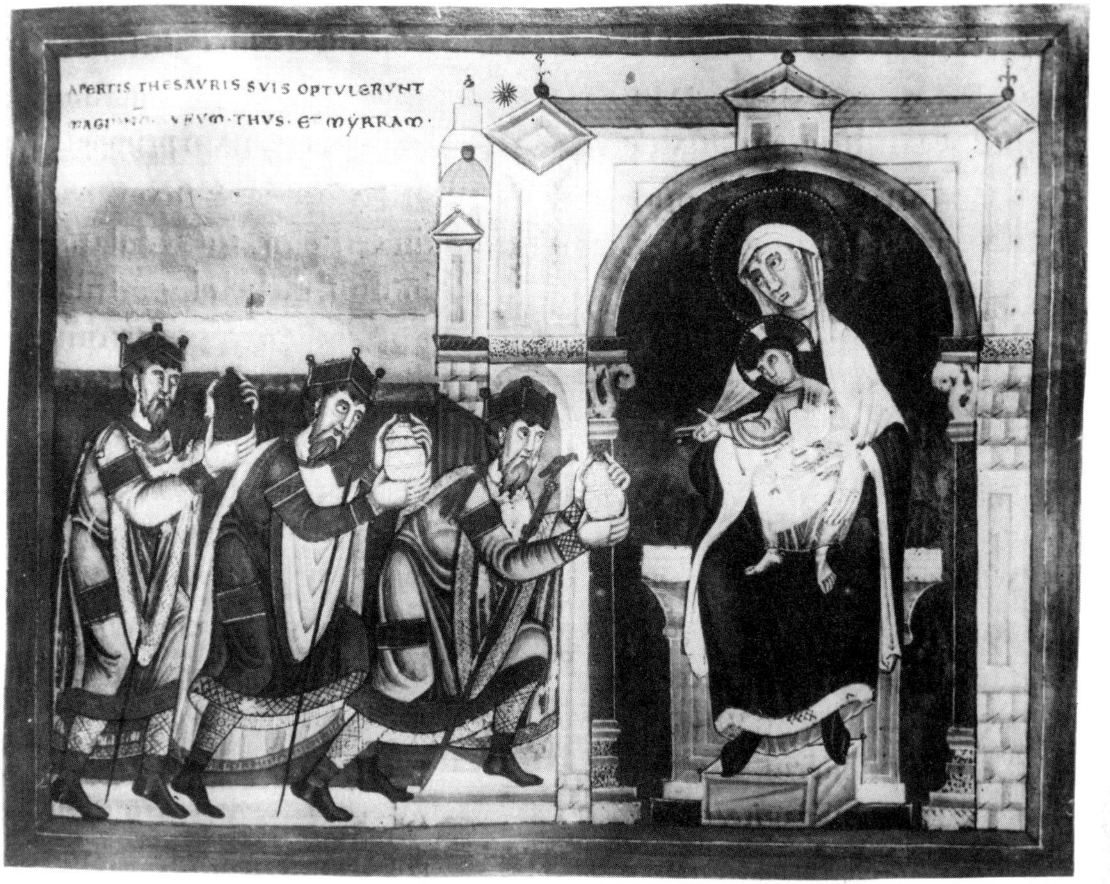

98 Escorial, Codex Vitrinas 17, fol.24r, Adoration of the Magi

99 London, B.L. MS Harley 603, fol.64v, Psalm CXXI

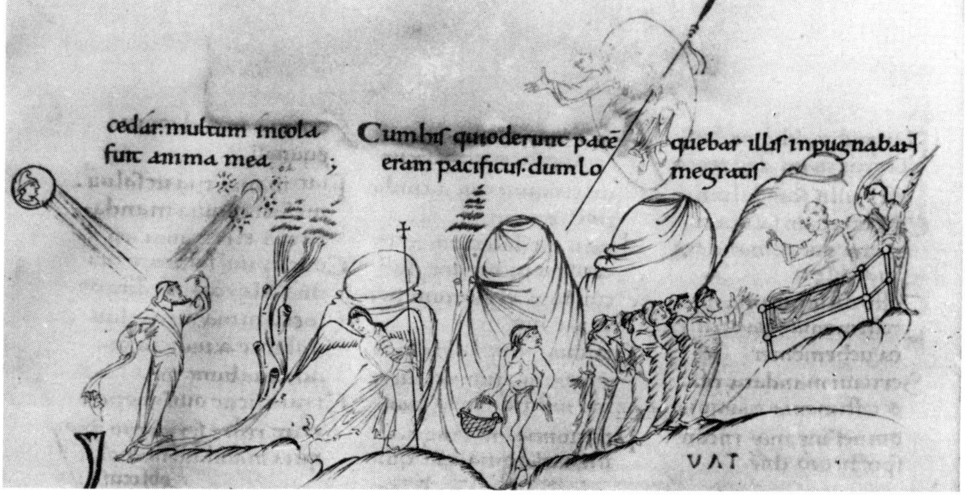

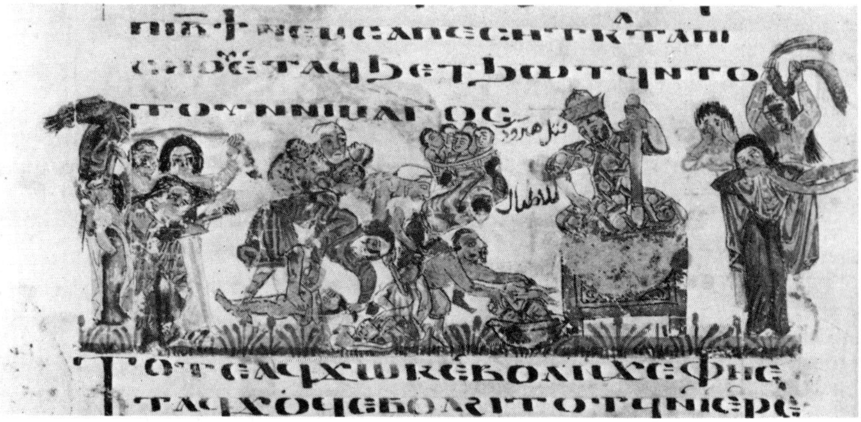

100 Paris, B.N., MS copte 13, fol.6v, Massacre of the Innocents

101 London, B.L. MS Add. 49598, fol.34v, the Presentation in the Temple

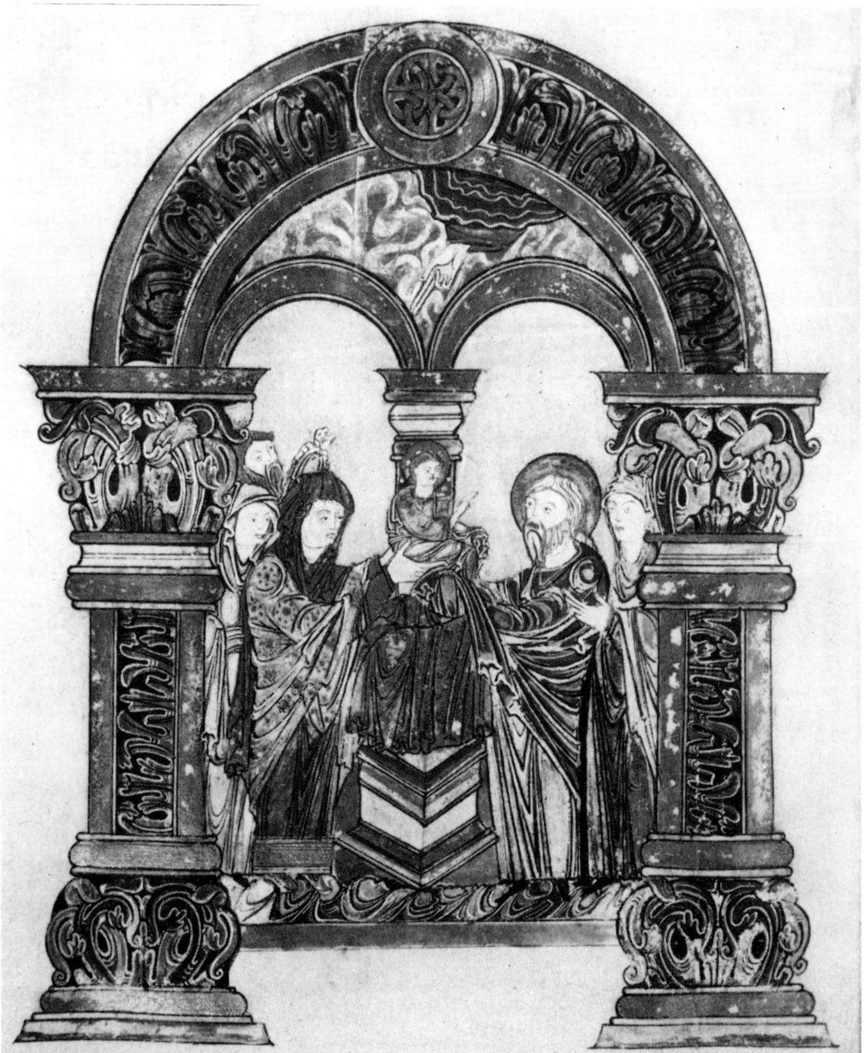

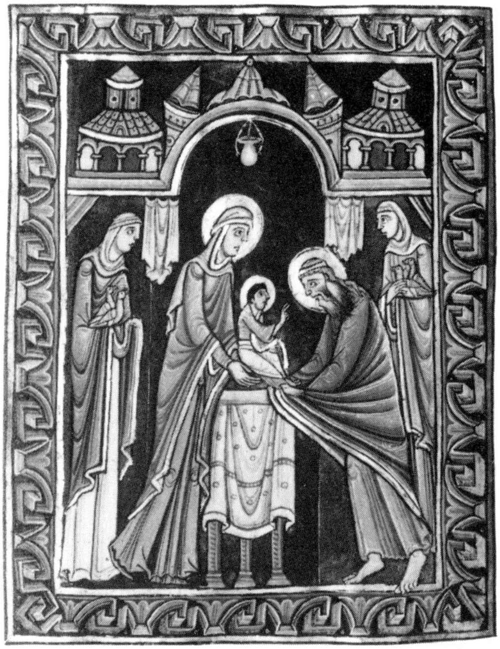

102 Hildesheim, St Godehard, p. 28, the Presentation in the Temple

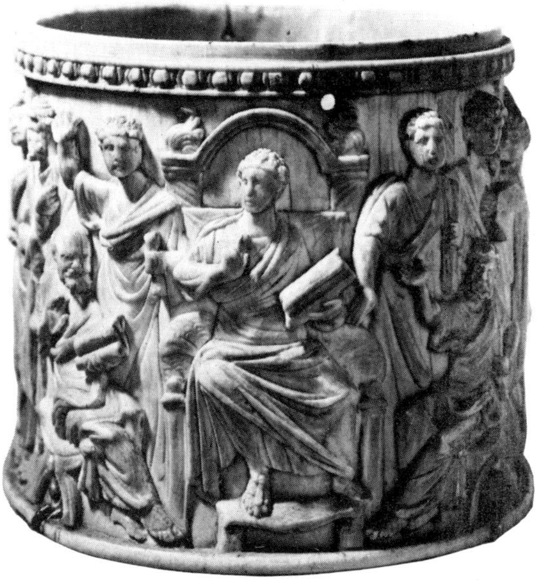

103 Berlin, Staatliche Museen, Skulpturenabteilung, ivory pyxis, Christ among the Doctors

104 Escorial, Codex Vitrinas 17, fol.97v, Christ among the Doctors

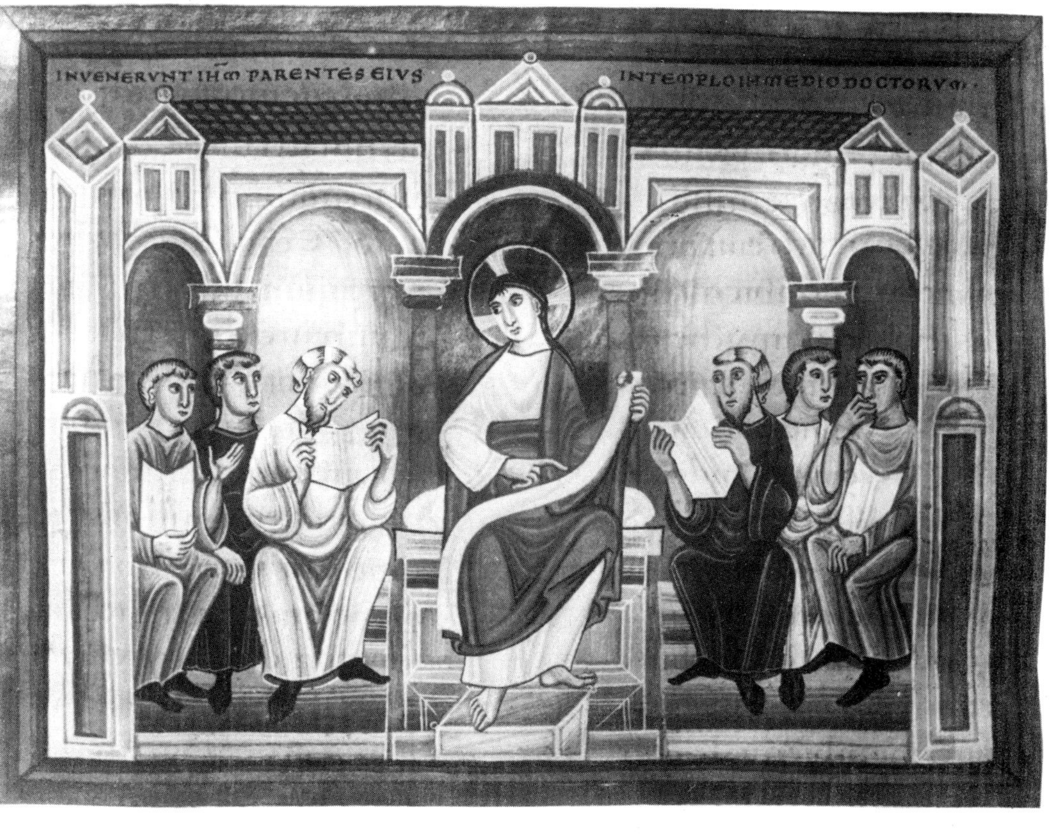

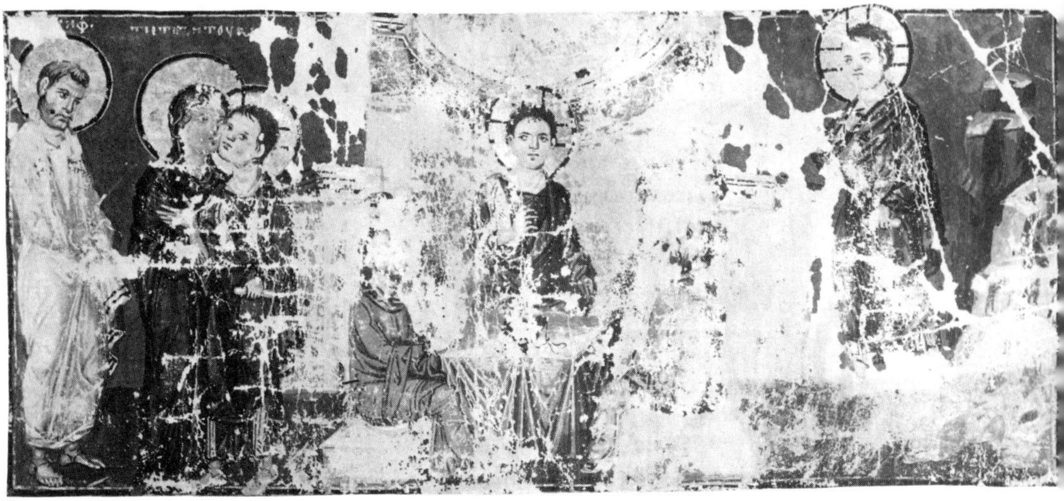

105 Paris, B.N., MS grec 510, fol.165r, Christ with his Parents

106 Chantilly, B.M. MS 7, fol.9v, the Baptism of Christ

107 Klosterneuberg, Abbey of St Augustine, enamel, the Baptism of Christ

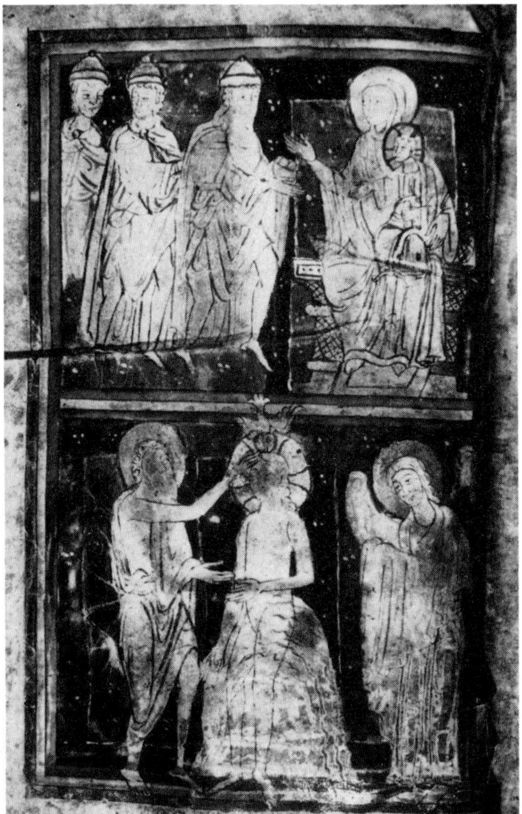

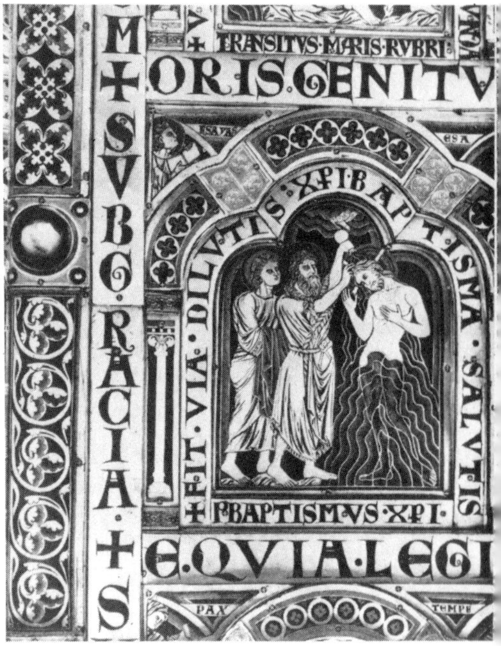

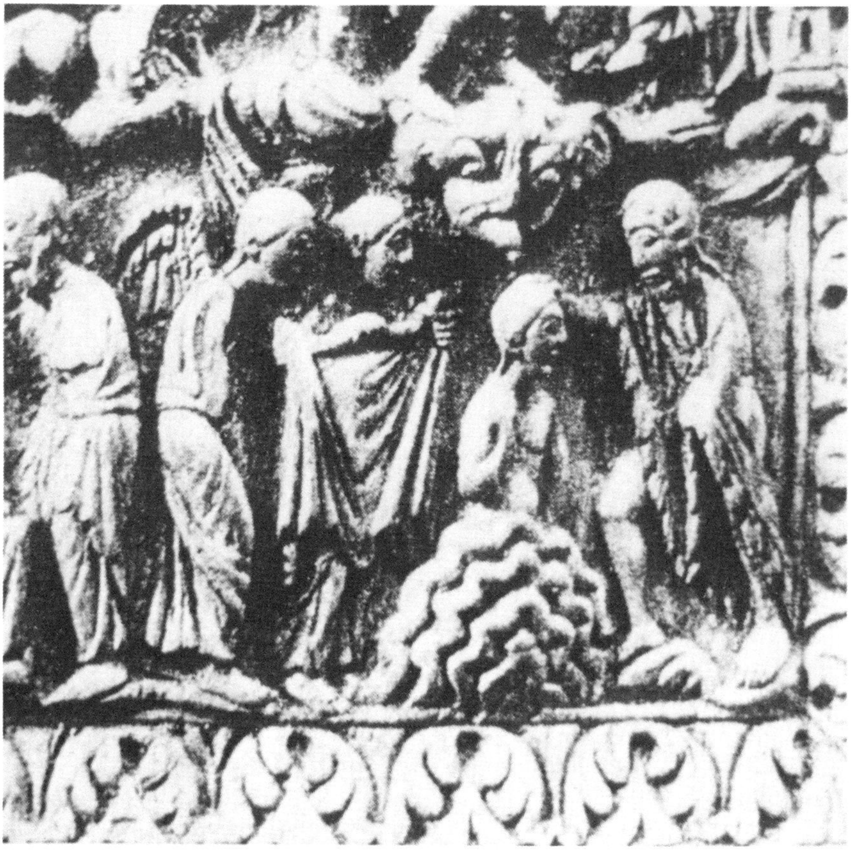

108 Berlin, Kaiser Friedrich Museum (formerly), ivory, the Baptism of Christ

109 Paris, B.N., MS grec 74, fol.170v, the Marriage at Cana

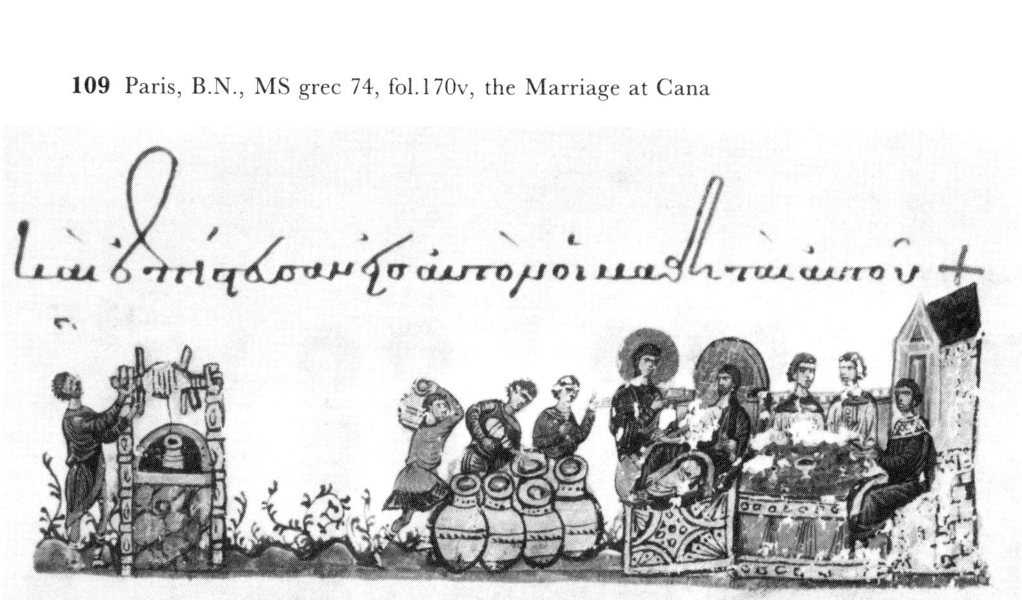

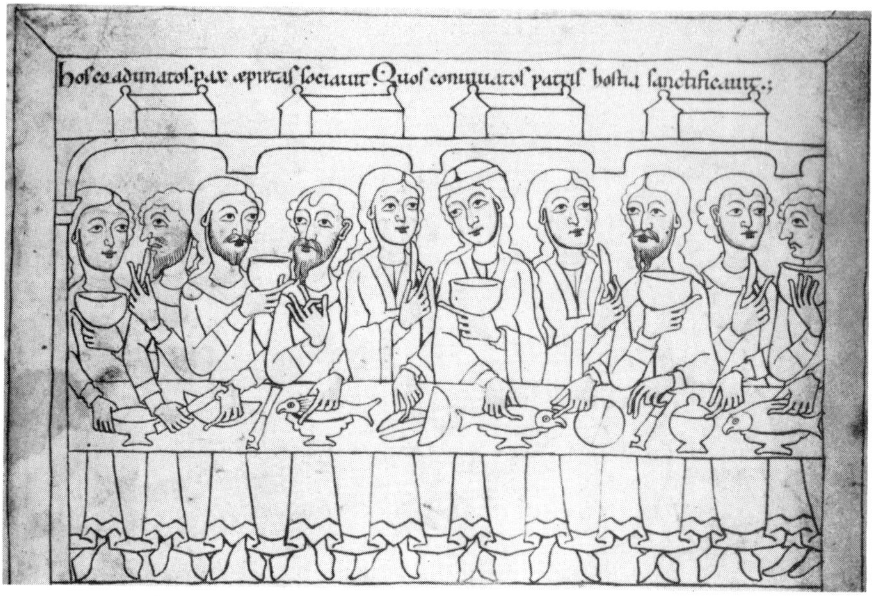

110 Paris, B.N., MS lat. 15675, fol.3r, the life of Job

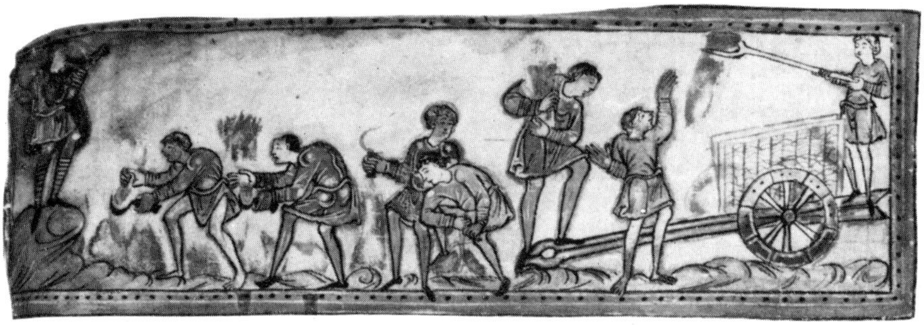

111 London, B.L., MS Julius B.V.I., fol.5v, calendar illustration

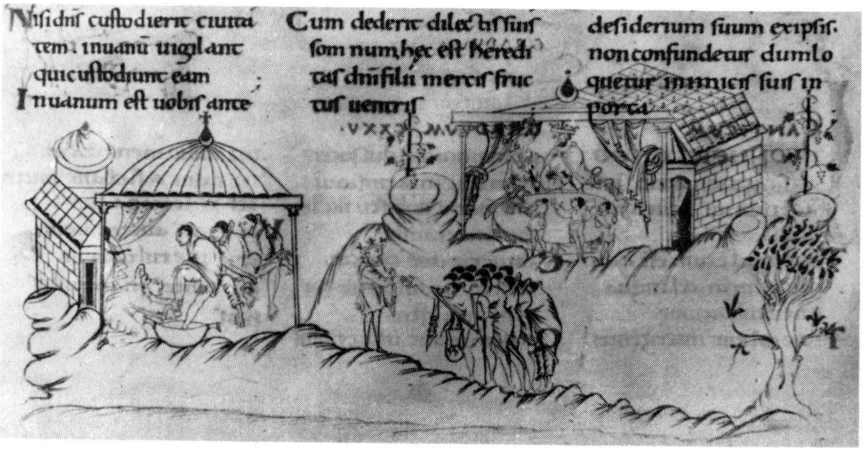

112 London, B.L., MS Harley 603, fol.66v, Psalm CXXVII

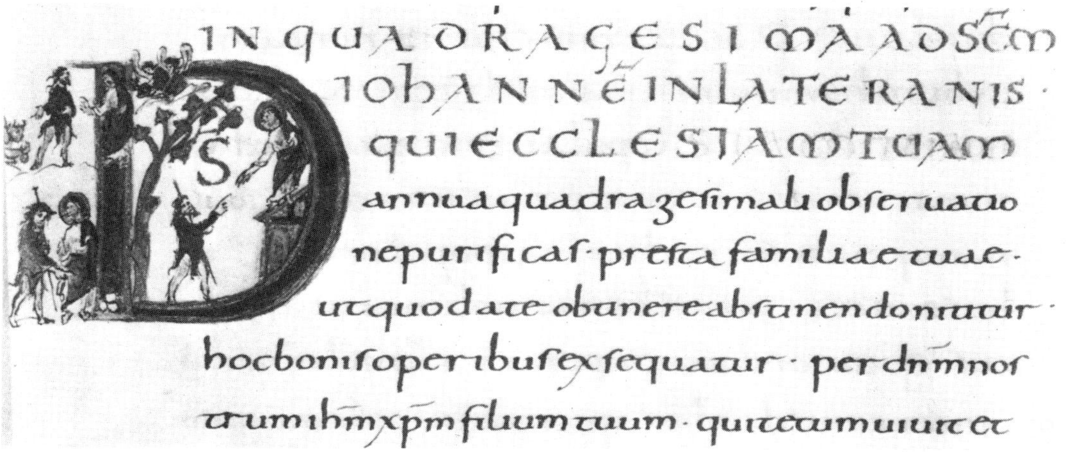

113 Paris, B.N., MS lat. 9428, fol.41r, the Temptations of Christ

114 Bremen, Universitätsbibliothek, MS b.21, fol.25v, the Temptations of Christ

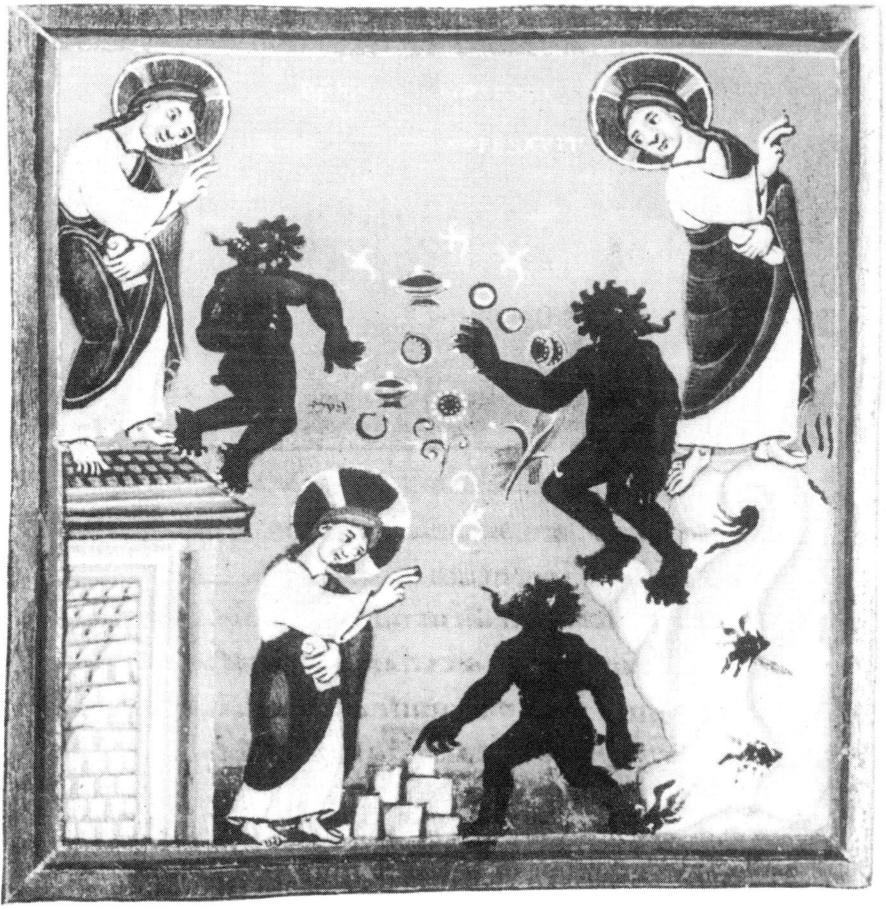

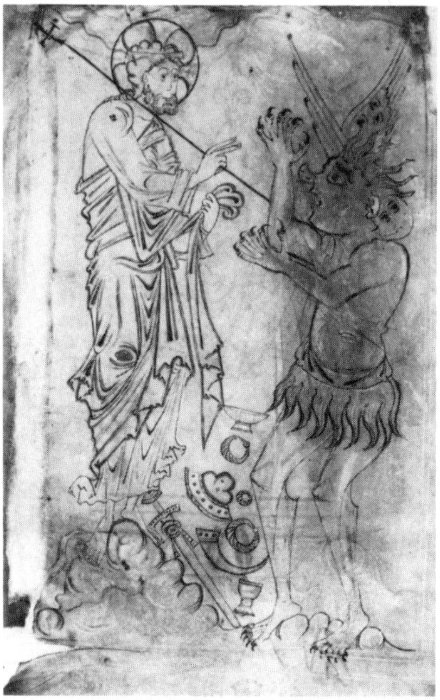

115 (above) London, B.L., MS Cotton Tiberius C.VI, fol.10v, the Temptations of Christ

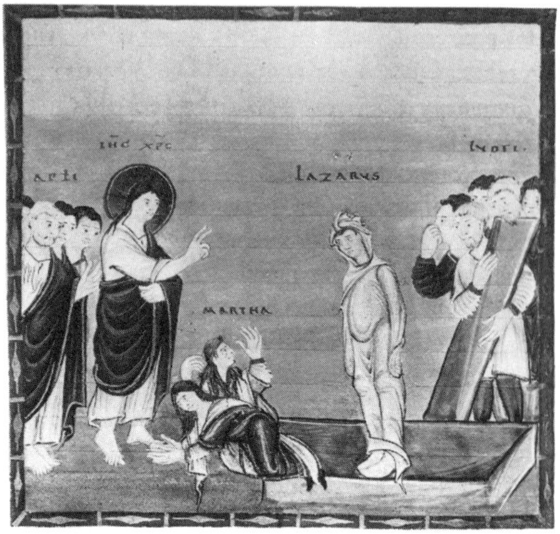

116 (above) Trier, Stadtsbibliothek, MS 24, fol.51v, the Raising of Lazarus

117 (below left) Escorial, Codex Vitrinas 17, fol.150r, the Raising of Lazarus

118 (below right) London, B.L., MS Add. 49598, fol.45v, the Entry into Jerusalem

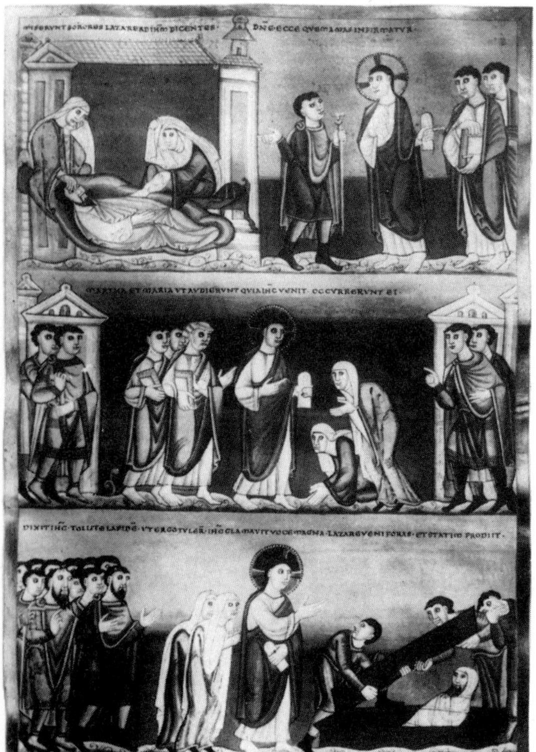

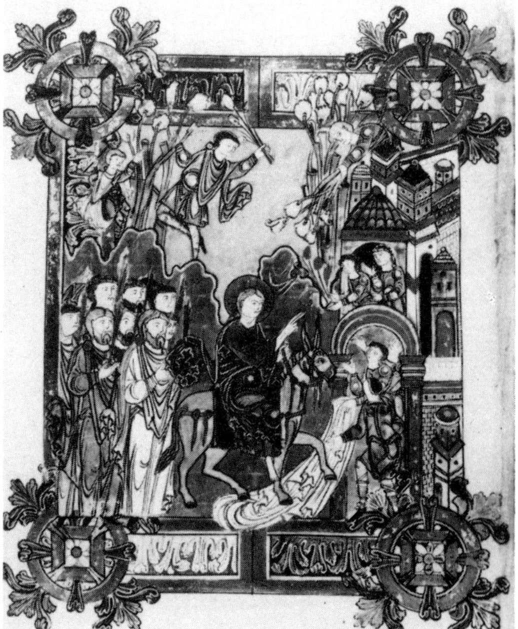

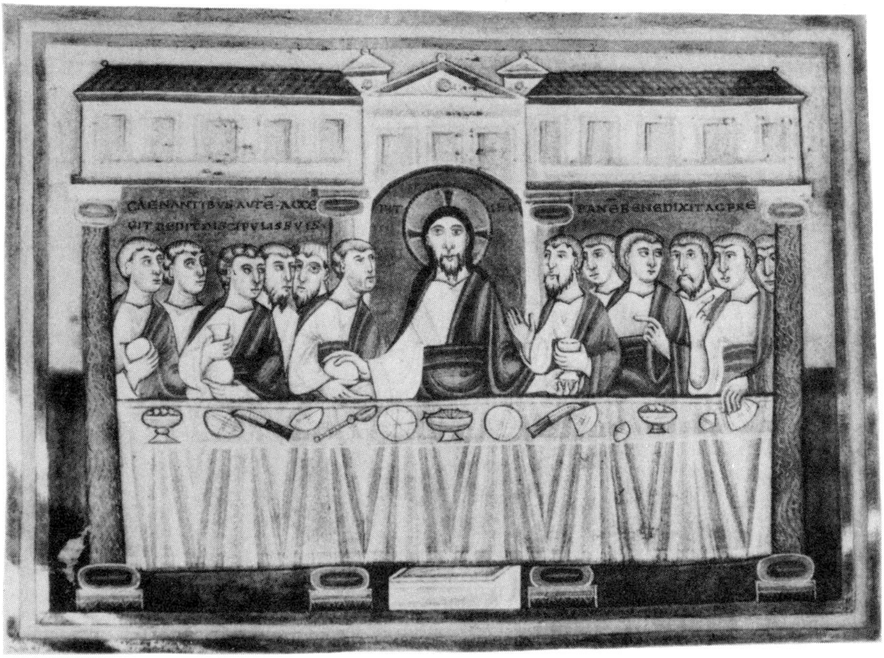

119 Escorial, Codex Vitrinas 17, fol.52r, the Last-Supper

120 Bremen, Universitätsbibliothek, MS b.21, fol.57v, the Last Supper

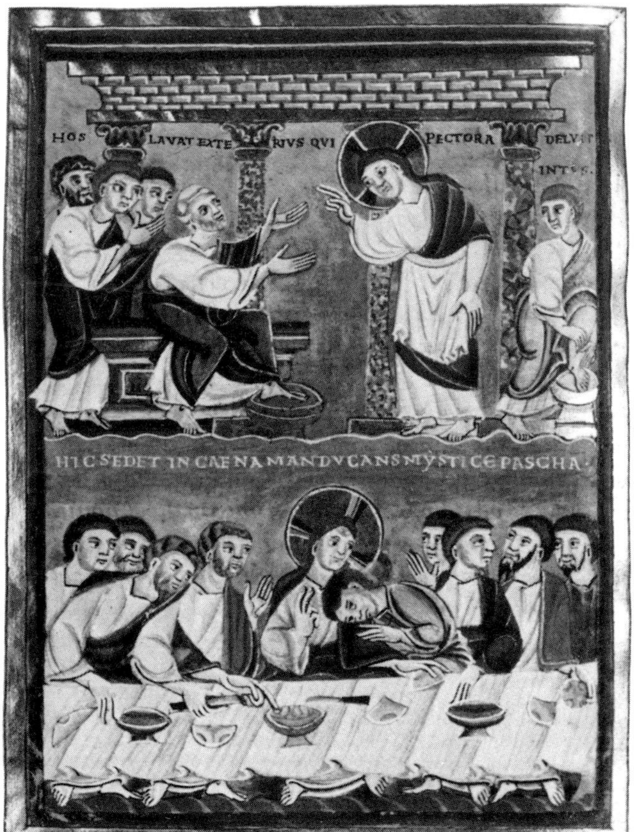

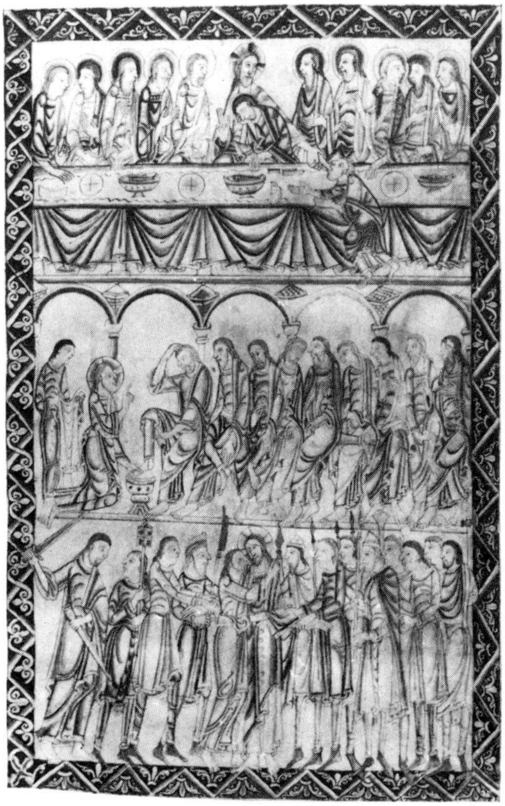

121 Cambridge, Pembroke College, MS 120, fol.3r, the Last Supper, Christ Washing the Feet of the Disciples, Betrayal

122 Escorial, Codex Vitrinas 17, fol.152v, Christ Washing the Feet of the Disciples

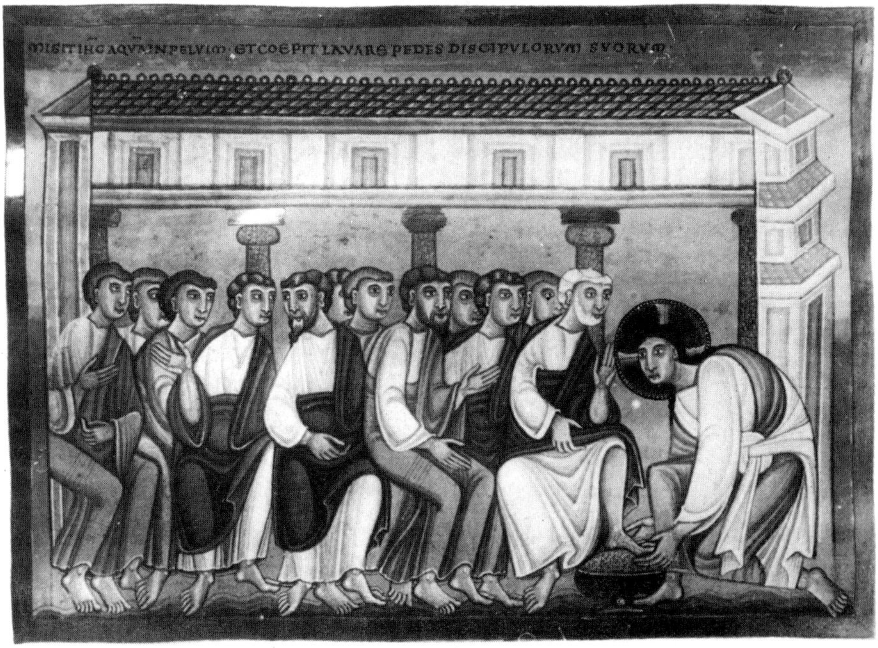

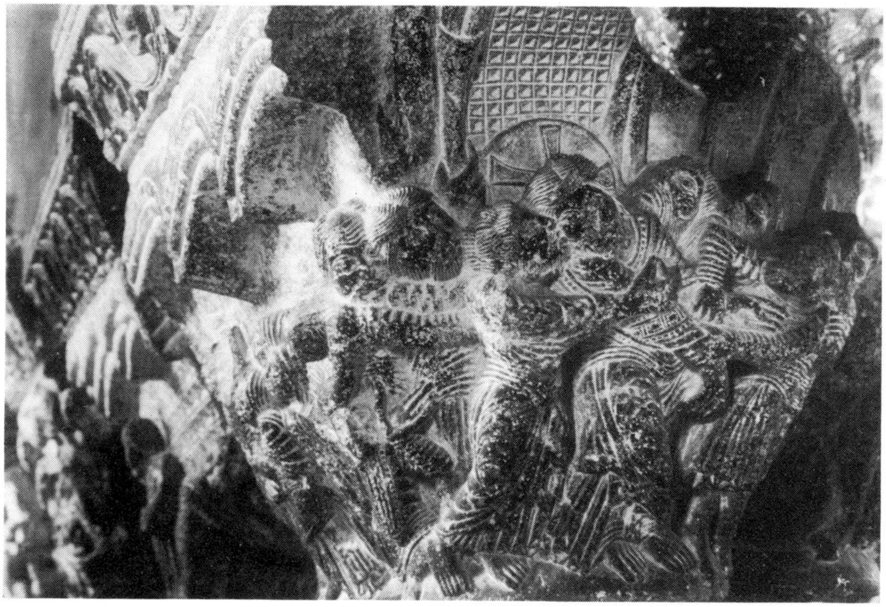

123 Toulouse, Musée des Augustins, capital from La Daurade, the Betrayal

124 Chartres, Cathedral, capital, the Betrayal

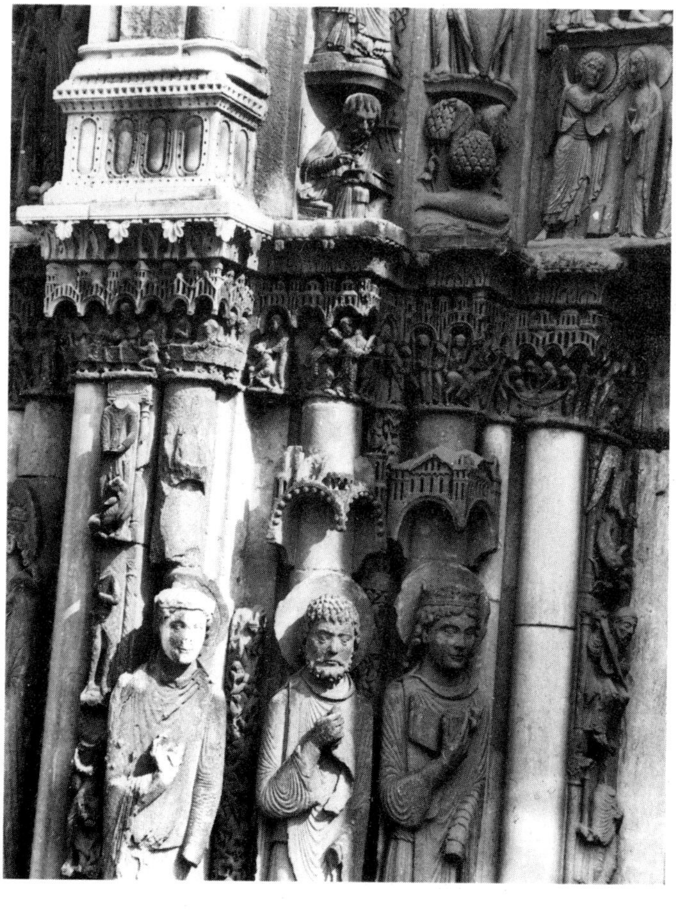

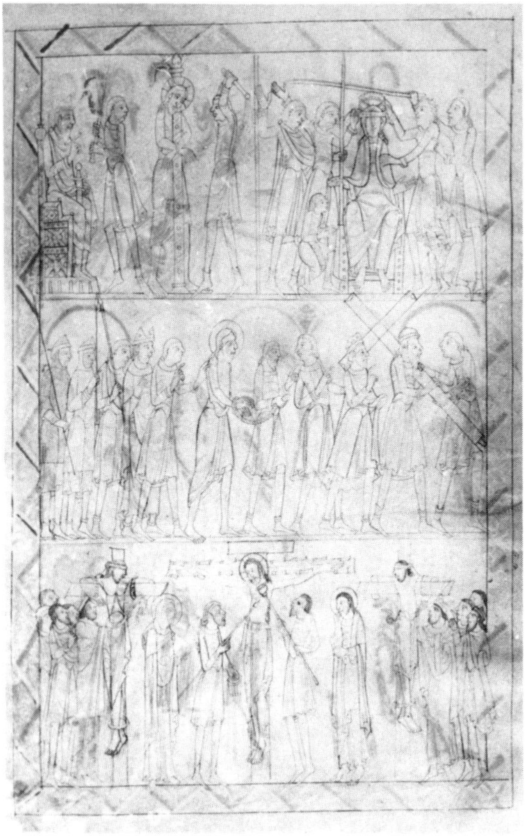

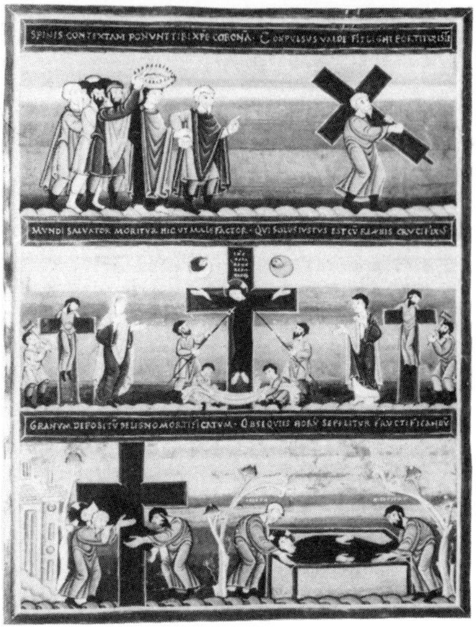

125 (left) Cambridge, Pembroke College, MS 120, fol.3v, the Flagellation, Crucifixion

127 (above right) Nuremberg, Germanisches-Nationalmuseum, MS 156142, fol.111r, the Crucifixion, Deposition

128 (below) Cambridge, Pembroke College, MS 120, fol.4r, the Deposition, Entombment, Women at the Tomb

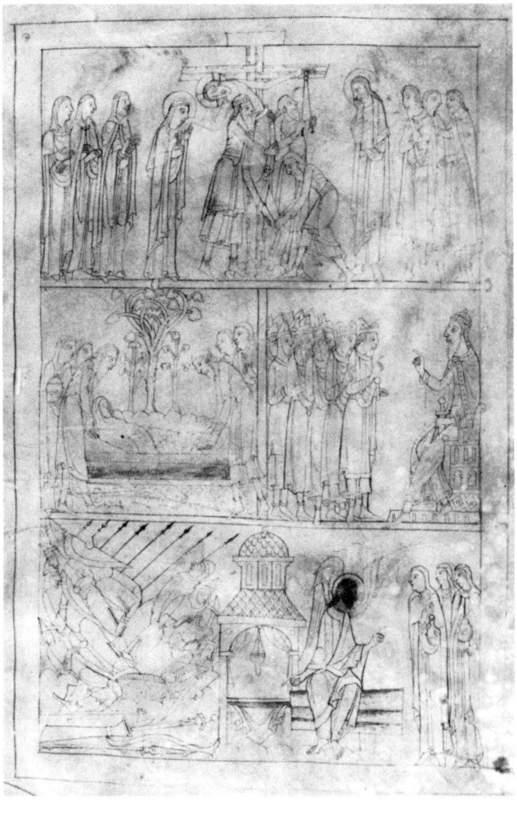

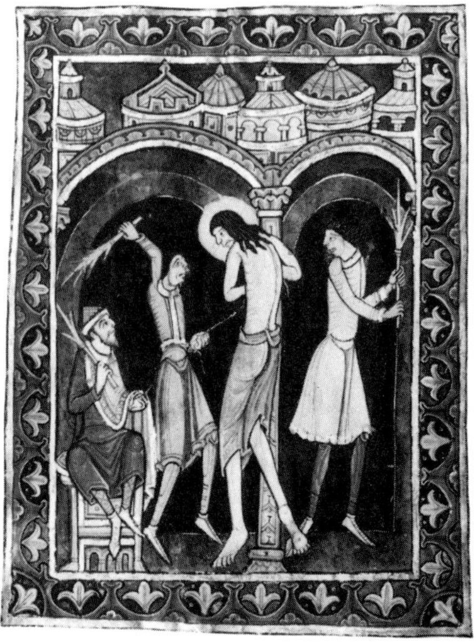

126 Hildesheim, St Godehard, p. 44, the Flagellation

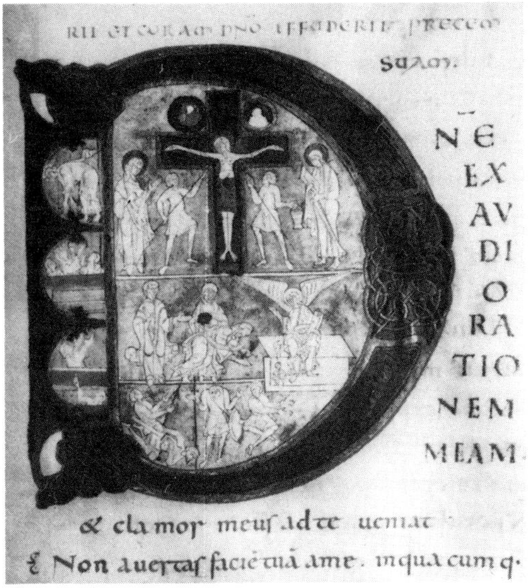

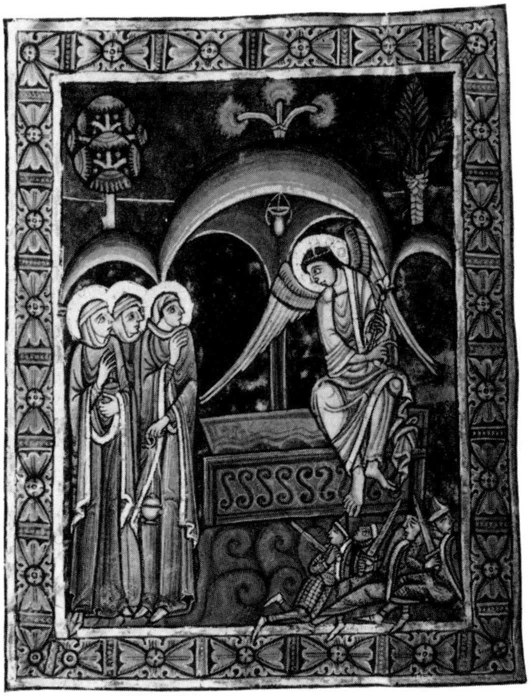

129 (above left) Boulogne, B.M., MS 20, fol.109r, the Women at the Tomb

130 (above right) Hildesheim, St Godehard, p. 50, the Women at the Tomb

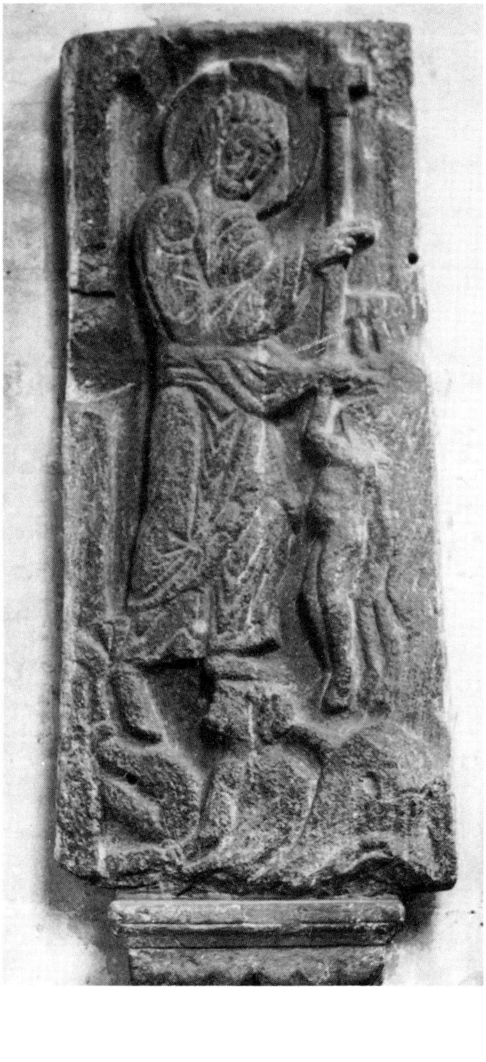

131 Bristol, Cathedral, relief, the Harrowing of Hell

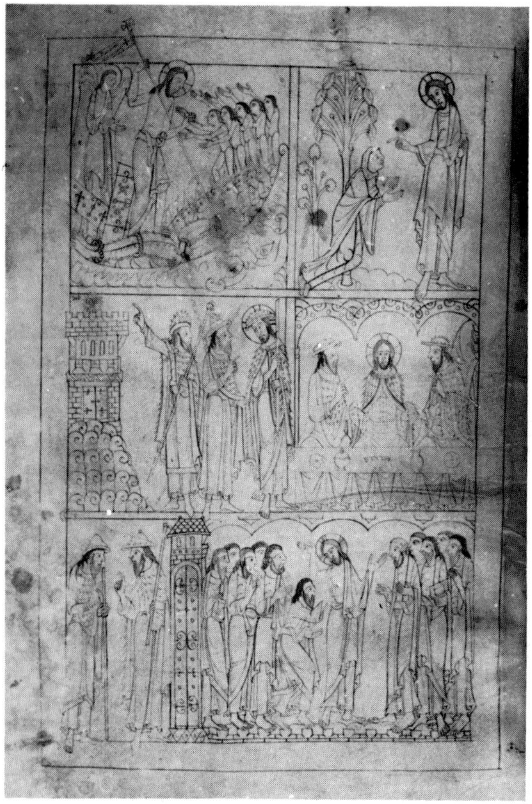

132 Cambridge, Pembroke College, MS 120, fol.4v, the Harrowing of Hell, *Noli me tangere*, Emmaus, Doubting Thomas

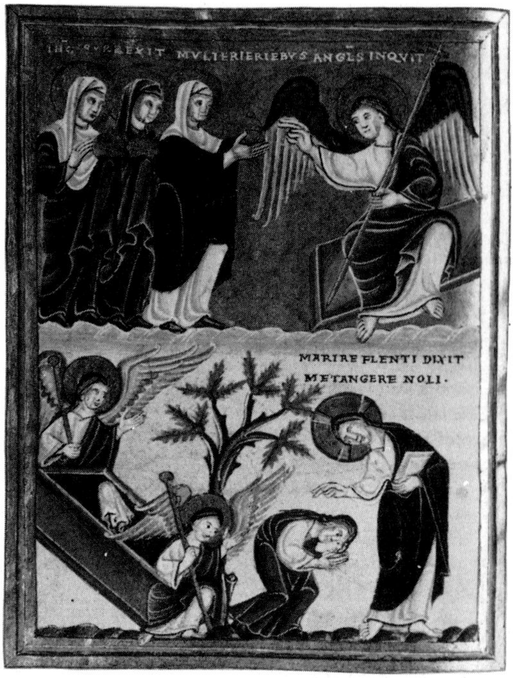

133 Bremen, Universitätsbibliothek, MS b.21, fol.62v, *Noli me tangere*

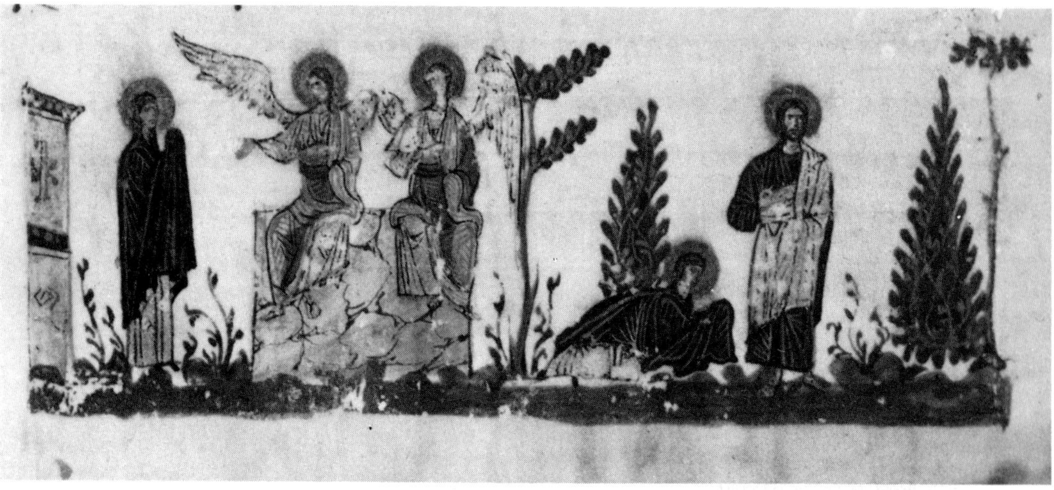

134 Paris, B.N., MS grec 74, fol.209v, *Noli me tangere*

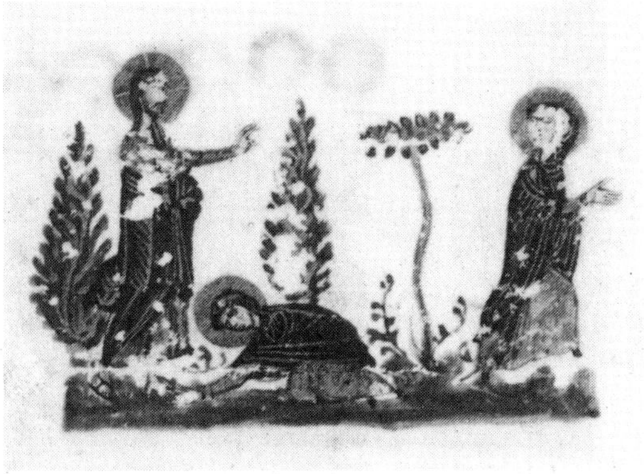

135 (left) Paris, B.N., MS grec 74, fol.101r, *Noli me tangere*

136 (below) Munich, Staatsbibliothek, MS Clm. 4453, fol.60v, Christ Giving the Keys to Peter

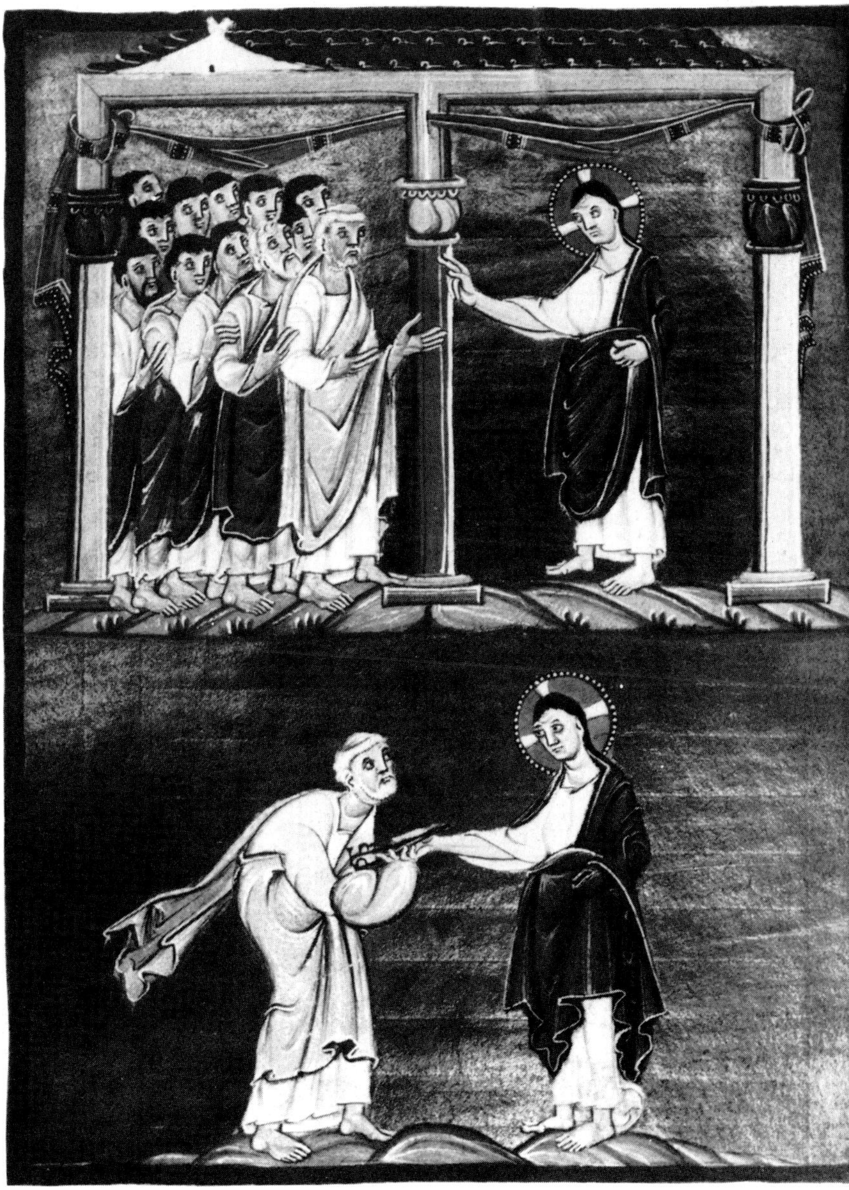

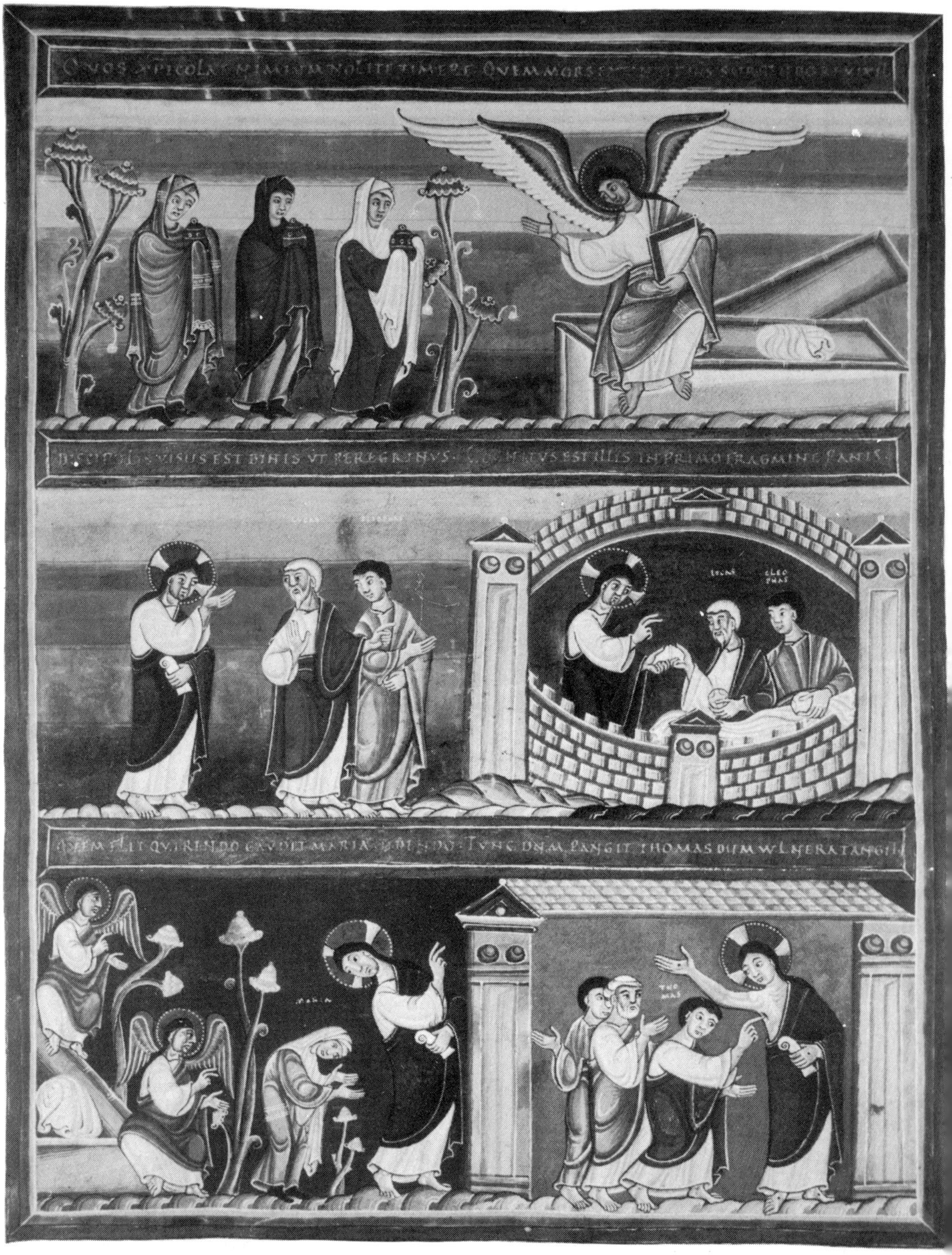

137 Nuremberg, Germanisches-Nationalmuseum, MS 156142, fol.11v, the Women at the Tomb, Emmaus, *Noli me tangere*, Doubting Thomas

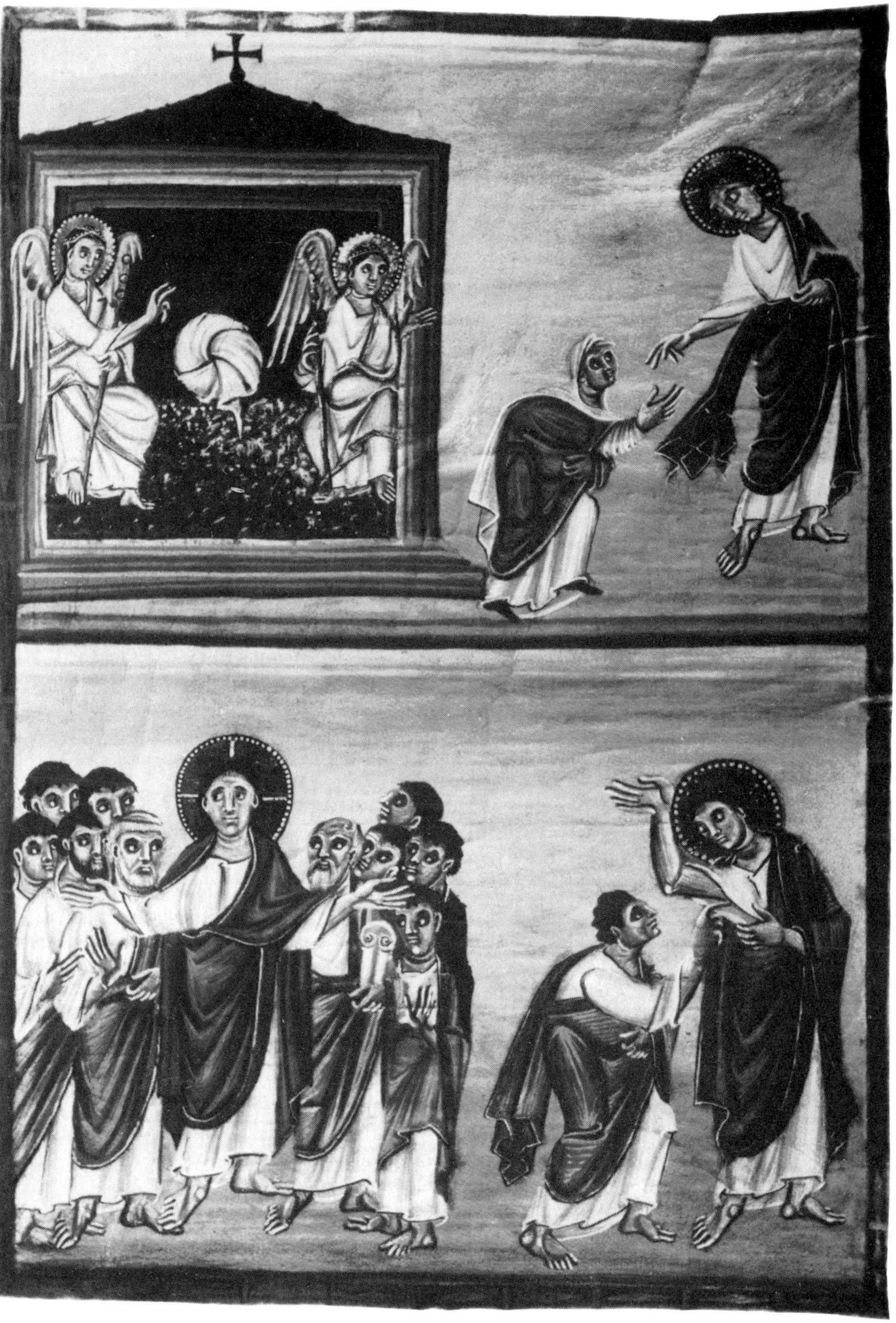

138 Munich, Staatsbibliothek, MS Clm. 4453, fol.251r, the Doubting Thomas

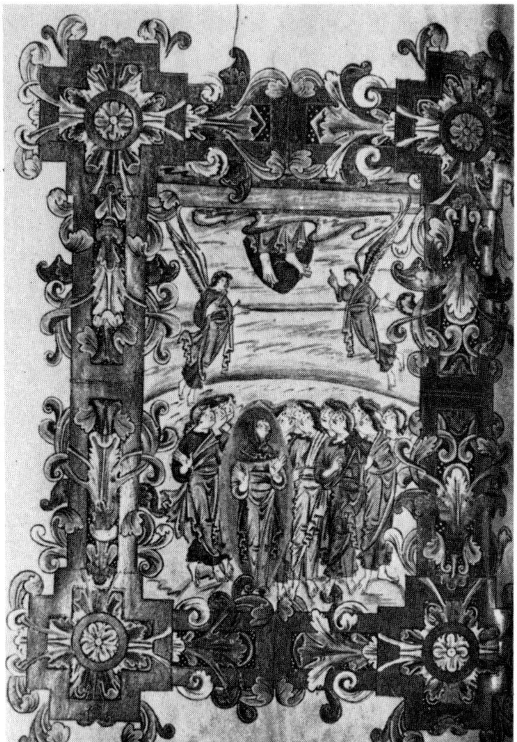

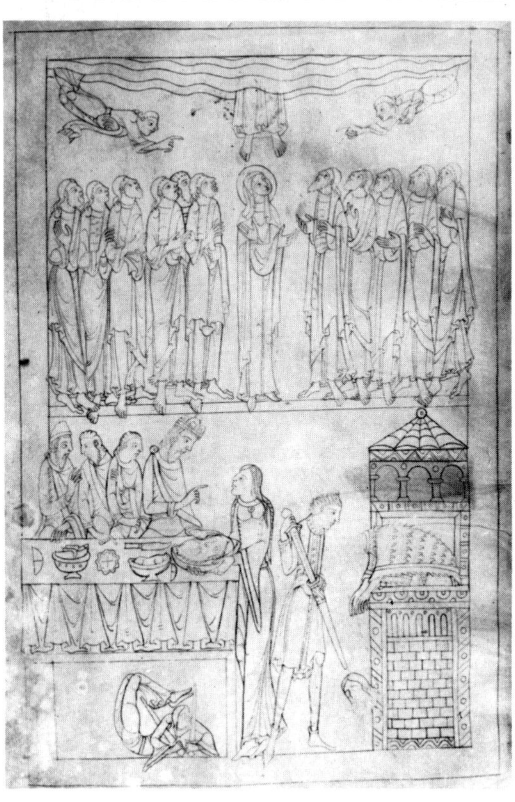

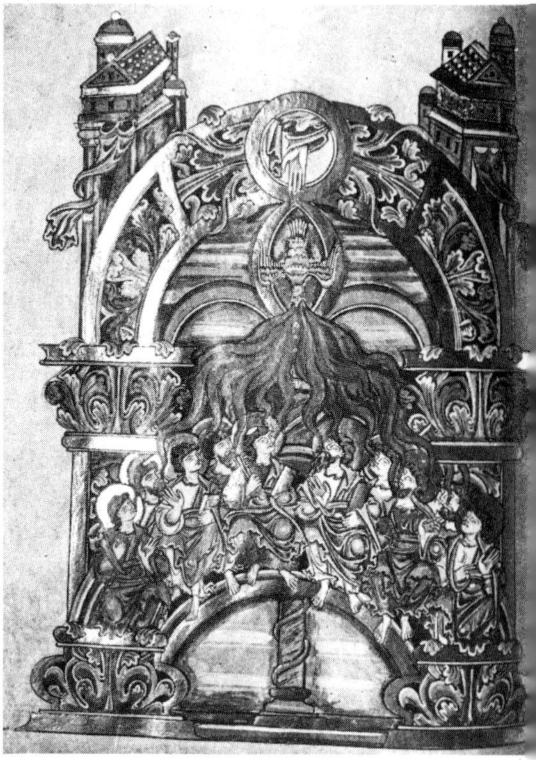

139 (above left) Rouen, B.M., MS Y.6, fol.81v, the Ascension

140 (below left) Cambridge, Pembroke College, MS 120, fol.5v, the Ascension

141 (above right) Rouen, B.M., MS Y.7, fol.29v, Pentecost

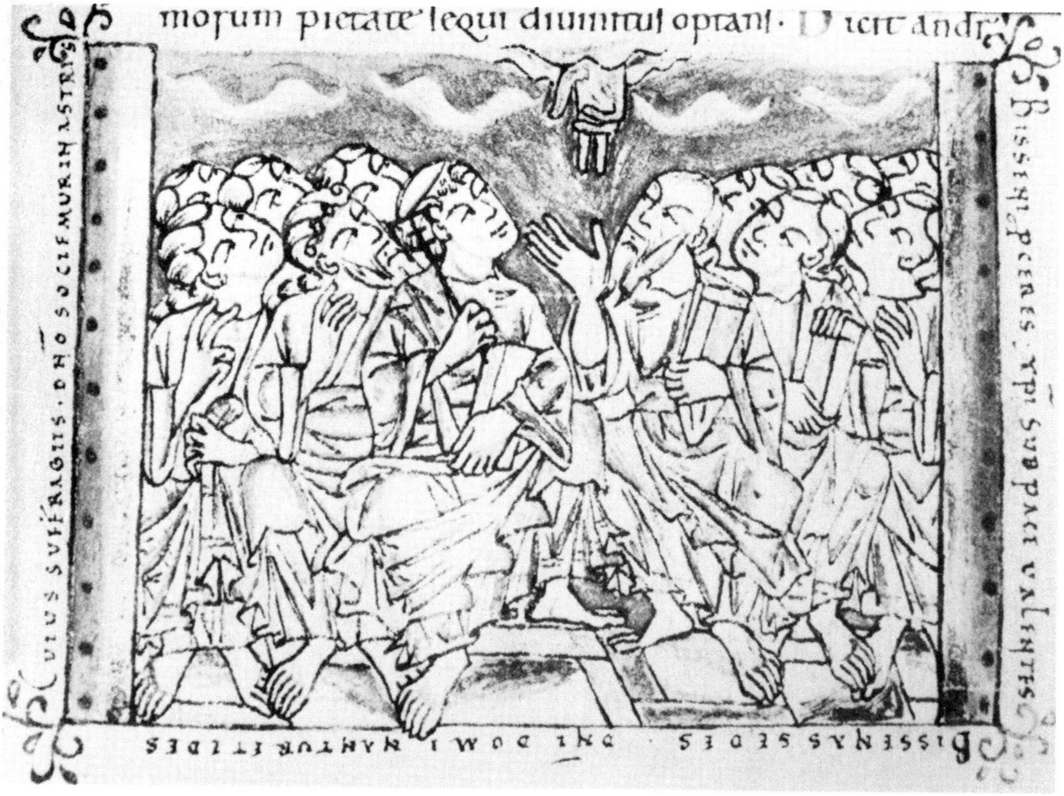

142 (above) London, B.L., MS Cotton Caligula A.XIV, fol.31r, Pentecost

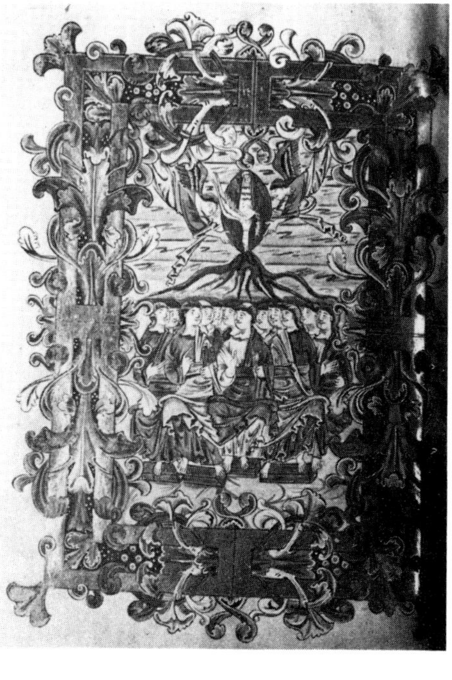

143 (left) Rouen, B.M., MS Y.6, fol.84v, Pentecost

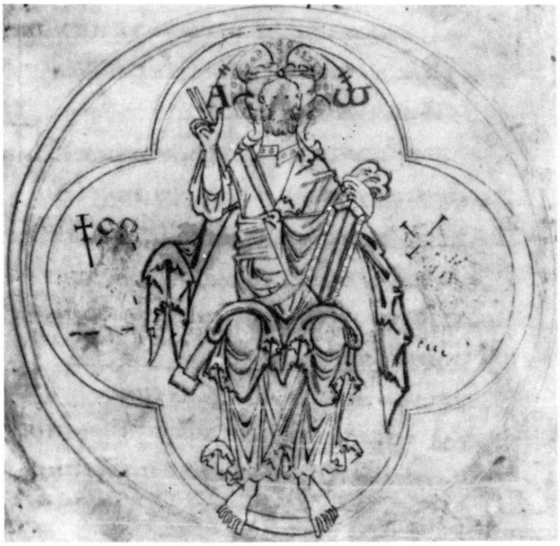

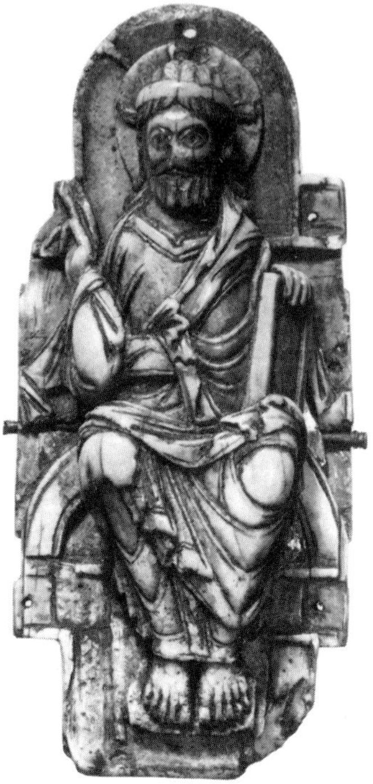

144 (above) London, B.L., MS Cotton Tiberius C.VI, fol.126v, Christ in Majesty

145 (above right) New York, Metropolitan Museum, ivory, Christ in Majesty

146 (below) Paris, B.N., MS grec 1208, fol.66v, the Virgin Enthroned

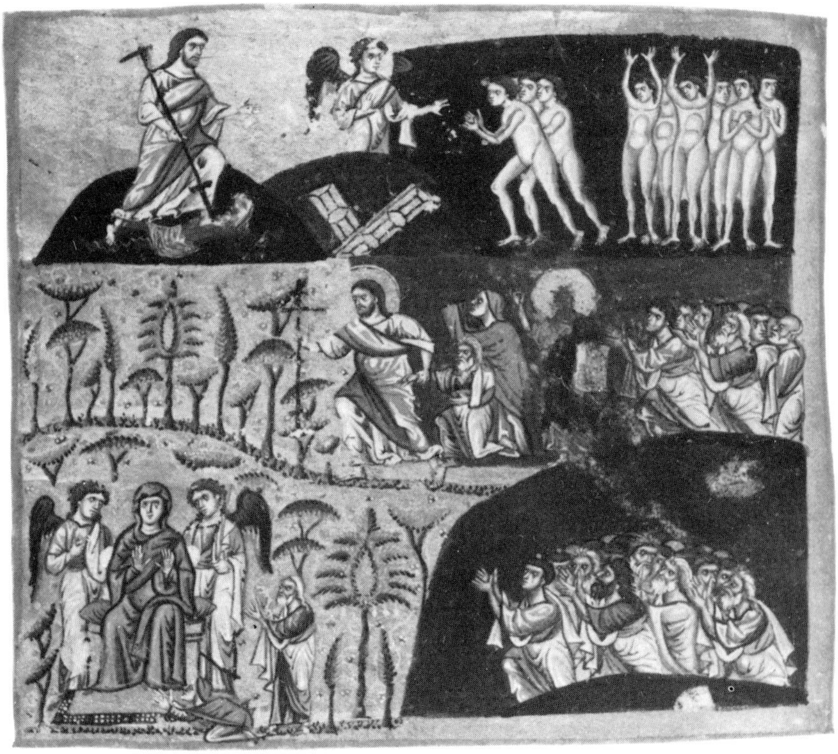

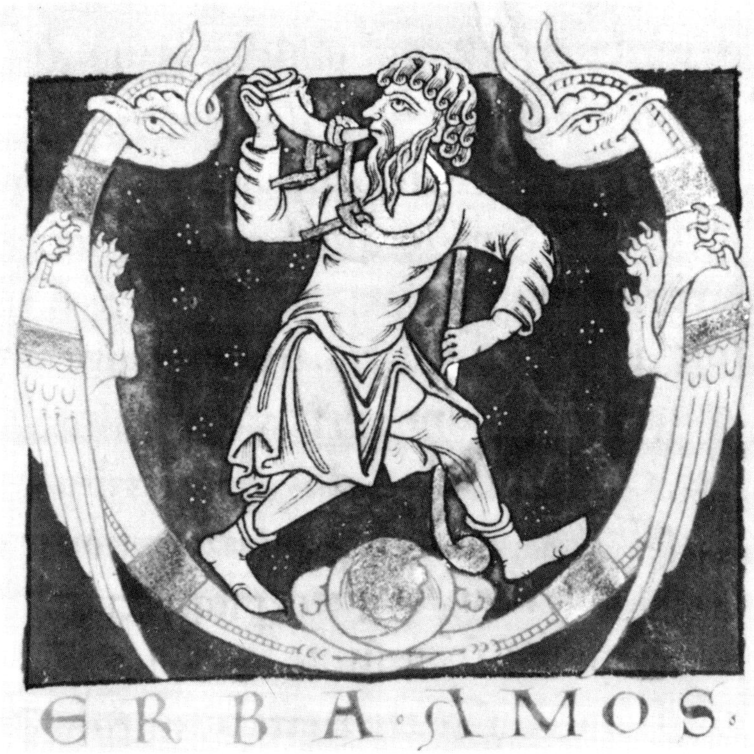

147 London, B.L., MS Add. 41790, fol.120r, initial

148 London, B.L., MS Harley 1585, fol.13r

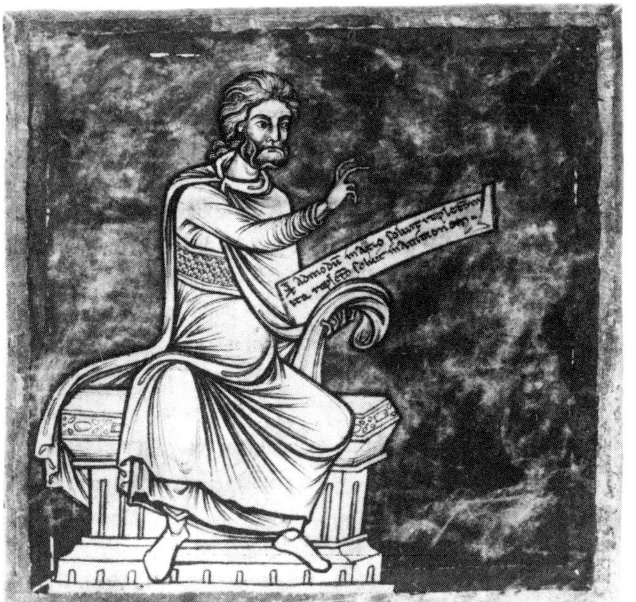

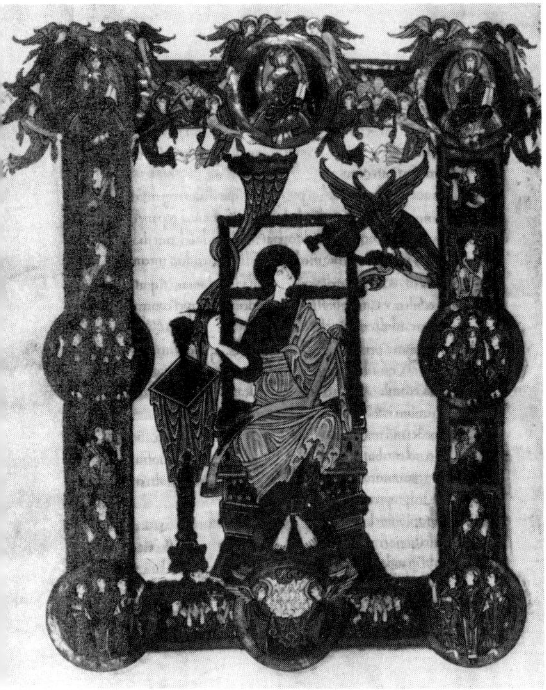

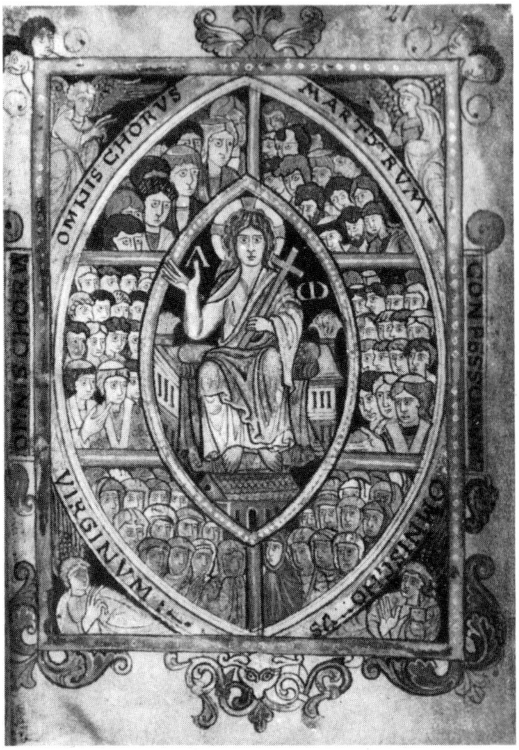

149 London, B.L., MS Add. 34890, fol.114v, Christ Enthroned

150 London, B.L., MS Cotton Galba A.XVIII, fol.21v, the Last Judgment

151 Clayton, wall painting, the Last Judgment

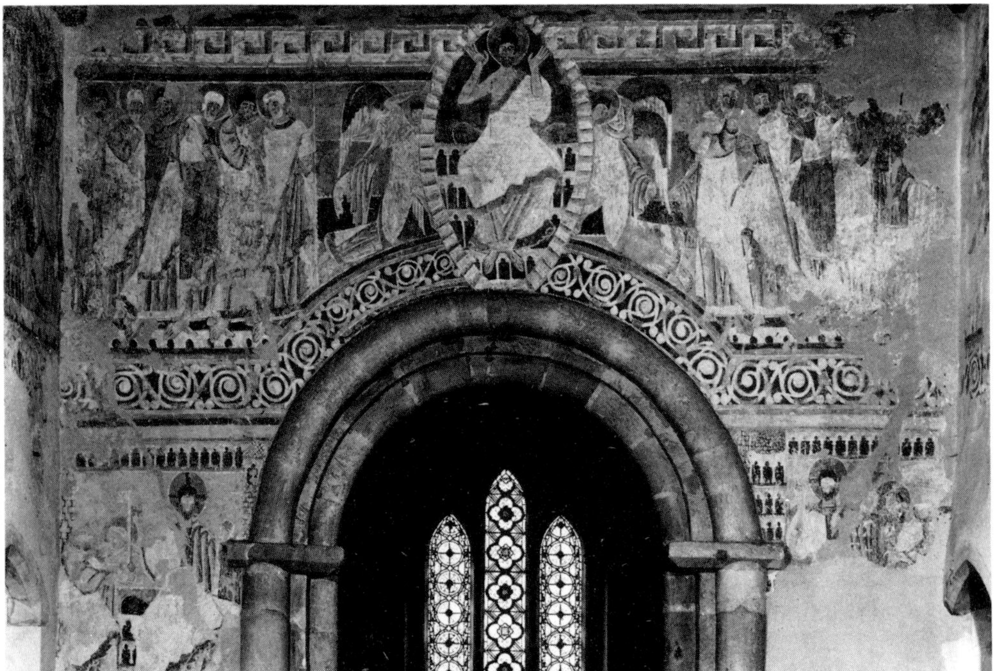

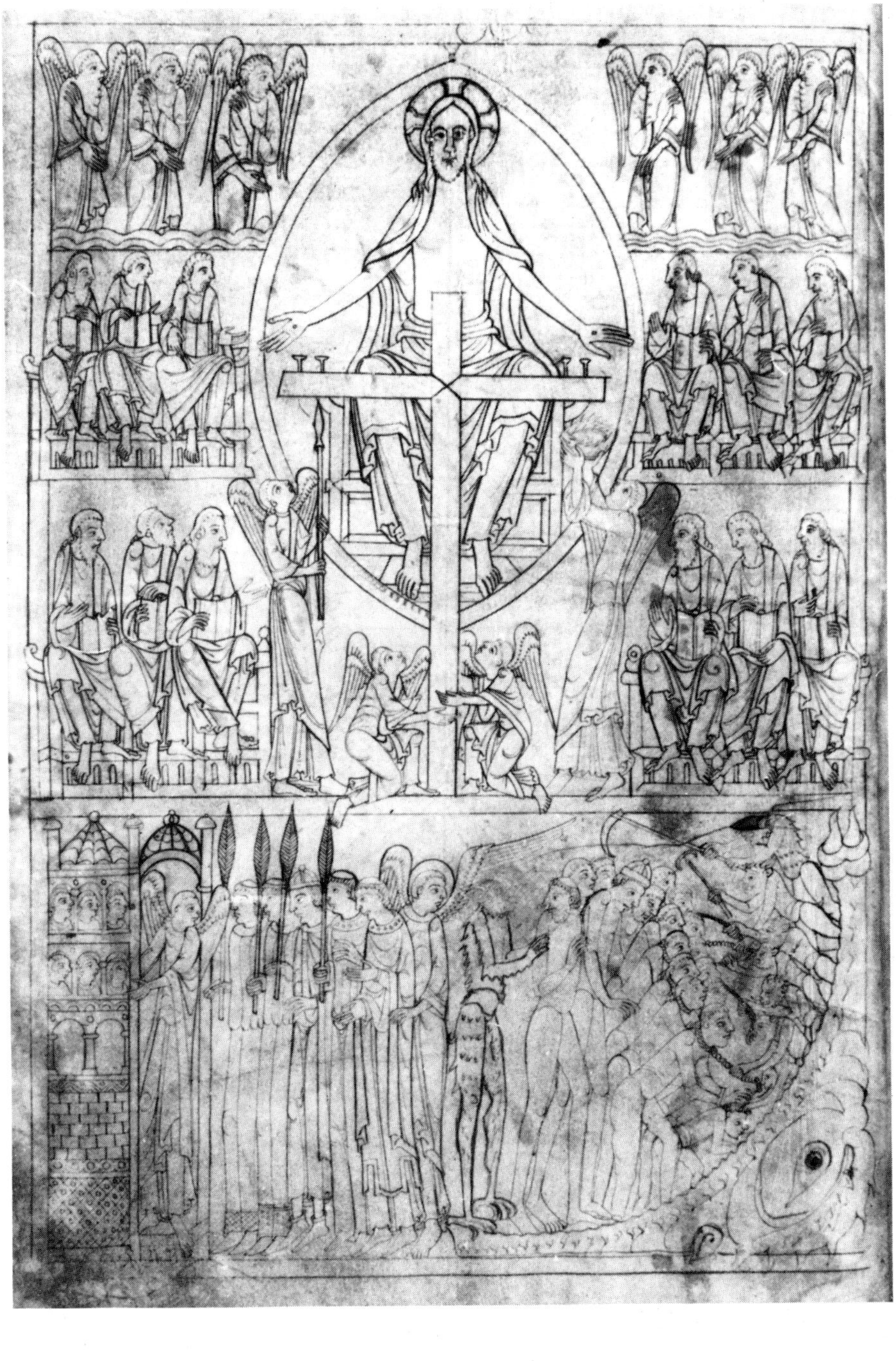

152 Cambridge, Pembroke College, MS 120, fol.6v, the Last Judgment

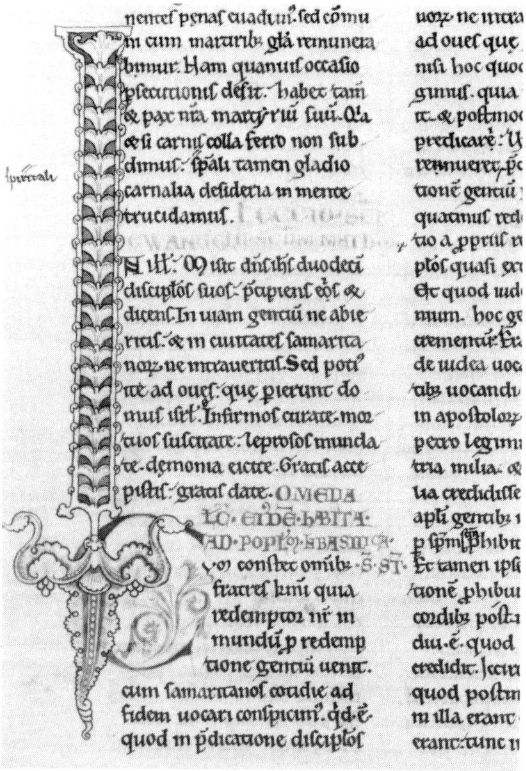

153 Cambridge, Pembroke College, MS 16, fol.7v, floral design

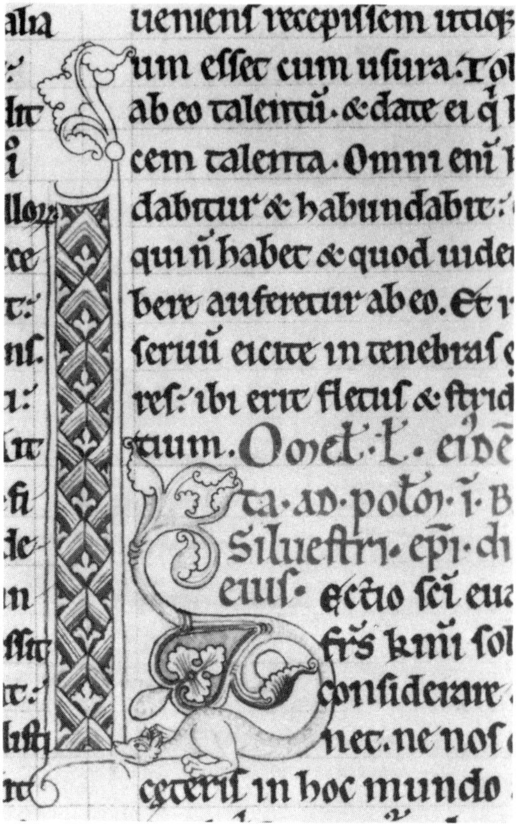

154 Cambridge, Pembroke College, MS 16, fol.17r, floral design

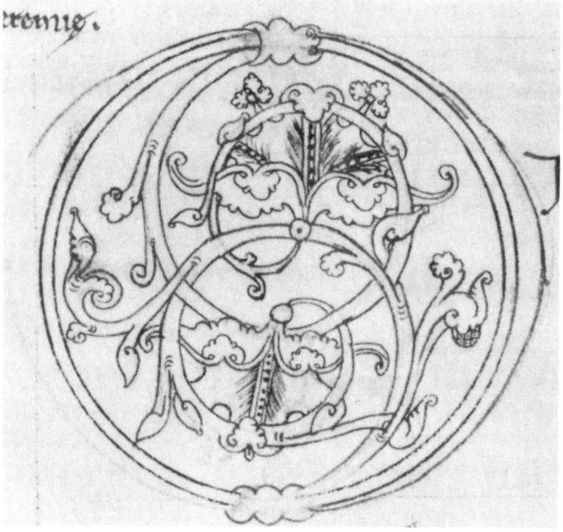

155 Cambridge, Pembroke College, MS 64, fol.148r, floral design

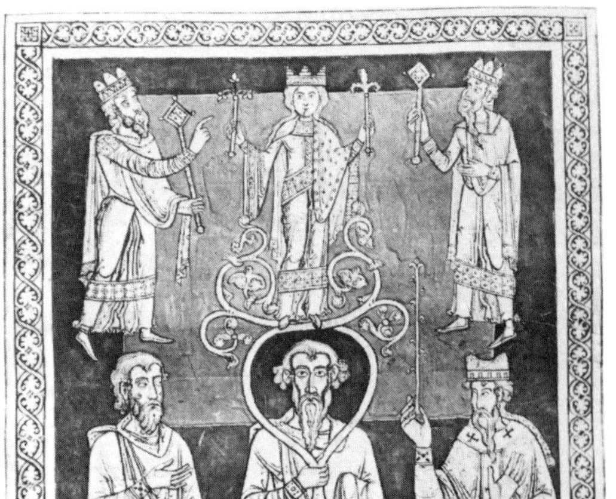

156 Salzburg, St Peter's Abbey, MS a.XII.7, p. 383, the Jesse Tree

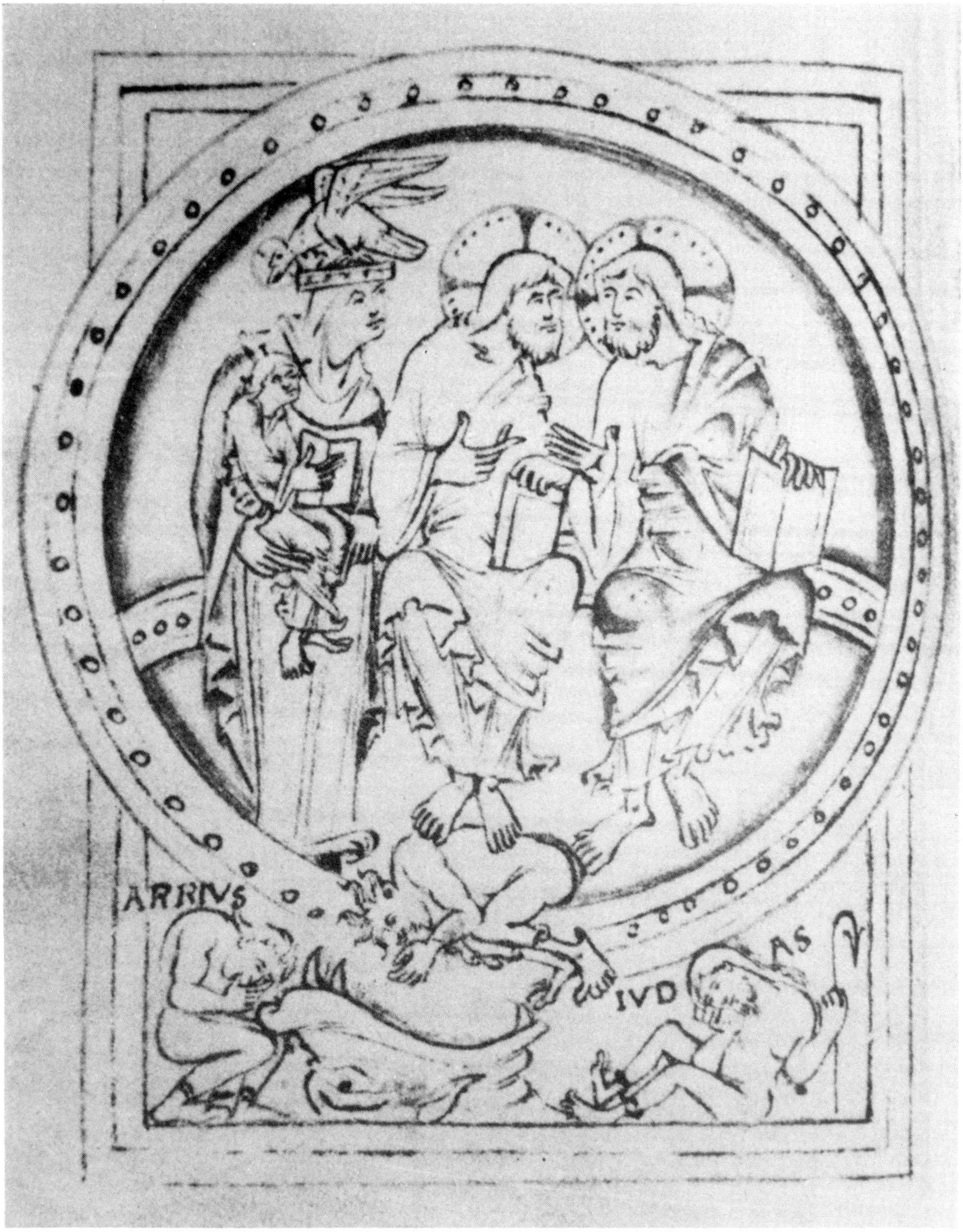

157 London, B.L., MS Cotton Titus D.XXVII, fol.75v, the Virgin and Child with the Trinity

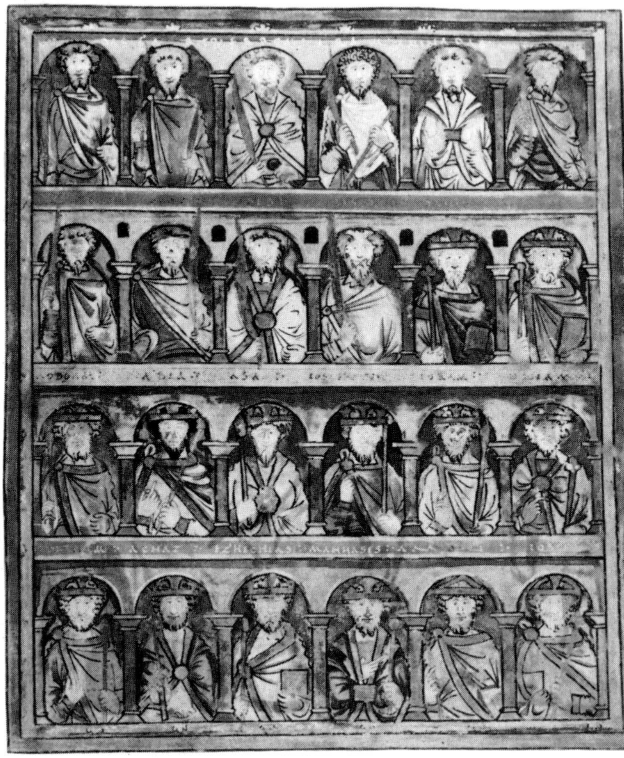

158 Boulogne, B.M., MS 11, fol.11r, the Ancestors of Christ

159 Monasterboice, high cross, *Traditio Legis*

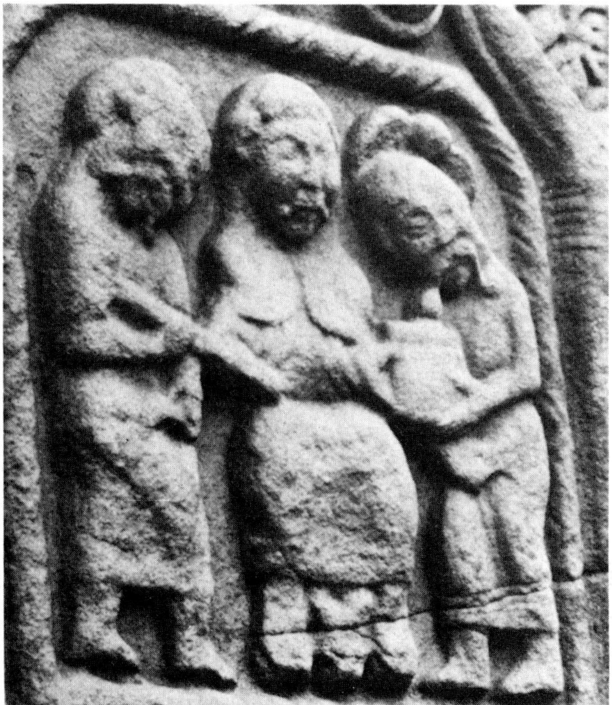

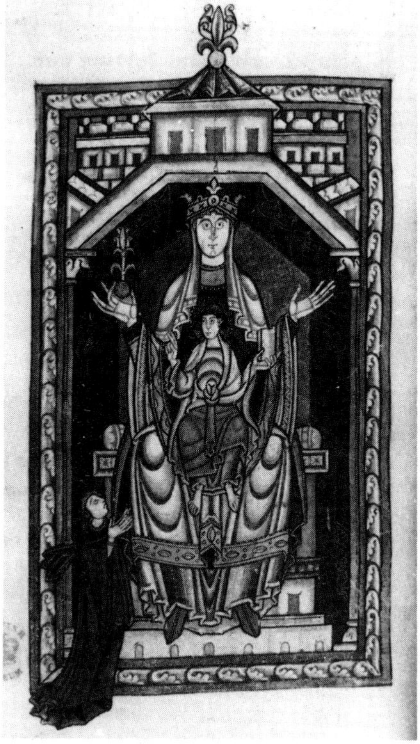

160 London, B.L., MS Lansdowne 383, fol.165v, the Virgin Enthroned

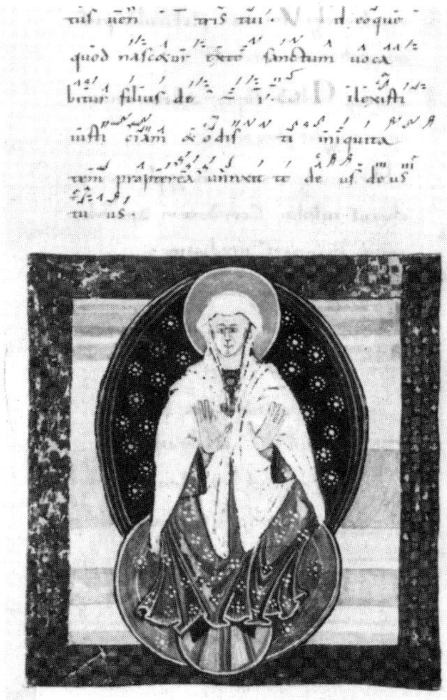

161 Paris, B.N., MS lat. 9448, fol.62v, the Virgin Enthroned

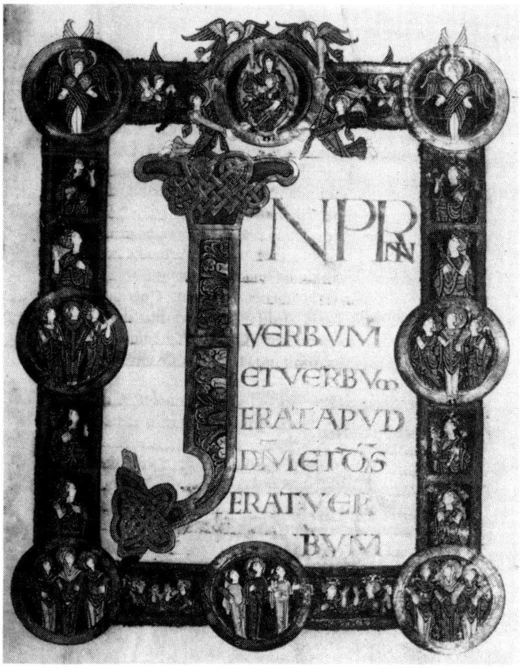

162 London, B.L., MS Add. 34890, fol.115r, *Maria, Regina Angelorum*

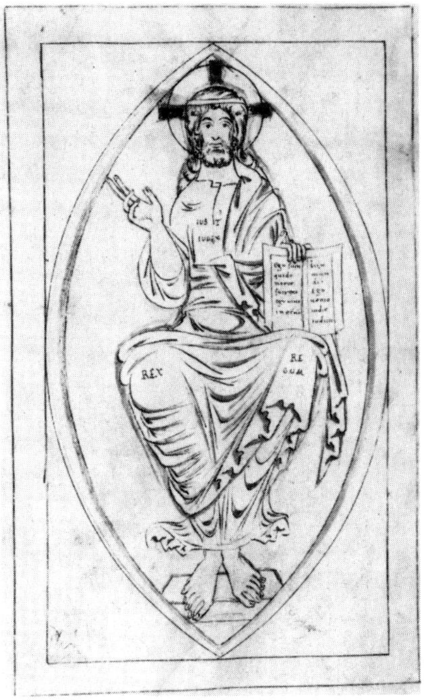

163 Cambridge, Trinity College, MS B.15.34, fol.1r, Christ as the Judge